# Aspects of the
# French Revolution

*by the same author*

Edmund Burke and the Revolt Against the Eighteenth Century

Rousseau and the Modern State

Dictatorship: Its History and Theory

The Crisis of Civilization

National Self-determination

The Debate on the French Revolution

Vichy France (in *Hitler's Europe*, ed. TOYNBEE)

Ambassadors and Secret Agents: The Diplomacy of the First
Earl of Malmesbury at The Hague

Historians and the Causes of the French Revolution

In Search of Humanity: The Role of the Enlightenment in Modern History

A History of Modern France, Vols. 1–3

The Social Interpretation of the French Revolution

# Aspects of the French Revolution

ALFRED COBBAN

GEORGE BRAZILLER
NEW YORK

Printed in Great Britain

# CONTENTS

5

# ACKNOWLEDGMENTS

I am indebted to the editors of the following journals for permission to reprint the papers which first appeared in their pages: the *English Historical Review* [6, 8, 9, 10, 11], *History* [3, 12, 15], Wesleyan University Press (*History and Theory*) [7], *The Times Literary Supplement* [13], the *Listener* [4]; also to the Council of the Historical Association [2], University College, London [5], the Johns Hopkins University Press [1] and Professor Roland Mousnier [14].

# INTRODUCTORY

## THE STATE OF REVOLUTIONARY HISTORIOGRAPHY

Any enumeration of the great movements in modern history must include, along with Reformation, Renaissance, Enlightenment, Industrial Revolution and the Communist Revolution, the French Revolution. The last of these may indeed be regarded as a focal point. As such it has justly received a concentration of historical attention such as can hardly be paralleled by that devoted to any other event in history. Revolutionary historiography has been marked both by its variety and its extent. It provides examples of practically every type of historical investigation and writing, from the most naïve chronicle to the most sophisticated metaphysical interpretation, from the anecdotal trivia of *la petite histoire* to the fundamental issues of human destiny.

For those who want their history to be a story the Revolution provides not only a great historic drama but a host of minor dramas within the greater one, ranging from the tragi-comedy of the diamond necklace to the plot which destroyed the republic of the Year III on the 18th of brumaire. And such episodes mattered. At any point the course of the Revolution could be diverted by a chance happening or an individual decision determined by a freak of personal character. No adequate general history of the Revolution can fail to bring before our eyes a host of individuals, marking with their own idiosyncrasies the events in which they participated. The records are so ample that the deeds and personalities of lesser men as well as of the great stand out clearly. At the same time, the historian whose bias lies in the detection of great impersonal forces can write the history of the Revolution in quite different terms. It would be a mistake to suppose that either approach is exclusively right. The right approach is determined only by the nature of the questions the historian is asking and the right answer by the material of which he asks them.

9

The circumstantial interpretation seems to be forced on us particularly when we look at the history of international relations during the revolutionary period. True, public opinion in all countries saw the struggle as an ideological one between revolution and established order; but those who actually determined international policies were free from this illusion, though they had to allow for and were prepared to make use of it in others. The history of the Revolutionary and Napoleonic Wars can be told almost exclusively in terms of power politics and explained by the traditions of the countries involved and the personalities of their rulers and ministers. The partly ideological underground war waged by revolutionary and counter-revolutionary propagandists and secret agents supplemented but was subordinate to this traditional power struggle. Continental powers kept ideology almost exclusively in the realm of propaganda. It played a certain part in the uneasy attempts at co-operation between the British government and the French royalists, but these all rapidly broke down, leaving nothing but the direct political conflict between states. However, apart from some recent work on Anglo-royalist relations,[1] little that is new has been written on the international history of the revolutionary period for a long time.

The frank recognition of the dominance of power politics in international relations has not been without its effect on the writing of domestic French history. One consequence is that the traditional admiration for Napoleon, and the effort to present him as something other than a military conqueror and dictator, has become difficult even for French historians. Emphasis on the ideological element in the policy of the revolutionary governments has also diminished and the desire for territorial aggrandisement, and even more for economic advantage, come to be seen as a dominant influence over their foreign policies. A similar tendency has operated in the study of the internal policies of the Revolution. The ideals which undoubtedly inspired many lesser men seem to have provided a weaker motivation for those engaged in the struggle for power at the top. Successively the revolutionary heroes of one generation of historians have been toppled and exposed as weak, foolish and above all self-seeking by the next. The ambition and lack of scruple of Mirabeau have long been well known. The constitutional monarchists of the opening phases of the Revolution have paid the price of their moderation in the eyes of historians as they did of contemporaries. No one has ever tried to make much of them. For those with royalist sympathies they were the traitors within the gates, or at best would-be reformers whose folly and weakness opened the flood-gates of revolution; while for orthodox revolutionary historians they were no better than half-hearted aristocrats. The Brissotins, Rolandists, Pétionists, Girondists, whose heyday was the disastrous time of the Legislative Assembly and the early Convention, have no admirers left. Danton's reputation can never more than partially recover from the vendetta waged in the name of Robespierre against him by Mathiez. Robespierre in turn has suffered the attacks of those for whom he is a petty bourgeois, a Social Democratic politician of the worst kind, the man who destroyed the *armées révolutionnaires* and overthrew Hébert and the sans-culottes. His Rousseauist ideas are written off as the sentimentality of the third-rate *littérateur* and his reforming social ideals as part of his all-embracing hypocrisy. No one, however, has attempted to make heroes out of Hébert and the leaders of the sans-culottes whom Robespierre overthrew. In the search for a revolutionary leader whose ideals can prove acceptable the final term has been reached in the present cult of Babeuf.[2] After him, and for those who cannot see him as a major figure, there is no remaining revolutionary hero left.

Individuals of course cannot be ignored, but the exploration of the internal history of France during the Revolution in terms of the ideas and actions of individuals has perforce largely been abandoned. One strongly urged alternative is that of R. R. Palmer, who puts forward the theory that the last three decades of the eighteenth century are to be interpreted as witnessing, in Europe and the Americas, a general democratic revolution, which he and J. Godechot have also called the Atlantic revolution.[3] In order to be able to envisage this as a single movement it has been necessary to put the emphasis on the ideas and methods of the revolutionaries, for the social structures of the many countries in which Palmer tries to see parallel developments were so different that the parallel in actual fact has often to be very forced. French historians, apart from Godechot, have been unwilling to see their own revolution reduced to being merely one among a number of similar revolutions, or to allow French to be submerged in Atlantic civilization; and the Palmer–Godechot thesis has won little acceptance beyond its original proponents. Yet it cannot be denied that the nations of Europe and the Americas were swept, from about 1770 onwards, by a series of revolutions which all have something in common, at least in their basic ideas. The trouble is that they operated in such different societies that Palmer's attempt to write their history as that of a single revolution can not do other than effect a distortion of their separate histories. Again, Godechot's emphasis on the 'Atlantic' nature of the revolution, which Palmer endorses, is justified as a recognition of the fact that the 'Democratic Revolution' was indeed much less general than their theory has tended to suggest, and that its influence in central and eastern Europe was very slight. But it is not easy to understand what the Atlantic has to do with this. The simple explanation is surely that the ideas inspiring the revolutionary age spread from Great Britain and France to the colonies in America. As for democracy, by 1815 aristocracy or monarchy had won the struggle everywhere except to a limited extent in the newly independent United States, and democracy seemed farther off than ever.

This is not to assert that there had been no revolution, and that nothing of any lasting consequence had happened in the revolutionary age. It is merely to insist that everywhere the main effect had been to consolidate the power of a ruling class or individual. If New England seems an exception to this statement, it is because it was already an exception before the revolutionary age began. The fundamental change was not in politics but in the ways of society, in dress, language and above all in the laws. To say this is frankly to reverse the trend of recent historiography and to admit that the real revolution was in the realm of ideas. This assertion must not be misunderstood. One of the few recent contributions in this field apparently shows the reverse, by demonstrating correctly how little influence the political ideas of Rousseau had in the opening years of the Revolution.[4] But it should be noted that this was essentially a study of political ideas. A distinction must be drawn between the political developments of the Revolution, which were evidently compatible in practice with rule by terror, oligarchy, military dictatorship, the dominance of a landed aristocracy and the restoration of monarchy and in which political ideals had little effect, and the legal and social reforms.

It was in respect of the latter that the Revolution was the heir of the Enlightenment. Considerable attention has been paid to the ideas of the Enlightenment in recent years,[5] but much less to the attempt to put them into practice. Historians, like contemporaries, have been fascinated with the age of revolution, so much that they have forgotten that it was also an age of reform. The Terror is a much more dramatic subject than the ending of legal torture or of religious persecution, or the anti-slavery movement. Moreover, while political developments varied from country to country and generalizations in this field are mostly misleading, attempts to reform social customs, the ways of the law and administrative procedures vary only in degree and are a proper subject for general history. It is unfortunate that the major essay in a general explanation should have been made by Palmer in the field of political history, which is most recalcitrant to this treatment.

Leaving general history on one side, however, let us look specifically at the historiography of the French Revolution. Here also the history of the age of revolutions as an age of reform remains largely to be written. In the realm of ideas, which have been treated on a less exclusively national basis, attention has been directed away from reforming ideas and emphasis laid on the European reaction against the Revolution and against the enlightened ideas which were generally held responsible for it. In this respect contemporary politics have doubtless not been without influence in diverting the direction of historical interest away from the more generous developments and towards the more brutal and tyrannical.

When the history of ideas is left on one side it is natural to assume that this is because of a greater concentration of attention on the more material aspects of the history of national and international economy. This explanation does not hold good of the recent historiography of the Revolution, for the slightness of work in the field of economic history is equally striking. Some local studies of the sale of *biens nationaux*,[6] and a detailed study of the little industrial town of Elbeuf,[7] form almost the sole exceptions to this statement. The many articles which have been written on the food crises of revolutionary France hardly fall into the category of economic history.[8] They are descriptive or narrative in nature and are directed mainly to illustrating the connection between food shortage or high prices of essential food-stuffs and popular disturbances.

To discover the prevailing tendency of recent work on the Revolution in France we have to look in a different direction. The name which dominates revolutionary historiography is that of Georges Lefebvre. Although he remained uninfluenced by the technical developments of contemporary sociology, his prime interest was in social history. It would be reasonable to expect his influence to have led to a marked development in this field. Curiously, those who have followed him, although the filiation is undeniable, instead of moving forward to a more thorough social analysis have rather withdrawn in the direction of politics. The new discovery has been 'history from below', and here by history is meant very specifically political history. An important contribution in this field was George Rudé's study of the revolutionary crowds,[9] revealing their constitution and their role in the onward movement of the Revolution. Soboul has done the same in much greater detail for the sans-culottes[10] and Richard Cobb has described the little *armées révolutionnaires* in two massive volumes.[11] These historians have demonstrated much more clearly and fully than ever before the major part played in the overthrow of successive revolutionary regimes by the militants of the Paris streets, composed largely of what might be described in modern terms as lower middle class or superior artisan elements, though not without a surprisingly large proportion of leaders from higher up in the social scale. In this way the machinery of political change has been revealed.

Having said this, however, we must recognize that here the new school stops. We are given no further economic or sociological analysis. Even as 'history from below' this is very limited. It takes us only a part of the way down the social scale. Beneath the level of political action there were the real poor, of town and country, and despite their numbers they have not yet emerged into the light of history. What the Revolution meant for them has hardly been examined. Even more surprising, since Lefebvre's magisterial contributions the peasants seem to have dropped out of the history of the Revolution. It is equally surprising that he himself never followed up his own initiatives in the study of provincial towns, his early work on Cherbourg and Orleans remaining for post-humous publication.[12] Research on the French provinces is also much neglected, apart from a recent work by Olwen Hufton on Bayeux,[13] so that what we call the history of revolutionary France remains for the greater part the history of Paris. The main exception to this statement is the Vendée.[14] This has naturally attracted attention because of the counter-revolutionary rising which occurred there. For the same reason any conclusions which are drawn from the history of the Vendée have to be treated as exceptional and not necessarily to be confirmed by other aspects of provincial history. Until more work has been done on the poor and the peasants, the history of the Revolution, even when it attempts a social analysis, is likely to prove inadequate in these respects. Moreover, in a country containing such wide divergences no Paris-based history can really tell us what was going on in other parts of the country.

What is more surprising is that even for Paris we learn from recent work much more about political developments than about the social pattern. Apart from an initiative taken by Norman Hampson,[15] the socially oriented history of the Revolution seems to have come to a dead end. The reason, as I have tried to show elsewhere, is not difficult to detect. History, if it is to be something more than pure chronology, has to be also something more than straight political history. It has to be the history of human activity in a specific form, such as religion or law or politics or production. By social history I understand the history of the changing patterns into which the life of man as a social animal falls. It demands equally a chronological explanation of the succession of relevant events and an analysis of the evolving pattern of the society which is being studied. The second of these has generally been lacking, with the result that up to the present a great quantity of factual discovery has been robbed of most of its value either by the lack of conclusions or by the trivial repetitiveness of conclusions which had been reached long before on the basis of much less adequate documentation.

The present state of revolutionary historiography as it emerges from this description is not an encouraging one. Work is doubtless under way which will change the picture, but at the moment we must look outside the history of the revolutionary age itself for the promise of future progress. Social history moves at a different pace from political history and needs to be envisaged on a different time scale. The political history of sixteenth-century France or of the Third Republic can throw little light on the politics of the Revolution: the social patterns of both can help us to understand Revolutionary society. It is gradually coming to be recognized even by historians of the Revolution that 1789, and still less 1799 or 1815, were far from being the great turning points in social history that they were in politics and were once supposed to have been in the social pattern. Major changes undoubtedly there were during the whole period, but to understand them we require to know more than we do of the society on which they were imposed and of that which emerged from them. Fortunately this is becoming possible. It is no paradox to say that the important contributions to the social history of the Revolution in recent years have come either from the history of the *ancien régime* or of the nineteenth century.

One detailed study of the pre-Revolution,[16] what Lefebvre called the *révolte nobiliaire*, although primarily political, and indeed *because* primarily political, has important implications for the social history of the Revolution. It shows the whole opening phase of the Revolution in France, in the hands of nobles, parlementaires and a few upper bourgeoisie, as in every sense an aristocratic revolution. Even when it ceased to be this it still kept more than a few of its aristocratic supporters.

Secondly, the same history of the pre-Revolution brings out, in the efforts of Calonne and Loménie de Brienne, the extent to which the Revolution followed on and indeed resulted from the failure of earlier attempts at administrative reform by royal ministers. In this field we have had recently only a study of the Ministry of the Interior under Roland.[17] A demonstration of the continuity of the struggle for administrative reform is provided by a study of the long attempt to make France into a single customs union by abolishing the network of internal tolls which were such a heavy burden on French trade and industry. Begun no later than Colbert, it was continued almost without intermission up to 1789 and finally achieved success under the Revolution.[18] This is an exceptional study. In general we must be struck with the inadequacy of the treatment of administrative questions, which has contributed in addition to the failure to see the Revolution as an age of reform.

This brings me finally to what, I believe, has been the greatest weakness in the historiography of the Revolution in recent years. Except in political history it has been excessively confined to the few short years of the Revolution proper. This, I suggest, is a main source of all the weaknesses to which I have drawn attention in this paper. The history of revolutionary ideas, the Revolution as an age of reform, its economic history, social history, including the history of those most resistant to change — the poor and the peasants, provincial history (always more slow-moving than that of Paris) — all these can only be brought out if we envisage them in a larger setting than the few years from 1789 to 1794. We can really only understand them when we know the changes that were already under way before 1789 and the true nature of the society which emerged from the revolutionary age. Fortunately this is becoming possible. Work under way or already produced is revealing the social pattern and changes both in the *ancien régime* and in nineteenth-century France. Social analysis, applied to pre- and post-Revolution society in France, is slowly moving in on the Revolution from both sides and in so doing it will inevitably expand our outlook on the Revolution itself, overcome the limitations, and break down the conservatism of revolutionary historians.[19]

# 1

## THE ENLIGHTENMENT AND THE FRENCH REVOLUTION

THE debate over the problem of the relation between the ideas of eighteenth-century France and the Revolution is not new. I have been aware of it ever since reading, as a schoolboy, what then seemed to me, and must still seem to many, the convincing explanation of Taine. 'When', he wrote, 'we see a man ... apparently sound and of peaceful habits, drink eagerly of a new liquor, then suddenly fall to the ground, foaming at the mouth ... we have no hesitation in supposing that in the pleasant draught there was some dangerous ingredient.'[1] The man, of course, was France, the liquor the Enlightenment, and the fit that overtook the unwise imbiber was the French Revolution. Similes are the camouflage of bad history, but Taine also puts it more succinctly. 'Millions of savages', he says, 'were launched into action by a few thousand babblers.'[2]

Does anyone read Taine now? Some sixty years ago Aulard said that at the Sorbonne a candidate for the diploma in historical studies or the doctorate would disqualify himself if he quoted Taine as an authority on any historical question.[3] Curiously enough, on the basic aspects of the problem under discussion here, Taine and his critic were in fundamental agreement. They both believed that an historian should be interested in causes, not as yet having learned from philosophers of history the impossibility of getting from one set of facts to another set of facts except by the interposition of a third set of facts, and so on *ad infinitum*; and they believed that ideas were the essential motive force in history. We should not be too critical of their interpretation of the relationship between the Enlightenment and the Revolution. The belief that the Revolution was caused by the spread of enlightened ideas is natural enough. It was put forward at the time by Burke and schematized by the Abbé Barruel in the form of a triple conspiracy — conspiracy being the easiest way of accounting for any great calamity of which one does not understand the origins. The three prongs of the conspiracy, as Barruel saw it, were (i) an anti-Christian conspiracy by the philosophers; (ii) these sophists of impiety were joined by the sophists of rebellion in the occult lodges of the Freemasons; (iii) impiety and anarchy became fused into a conspiracy against all religion, government and property in the sect of the *Illuminés*. The heads of the conspiracy were Voltaire, d'Alembert, Frederick II and Diderot, its chief weapon the *Encyclopédie*, and its active agent the club of the Jacobins.[4]

The historians of the nineteenth century continued the same basic assumption, except that instead of regarding the Revolution as a disaster, they began to regard it as a good thing, and hence not the work of conspirators spreading dangerous ideas but the people inspired by noble ones. Thus, for Lamartine the Revolution came into existence the day when printing was invented, for this made public opinion possible: eighteenth-century philosophy was the code of civil and religious liberty put into action in the Revolution by the people.[5] Michelet is more specific. He says, 'When these two men [Voltaire and Rousseau] had formed their ideas, the Revolution was accomplished in the high realm of the mind.'[6] But this was only because they expressed the thought of the masses, 'the chief author was the people'.[7] Of course, the eighteenth century could not have seen the Revolution as the revolt of the masses, since the masses did not exist before the great growth of population and urbanization that characterized the nineteenth century. The eighteenth-century belief in the primacy of ideas, however, persisted, even when the newer conditions of the nineteenth century had brought economic motivation to the fore, as it was in the history of Louis Blanc. Writing, like Karl Marx, in that great incubator of revolutionary thought the British Museum, Louis Blanc used the Croker collection of pamphlets, from which, aided by his own experience of France under the July Monarchy, he discovered the contempt of the revolutionary bourgeois for the people and the hatred of the people for the bourgeois.[8] This, added to the struggle of the *tiers état* against the privileged orders, could have been interpreted in terms of a class struggle and conflict of economic interests, but Louis Blanc, for all his socialist ideology, still puts the revolutionary struggle as one of conflicting principles

— authority, individualism and fraternity, corresponding respectively to noblesse, bourgeoisie and people. There were few students of the revolutionary period who, like de Tocqueville, saw social and political factors as more powerful than ideas.[9] Even socialist historians, such as Jaurès, Mathiez, Lefebvre and Labrousse, for all their awareness of economic factors, still seem to interpret the Revolution as basically a conflict of principles, a struggle for the hearts of men. 'All historians agree on the influence of *lumières* on the Revolution,' wrote Professor Jacques Godechot recently, 'but disagree whether their influence is essential, or secondary to economic factors.'[10]

The problem adumbrated here is not one which is peculiar to the French Revolution. The degree of influence to be attributed to ideas is an unresolved question in respect of all great historical movements — Renaissance and Reformation, Industrial Revolution, benevolent despotism, as well as French Revolution. The attempt to dispose of this difficulty by treating ideas as merely the ideologies of social classes underestimates the elasticity of principles, what Whitehead called the 'adventures of ideas'.[11] They cannot be identified with social forces; for once an idea has been let loose on the world, no one knows where it will settle or what new movement it will start. This is not a reason for abandoning the attempt to establish connections between changes in ideas and political and social developments, but it does suggest that these connections need to be examined with as much care and criticism of the evidence as would be applied to any other historical problem. Although contemporaries and historians have agreed on the causal relation between the thought of the eighteenth century, or more specifically the Enlightenment, and the Revolution, it has usually been on the basis of assumptions about both that have hardly survived more recent historical analysis.

What do we now understand by the Enlightenment? Its enemies, from the time of Burke and the Abbé Barruel, have condemned it for dealing in abstractions, to which the real interests of actual men and women are sacrificed. It can hardly be denied that the Enlightenment, though scientific and empirical on the one hand, was also a system of abstract, generalizing thought which tried to substitute impersonal for personal forces over a large range of human life: indeed the measure to which it succeeded in doing this is the measure of its success in changing much of the social ethic of Western civilization. If we look for rational, physical causes of misfortunes instead of attributing them to witchcraft, if we accept the impersonal wage system in place of personal slavery, if we reject the torture of individuals as a means of eliciting the truth and use instead the impersonal rules of the law, if we do not regard personal salvation as so important that we are prepared to burn people in order to achieve it for them as well as for ourselves, if we do not believe that the stars are concerned with our individual fortunes, and so on, we are tacitly acknowledging the influence of the Enlightenment over our assumptions and actions; for the opposite was in each case the normal view before what has so often been condemned as the abstract thought of the Enlightenment extended the scientific, generalizing approach from physical nature to human actions. The Enlightenment was the end of a spiritual world ruled by angels and demons, cherubim and seraphim, Beelzebub and Satan. 'Farewell rewards and fairies.' In religion, the Enlightenment substituted the impersonal god of deism for a personal deity, and scepticism about the dogmas of revealed religion was followed by toleration. Systems of ethics based on religious authority and sanctions were replaced by ideas of utilitarianism and humanitarianism and the search for a new ethic. There is a paradox by which the ages most condemned at the time for immorality are in fact those most concerned with morality. Such were fifth-century Athens and eighteenth-century Western Europe.

It is not my purpose, nor is it necessary here, to provide a detailed survey of the ideas of the Enlightenment; but any account, however brief, cannot fail to point out that one element is the strong current of political liberalism that runs through it. This is particularly important for the present argument, in that the Revolution, whatever else it may have been, was also a struggle for political power. In the course of this were revived many of the political concepts employed by the political writers of seventeenth-century England to justify the revolutions of that century. Locke's political ideas, in particular, were introduced into eighteenth-century France in the translations and commentaries of Burlamaqui and Barbeyrac. They were reproduced by the chevalier de Jaucourt in his contributions to the *Encyclopédie*. They appear in a modified form in the writings of Montesquieu, Rousseau, d'Holbach or Mably, and are not absent from those of Voltaire and Diderot. However, the political content of the French Enlightenment must not be exaggerated. If we exclude Montesquieu and Rousseau, we are left for the most part with general sentiments about the desirability of liberty and the undesirability of despotism, with especial reference to freedom of thought and religion. The influence of Montesquieu's emphasis on the virtues of the English constitution did not outlast the third quarter of the century, and his famous *Esprit des lois* was often, though not quite correctly, interpreted merely as a defence of the claims of the French *parlements*.[12] Rousseau's *Contrat social* had no ascertainable influence before the Revolution and only a very debatable one during its course.[13] True, there is the oft-repeated story of Marat reading it to enthralled crowds at street corners,[14] but anyone who could believe this could believe anything.

Alternatively, there has been the suggestion that the *philosophes* were the theorists of benevolent despotism. This view has been too effectively dealt with elsewhere to require any further demolition here.[15] In so far as it ever appeared to have any plausibility, this was due to the confusion of the *philosophes* with the small group of Physiocrats, and only with the first generation even of these.

It must be recognized that the French Enlightenment was on the whole lacking in systematic political theory; it was hardly to be expected in a country which had no active politics. Since the French Revolution was primarily a political revolution, this must cast doubt upon its supposed causal relationship with the Enlightenment. But we are left with the need to ask, if they did not come from the Enlightenment, what were the sources of the political theories of the Revolution, which if they did not cause it — and this would be difficult to prove in any case — at least were used to justify it. Framed in these terms, however, this is a problem that is not susceptible of a single answer. There is now general agreement that the picture of the French Revolution as a bloc with one inspiration, though used in the propaganda both of supporters and opponents of 'the Revolution', is invalid. The historic reality is a series of revolutions, very different in their aims and therefore in any theoretical affiliations they may have had.

The revolutionary period opened, in 1787, with what has been termed the *révolte nobiliaire*. This was in effect an attempt on the part of sections of the privileged classes to take over the government of France. It was an aristocratic movement, using the term in its strictly political sense of government by those who believed in rule of an aristocracy. Thus one could have a 'bourgeois aristocrat' or even a 'peasant aristocrat', and on the other hand a patriot noble.[16] The theoretical justification for such a polity evidently cannot be sought in the Enlightenment. There is an obvious ancestry — without venturing into any speculations about causal connections — in the political literature of the Fronde and of the so-called faction of the duke of Burgundy under Louis XIV.

A second revolution, the peasant revolt of 1789, which has been correctly singled out by Lefebvre as a separate and autonomous movement, was a practical revolt against practical grievances. It could have occurred at any time when circumstances were favourable, and no theory was needed to instigate or justify it. There had been a paper attack on 'feudalism', it is true, running through the century,[17] but this bore remarkably little relationship to the ills of the peasantry, and when it was employed on the famous night of the Fourth of August, it was used in an attempt to save what could be saved of the seigneurial rights and dues by limiting the definition of 'feudal' rather than to promote the rising against them.[18]

What made the peasant revolt possible, however, had been a third revolutionary movement, that of the *tiers état*, which followed on the *révolte nobiliaire*. Here we certainly meet with political ideas in abundance, at least of expression. This is not the place for a detailed analysis of the ideology of the *tiers état*. It can hardly be questioned, however, that its central theme was the idea of popular sovereignty, which was given its fullest expression by the Abbé Sieyes in the most famous pamphlet of the Revolution, which, because it embodied the wishes of the Third Estate, obtained unprecedented circulation. In *Qu'est-ce que le tiers état?* Sieyes stated the new political ideology in uncompromising form. 'The nation', he wrote, 'is prior to everything. It is the source of everything. Its will is always legal. The manner in which a nation exercises its will does not matter; the point is that it does exercise it; any procedure is adequate, and its will is always the supreme law.'[19] The logical consequence of this extreme assertion of popular or national sovereignty, as I have suggested elsewhere, is to identify the people with the government, the rulers with the ruled.[20] The result of apparently removing the need for any check on government must be something very like what Professor Talmon has called totalitarian democracy. It should be noted in qualification that the application of this idea in the French Revolution was nothing like as extreme as it has been subsequently, and that totalitarianism, even in an embryonic form, is more easily associated with the Napoleonic dictatorship than with the revolutionary assemblies.

For our present purpose, however, the problem is whether, or how far, the revolutionary idea of popular sovereignty can be derived from the thought of the Enlightenment; and the answer must be that it is not easily to be found in the writings of the *philosophes* or of their seventeenth-century predecessors. Locke, who summed up the political thinking of the seventeenth century and passed it on to the eighteenth, directed his whole argument to limiting sovereignty of any kind. The same can be said of Montesquieu, de Jaucourt, Voltaire and d'Holbach. To Rousseau alone is it even plausible to attribute any conception of the sovereignty of the people; and it is not difficult to see that even in his case the attribution rests upon an elementary, though common, misunderstanding of his thought. Sovereignty for Rousseau resides in the General Will, and the General Will is an ideal will — what would be willed by the people if it were willing only in the common interest, enlightened and disinterested. Even so the General Will is restricted by him to the function of making general laws. Government, involving individual acts, does not enter into its scope.[21]

Indeed any theory of absolute sovereignty is incompatible with the political liberalism of the Enlightenment. The supremacy of the interests of the people is another matter, and this indeed can be attributed to the thinkers of the Enlightenment, who were all more or less explicitly utilitarian in their social philosophy. The revolutionary theory of popular sovereignty only appeared when the belief that government should be in the interests of the people was fused with the principle of sovereignty, deriving from quite a different source. Eighteenth-century France learned the idea and the practice of sovereignty from the absolute monarchy. It was not difficult, when the leaders of the *tiers état* made their bid for power, to envisage their aim as the transference of the sovereignty from the monarchy to the people. That this was so was tacitly acknowledged when they substituted *lèse-nation* for *lèse-majesté*.

The Revolution, thus, was inaugurated not by the application of an old political idea but by the invention of a new one. Even this might not have been so decisive if it had not been applied also in a new political and social situation, for in the last quarter of the eighteenth century romanticism and the religious revival were creating new political conditions. They gave emotional content and organic unity to the idea of the people, and so made possible the rise of what might loosely be called totalitarian thought. It is significant that even in the contemporary world, totalitarian regimes have only been successfully established in countries with strong religious orthodoxies, such as Italy, Germany and Russia.

The end of the eighteenth century may truly be said to have witnessed a partial transition from an individualist to a collectivist view of society; but this was not a continuation of, but a break away from, the ideas of the Enlightenment. For Locke and his followers a state had been a society of individuals associated together by voluntary choice for the pursuit of common interests and ideals. Rousseau's people was a *corps moral*, that is to say an artificial body, a collection of individuals.[22] With the romantic movement the idea of the people gained historic dimensions and organic unity. It became the nation. In Lockian and enlightened thought the state had existed for the sake of the individual. Now the view began to grow that the individual existed for the sake of the nation. It was a sign of the new age when, in the first revolutionary constitution, the king of France became the *roi des Français*. The Revolution ends the age of individualism and opens that of nationalism. At the same time, politics became more emotional, now that it had to appeal to large numbers. Journalism assumed its modern role of whipping up popular passions and lowering the level of political discussion. Wars became national and therefore much more bitter. In all this can be seen not the fulfilment but the frustration of the Enlightenment. It has always been difficult to believe that the liberal political ideas of the Enlightenment were the source of revolutionary terrorism, oligarchy and military dictatorship. It ceases to be a problem if we realize that such developments were indeed not the result of the Enlightenment but of the new social and political trends that appeared in the last quarter of the eighteenth century.

The revolutionary period, which in the past has been most often linked with the Enlightenment, cannot be understood unless we realize that it was also the period of the romantic and conservative reaction. In the Revolution itself, historians have in recent years discovered the presence of conservative and even reactionary trends, and this has involved much rethinking and rewriting of its history. Now, being invited to think in new ways about subjects which one had thought were safely docketed and pigeonholed can be very distressing, as is shown in an article by Mr Franklin L. Ford.[23] A lecture I gave some ten years ago suggesting the need for revisionism in revolutionary history seemed to him to cast doubt on the fundamental reality of the Revolution, and in his article Mr Ford set out to reassert that there *was* a revolutionary age. The article is hardly likely to have a major influence on historical thought, and I would not have troubled with it if it did not also illustrate a common form of confusion which is relevant to the present discussion. To prove that there really was a French Revolution that effected revolutionary changes throughout the whole gamut of European society, Mr Ford lists the developments of the turn of the century in literature, music, the visual arts, administration and institutions, social structure, the strategy of war, and so on. That there were these and many more changes is undeniable: they can be found in any textbook. But Mr Ford's anxiety to rehabilitate the French Revolution led him into making the assumption that all these changes – revolutionary, counter-revolutionary, non-revolutionary – were identified with, or resulted from, the French Revolution. Therefore, the conclusion is, 'In 1789, after long, confused preliminaries, the old Europe began a transformation, convulsive, bewildering, to some of the participants wildly exhilarating, to others bitterly tragic.'[24]

The history of a period that is full of such a variety of currents and cross-currents is more complicated and requires a more sophisticated analysis than this simple approach allows for. For the same reason, any attempt to link the Revolution – or, to be more exact, any of the successive revolutions – with the Enlightenment, as a single case of cause and effect, is unacceptable. To do this would be to distort the ideas of the Enlightenment and to reduce the history of the Revolution to a myth. It does not follow from this that we must write off the Enlightenment completely as an influence in the Revolution. Agreed that the Enlightenment had no identifiable part in causing any of the successive revolutions between 1787 and 1795, and that the revolutionary ideology of popular sovereignty ran counter to its basic political ideas, even so there was a great deal more in the Revolution than this.

To see only the principle of sovereignty in the political ideology of the revolutionaries is to ignore the strong elements of liberalism, derived from the Lockian tradition of the Enlightenment, in it. It would also be a wilful disregard of patent facts to pretend that when the members of the *États Généraux* and the subsequent revolutionary assemblies came to Versailles, they did not bring along the effects of their education and their reading in the literature of the eighteenth century. They were inevitably the children of the Enlightenment, and if, as I have suggested, they could get little in the way of specific political theory from the *philosophes*, they could get much in the way of humanitarian ideas and legal reform. Thus, torture as an element in judicial procedure, which reached its height between the fifteenth and seventeenth centuries, was eliminated from the law and very largely from practice. Despite the opposition of powerful vested interests, the Revolution saw the inauguration of a campaign for the abolition of both slavery and the slave trade, though it achieved success in France only in 1848. Religious toleration and the extension of civic rights to non-Catholics had made some progress before the Revolution: it was carried through to completion in the course of the revolutionary secularization of the state. The codification of the laws, which the revolutionary assemblies set in hand and Napoleon completed, represents the fulfilment of an ideal of Voltaire. And, not to go into further detail, the positive creed of the Enlightenment, the search for happiness (*bonheur*) was also one end of the Revolution. 'Un peuple', declared St Just on November 29th, 1792, 'qui n'est pas heureux, n'a pas de patrie.'

But in reaching this utilitarian ideal we have also reached the point at which the Revolution broke away from the Enlightenment. Here, Bentham and utilitarianism carried forward its true inheritance. The Revolution, meanwhile, strayed from the primrose path of enlightened happiness to the strait and narrow road of Jacobin virtue, from the principle of representative and constitutional government to the rule of an authoritarian élite, from the *philosophes'* ideal of peace to the revolutionaries' crusading war and the Napoleonic dream of conquest. Nothing could have been more alien to the Enlightenment than this transition from the ideals of democracy and peace to a policy of dictatorship and war. It has been said that the principles of the *lumières* light up the Revolution intermittently, like the beam of a lighthouse swinging round brilliantly and then disappearing. The influence of the Enlightenment cannot be disregarded in any history of the French Revolution; but the revolutionaries did not set their course by its light in the beginning, nor did they steer the ship of state into the haven of the Enlightenment in the end.

# 2

## HISTORIANS AND THE CAUSES
## OF THE
## FRENCH REVOLUTION

HISTORY is essentially a story: that is a platitude and like most platitudes tells us little. The unstated assumption is that the links in the story are connected together. If an event could be conceived as existing in isolation, unconnected with other events by a chain of causation, it would not be a part of history. The analysis of causes and consequences, therefore, lies at the very heart of historical studies. To say that a particular event, or series of events, is historically significant, is a way of saying that it is a focal point in the relation of cause and effect, a knot in the skein, towards and away from which many threads of historical development can be traced. Few chapters in history have equalled in such significance the French Revolution. The discussion of its causes has therefore naturally dominated writing on the history of eighteenth-century France. My object in this essay is to pick out and examine some of the better-known treatments of this theme.

The problem of the cause, or causes, of the Revolution was first stated, and a solution offered, before the Revolution itself had proceeded very far on its way, by the greatest political writer of the age, EDMUND BURKE, whose interpretation of the Revolution gave a bias to historical studies from which they have hardly recovered even at the present day. It must be premised that any attempt to summarize the arguments of his *Reflections on the Revolution in France* necessarily robs them of the emotional quality which is their great strength. Burke saw the Revolution as the expression of a view of the world which would be fatal to what he regarded as the two foundations of society, religion and landed property. But he also saw it, almost from the beginning, as an outbreak of popular violence and wanton cruelty, of what he would have called sadism if the Marquis de Sade had yet provided it with a name. The profound humanitarian spirit which he shared with the best minds of his age, and the eighteenth-century devotion to the rule of law, combined to produce a conviction in his mind that the Revolution was the embodiment of evil. Burke's mind was completely made up when he wrote the *Reflections*: the Revolution was a bad thing. Being bad, it was also unnecessary. This was the fundamental assumption underlying all that he had to say of its causes.

France, he claimed, possessed before 1789 the elements of a constitution nearly as good as could have been wished. He paid tribute to the virtues of the king and queen, clergy and nobility, in eloquent passages. France was prospering in its economy. The absence of fundamental dissatisfaction with the regime was evidenced by the *cahiers*, which asked only for specific reforms; and indeed reforms were already being introduced by one of the mildest governments in Europe. There was much that was plausible in this, but if it represented the whole story even the contemporary reader was bound to ask why there was a Revolution at all. Burke's answer was that it arose not out of the need for reforms, nor even out of the demand for a new constitution, on which he admitted, rather inconsistently, there was general agreement in France. It arose, to use his own words, out of the preference of a despotic democracy over the principles of the British Constitution. The Revolution, he claimed, was the consequence of the calling of a National Assembly which represented the 'enterprising talents' of the nation instead of its property. Behind the petty lawyers, doctors, curés, professional men and the like, of the Assembly, Burke detected two sinister influences. The first was constituted by that clique of literary men which had conducted so long and infamous a campaign against religion. The second was the growing monied interest, which, moved by its jealousy of the old aristocracy, joined in an infamous alliance of destruction with the disciples of Voltaire and Rousseau for the purpose of uprooting French society from its foundations.

This is a familiar analysis, which has appeared many times since Burke first invented it. What can be regarded as valid in it and what has to be discarded? First, it must be said that the initial assumption, that in France before 1789 there were legitimate constitutional checks on royal authority, while it would have been accepted by the *parlements* — the courts of venal, hereditary magistrates who thought that they embodied in themselves the constitution of France — would have been repudiated by the reformers and contested by the upholders of royal power. The thesis of the royal lawyers of the seventeenth century had been that the whole law and government of France resided in the bosom of the king, and that there was no such thing as a constitutional check on royal power. Reformers agreed with this as a statement of the facts, though they wished to change them. The pre-1789 constitution, on which Burke laid so much store, amounted to no more than the claims of the narrow and selfish caste of lawyers entrenched in the *parlements*, and the political ambitions of a decadent *noblesse*. He had swallowed the propaganda of the aristocratic reaction, which was in fact the first stage in the Revolution, entire and without question.

What Burke said of the virtues of the king had much truth in it, but absence of vice, accompanied by the absence of almost every other positive quality, was hardly an adequate qualification for a technically absolute monarch. As for Marie Antoinette, poor woman, one would never suspect from Burke's glowing, romantic eulogies that *her* reputation had long been reduced to tatters by her own lack of discretion and the campaign of scurrility waged against her by her enemies of the Court, headed by the princes of the blood. One would suppose that Burke himself was ignorant of the attacks upon her, were it not for a passing mention, in the *Reflections*, of the slanders of wretches branded with the *fleur de lis*, which obviously refers to the mendacious memoirs of Jeanne de la Motte Valois, the shady heroine of the affair of the diamond necklace. But for Burke a queen was by definition virtuous. In the same way he was anxious to emphasize the virtues of the privileged classes. His praise of the moral elevation of the higher clergy — 'I believe the instances of eminent depravity may be as rare amongst them as those of transcendent goodness' — is not without disingenuousness. The curés, who were not on the whole unworthy of respect, were precisely those whose presence in the National Assembly he condemned. As evidence of the virtues of the *noblesse*, he drew attention to a few exceptional men from among the liberal aristocrats. Describing the government of France before the Revolution truly as a reforming government, he refrained from adding how many of the projected reforms had been frustrated or rendered ineffective by the opposition of the privileged classes and the weakness of the king.

To complete his rosy picture of the *ancien régime* Burke emphasized, correctly, the natural wealth of France and the increase in economic activity during the eighteenth century. But, like most of his contemporaries, he failed to observe the problem of a population growing more rapidly than food supply, the distress caused by failures of the harvest, or the steep rise in prices, unaccompanied by a corresponding rise in wages, during the years immediately before the Revolution. Indeed, Burke left on one side the whole economic aspect of the problem; the question of taxation he slurred over, and the grievances of the peasants went unmentioned.

As for the explanation offered in the *Reflections* for the outbreak of the Revolution, for the moment it must be enough to say that no serious student could today accept Burke's views on the influence of eighteenth-century writers without the most extensive qualifications. The other revolutionary element that Burke detected in French society was the monied interest. Unfortunately, whether because of lack of detailed knowledge, or because money, after all, was property, and to present the Revolution as a civil war between two forms of property was hardly in keeping with his plan, Burke made no attempt to follow up this argument.

In so far as the *Reflections* deal with the causes of the Revolution, then, they are not merely inadequate, but misleading. Apart from Burke's violent *parti pris*, it is not difficult to see another reason for the failure of his analysis in this connection, compared with his success in discussing other movements of his time. On the American colonies he had been one of the best-informed men in England; he knew the facts of the Irish problem at first hand; he at least did his best to prepare himself for his speeches on Indian affairs by a thorough study of all the sources of information available to him. On the other hand, his one visit to France had left him with strong prejudices, which the information provided by émigrés, especially priests, did not correct. His knowledge of France was limited and it is difficult to believe that he ever understood the pre-revolutionary situation. As literature, as political theory, as anything but history, his *Reflections* are magnificent.

As a study of the causes of the Revolution they amount to little more than an elaboration of the 'plot' theory favoured by the émigrés.

As early as 1790 the idea that the Revolution was the result of a conspiracy had begun to appear in royalist literature. This thesis received its fullest exposition in the *Mémoires pour servir à l'histoire de Jacobinisme* of the abbé Barruel in 1797–9. Barruel uncovered a triple conspiracy of *philosophes*, freemasons and *illuminés*, headed by Voltaire, d'Alembert, Diderot and Frederick II, which has haunted the history of the causes of the Revolution ever since, but which need not be taken very seriously. The conspiracy thesis represents the common reaction of contemporaries to any development which they deplore but do not understand. In this respect Burke was no wiser than the rest. It is odd to reflect how much more successful he was in prophesying the consequences than in analysing the antecedents of the Revolution.

*

A striking contrast with Burke is provided by the modest observations of a contemporary who discussed the causes of the Revolution only incidentally. One could hardly find a wider divergence than that between the violent denunciation of the Revolution by Burke and its treatment by Arthur Young in his *Travels in France*. Burke started with a series of prejudices and a case to prove. ARTHUR YOUNG had no preconceived views; he simply began with the facts that were evident to an acute and honest observer who happened to tour France during the crisis. His *Travels* are a case-book on the agricultural condition of France, with a running commentary on politics and an appended study of the causes of the Revolution. He was able to appreciate from personal observation all over the French countryside the reality of grievances arising out of royal taxation, militia service, *corvées*, *gabelles*, *capitaineries*, seigneurial dues, tithes and the like, about which Burke was silent. He was impressed by the appearance of general poverty among the people, the lower standard of living compared with that of England, the high price of bread, and the extent in 1788–9 of unemployment. He did not slavishly believe everything that he was told. His observations are a corrective to some generally accepted views of the time. For example, he points

out that the *lettres de cachet* did not constitute a widespread grievance, and in any case had almost fallen into disuse under Louis
XVI. He draws attention to the fact that many of the nobles,
instead of being mere court parasites, lived similar lives as country
gentlemen to those of the corresponding class in England. He
was struck, however, by the intensity of the caste spirit in France.
Witnessing the Revolution on the spot and while it was in its
early stages, he had no doubt that existing evils amply justified
it. But he also realized that revolutions do not arise from grievances without someone to lead and direct them, and his comments
on the revolutionary agitation exhibit the acuteness of his observation. He appreciated the large part played by the *parlements* in
creating a revolutionary situation, and at the same time their
purely selfish and reactionary motives. He did not believe in the
spontaneous outbreak of revolt in Paris and other towns, and
recorded the general view that the mobs were raised with the aid
of financial support from the bourgeois leaders of the *tiers état*.
He commented also on the widespread suspicion of the intrigues
and ambitions of the duke of Orleans. The *Travels in France* of
Arthur Young are not a history, but his capacity for keen and —
apart from a certain tendency to compare things French and
English, usually to the advantage of the latter — unprejudiced
observation, makes them one of the most valuable sources on the
condition of France on the eve of the Revolution. He had a shrewd
idea of many of the elements that had contributed to making a
revolutionary situation, and he did not try to sum them up in
any simple, all-embracing formula.

*

It may be said that so far we have not yet arrived at what can
properly be called history. But contemporary, or near-contempo-
rary commentators are important, not only because they provide
source material, but also because they are apt to set the pattern
which historians later, consciously or unconsciously, follow. The
generation after the Revolution, though it witnessed a great
development in historical writing in France, added little to contemporary comment on its causes. Alison, in England, wrote a
history of the Revolution for the purpose of demonstrating the
dangers of political change; and a school textbook, in France,

summed up the last twenty-five years of French history in a single sentence: '1789–1815 — During this period France was a prey to disorder.'

As the Revolution receded into the past it became possible for historians to envisage it with a degree of cautious sympathy, and to begin to assess its causes more objectively. But the first two notable historians to tackle the problem, Thiers and Mignet, both wrote their histories of the Revolution partly as contributions to the political campaign against the Bourbons. THIERS began by taking over the work of a hack writer employed by a bookseller to turn out historical textbooks, so the early pages are not the best. Apart from this, an historian who keeps as persistently to the surface of events as Thiers is not likely to have much of interest to say on the causes of anything. He traces the general demand for the calling of the States General to a joke made by a councillor. His explanation of the outbreak of the Revolution amounts largely to the view that it was a chapter of accidents; but his closeness to actual events enabled him to pick out one important factor, which his successors forgot. If the king, he wrote, had established some equality in official appointments, and given some guarantees, all discontent would have been appeased. Behind this judgment was the superficial assumption that the revolutionary politicians were ambitious career-hunters like himself — and of course a fair number of them were.

*

MIGNET's is a much greater name among historians, and even in his early work on the French Revolution the reason why can be seen. His limpid narrative runs swiftly down a well-marked course. For the causes of the Revolution he looks mainly to political motives. He regards the royal government as arbitrary and decadent, and detects the fatal influence of Maurepas behind the weakness of Louis XVI. He sees that the opposition of the *parlements* initiated the Revolution, and that *parlements* and *noblesse* only demanded the calling of the States General in the hope of using them against both crown and people. What the privileged classes had failed to appreciate, he notes, was the rise of the Third Estate, which by 1789 had become a force that could not be overthrown. The experience of the revolutionary and Napoleonic era had imprinted on the historical mind of France a strong sense of fatality, and of individual powerlessness to change the course of events. 'When a reform has become necessary,' writes Mignet, 'and the moment to achieve it has arrived, nothing can stand in its way and everything serves its progress.'

*

In the absence of the detailed evidence from which a plausible sequence of events could be derived, it was natural that historical explanation should take the form first of a hypothetical conspiracy, and then of the great forces of irresistible destiny. These two alternative explanations have dominated historical interpretation of the causes of the Revolution to the present day. In the earlier years they are presented in a rather crude and simple form. By the 'thirties, however, printed sources for the history of the Revolution were beginning to accumulate and more detailed treatment was possible. These were exploited first by English writers, in the shrewd essays of Croker and others, and more notably in CARLYLE's *French Revolution*, the first four books of which are devoted to the period preceding the Revolution. But if Burke leaves us with such a favourable impression of the *ancien régime* that we are forced to ask how, save by a spontaneous outburst of madness, the Revolution ever came about, Carlyle draws it as a phantasmagoria which it is difficult to believe ever existed at all, outside the pages of the *Arabian Nights*. His description is a parody of French eighteenth-century society, with the oracular judgments of a minor prophet as running commentary. Carlyle's main sources were the memoirs of the courts of Louis XV and Louis XVI. His standpoint was fixed by ideas imbibed partly from the French Saint-Simonians and partly from the German romantic writers. From the former he acquired the theory of the progress of history by the alternation of critical and creative periods, and from the German romantic movement he learnt to look on the eighteenth century as an age of decadence. His picture of the luxury of French society in its higher levels presents a melodramatic contrast with that of the hordes of starving wretches, 'five-and-twenty labouring millions', composing the ulcerated body of the nation. Everything is corrupt. Monarchy is Mumbo-jumbo. The nobles, presumed supports of the throne, are 'singular gilt pasteboard caryatides in that singular edifice'. Under Louis XV all is a 'mouldering mass of Sensuality and Falsehood', and when Louis XVI's reign opens with philanthropy and hope, what is this but mere diseased sentimentality?

Eighteenth-century France is so rotten an edifice in Carlyle's description that one wonders why he takes the trouble to provide any specific reasons for its collapse. However, he adduces bankrupt finance and bad philosophy as the agencies through which nemesis was to descend on the *ancien régime*. His view that the extravagances of the court were the chief cause of the deficit is hardly to be criticized too severely, for it was commonly believed at the time. The financiers naturally did not publish the fact, even if they were aware of it, that the interest on loans — mostly incurred to finance the American war — was responsible for approximately one-third of the annual expenditure and the whole expenses of the court for only about one-ninth. As for 'French philosophism', he has no good to say of that. 'Here, indeed, lies properly the cardinal symptom of the whole widespread malady.' He has the true German romantic contempt for the age of enlightenment. He lashes the scepticism of the *philosophes*, the 'thin wiredrawn intrigues' of *Figaro*, the 'prurient corruption' of *Paul et Virginie*. True, Rousseau and the political writers, he imagines, have substituted a new Faith for the old scepticism, but it is no more pleasing to him. Social contracts and constitutions are not for the prophet of the leadership-principle. 'Theories of government!' says Carlyle with scorn, 'Such have been, and will be; in ages of decadence.'

In two points Carlyle's account of the origins of the Revolution is deserving of respect. He realized the important share of the *parlements* in the events leading up to the Revolution, and here at least his contempt for assemblies of any kind, and his natural foible for tyrants, enabled him to see them as the venal and selfish defenders of their own vested interests that they were. Secondly, the same natural bias enabled him to appreciate and attribute due importance to the weakness of authority that amounted almost to absence of government in France before the Revolution. When we have said this, however, we have said all that we can adduce in favour of Carlyle's presentation of the antecedents of the Revolution. His version of its causes is a fitting preamble to that Hollywood scenario which he called *The French Revolution*; and at the same time it lacks the sense of uncontrolled passion, the picture of human confusion, as of an ant-heap stirred up by a stick, its inhabitants scurrying frantically this way and that in constant, meaningless motion, which gives a fevered vitality to his description of the Revolution itself.

\*

The superficiality of Carlyle's estimate of the causes of the Revolution derives, I think, from his Calvinistic conception of the world as the battle-ground of a simple, uncomplicated struggle between good and the hosts of evil. French historians, at the same time, also saw the Revolution as the climax of a spiritual battle, and they were as absolute as Carlyle in their application of the labels good and evil, only they applied them to the contrary parties. The French historian who comes closest to Carlyle is MICHELET, though for Carlyle the Revolution was purely destructive, while Michelet saw it as a great creative effort. His approach to the Revolution is likely to seem a little obscure to readers who are not familiar with the conflict which underlies modern French history, between the Catholic Church and the tradition of the Revolution, or, to use Michelet's own terms, between the doctrine of Grace and the principle of Justice. By Justice he means the rights of the people, and his account of the origins of the Revolution is written in terms of the progressive recognition of these rights. His starting point is medieval society, in which the people, oppressed and living in the depth of misery, yet manifest only trust and devotion towards those spoilt children of heaven, the priest and the lord. If salvation is the reward of patience, writes Michelet, forgetful of a long history of peasant revolts, then the people truly surpassed all the merits of the saints. In his dramatic sketch of pre-revolutionary France, the condition of the people is ever more wretched. The nobles have gone to Versailles — a remarkable assertion in the light of the fact that the number of noble families on one calculation was about 80,000. The Church has abandoned its charitable duties. The only hope lies in the king, to whom *philosophes* and economists have turned in the illusory hope of a revolution presided over by a king. But who and where, asks Michelet, is the king? He is Louis XV, and has retired to the

Parc-aux-Cerfs, there to indulge his vicious pleasures at the expense of the daughters of the people. Louis, formerly the *Bien-aimé*, is no protector of his people but their bitterest enemy, a hard, egotistic, heartless sensualist, *sans entrailles*. This traditional picture of Louis XV, drawn from the memoirs of disappointed courtiers, dismissed ministers and gossiping lawyers, and written up, for propagandist reasons, during the Revolution, is accepted by Michelet without question. To complete the sketch of a tyrant he adds the material embodied in the Red Book of pensions and gifts, and the horrors of the *lettres de cachet*, for which he relies mainly upon the quite unreliable journalistic *Memoirs of the Bastille* by Linguet.

Such is the nature of the rule of Grace. On the other side, Michelet sets up the prophets of the cause of Law and Justice — Montesquieu, Voltaire and Rousseau. Montesquieu is the interpreter of the rule of law, Voltaire its advocate, Rousseau its founder. The divergences and contradictions between their respective systems of thought do not occur to him. With their writings the Revolution has already triumphed, says Michelet, 'in the high realm of the mind'. His explanation of its outbreak is simple to a degree: into the explosive mixture created by the combination of the misery of the people with the tyranny of the government is dropped the spark of new ideas. Of the part played by political and economic developments in precipitating the Revolution he says little; in fact he fundamentally falsifies the situation by representing the Royal Council as taking the initiative in its long struggle with *parlements* and *noblesse*. If he is right in believing that the Crown opened the gates to the Revolution by summoning the *États Généraux* in the hope of gaining the support of the people against the privileged classes, he does not conceive of the people as possessed of separate, divergent interests. The only distinction he admits in the ranks of the *tiers état* is that between the literate and the illiterate, and even here his argument is that while the educated classes speak and write, they express the thoughts of those who are not vocal. With the corruption and tyranny of the old order on one side, the principles of liberty and justice on the other, Michelet's interpretation of the outbreak of the Revolution, like Carlyle's, is at bottom apocalyptic. The Revolution is the Day of Judgment on the *ancien régime*; but whereas Carlyle's is a calvinist creed and his Revolution represents the culmination of an age of scepticism in which evil casts out evil and all are damned, for Michelet, while the religious faith of old France is drowned by the Revolution in a sea of blood, the cause of Justice and the People takes its first mighty step towards ultimate triumph.

\*

Lamartine, who falls into the same group as Carlyle and Michelet, is too light-weight an historian to measure in our scales, but it would be wrong to neglect Louis Blanc. One of the earliest theorists of state socialism, frustrated and proscribed after the revolution of 1848, writing his many-volumed history of the Revolution of 1789 in exile, Louis Blanc never abandoned his faith in the triumph of right. He is interesting because while he still describes the revolution, like his contemporaries, in terms of the struggle of great spiritual principles, he begins the process by which these were to be transformed into social and economic forces. In a sense, because he is almost the first to perform the trick of conjuring ideological into economic, and does it rather crudely, he gives the game away. Basically he sees history in terms of the successive rule of three great ideas: authority, individualism, fraternity — a triad which has merely to be translated into different terminology to become the familiar sequence of feudalism, the rule of the bourgeoisie, and socialism. He takes one important step beyond Michelet in his analysis of eighteenth-century thinkers. He divides them into those who, with Voltaire, seek liberty through the emancipation of the individual, and those, principally Rousseau, who seek it through the rise of the spirit of fraternity. This is not exactly a valuable contribution to the history of thought; but the importance of this distinction, projected forward, is that it disintegrates the unity of the Revolution, which thus ceases to be an indivisible entity, to be approved or condemned *en bloc*. Louis Blanc was also the first historian to exploit the great mass of revolutionary journals and pamphlets in the British Museum, material which enabled him to detect factors in the French situation which had been hidden from most of his predecessors. He saw the importance of the *parlements* as a constitutional check on the *ancien régime*, he was aware of the efforts at reform of such ministers as St Germain, he realized the factious nature of the aristocratic campaign against Marie Antoinette and the covert ambitions of the king's brothers. Yet at the same time he accepted legends such as Barruel's inane masonic plot, the queen's guilt in the affair of the necklace, and the *pacte de famine* according to which famines were artificially induced to make profits for the royal treasury.

*

From such historians as Michelet or Louis Blanc, even when they continued their writing well into the second half of the nineteenth century, to DE TOCQUEVILLE, is a far cry, not in the passage of years but because between them lies the great gulf of the Revolution of 1848, which brought disillusionment to so many high democratic hopes in France and elsewhere. The people, whom Michelet idealized, had materialized in the form of the ragged and desperate proletariat of the great cities of Europe. Carlyle, with the social conditions of the London of the 'thirties before his eyes, had seen it earlier; but for many of the French liberals the consciousness of social realities burst like a thunderclap in the June Days of 1848. They saw the first attempt at social revolution crushed in a welter of bloodshed far exceeding anything that the Paris of the Terror had witnessed; and when the voice of the people was heard in the presidential election it was with an overwhelming vote for the name of Bonaparte. De Tocqueville undertook his great work under the impression of these events. As its title implies, his book is not a history of the Revolution, but an attempt to establish the nature of the relationship between the *ancien régime* and the France which emerged in the Revolution. Examining both from the point of view of an aristocratic liberalism de Tocqueville saw in the Revolution primarily the substitution of one despotic sovereignty for another, a process which he envisaged in the light of the *commissaires* of the Second Republic, the plebiscitary dictatorship of Louis Napoleon, and the indiscriminate levelling that he had described in *Democracy in America*. Not that he was hostile to reform. His fundamental criticism of the Revolution was that it was not revolutionary enough, that it merely accepted and continued the process of reducing individual liberties and building up the power of the centralized state, which had already progressed far before 1789. The great virtue of his

41

history was that it was the work of a man who had thought long and deeply on the problems of government, and that it was also the first history to be based upon a study of some of the administrative records in which the *ancien régime* was so rich.

With de Tocqueville we escape both from the conspiracy thesis and from the overriding forces of destiny, and begin to learn some of the facts of social history. His aim was to show the Revolution as the natural conclusion to the long-term evolution of the *ancien régime*. He saw that increasing resentment at seigneurial obligations might have been the result not of deteriorating, but of improved conditions among the peasantry, and of the fact that the privileged classes kept their social and economic privileges when they had lost all powers of government. He was right in laying great emphasis on the cleavages between the various classes which weakened the whole fabric of society, and particularly on the hostility of the nobles towards the royal administration. In the reign of Louis XVI, when the need for reform was generally admitted — and de Tocqueville truly observed that the moment when a bad government tries to reform itself is always the most dangerous — the Crown and the privileged classes were busily engaged in casting on one another the responsibility for the grievances of the country. The Royal Council, in the preambles to its decrees, itself advertised the evils of existing conditions and the urgency of drastic changes, which it yet proved incapable of introducing. Its biggest attempt at reform, the establishment of provincial assemblies, though laudable in itself as an attempt at decentralization, had the effect of throwing the whole administration into disorder. Perhaps de Tocqueville was not quite fair here, for the virulent aristocratic reaction against the royal administration undermined what might have been a useful reform.

On the oft-denounced influence of the ideas of the century, de Tocqueville was sounder in his judgment than most of his predecessors, though his version of the actual aims of the *philosophes* is not acceptable. He assumed that their campaign was not primarily anti-religious, but was directed against the Church as a political force, that it was, in fact, merely one aspect of a general onslaught against outworn political and social institutions. This is to underestimate the hostility of the *philosophes* to religion, and especially to Catholicism. The criticism of the *philosophes*, he thought, was mainly legal and social in its impact, and in favour of administrative reform rather than political change. The idea of political liberty was that which appeared last and disappeared first. The school of thought which best represented the practical political tendencies of the Revolution to his mind was the physiocratic school, in whose writings the idea of absolute sovereignty in the state was fundamental, and whose only safeguard against the abuse of power was education. The centralization of authority, and the destruction of local liberties, had already been achieved by the monarchy. When the desire for political liberty awoke in France — and it was far stronger among the revolutionaries than de Tocqueville allows — he believed that the country had already acquired ideas and was dominated by traditions of government which were not reconcilable with it. The two passions of the revolutionaries were for liberty and equality; but, for a moment allied in the wave of disinterested patriotism with which the Revolution began, they soon parted company, and while the desire for equality survived, the love of liberty died. Across the whole of de Tocqueville's analysis lies the shadow of Bonapartism. He sees the Revolution as not so much a revolt against the *ancien régime* as a stepping-stone from the milder absolutism of the Bourbons to the tyranny of Napoleon.

Since de Tocqueville wrote, nearly a century ago, historical research has added a mountain of detail to the little heap of facts he had garnered, yet his remains one of the best books on the Revolution that has ever been written. Some of the books on our list illustrate the dangers of writing history to a theory. Many literary histories of the Revolution have now not even a literary value. De Tocqueville's work shows that intellectual content and historical integrity, even without the highest literary qualities, can give a history a place in the small and select rank of historical classics.

\*

The critique of revolutionary democracy, which found a moderate and reasonable exponent in de Tocqueville, turned into a violent polemic when it was taken up by HIPPOLYTE TAINE. Of all those who have written histories of the Revolution, Taine possibly possessed the greatest genius and produced the worst history. His *Origines de la France contemporaine* consists of an introductory volume on *L'ancien régime* and five volumes on the Revolution. It is written in a brilliant style, rising at times to real heights of eloquence. Its power of intellectual analysis is dazzling, and its emotional force carries the reader away, as it was meant to do. No writer since Burke, of whom Taine reminds us in some respects, has done so much to implant his own interpretation of the Revolution on the educated mind. If his work were presented as anything but history it would be worthy of the highest admiration. Even Aulard, who devoted a whole book to tearing Taine's historical reputation to tatters, confessed the fascination that he exercised over more than one generation of young Frenchmen. And if his gems have proved paste, their brilliance still dazzles and their intellectual stimulation is still strong. The trouble with Taine was that his object was at bottom not historical. His letters show that his verdict on the Revolution had been passed before he began its detailed study. Though basically his views had been fixed earlier, the event which dominated his mind when he set out to trace the origins of the France of his day was the Commune of 1871, and his approach to the problems presented was by way of psychology and not of history. For Taine history was a form of applied psychology. The lesson he drew from his study of contemporary events was that not far beneath the surface of society violent passions seethed, ever ready to break out when the constraints of government were relaxed. It would almost be true to say that the one thing he saw in the Revolution, from beginning to end, was the Terror. The aim of his history was to find an explanation for the bursting of the bonds of society and letting loose of the forces of anarchy. In a way, then, he was asking the same question as Burke, and though his mode of thought was very different, it is not surprising that he reached the same result. His volumes on the Revolution are the anatomy of terrorism, and the first volume, describing the *ancien régime*, offers his analysis of its causes.

Taine's method of approach was analytical and psychological. He found the source of revolutionary terrorism in a state of mind, in that spirit of criticism and destruction which was born of the abstract and universalizing *raison raisonnante*, which in its turn arose out of the combination of what he called the scientific and the classic spirits. It is not possible here to discuss at length the defects of this analysis, but it must be said that if Taine had studied the thought of the eighteenth century with an open mind, he would have discovered that its revolutionary content arose from precisely the opposite qualities. By classic he meant deductive, and by scientific mathematical. Now it is perfectly true that French thought since Descartes has tended to aim at establishing general principles, or laws, on abstract grounds, and then regimenting the facts into conformity with these principles. But the empirical, practical spirit of the so-called *philosophes* embodied, in fact, a break-away from precisely these abstract, universalizing tendencies. Taine himself, on the other hand, was a notable representative of the intellectual sins he denounced. His prime weakness as an historian was that he envisaged the process of history in mechanistic terms. He saw it unrolling in obedience to inflexible and eternal laws, and, logically enough, envisaged the establishment of these laws as the historian's chief task. His method, however, was to decide the formula governing a particular development first, and then subsequently to search for facts to support it. His historical method was vicious from its foundation, and this was a pity, for in two respects he had important contributions to make to the progress of historical studies. In the first place, he realized that the Revolution was accompanied throughout by the Terror, and that this was not an accidental aberration but an essential and inseparable element in it. But his attempted explanation in terms of the bestial passions of the masses was not merely pathetically inadequate, but plainly and simply wrong; even when they were the agents, it was not the masses who were mainly responsible for the Terror. Secondly, Taine saw that a great historical movement like the Revolution was not to be explained in terms of a simple political narrative, but only by means of the analysis of social forces. His inquiry into the origins of the Revolution, which began as a study of the conflict of classes in the *ancien régime*, might have been of great value had not his prejudices predetermined the results of his researches. Moreover, unconsciously he abandoned this line of thought halfway through. Given the two facts of the existence of acute social tension in France, culminating in a revolutionary outbreak, and the seizure of power in the course of the Revolution by a small minority of active politicians, he disregarded the order of their appearance, and turned the consequence into the cause, by making the revolutionary outbreak itself the work of this minority, which in fact did not exist before 1789. In other words, reading his history backwards, instead of seeing in the revolutionary minority the agency through which great social forces found expression, as on his own principles he should have done, in effect he jettisoned his analysis of causes and reverted to the old conspiracy thesis of Burke and the abbé Barruel. Like them he laid his chief stress on the influence of a handful of literary men, ignoring the fact that their political views had been marked by a singular moderation. On the other hand, he paid no attention to the long and bitter struggle, ending in open rebellion, which the *parlements* had waged against the Crown, or to the part played by the provincial *états* and assemblies in the conflict of 1788–9. In fact the whole aristocratic revolt with which the Revolution began is bowdlerized out of his pages.

Taine's *Ancien régime* is not disfigured by the violent partisanship of his later volumes, but in addition to those I have mentioned, it suffers from other defects. He was proud that he had drawn so much of his material from the archives, but Aulard has shown how unsystematic was his treatment of them. His literary sources he accepted and used quite uncritically. His analysis is innocent of any attempt at chronological sequence: the court of the Regent and that of Louis XVI, the *noblesse* of Saint-Simon and of de Ségur, equally provide him with material. He selects his illustrations indiscriminately from any period in the century, and makes no allowance for development in the social scene. Again, he sees only the three elements — privileged classes, bourgeoisie and peasants — in French society, which is far too simple a schematization of a complex social situation.

As I have already said, Taine's method of exposition was to decide in advance on the view which he wished to establish, and then to prove it by collecting references to support his argument — what he called 'de tout petits faits bien choisis'. He saw everything in black and white. It gives an illusory appearance of fairness when, for example, he describes the Court as the central point of a great social abscess, the swollen core of the evil; but he subsequently ignores his own condemnation and sums up the *ancien régime* as merely 'un peu faible de constitution'. He paints a dark picture of the miseries of the peasantry, but it does not affect his judgment on the outbreak of rural terrorism. 'Several million savages', he writes, 'are thus impelled into action by a few thousand thinkers ... Radical dogma takes service under the banner of brute force.' The inconsequence is glaring; for all Taine's love of logic, his history proceeds not by logical argument but by a succession of epigrams. At the Sorbonne, declared Aulard, a candidate for the diploma in historical studies or the doctorate would disqualify himself if he cited Taine as an authority on any historical question. The greatest charge against him, however, does not lie in the defects of his historical method, but in the prostitution of talents amounting to genius to the service of an impassioned partisanship. Seldom has bad history been better written. Taine is the last, and perhaps the most stimulating of the great primitives of revolutionary historiography. After him, history proper begins, and unfortunately, for the most part, literature ends.

\*

The influence of Taine determined the trend of the debate over the origins of the Revolution for another two generations. It established for a time beyond challenge the belief that the propaganda of the *philosophes* was the cause of the Revolution. The only problem was whether this was a good thing or a bad thing. A counter-blast to Taine, though not comparable with his work in intellectual quality, was the study by ROUSTAN entitled, in its English translation, *Pioneers of the French Revolution*. To prove that the Revolution was the work of the *philosophes*, Roustan adduced one argument and one alone. He pointed out that d'Argenson and other observers were declaring in the middle of the century that France was on the brink of revolution. Why, then, he asked, did it break out, not in 1753, but only in 1789? Some new factor must have appeared in the interval. This new factor was the agitation of the *philosophes*, who therefore may be considered to have brought about the Revolution. This rather simple argument is the only one Roustan produces in support of his view, and it is certainly not sufficient to justify Laski's statement in the introduction to the English translation that he makes good his case.

Apart from this bald assertion, Roustan's book does not discuss the question which is presented as its main subject at all. It is an interesting, readable, rather superficial account of the attitude of the *philosophes* to, and their relations with, the various elements in eighteenth-century French society — the monarchy, nobles, magistrates, financiers, the *salons*, the bourgeoisie and the people. On all of these there is interesting material, though a weakness of the book is its almost exclusive reliance on memoirs. At times it degenerates into a collection of quotations and anecdotes, recited uncritically. A long chapter on the royal mistresses has a little justification in the patronage of the *philosophes* by Mme de Pompadour, but greatly exaggerates the importance of Mme du Barry. The chapter on the bourgeoisie relies almost exclusively upon a single source, the memoirs of Barbier. Roustan, like Taine, attributes to the *philosophes* an influence over the largely illiterate peasantry for which there is no proof and which is in the nature of things inherently improbable. Indeed, one has only to look at the parish *cahiers* of 1789 to see how exclusively the attention of the peasants was concentrated upon the redress of practical grievances. On their possible influence over the people as a whole, Roustan quotes Morellet, who wrote, very truly, 'The people, immersed in toil, cannot read, and have neither time nor wish to read. No metaphysical works, however eloquent, could have led this great mass to the terrible movement of the last three years ... The writings of the *philosophes*, not being read, nor being within reach of the multitude, could not have produced such great consequences.' In spite of the obvious common sense of this verdict, Roustan continues to assert that the *philosophes* trained the people in new ideas, and that their influence was 'real and decisive: they brought about the French Revolution'. But this is no more proven at the end than at the beginning of his study. With much of incidental interest, it adds nothing of value to the debate over the causes of the Revolution. Judged on its main theme it is a prolonged *non sequitur*.

*

It is appropriate that the cycle of historical interpretation which began with Burke should end with ACTON. His *Lectures on the French Revolution* were delivered at Cambridge from 1895 to 1899, though they were only printed in 1910. They begin with a chapter on the 'Heralds of the Revolution', in which pride of place goes to the Jansenist Domat, the Calvinist Jurieu, and the Catholic Fénelon. The more familiar names of the *philosophes* appear subsequently, but Acton seems to attribute more influence to the former minister d'Argenson, whom he describes as the earliest writer from whom we can extract the system of 1789, and the intendant and Controller-General Turgot. This is odd, to say the least. For the cathartic agent which translated thought into action, he looks farther afield — to the American Declaration of Independence. Although Louis XVI was a reforming monarch, the imminence of financial disaster, which forced the calling of the *États Généraux*, found him with no policy. 'Monarchy transformed itself into anarchy to see what would come of it.' This is an interesting summary so far as it goes, but it does not go very far. Acton is held back partly by the inadequacy of the facts he had accumulated: without much more information than he possessed no discussion of French Revolutionary causes could be more than a slight sketch. But also it is fair to point out that his account of the causes of 1789 is governed by his belief in the primacy of ideas in historical development.

*

Already, however, the study of the Revolution by modern methods of systematic historical research had begun in France with AULARD, who was an inexhaustible, if sometimes rather slapdash, editor of manuscript material, and who, in his *Political History of the French Revolution*, produced the first standard modern history. Aulard wrote at a time when the Third Republic had overcome its early difficulties and was beginning to acquire confidence. His political ideal was embodied in the bourgeois, anti-clerical republicanism of the Radical Socialist Party, and with him the pendulum swings from right to left, away from Taine and back to Michelet. Aulard saw the Revolution as sowing the seed which had reached fruition in the Third Republic. He treated it on political lines, and paid little attention to economic or social factors in its course or causation. His discussion of the origins of the Revolution is confined to one short chapter.

He begins by rejecting the old theory that the Revolution was the result of an organized effort on the part of the writers of the century to convert France to a democratic, republican regime. As he says, these writers did not advocate republicanism and in 1789 there was no republican party in France. He proceeds to argue that though the *philosophes* and other writers were not advocates of a republican regime, yet they created a republican spirit, as a result of which there was a general desire to limit the power of the monarchy. To this statement Aulard adds the — at any rate superficially — contradictory view that the increasing disrespect for monarchy arose not because of its tyrannical exercise of power, but because of its weakness. This weakness was exhibited particularly in the conflict of the Crown with the *parlements*. Without following up this point, however, he returns to the influence of ideas, this time with reference to English sources. Undoubtedly, English influence had been strong over French thought in the earlier part of the century. Aulard did not realize that in the years before the Revolution the English example had largely been discredited. The French interest in the American Revolution, and the circulation in France of the Declaration of Independence and of the constitutions of the Union and the states, however, he rightly remarked as an important influence over opinion in the pre-revolutionary period.

By far the greatest emphasis, thus, in Aulard's account of the origins of the Revolution, is given to the influence of ideas. Like Michelet, he approves of this, whereas the school of Taine regarded it as a national disaster. To neither side in the controversy had it as yet occurred that the one point on which they were in agreement — that the influence of the writers could and did cause a revolution — was precisely that which required the most careful historical investigation — which it has not received even now. Aulard saw that the masses of the people were illiterate, pious and despised by the advanced thinkers. How they come into the Revolution he does not explain. Indeed into his Revolution they hardly do come: it is an almost purely bourgeois phenomenon. Other studies show that he was not unaware of some of the factors which he omits in the first chapter of his *Political History*. Perhaps he felt that to give full weight to them would be to open the door to interpretations that he preferred to exclude from the revolutionary canon. Perhaps he really in his heart believed that history began in 1789, and that the question of causes was therefore not of major importance.

\*

The work of Aulard did not bring right-wing history to an end in France, and its influence was slow in penetrating into historical studies in Great Britain. Of all French historians of the Revolution the best known and most read in this country was until recently MADELIN, perhaps because he makes the least demand for intellectual effort on the part of his readers. His discussion of the causes of the Revolution has an air of frankness and exhibits an apparent willingness to see both sides of the question. He begins by recognizing the existence of a general desire in France before 1789 for what was called a constitution, which he interprets as meaning a rational organization of the powers of the state. It should be noted that with this definition, Madelin, by implication, excludes the idea of political liberty from the motives of the Revolution. This implication is underlined by his next point, which is that the king, in theory absolute, was in fact the slave of the system of which he was the nominally despotic head. The weakness of the monarchy, its absence of policy, and the inability of Louis XV and Louis XVI to wield the mighty instrument that Louis XIV and his ministers had created, was the crucial fact. Along with this went the incompetence of the *noblesse*, uprooted and its self-confidence undermined by the new ideas of the age, and the mediocrity of the Church. On the other hand, the royal tax-collectors, the Church and the *noblesse* continued to levy toll upon the unprivileged sections of the community. All this Madelin frankly recognizes.

One might have expected him to follow up his statement of the defects of the *ancien régime* by arguing that the opposition of an increasingly weak royal authority to an increasingly keen sense of grievance on the part of the great mass of the nation had created an explosive mixture which sooner or later was bound to be fired by a combination of political and economic circumstances. He does not draw this conclusion. Instead he returns to the old conspiracy thesis. The strength of the *ancien régime*, he says, lay in its traditions, and these had been systematically discredited by the *philosophes*. The Revolution was propagated by a group of 'writers

51

who believed themselves to be thinkers', in whose writings sham classicism combined with baleful foreign influences — by which he means English and American — to produce a cosmopolitan cult of humanity leading only to the guillotine. Madeline's onslaught is summed up in the condemnation of eighteenth-century thought as purely destructive. Now clearly, while it was bitterly critical of many of the religious, social and to a lesser extent political institutions of the day, it also laid the intellectual foundations on which modern liberal states were subsequently built. To condemn it as purely destructive is therefore a way of passing judgment upon the ideals and methods of modern liberalism, and one cannot but feel that this, though unacknowledged, is Madelin's implicit aim. It is not for us to discuss whether the Western world did or did not take the wrong turning when it abandoned the principles of the *ancien régime*; but it is justifiable to point out that whereas Taine's *Histoire des Origines de la France contemporaine* is specifically devoted to the discussion of this problem, Madelin, more disingenuously, gives his answer disguised as impartial, unideological history.

From the importance which Madelin attaches to eighteenth-century ideas it might be supposed that he intends to present the Revolution as a crusade of destruction instigated by the *philosophes*. But what section of society was most influenced by their ideas? He answers, the bourgeois, and when he comes to discuss their motives, instead of the influence of the new ideas over them, he emphasizes their resentment at the social inequalities of the *ancien régime*. The Revolution, he holds, was far more against inequality than against despotism, but this does not mean that the object of the men of 1789 was general equality. They had the utmost scorn for the masses, and they only demanded equality in order that they might obtain dominance. To achieve this end they played upon the peasants' sense of grievance and the wretchedness of the town workers, distributed model *cahiers* and managed the elections. This is cynical but not altogether unfounded. It is an anticlimax after this to be told that the general demand of the *cahiers* was only for reform, and to learn from the epilogue to his history that Madelin apparently did not regard as unreasonable the initial achievements of the Revolution — equality in justice and taxation, abolition of feudal dues, and the reorganization of government.

His argument is that these reforms summed up all that nine-tenths of France desired, and that they had been achieved by August 1789. This may be true, but then what becomes of the evil influences of the *philosophes* and the crusade of destruction? Instead of producing the Revolution, these now produce the perversion of the Revolution by the Jacobins through the agency of the Terror. Ambitious politicians make insurrection chronic, and after ten years of anarchy, in the end Bonaparte comes to rescue France from the clutches of a corrupt oligarchy and give the nation the government and the reforms it desires. The whole revolutionary period is for Madelin but a bloody prologue to the greatness of Napoleon. His discussion of the causes of the Revolution achieves the appearance of moderation by a series of self-contradictions. If these are allowed to cancel one another out we are left with precisely nothing.

\*

If Madelin was moved by prejudice against the traditions of the Revolution, it may reasonably be urged that the official school of historians, led by Aulard, was inspired by an equally strong dogmatic faith in its principles. Why should Aulard, it may be asked, who wrote as a whole-hearted supporter of the bourgeois revolution, be regarded as a more respectable historian than Madelin, who was the favourite historian of the right-wing parties until more extreme writers usurped his place? The answer is that Aulard attempts a coherent explanation and that while his interpretation may be open to criticism, his facts are substantiated from contemporary sources and his history is well documented. Madelin scorned the scholarly encumbrances which are a barrier to popularity. Greater scholarship, without any sacrifice of literary graces, was exhibited by FUNCK-BRENTANO, with whom we return to the tradition of Taine, many of the vices and merits of whose approach he inherits. Funck-Brentano's *L'ancien régime* similarly draws on illustrations from widely separated periods to support his arguments. Mercier and Rétif de la Bretonne rub shoulders with Saint-Simon and Mme de Sévigné; he takes his evidence from the reign of Henry IV or from that of Louis XVI, or even from the Napoleonic period. The ground plan of his argument is a very idealized version of medieval society, on the strength of which he contrasts the liberties of the old order with the despotism of the modern state. This interpretation is not mere paradox, but what there was of truth in it had long before been put by de Tocqueville. Funck-Brentano brings out well the 'popular' nature of the monarchy before 1789. The whole life of a king of France, from birth to death, was a public show, played out literally before the eyes of his people. He omits to point out, however, that Louis XVI and Marie Antoinette had withdrawn very much into private life, and that herein in fact was a minor cause of the Revolution. Of the rulers of the eighteenth century he paints a flattering picture. If Louis XV and Mme de Pompadour deserved to be rescued from an excessive load of obloquy, a verdict on their successors which neglects the irresponsibility of Marie Antoinette and the incapacity of Louis XVI cannot be regarded as other than special pleading.

The description of the social and political institutions of the *ancien régime* in Funck-Brentano is selective and designed to prove a case. Considerable space is given to the *lettres de cachet*, on which he had himself made detailed researches which put them in a new light and showed that they were largely used for the purpose of protecting the interests of the family. But the argument that since the *lettres de cachet* were also a means of asserting royal authority, and royal authority was the essential condition of liberty in France, therefore they were an instrument of liberty, is at least far-fetched. In some respects Funck-Brentano is not even willing to make the concessions that Taine does. In particular, he gives a much more favourable verdict on the conditions of the peasantry. His chief source here is Rétif de la Bretonne, and while he is justified in arguing that Rétif, being the son of a peasant, unlike most other writers knew what he was talking about, he refrains from adding that his father was a *laboureur*, that is to say a fairly well-to-do farmer, and far from typical of the masses in the countryside. He is similarly optimistic in his estimates of the division of land among the peasants and of the extent of literacy among them, on the strength of figures which are mere guesses. Material on which a more reasonable verdict could be framed has more recently been produced by the researches of Lefebvre on the division of land, and of Mornet on literacy. From their work there has emerged one point which earlier historians, including Funck-

Brentano, failed to allow for — the wide local variations which make any generalization on such questions misleading. Another characteristic feature of Funck-Brentano's picture of the *ancien régime* is his emphasis on the power of public opinion, for example in the appointment and dismissal of ministers. This fits in with his praise of the eighteenth century as the age of liberty, but it will appear in a different light to anyone who has viewed, even in passing, the network of intrigue through which ministers rose or fell.

This description of the *ancien régime*, though more detailed than that of Burke, leaves us asking the same question — Why then was there a Revolution? In a few pages at the end, Funck-Brentano sums up its causes as, first, the decline of the old French family spirit, and, secondly, the economic progress of France, which led to a demand for a greater unification of the country and the creation of an administrative regime. This is patently inadequate. His book is readable in a high degree, it is packed with picturesque detail and witty anecdote, it brings out in relief many facts which are a useful corrective to common prejudices about the *ancien régime*. But its historical methods are unsound, the picture it draws one-sided, and its treatment of all the real historical problems superficial.

\*

We pass a stage beyond Funck-Brentano in the path of right-wing history when we come to GAXOTTE. His chief merit is to have brought the counter-revolutionary version of the Revolution up to date by incorporating some of the results of modern research, though in his general interpretation he introduces nothing fundamentally new. Gaxotte was the historian of the right-wing nationalist parties in the unhappy years that preceded 1939. His history of the Revolution begins with a tribute to the monarchy as the creator of French national unity. He adopts de Tocqueville's contrast between the infinite variety of the *ancien régime* and the sameness, uniformity, of the modern bureaucratic state; but being conscious that historians have more recently shown that there was a great development of the administrative services under Louis XV and his successor, he adds the claim that France before 1789 already possessed the most efficient administration it has ever had, which Napoleon had merely to revive and expand in order to achieve his so-called reorganization of France. This is rather exaggerated. Borrowing from modern economic historians, Gaxotte shows that France in the eighteenth century was not economically exhausted, but in the full flight of commercial expansion. On the peasantry he merely echoes Funck-Brentano's inadequate verdict. Gaxotte's facts and arguments, so far as they go, are reasonably sound — he borrows them from the best historians — but they are carefully selected. We cannot feel any confidence in a discussion of the conditions of the peasantry which refrains from mentioning *capitaineries, gabelle, corvée* or militia. In all, Gaxotte is only willing to admit two flaws in the fabric of the *ancien régime*: the survival of vestiges of feudal rights, and the deficit in the national finances, which he attributes exclusively to the borrowing policy of Necker. Both these, he holds, would have been capable of solution if it had not been for the intellectual and moral crisis which had smitten the French mind in the course of the eighteenth century. With this we return once more to the traditional theme, though Gaxotte gives it a twist more in line with nationalist and *Action Française* propaganda by tracing back the 'destructive individualism and republican sentimentality' of the Revolution to the influence of the Protestant Reformation, reinforced during the seventeenth and eighteenth centuries by foreign influences from the Dutch Republic, England and the American colonies. He adopts the theory of Cochin on the organization and dissemination of the new ideas by *sociétés de pensée* and Masonic lodges. Under Louis XVI the new ideas, he alleges, even came to dominate royal policy. In his condemnation of the sentimental idealism of Louis XVI Gaxotte comes nearest to introducing an original argument into the traditional story, but we can hardly be expected to accept a picture of the king as penetrated with subversive ideas derived from Fénelon and Rousseau.

Gaxotte recognizes that the actual revolt against the monarchy began with the *parlements*, for which he has no love, and with the *noblesse de province*, but he represents this as a superficial agitation which could easily have been mastered. He admits that there was an economic crisis, but ridiculously underestimates it, attributing it simply to the Vergennes commercial treaty with Great Britain. Behind the elections to the *États Généraux*, rioting in the larger towns, *Grande Peur* in the countryside, he sees the hidden hand of the anti-religious, anti-monarchical Masonic clubs, the greed of the financiers and the ambitions of the duke of Orleans. His history provides an interesting variant to the republican bias of the school of Aulard. It is cleverly done. Most of what Gaxotte writes is true, but it is carefully selected to prove a case; anything that does not prove it is quietly omitted. To say that he has written political propaganda disguised as history would be severe, but not too severe.

*

Meanwhile, on the other side, a school of left-wing history of the Revolution had grown up under the inspiration of the Socialist leader JEAN JAURÈS, who began his *Histoire socialiste* in 1901. That the writing of this history was a political act may be seen, not merely from the fact that its author was an eminent party politician, but from the triple inspiration which he acknowledges in his introduction — Marx, Michelet and Plutarch. From Plutarch he derived the didactic purpose of his history, from Michelet its democratic idealism and from Marx his interest in economic facts and the basic interpretation with which the Revolution had to be reconciled. His dependence on an *a priori* pattern is not altogether surprising. Although Jaurès forcefully defends the writers of the eighteenth century from Taine's condemnation of their thought as abstract and generalizing, in the course of this defence he reveals that he himself, like Taine, shares the deductive, theoretical attitude of mind with which the eighteenth century is charged. The alleged contradiction between its scientific, empirical mode of thought and that of classic Cartesianism, Jaurès declares, is a false one: in all fields of thought we should try to disengage (*dégager*) the most general ideas, the broadest and simplest concepts. These will embody historical truth. This was just what Taine believed.

The general idea in which Jaurès sums up the causation of the Revolution is the rise of the bourgeoisie, which 'through its economic growth inevitably took the road of its revolutionary destinies'. Starting with Marxist assumptions, he takes the French bourgeoisie to be a class of wealthy capitalists and financiers, with a satellite class of *rentiers* — investors in state funds. He devotes many pages to illustrating the rise of this class through the prodigious growth of French industry, overseas commerce and internal trade in the eighteenth century. Unfortunately the material for a serious economic history of the period did not yet exist, and Jaurès' illustrations, though more respectable than Taine's '*de tout petits faits bien choisis*', belong in the same category. An example of his method of argument — admittedly it is usually not as bad as this — is his use of the fine highways that had been built during the eighteenth century to demonstrate the great extent of internal trade that must have existed to make them necessary. If Jaurès had read Arthur Young he would have seen his comments on the almost deserted condition of these fine roads, even within a short distance of Paris or other large towns.

Jaurès' bourgeoisie is made to fit an hypothesis, but, whoever they were, against what were they rebelling? The usual answer is 'feudalism', and Jaurès presumably intended to give this answer, for he began his history with the analysis of seigneurial justice, fiscal privilege, *corvées*, *banalités*, seigneurial dues and so on. But he was a conspicuously honest thinker and at the end of the enumeration frankly confessed that it did not add up to the expected total. 'What remained of feudalism in our institutions and customs', he wrote, 'was already no more than a survival. Monarchical centralization had played a revolutionary role in relation to feudal authority, and a new revolution was not needed to tear up its last roots.' As for the abolition of these remaining burdens by the bourgeois Constituent Assembly on the night of the Fourth of August, the Assembly left to itself, says Jaurès, would have ended tax exemptions and personal servitude and at most decreed that seigneurial dues should be purchasable. The bourgeoisie was not interested in the fact that the relics of seigneurial rights oppressed the peasantry. Its grievance was that the *noblesse* and the Church had twisted royal authority to their own advantage, regardless of public interest, and were pillaging the state. If it had not been for this, says Jaurès, the French Revolution of 1789 would probably never have broken out.

The conclusion which emerges from his discussion is thus much more restricted and reasonable than his use of big words like bourgeoisie and feudalism would suggest. It is that the Revolution represented the final elimination of the privileged classes from a position of dominance in which they could exploit the state for their own financial and social advantage. Though Jaurès does not deny that ideas could have a revolutionary influence, he has little to say about them, apart from defending eighteenth-century thought from the indictment of Taine. His great contribution to revolutionary history lies not so much in the answers he gave as in the questions he stimulated later historians to ask, and to which, he insisted, only detailed, documentary research, above all in the economic history of France, could provide the answers.

*

The work of HENRI SÉE well illustrates the virtue of checking generalizations by detailed research. The simple pattern of privileged classes, bourgeoisie and peasantry, which satisfied earlier writers, disintegrates as a result of Sée's closer study into a complex mosaic of overlapping classes and interests. Economic history, by substituting the microscope for the brush of the romantic historian, and statistics for prejudice or guesswork, has modified or destroyed many formerly current generalizations. We find, for example, that the estates of the Church, which in one or two provinces of the north of France constituted as high a proportion as 40 per cent of the property, on an average of the whole country may have amounted to only some 6 per cent. Nine-tenths of all the proprietors of France were peasants, but the proportion of the land owned by them varied greatly. In Brittany and Normandy it may only have been one-fifth, in Languedoc as much as one-half. Again, it must not be supposed that the peasantry formed a single, undifferentiated class. Among them the *laboureurs*, owners of farms sufficient to maintain themselves and their households, were a kind of peasant aristocracy. The lot of the agricultural population, Sée concludes, was hard, but not quite so desperate in the eighteenth century as the highly-coloured picture of Taine had suggested. Whereas the reign of Louis XIV was punctuated with peasant revolts, there were none of any note between 1715 and 1789.

At the other end of the scale the *noblesse* was equally far from being a homogeneous body. The arrogant and rich *parlementaires* must not be classed with the *avocats*. In the towns there was an urban patriciate which, although *roturier*, had most of the characteristics of a privileged class: the bourgeoisie was itself divided into privileged and unprivileged sections. Sée did not provide a discussion of the causes of the Revolution. He did what was more valuable: he continued the process which de Tocqueville had begun, by which the traditional fancy picture of the *ancien régime* was to be transformed into the likeness of a real society that once lived and functioned.

\*

Jaurès was followed by ALBERT MATHIEZ, who provided a basically similar, but fuller, explanation of the outbreak of the Revolution. Revolutions come, he premised, out of the divorce between social facts and institutions, between the letter of the law and the spirit of society. Such a divorce had grown up in eighteenth-century France. He paid tribute to the efforts of the royal administration to cope with the problem, but recognized that its efforts at reform only stimulated general discontent. Admitting the primacy of the financial difficulties, Mathiez incorporated the correction of older views by those economic historians who had shown that the burden of debt which proved overwhelming was the result not of the extravagance of the court, but of the loans with which Necker financed French intervention in the American War of Independence. The conflict between the Crown and the privileged classes became acute in consequence of financial difficulties, but Mathiez saw that it was much broader and more fundamental than the simple dispute over taxation which brought it to a head. There was what has been called a 'feudal reaction' in the reign of Louis XVI. The princes of the blood, and particularly Orleans, played an important part in stimulating this aristocratic opposition. The particularism of the *pays d'état* provided a nucleus for the revolt of *noblesse* and *parlements*, but they would never have dared, Mathiez believed, to venture on an open conflict with the Crown if its powers of resistance had not been undermined by the infiltration of nobles into the ranks of the administration. By 1789 the great majority of the ministers and officials were themselves nobles, while the higher officers of the army were also noble. Amongst them all the *frondeur* spirit was strong.

In the early stages of the struggle the privileged classes were able to appeal to the support of the bourgeois. These had been rapidly growing in importance. While the finances of the Crown were deteriorating, the commerce of France had been flourishing. A wealthy bourgeoisie had grown up, whose members were not prepared to play second fiddle to the aristocratic *frondeurs*. Mathiez does not specifically indicate who these bourgeois were, but the impression, as in Jaurès, is that they were a class of capitalist manufacturers, merchants and financiers. In the winter of 1788–9 they repudiated the leadership of the privileged classes and struck out for their own ends. These were not summed up in abstract ideas imbibed from the *philosophes*. As Mathiez says, 'The class which was going to take control of the Revolution was fully conscious of its strength and its rights. It is not true that it allowed itself to be seduced by an empty ideology. It well appreciated the realities of the situation.' The Royal Council had hoped to play off the bourgeoisie against the privileged classes, but the weak character of the king and the mistakes of Marie Antoinette, coupled with the influence of the court circle, prevented the plan from being put into effective operation. Finally, the increasing economic crisis, added to the general agitation, brought into action the working classes of the towns, and last of all the peasantry.

This is an excellent brief summary of the causes of the Revolution. It is unaffected by the prejudices which may be considered to have distorted Mathiez' history of the Revolution — the vendetta against Aulard, passionate denigration of Danton and idolization of Robespierre. Yet so far as concerns the problems which Jaurès had left on the agenda, and which could only be dealt with on the basis of fundamental research, Mathiez carried the discussion little further. His analysis consists of the same large, undifferentiated elements — economic, social, ideological — arranged in a pattern which is essentially *a priori* and shows signs of hardening into a dogmatic formula.

\*

Detailed research still tended to concentrate on the Revolution itself, particularly the period from 1789 to 1794, rather than on the events leading up to it, and this is probably the reason why the explanation formulated by the historians of the last generation has remained largely unchallenged. Attention has been drawn to developments in the provinces by the work of Professor Egret and this has reinforced the interpretation of the first stage of the Revolution as a revolt of the privileged classes against the monarchy. New light was thrown upon the economic situation of France on the eve of the Revolution by the detailed study of price trends made by Professor C. E. LABROUSSE. He showed that the eighteenth century was marked by a slow increase in prices, up to about 1778, which stimulated economic activity. This, along with the growth of population, involved an increase in agricultural prices, which however was beneficial only to certain sections of the agricultural population. The seigneurs gained by the increased value of seigneurial dues or tithes paid in kind, and by their ability to hold up grain until prices rose. Farmers paying money rents also gained, for these rose more slowly than wages. The mass of the peasants, on the other hand, having to feed themselves out of their crop, save one-quarter or one-fifth of it for seed and often pay their dues in kind, apart from the vine-growers gained little or nothing from the rise. As for the rapidly increasing population of wage-earners in the towns and landless labourers in the country, the static tendency of wages and the excess supply of labour seems to have resulted in a fall in their standards of living. As a picture of the whole century it must be confessed that this is a little too neatly schematized, and rests too much upon statistical arguments in a pre-statistical age to be completely convincing, though it may be highly probable. There need be little reservation about the last phase in the economic history of the *ancien régime*. In the twelve years before the Revolution most agricultural prices fell. It is not easy to see the reason for it but the fact seems certain. In a predominantly agrarian economy the result was naturally a general recession and growing unemployment. The bad harvest of 1788, coming on top of this, produced an economic crisis, of which the financial crisis which precipitated the Revolution was part; for the burden of taxation, bearable in time of prosperity, became unendurable in time of general distress. In this sense, Labrousse argues, the Revolution was, as Michelet had believed, and contrary to the thesis of Jaurès and Mathiez, a 'révolution de la misère'. But all classes attributed their distress to the state and sought for a political remedy. To this acute analysis, Labrousse adds a somewhat unexpected appendage. The economic progress of the eighteenth century, he says,

is the really important development and the difficulties of the
reign of Louis XVI a mere episode. The real revolution is, after
all, not a revolution of distress but one of prosperity: it is the
culmination of the rise of the bourgeoisie. It may be; but whereas
the picture Labrousse draws of the economic crisis is based on
extensive and fundamental research, this conclusion is merely a
theory.

*

The established and generally accepted theory of the bourgeois
revolution lies also at the heart of the interpretation of Professor
GEORGES LEFEBVRE, the most recent of the greater historians of the
French Revolution.

For him, as for Mathiez, the financial crisis precipitated the
Revolution, the offensive was taken by the privileged classes in
the form of a 'feudal' reaction and a revolt against the Crown.
The bourgeoisie, which had been rising to wealth and influence
in the course of the century, revolted against the aristocracy, and
the economic crisis brought in the people. The Revolution marks,
Lefebvre says, the end of the struggle of the aristocracy against
the monarchy and the rise of the bourgeoisie to triumph over
both: in this way it constitutes 'a stage in the destinies of the
Western world'. One would think that there is no more to be
said: the Revolution is neatly parcelled, tied up and delivered to
the address designated in the historical philosophy of Karl Marx.

But Lefebvre is far too good an historian to be content with the
mere illustration of a formula; and his own extensive and penetrating researches have opened a new phase in the history of the
Revolution. One result of his work has been the further disintegra-
tion of the traditional picture of aristocracy, bourgeoisie and
people. He points out that the bourgeoisie properly so-called of
eighteenth-century France was a comparatively small class of
wealthy men 'vivant noblement et de leur bien', who far from
triumphing in the Revolution suffered from it. Those who gained
were the hosts of officials of the royal bureaucracy and law courts,
along with the more successful members of the legal and other
professions, and — on a lower social level — the financiers and men
of affairs. What they gained was a position in the state based on
wealth and talent, breaking the — possibly increasingly rigid —
monopoly of the aristocracy of birth.

Attempts are still made to identify the actual historical French Revolution with the capitalist revolution of Marxist theory, itself based mainly on an interpretation of English history which is in process of drastic revision. Even Lefebvre can say: 'The capital fact is that, for the first time in Europe, [the Revolution] proclaimed liberty of enterprise'; it opened the door to capitalism. Such a generalization represents a throw-back to the deductive historiography of the nineteenth century, as becomes evident the moment an attempt is made to support it with historical evidence. Thus Lefebvre himself draws attention to the fact that the Declaration of Rights does not mention economic freedom, although, he believes, the bourgeoisie held to this above all other rights. His explanation is in part that since the time of Turgot the *ancien régime* had not been hostile to economic reform, and so there was no urge to proclaim it, which is not very convincing; and in part that the Third Estate was divided in opinion on the matter, for example on the subject of corporations, which is true but rather weakens the argument.

Many more contradictions and qualifications can be found. The financiers had achieved 'freedom' long before the Revolution; so had employers in many trades in dealing with their journeymen. The decline of gilds and corporations, and of the great trading companies, was already well advanced in the second half of the eighteenth century, though it was to be completed during the Revolution. On the other hand, the control of the state over industry and trade was enhanced during the revolutionary and Napoleonic period. The abolition of internal customs, long fought for, was achieved early in the Revolution; but the protectionist policy on the frontiers was intensified. The comparatively few large employers and merchants may have been all for freedom from such controls as they thought to be against their interests. Lower down the social scale, the small employers, master craftsmen, and the peasants, without whose participation the Revolution would have been inconceivable, were those who were most bitterly opposed to capitalist industry and economic liberty, as Lefebvre has pointed out. Though politically they emerge only momentarily, the state could not disregard their economic interests and prejudices. All in all it may be that the Revolution, instead of promoting free enterprise and new methods, contributed to the backwardness of agriculture and industry in the nineteenth century and the slowness of capitalist progress in France. The supposition that the Revolution was promoted by and directed in the interests of industrial and commercial capitalism has so far been supported by no more than isolated facts in the fashion of Taine, while there is much to be said on the other side, which must either be explained or explained away.

Lefebvre's comments make us realize that the contribution of ideas to the revolutionary nexus also requires more detailed examination. He tells us that the 'experimental rationalism' of the *philosophes* provided the bourgeoisie with a philosophy, but also that the appeal of the *philosophes* to the rule of law and equality of rights was more effective than the desire for economic reform. This should lead us to reflect further on the nature of the 'bourgeois' revolution.

Indeed, as qualification after qualification is introduced, the outlines of the accepted picture of a revolution of bourgeois merchants, financiers and industrialists become more and more obscure. It begins to look more like a revolution of officials and professional men, backed by lesser army officers and non-commissioned officers, small employers and the better-off peasants. Some of the wealthier elements in society, temporarily submerged, reappear under Napoleon and the Restoration, or even earlier under the Directory. The aristocratic landlords lose their fiscal privileges and seigneurial dues, but keep much of their land. The power of the state machine over its subjects is greatly increased.

We begin to envisage the Revolution now, I think, in terms which are not reconcilable with the established formula. Its causes become much more complex. 'Class interests and personal interests, humbled pride, mass suffering, philosophical propaganda, all made their contribution', writes Lefebvre: but a contribution to what? If the causes are changing, so is the Revolution itself. No historian, in the light of modern research, can seriously write, as he used to be able to, that the Revolution does this or that. As a personified entity it has too long haunted the pages of history. The conception of the Revolution as an indivisible unity, a *bloc*, is increasingly untenable. It has become a complex of different and even opposed developments, the origins of which are likely to have been equally complex. The problem of its causes is no longer to find an equation $a + b \pm c = d$, but to analyse, as well as one can, the elements in an enormously complex and changing historic situation, and to trace the process by which it was translated into another situation, equally complex and changing. The result may be something which it is difficult to list as a series of causes in a textbook, and in this sense the search for causes of the French Revolution may well be at an end.

There is another respect also in which the conditions of the problem have been changing. History is now a little less confined within national boundaries than it used to be. Historians[1] have recently been drawing attention to the international character of the revolutionary movements in the latter part of the eighteenth century. It will be difficult henceforth to discuss any one of these movements in isolation from the others. This is not altogether a new idea; but there are signs that it is now more likely to affect the history of the Revolution than it has done in the past. And here is another reason why — though there is still need for research on the events leading up to the outbreak of the Revolution in France — the study of the causes of the French Revolution has passed into a new phase, while the study of the origins and nature of this wider revolution has hardly yet begun.

## LIST OF BOOKS

EDMUND BURKE, *Reflections on the Revolution in France* (1790).
ARTHUR YOUNG, *Travels in France and Italy during the years 1787, 1788, 1789* (1792–4).
THIERS, *Histoire de la Révolution française* (1823–7).
MIGNET, *Histoire de la Révolution française* (1824).
CARLYLE, *The French Revolution* (1837).
MICHELET, *Histoire de la révolution française* (1847–53). Translated as *History of the French Revolution* (1860).
LOUIS BLANC, *Histoire de la révolution française* (1847–62).
A. DE TOCQUEVILLE, *L'ancien régime et la révolution* (1856). Translated 1856, 1888, 1933.
HIPPOLYTE TAINE, *Les origines de la France contemporaine*, vol. I, *L'ancien régime* (1876). Translated as *The Ancient Regime* (1896).

M. ROUSTAN, *Les philosophes et la société française au XVIIIe siècle* (1906). Abridged and translated as *The Pioneers of the French Revolution* (1926).

LORD ACTON, *Lectures on the French Revolution* (1895–9) (1910).

F. V. A. AULARD, *Histoire politique de la révolution française* (1901). Translation of third edition as *The French Revolution, a political history, 1789–1804* (1910).

LOUIS MADELIN, *La révolution* (in *L'Histoire de France racontée à tous*, ed. F. Funck-Brentano) (1911). Translated as *The French Revolution* (1916).

F. FUNCK-BRENTANO, *L'ancien régime* (1926). Translated as *The Old Régime in France* (1929).

P. GAXOTTE, *La révolution française* (1928). Translated as *The French Revolution* (1932).

JEAN JAURÈS, *Histoire socialiste (1789–1800)*: vol. I. *La Constituante (1789–91)* (1901). Edition revue par A. Mathiez (1927).

HENRI SÉE, *La France économique et sociale au XVIIIe siècle* (1925). Translated as *Economic and Social Conditions in France during the Eighteenth Century* (1927).

ALBERT MATHIEZ, *La révolution française* (1922–7). Translated as *The French Revolution* (1928).

C. E. LABROUSSE, *La crise de l'économie française à la fin de l'Ancien Régime et au début de la Révolution* (1944).

GEORGES LEFEBVRE, *Quatre-vingt-neuf* (1939). Translated by R. R. Palmer as *The Coming of the French Revolution* (1947).
*La Révolution française* (Peuples et civilisations, ed. Halphen et Sagnac, t. XIII), new ed. (1951).
'*Le mythe de la Révolution française*', in *Annales historiques de la Révolution française*, t. 145, pp. 337–45 (1956).

# 3

## THE *PARLEMENTS* OF FRANCE IN THE EIGHTEENTH CENTURY

I f we compare the French monarchy in the eighteenth century with practically any other European monarchy of the same period, the striking fact that emerges is the comparative effectiveness of the limitations on royal power in France, and this in spite of the fact that, in the absence of other checks, organized opposition to the Crown was concentrated in a single institution. The royal courts of law, known as the *parlements*, stood out in proud isolation as the last great relics of the medieval French constitution.[1] The *parlement* of Paris still retained much of the prestige won in the centuries when it had co-operated with the monarchy in the glorious task of building up the unity of France. 'Il faut confesser', wrote Loyseau, 'que ç'a esté le Parlement, qui nous a sauvé en France d'être cantonnez et démembrez, comme en Italie et Allemagne, et qui a maintenu ce Royaume en son entier.'[2] On the model provided by Paris twelve other *parlements* and four sovereign courts had in due course been established in the provinces between the fifteenth and the eighteenth centuries. The *parlement* of Paris, however, by virtue of its priority in time, its situation, and the vast extent of its jurisdiction, covering one-third of the country, was by far the most important.

The members of the *parlements*, altogether some eleven hundred, constituted the famous and powerful corporation known as the *noblesse de robe*, headed by great families like the d'Ormesson, Lamoignon, Molé, who rivalled in wealth and influence all but the greatest of the *noblesse de l'épée*. In earlier centuries recruited from the bourgeoisie, during the eighteenth century the *parlementaires* cut themselves off from their humble origins. Thus, for admission to the *parlement* of Brittany in the eighteenth century, noble birth was required.[3] By a verbal decree of 1777 the *parlement* of Normandy excluded all who were not of noble birth or the sons

of magistrates.[4] The *parlement* of Aix insisted on either four degrees
or a hundred years of nobility.[5] At Bordeaux the *parlement*, protesting against the appointment of a new president, declared that
for this office either a hundred years of nobility, or three generations of magistracy, was required.[6] Apart from birth and wealth
the qualifications for membership were not onerous. It was necessary, in theory, to be twenty-five years old, but exemption from
this condition was easily obtained. Of twelve new magistrates
admitted at Bordeaux between 1785 and 1789, two alone were
over twenty-five;[7] among one hundred and sixty-five admitted at
Aix between 1700 and 1789, only sixty-one were of the requisite
age, and nine were under twenty.[8] The candidate had to possess a
licence from a university as a doctor of laws; but the eighteenth
century was free from the fetish of examinations, and the degree
could be bought or a letter of dispensation obtained. The further
condition of an examination by the *parlement* itself was no more
serious a test. There was, in fact, considerable justification for the
satiric clause in the mock testament put out under the name of the
duchesse de Polignac, 'I bequeath to all the *parlementaires* having as
yet neither beard nor sense, and it is unfortunately the greater
number, the Corpus of the Roman Law.'[9] The essential qualifications for membership thus were birth and money. The *noblesse de
robe* of the eighteenth century has been described not unfairly as a
plutocracy, though one closely bound by *esprit de corps* and family
relationships.[10]

Originally the members of the *parlements* had been royal nominees, but it had come to be recognized that they had the right of
resigning office in favour of their heirs. To guard against the risk
of a sudden death preventing the transfer, the payment of a fee
was introduced, in return for which the *survivance*, the right of
bequeathing the office, was obtained. In 1604 hereditary rights
were finally safeguarded by the imposition of an annual tax of
one-sixtieth of the value of the office, called the *paulette* after
Charles Paulet, under whom it was introduced. This completed
the process by which membership of the *parlements* became an individual property right like the ownership of an estate. As such it
could be bought and sold. High prices were paid for office in the
*parlements*, though in the eighteenth century, both because other
openings were available to men with money, and because the

restrictions on membership imposed by the *parlements* themselves limited the market, there was a considerable fall in their value.[11] The most important consequence of the venality of the *parlements* was the fact that the Crown, in return for a petty financial advantage, had abandoned its control over the membership and recruitment of the chief law courts of the realm. Moreover, in all these conditions it was almost inevitable that the standards of the *parlements* should decline. Family tradition was strong, and there were, of course, always men of integrity and intellectual distinction amongst the *parlementaires*, but the unfavourable verdict on them in the eighteenth century is too general to be ignored. Arthur Young, on the eve of the Revolution, wrote,

> Upon the question of expecting justice to be really and fairly administered, everyone confessed there was no such thing to be looked for. The conduct of the parliaments was profligate and atrocious. Upon almost every cause that came before them, interest was openly made with the judges: and woe betide the man who, with a cause to support, had no means of conciliating favour, either by the beauty of a handsome wife, or by other methods.[12]

The attraction of membership of a *parlement* rested largely on the social prestige and influence it conferred, and to a less extent, on the whole, in the financial advantages, though there were many complaints of exorbitant *épices* — originally voluntary presents of sweets or spices, which had become money payments and obligatory. As they were fixed in proportion to the time taken over a case, there was no undue temptation to shorten proceedings.

The powers of the *parlements* fell into three categories. First came their strictly judicial duties as law courts. Secondly, they had a wide range of police powers, which brought them into rivalry with the royal *intendants*.[13] Most important of all, in the eighteenth century, were their political claims. Registration by the *parlements* was the traditional method of promulgation for royal decrees, each court having the exclusive right of registration within its own *ressort*. When a *parlement* found cause for objection in the king's decrees it drew up *remontrances*. The king could reply to these by *lettres de jussion*, ordering that his decrees should be registered, and if the *parlement* remained recalcitrant its resistance could be overridden by the procedure of *lit de justice*.[14] In the last resort, if the *parlement* refused to recognize the *lit de justice*, reiterated its remonstrances, or suspended its sessions in protest, the Crown could take action against individual magistrates by *lettre de cachet*, ordering imprisonment or removal to another town, or in extreme cases the exile of the court as a whole. Exile, i.e., compulsory removal to another town, was, however, more an inconvenience than anything else. Barbier, who was an *avocat*, wrote, not without malice, in 1732, 'Such an exile will not fail to punish a bit our *robins* [gentlemen of the robe]. Some were wanting to go to see to their affairs in their estates; others leave young wives and risk being sorry for it; others will regret Paris, the theatres, their mistresses, picnics in the country, and it will cause them all, more or less, a very inconvenient expense.'[15]

This is, inevitably, a simplified account, omitting many details, but it may serve as an explanation of the traditional procedure, and indeed of the practice of the eighteenth century. During the previous century, however, a very different situation had been established by Louis XIV, who never forgot the Fronde, or forgave the *parlements* for their part in it. His reign is proof of the fact that the *parlements* were strong only when the monarchy was weak. 'Louis XIV', says Pagès, 'did not have to crush the opposition of the *parlements*; he showed that he did not fear it, and that was enough.'[16] So long as he lived the *parlements* did not venture to challenge his authority, and it might reasonably have been supposed that their history as a political power was at an end. Thus Montesquieu wrote,

> The *parlements* resemble those ruins which one treads underfoot, but which still recall the idea of some famous temple belonging to the old religion of the people ... These great corporations have followed the destiny of human things: they have given way to time, which destroys all; to the corruption of manners, which has enfeebled all; and to the supreme authority, which has brought all low.[17]

On the contrary, however, the regency of Philip of Orleans was to inaugurate a period of incessant febrile activity, which was to cease only when *parlements* and monarchy fell together in the catastrophe of 1789. The terms of Louis XIV's will were known to favour the royal bastards at the expense of the regent, who, to establish his authority in legal form, turned to the *parlement* of Paris, which set aside the will, and in return obtained recognition once again of its former rights of *remontrance*.[18] This episode was destined to be the prologue to a long conflict between Crown and *parlements*, which dominated the internal situation of France so long as the *ancien régime* lasted. Already during the regency the two issues over which the main battles between monarchy and *parlements* were to be fought, the control of finance and religion, had appeared. These may, for the sake of clarity, be treated separately, though in fact the religious and financial quarrels overlap and react upon one another continually.

One of Louis XIV's last acts, and the first since the early years of his reign to arouse the long intimidated *parlements* to a show of resistance, had been the enforced registration of the bull *Unigenitus*, condemning one hundred and one propositions from a devotional work by Quesnel as Jansenist.[19] Of course, by the time when the bull was issued Jansenism proper had already been extirpated. The Jesuits had had their revenge for the literary triumphs of Pascal. The heresy of Jansen had been proclaimed by Rome; the small group of aged nuns, all that was left of the community of Port-Royal, had been dispersed, its buildings razed to the ground, the plough driven over the ruins, and even the inhabitants of the cemetery somewhat indecently scrabbled up and deposited elsewhere. The Jesuits were not content with this, and the bull *Unigenitus* was seen as a means of consolidating their victory. This bull, attacking a popular religious work, however, aroused widespread opposition. France was divided into *acceptants* and *refusants*, and among the latter were the *parlements*. Of course, the Jansenism of the *parlementaires* was of very doubtful quality. What was not doubtful was their traditional Gallicanism, jealousy of the independence of the clergy, and hostility to the influence of Rome; and all these sentiments led the *parlements* into the camp opposed to the bull. The *parlement* of Paris defined Gallican principles in a declaration of 1731,

1. That the temporal power, established directly by God, is absolutely independent of every other power ...
2. That the regulations and canons which the Church has

the right to make, do not become laws of the state until they have been clothed with the authority of the sovereign.

3. That jurisdiction with the right to employ visible and external force to constrain the subjects of the king belongs to the temporal power alone.

4. That the ministers of the Church are accountable to the king ... [20]

The *parlements*, indeed, were destined to play the leading part in the new Jansenist controversy. Endemic throughout the reign of Louis XV, it became particularly acute in the 'thirties as a result of the wave of religious enthusiasm produced by a very inconvenient, though well authenticated, outbreak of miracles at the tomb of the Jansenist deacon Pâris. Conflict between the *parlements* and the Church was further intensified by the policy of the archbishop of Paris, Christophe de Beaumont, a virtuous, charitable, not very intelligent prelate, and a fanatical partisan of the bull *Unigenitus*, who ordered his clergy to refuse the last sacraments to all persons suspected of Jansenism, unless they could produce a *billet de confession* signed by a priest who had accepted the bull. Since opponents of the bull could not be prevented from dying, a better means could hardly have been found of maintaining a continual flow of incidents and perpetuating unrest. The *parlements* protected the Jansenist clergy and took legal action against those who obeyed the archbishop's orders to withhold the sacraments. The court being largely under the influence of the *dévot* party, the royal council supported Christophe de Beaumont. It attempted to still the Jansenist agitation by decree after decree, but never persisted long in any one policy. We need not trace the long series of *remontrances*, *lits de justice* and exiles, followed by weak royal withdrawals.[21] In turn the *parlements* successfully resisted the archbishop of Paris, the Crown and the papacy. Finally they turned their main attack against the Jesuits, the traditional enemies of Jansenists and Gallicans alike. The story of the fall of the Jesuits is too well known to require re-telling. In 1764 the king yielded to pressure from many quarters, and the long campaign of the *parlements* reached its triumphant conclusion. With the dissolution of the Society of Jesus in France the struggle came to an end, and Jansenism ceased to occupy the centre of the political stage.

In their embittered warfare with the Church, the *parlements* had undermined one important pillar of divine-right monarchy, and given a lesson in successful disobedience. At the same time they were engaging in direct warfare with the monarchy through their constant opposition to all attempts on the part of the royal administration to reform its finances. It is hardly too much to say that every project for financial reform between 1715 and 1789 broke on the rock of the opposition of the *parlements*. After various indecisive skirmishes, a serious dispute arose with the appointment, in 1745, of possibly the ablest financial minister of the century, Jean-Baptiste de Machault, to face the problem of financing the War of the Austrian Succession.[22] Since existing taxes, with all the exemptions allowed to the privileged classes, could evidently not produce sufficient revenue, the obvious solution lay in a new tax which should be free from such exemptions. In 1749, therefore, Machault presented an edict creating the *vingtième*, a tax on income to be imposed on all proprietors. The battle against the *vingtième*, begun by the *parlements*, was taken up by the clergy, who through the influence of the *dévot* party at court succeeded in obtaining exemption for the property of the Church. In effect this meant the ruin of Machault's plans. The *vingtième* was subsequently so riddled with exceptions that it became little better than merely another tax upon the unfortunate peasantry. It was a long time before another controller-general was found to attempt a fundamental reform.

Not only in finance, but wherever they could make their influence felt, the *parlements* stood in the way of reform. They exhibited the conservatism of a close professional oligarchy in the preservation of their laws and procedure with all their traditional complication and local variety. They maintained with peculiar devotion the brutal and inefficient criminal laws. The only legal reform with which they can be associated is the abolition of *lettres de cachet*, which they continually demanded, though individual *parlementaires* frequently made use of them.[23] To be sure, no great enlightenment was needed to reinforce their professional bias against a procedure which took cases out of their cognizance, and was indeed sometimes used to save accused persons from the excessive and cruel punishments to which the jurisdiction of the *parlements* would have subjected them.

By the exercise of their judicial authority for the enforcement of seigneurial claims, the *parlements* constituted one of the bulwarks of the *ancien régime*. The alliance of *parlements* and *noblesse* was cemented by a joint interest in the defence of feudal rights.[24] But even where their interests were not affected the *parlements* manifested the same opposition to reform, as, for example, in the notorious decree of the *parlement* of Paris condemning the practice of inoculation against smallpox. They joined with their enemies of the clergy in preventing concessions to the Protestants, though the result of trials such as those of the Calas family, Sirven and La Barre has been attributed to the vices of their judicial procedure as much as to the influence of religious bigotry.[25] At the same time the *parlements* waged a continual war against the writings of the *philosophes*, being as zealous in the defence of orthodox religion as they were in opposition to its ministers. Their efforts had little effect in this connection, save that of giving publicity to the books they condemned.[26] Ideas found a way of escaping the net, though practical reforms were effectively held up.

It may fairly be said that the *parlements* presented an unyielding barrier against which the reforming spirit of the century broke itself in vain. The writings they condemned, though packed with plans for reform, were far from revolutionary. In the royal administration there was a machine ready made for putting the plans of the reformers into operation. A reforming bureaucracy is a rare thing in history, but such was the French bureaucracy in the eighteenth century.[27] For the frustration of reform, and its eventual translation into revolution, the *parlements* bear no small share of the responsibility. In the words of Aulard, 'If they prepared the Revolution ... it was not only because they weakened the monarchy by the fact of their disobedience, it was also because they prevented it from evolving and creating new institutions better related to the spirit of the time.'[28]

With the successful resistance of the *parlements* to ministerial attempts at financial reform, and their triumph over the clergy, symbolized in the destruction of the Society of Jesus, it may be said that one stage in their history in the eighteenth century was completed. At this point we may pause to examine the ideas which inspired their actions and gradually developed into a full-blown constitutional, and even revolutionary, theory. To Saint-Simon

75

must be given the credit for his early appreciation of the dangers that would result from the reborn pretensions of the *parlements* under the regent. But at the same time he opposed the project of substituting for them a nominated court, because he saw no other barrier in the state against royal despotism and clerical interference.[29] If Saint-Simon, who bitterly hated and despised the *parlements*, could admit so much, it is understandable that the general public, and even more the magistrates themselves, should have believed that they had a role to play in the life of the state, and a moderating influence to exercise over the monarchy.

It was some time, however, before the *parlements* came to their more exaggerated claims. In their remonstrances they repeatedly acknowledged the divine right of the monarchy, and the king's responsibility only to God.[30] On the other hand, they never recognized the title of the Crown to absolute sovereignty, but maintained that France had always been a constitutional monarchy. If the other constitutional organs of the Middle Ages were defunct, the responsibility resting on the *parlements* to safeguard constitutional principles was all the greater. They substantiated their claims by tracing their ancestry back to the earliest days of the monarchy. A *mémoire* on the *généralité* of Paris, prepared for the *intendant* in 1700, declared, 'The *parlement* of Paris was instituted in the year 755 by Pepin.'[31] The claim that the *parlements* represented the ancient *curia regis* had been put forward by Claude Joly during the Fronde, and in Hotman's *Franco-gallia* during the Religious Wars,[32] and by right of descent from the medieval *curia* they claimed to be the guardians of the fundamental laws of the country.[33] In 1753–4 the *avocat* Le Paige asked himself what the *parlement* was, and answered, 'All that it was in the time of Clovis.'[34] For contemporary support they appealed to the great name of Montesquieu after the appearance of *De l'esprit des lois* in 1748. They borrowed from him phrases such as 'dépot des lois' and 'corps intermédiaires', and bolstered up by his authority their conception of themselves as an intermediary power between the King and the nation.[35]

The *Grandes Remontrances* of April 9th, 1753, may be regarded as opening the second stage in the campaign of the *parlements* against the monarchy. In these the *parlement* of Paris speaks of 'une espèce de contrat' between the sovereign and the people, and asserts that 'if subjects owe obedience to kings, kings for their part owe obedience to the laws.'[36] They now cease to rely mainly on their historical claims and begin to appeal to the rights of the nation, of which they regard themselves as the representative. If we are looking for an agency through which the ideas of the contractual school of political thought could have been brought into the minds of the members of the revolutionary assemblies, among whom, it must be remembered, a large proportion were *avocats*, here is a much more palpable one than the little-read and less understood *Contrat social* of Rousseau. Nor should we turn to the *philosophes* or physiocrats, whose writings were more strongly influenced by the ideas of the newer utilitarian trend of thought. It is not unreasonable to suggest that the *parlements* played a large part in spreading the idea that the people is the only rightful source of power. On the eve of 1789 they were even talking, however inappropriately for such bodies, of liberty and equality — 'that man is born free, that in origin men are equal, these are truths which do not need to be proved'; and of the authority of the general will — 'One of the first conditions of society is that the individual will shall always yield to the general will.'[37]

Finally, while our discussion has mainly referred to the struggle between the Crown and the *parlement* of Paris, it must be pointed out that this does not mean that the other *parlements* were inactive. They played only a minor part in national politics during the earlier part of the century, but in the second half a conflict, with whichever *parlement* it had originated, was liable to be taken up by the others, and a victory in one province was an encouragement and incitement to all the rest. While the *parlement* of Paris fought a succession of controllers-general, the provincial *parlements* engaged in bitter and prolonged struggles against the *intendants* of their provinces, often with equal success.[38] Under Choiseul it is almost true to say that capitulation to the *parlements* became official policy,[39] but their apparent triumph, far from satisfying them, merely evoked more reckless opposition to the government. It became evident that the policy of conciliation was merely producing a progressive weakening of royal authority.

The fall of Choiseul, and his replacement by Maupeou in 1770, was to lead to a revolutionary change.[40] For the first time Louis XV had given his confidence to a strong minister, who was determined to crush opposition. He had an equally determined colleague in the abbé Terray,[41] who, as controller-general, proceeded to deal with what had become a critical financial situation by a wholesale repudiation of obligations and a forced loan. These measures, which were in effect a declaration of royal bankruptcy, were directed mainly against the wealthy bourgeois, for whom the *parlements* had no love. To these steps, therefore, they offered only a perfunctory resistance. But the king had now a minister who was prepared to take the initiative and crush the opposition of the *parlements* once and for all. Maupeou flung down a deliberate challenge, to which the *parlement* of Paris replied by suspending its sessions, and refusing to resume them, although four times summoned by *lettres de jussion*. In January 1771, Maupeou proceeded to have the magistrates exiled and their offices confiscated. A royal court was substituted for the *parlements*, taking their name and functions. Protests showered upon the ministry, but undeterred, Maupeou next turned the axe against the provincial *parlements*. At the same time, the opportunity was taken to divide the huge *ressort* of the *parlement* of Paris by the creation of six new courts. Maupeou also had plans for fundamental judicial reform. To begin with, the purchase and sale of offices in the new *parlements*, and the taking of *épices*, were forbidden. Further projected legal reforms were destined not to be realized until his secretary, Lebrun, was able to introduce them in the year VIII, under the consulate of Bonaparte. Freed from the opposition of the *parlements*, however, Terray was able to introduce important financial reforms. By 1774 he had reduced the deficit to manageable proportions.

A virulent war of pamphlets was waged against Maupeou, and the exiled magistrates were able to pose, with greater success than ever before, as the victims of a despotic minister and the defenders of public liberties. In spite of widespread agitation the new courts were functioning, however, and the reform seemed to be definitive. There was no sign that Louis XV would desert the minister who had rid him of the turbulent *parlements*, when the whole situation was changed by the king's death. Whatever ill services Louis XV had done the French monarchy by his life, the greatest was in the moment of his death, when, if he had lived a few more years, time would have been gained for the new courts set up by Maupeou to consolidate themselves and his work could not have been undone.

The young king and Marie Antoinette were determined to break with the tradition of the disreputable old king. Maupeou and Terray lost office in August 1774, and in November the *parlements* were restored. The ministry did not intend this to be an unconditional surrender, and a number of precautionary measures were decreed, which proved completely ineffective. The best comment on the whole episode was perhaps the sarcastic observation of Voltaire,

> At last all the *parlements* were reformed and it was hoped that we would see the reform of the laws likewise. We were mistaken: nothing was reformed. Louis XVI in his wisdom re-established the *parlements* that Louis XV with justice had destroyed. The people witnessed their return with transports of joy.[42]

The result of the recall of the *parlements* was that the royal government lost the advantages it had gained by Maupeou's coup d'état, while it continued to suffer from the odium of having proved itself an arbitrary despotism and from a further loss of prestige by its capitulation.

The *parlements* soon showed the use they intended to make of their victory. Turgot, who had been made controller-general, initiated a programme of reform. A former *intendant*, he belonged to that administrative magistracy which the *parlements* regarded as their natural enemy. As his measures appeared they encountered a series of protests from the *parlements* and refusals of registration, until the hostility they aroused gathered so many forces into the opposition that the king abandoned him.[43] Turgot's was the first of a series of attempts at financial reform, continually frustrated by an increasingly close alliance of all the privileged interests, with the *parlements* in the vanguard of resistance.

The reign of Louis XVI saw the final crystallization of the constitutional doctrine of the *parlements*. In their conflict with the Crown they had come, almost without realizing it, to recognize the people as the source of their own authority. Without contemplating abdication from the position they claimed for themselves as '*corps intermédiaires*' in the state, they appealed to the idea of the

*États Généraux*.[44] This appeal was taken more seriously by the people than it was perhaps meant by the *parlements*. In the public mind the *parlements* henceforth sank into second place, and attention was concentrated increasingly on the idea of a revival of the *États Généraux*. 'Instead of demanding the re-establishment of the former *parlement*, it is the convocation of the *États Généraux* that should be called for.'[45] The traditional monarchy, even if it accepted the constitutional check of the *parlements*, was no longer a satisfactory halfway house. The choice was henceforth between an enlightened despotism and the legislative sovereignty of a representative assembly.

So long as Necker, who succeeded Turgot, attempted no reforms, and pursued his policy of borrowing on an unprecedented scale, he encountered no serious opposition from the *parlements*, and their demand for the *États Généraux* was forgotten. When he took the first step towards reform their hostility revived and it became impossible for him to obtain the registration of further loans. Recognizing defeat, he put forward proposals which he knew the royal council would reject, thus enabling himself to resign with honour and the reputation of having sacrificed office to his desire for reform.[46] Calonne, who became controller-general in 1783, also met with little opposition while he continued the policy of borrowing. When the sources of loans began to dry up, and he was faced with the urgency of new taxation, he attempted to circumvent the inevitable opposition of the *parlements* by calling an assembly of notables. This device, however, proved fruitless and his successor, Brienne, reverted to the attempt to obtain registration for fresh taxes from the *parlements*, with the usual result.

Having tried conciliation, and even corruption, in vain, Brienne, or rather his colleague Lamoignon, fell back on strong measures in the form of a revival of the policy of Maupeou. On May 8th, 1788, the process of *lit de justice* was used to set up forty-seven new courts to take over practically the whole judicial business of the *parlements*, with a *cour plenière* at Paris to verify and register the laws.[47] The conflict was now frankly a political one, between the supporters of the absolute monarchy and the privileged classes led by the *parlements*. The words unconstitutional and anti-constitutional, which are hardly met with before 1788, become frequent.[48] Open revolt breaks out in several of the provinces. With clergy, *noblesse*, bourgeoisie and the mobs of the towns all on the side of the *parlements*, the Crown once again gave way. The queen reluctantly abandoned her support of Brienne, and public opinion forced back into office the one man whose genius was supposed to be equal to the task of solving the financial problems of the country. On September 23rd, 1788, Necker recalled the *parlements* and abandoned the scheme of Lamoignon. All parties were agreed that there was only one final recourse now: the *États Généraux* were summoned for the following year.[49]

The *parlements* came back on the crest of a great wave of public feeling. Steadily throughout the century they had appealed to the people against royal authority. The *remontrances*, which were supposed to be addressed privately to the king,[50] they had turned into public manifestos and circulated widely. Of the *Grandes Remontrances* of 1753 more than twenty thousand copies had been sold within a few weeks.[51] The *remontrances* were often written in highly emotional language for the purpose of inflaming opinion, and Mathiez is surely right in attributing to them a far greater influence in spreading disrespect for the monarchy and the established order of government than was exercised by the writings of the *philosophes*, which were for the most part far from anti-monarchical.[52] Alexandre de Lameth asked, 'Who had accustomed the people to unlawful assemblies and to resistance?', and answered 'The *parlements*.'[53] Yet the moment of the triumph of the *parlements* was the moment of their downfall. It was at this point that the falsity of their whole position was revealed. When they registered the royal decrees convoking the *États Généraux*, they added the condition that the forms of 1614 should be observed. They followed this up by rejecting a proposal in favour of the right of the *tiers état* to deliberate on all subjects. In so doing they revealed themselves as the mere spokesmen of the privileged orders, and brought the fundamental opposition of interests between themselves and the *tiers* to the surface. Protests against the attitude of the *parlements* poured out. The leaders of the *tiers* launched a violent campaign against them, stirred up popular agitation, and directed the mob against the *parlements* in their provincial strongholds.[54] Neither the privileged classes, nor the bourgeoisie, it must be observed in passing, realized how dangerous a game they were playing, in letting loose popular passions just at the time when a series of bad harvests, following on a period of economic regression, had produced an economic crisis of the utmost severity.[55] Without the economic crisis, indeed, the political crisis might not have been possible. Most sections of the country were suffering from it, and since the royal administration was still the responsible government of the country, they all tended to place the blame for the economic ills, the real sources of which they failed to understand, on the king's ministers.

The *frondeur parlements* had blocked the road to reform for so long, while at the same time exciting the demand, that now they were faced with revolution. Not for themselves had they laboured to bring down the absolute monarchy. Now was seen what Mirabeau had prophesied in a letter of April 1788, to Montmorin. 'Suddenly the *parlements* by the force of circumstances will be reduced to their true stature ... Their whole strength lies in the distress of the government and the discontent of the people.'[56] By 1789 they had completely lost all influence over the course of events and had sunk into the background. The last stage in their history is the story of their unresisted elimination by the National Assembly, which thus achieved, almost without effort, what the monarchy had struggled so long to do in vain.

On November 2nd, 1789, on the proposal of Alexandre de Lameth, the vacation of the *parlements* was indefinitely prolonged and the *chambres des vacations* took over their duties. A year later they were formally suppressed. Thus was consummated the prophesy of the cardinal de Retz in 1649, 'Les parlements, qui soufflaient sur le feu, en seraient, un jour, consumés.'

# 4

## THE AFFAIR OF THE DIAMOND NECKLACE

THERE is a tendency these days to underestimate the part that the trivial, the apparently irrational, the accidental, plays in history. At times, not least when great tragedies are preparing, the spirit of chance seems to me to get out of hand, and to reduce the dignity of history for a moment to the level of farce. It did so in the episode I am going to describe. Everyone has heard of the affair of the diamond necklace, but I wonder how many have more than a vague idea of the story, or have thought of it as more than a story.

It is a good one, of course, even for the eighteenth century. A young French provincial lawyer named Beugnot can begin it. One day, in the autumn of 1782, he says, visiting Bar-sur-Aube, he heard a rumour that a princess, escaped from a convent, had taken refuge in the most wretched inn of a town which had not a single good one. When Beugnot returned home he told the rumour to his father as a joke. But he found that the old man took it seriously.

His father told him that fifteen years ago, at Bar-sur-Aube, there had been three miserable, half-starved children, living in a hut like little naked animals, on scraps provided by charitable neighbours. Yet it was discovered that they were descended from the ancient royal house of Valois. Local gentry became interested in them, and had the boy put in a school for naval officers, and the two girls sent to a convent to be educated with a grant from the Crown. Perhaps the alleged princess was one of these children. She was indeed. She was the elder girl, Jeanne de Valois, who believed herself destined for a larger fate than life in a convent. 'I wasn't made', she wrote in her memoirs, 'to live in the pious prison in which my sister and I had been put. I fled, to win back my estates, my position, my rightful heritage.'

She had qualities to help her in the task besides her descent and her ambition. Beugnot says she was not beautiful, but she was slender and shapely, with lovely hands and little feet, blue expressive eyes, black arched eyebrows, a clear complexion, a generous mouth, and — 'what', he adds, 'is the real charm of her type of face' — an enchanting smile. She had little education, but a quick and penetrating mind, and incredible powers of invention. Yet her first move was a mistake. Judgment, self-control, she never possessed. She married in a hurry a penniless young Gendarmerie officer, Marc-Antoine de la Motte. The young couple became known as the Count and Countess de la Motte. Titles were easily come by: you simply moved to another town and adopted one.

Versailles was Jeanne de la Motte's goal, but accident, the presiding genius of her life, took her first to Strasbourg. There she sought the help of the Cardinal Prince Louis de Rohan, Archbishop of Strasbourg and Grand Almoner of France. He was a handsome, distinguished, wealthy, extravagant prelate, not devout though devoted to the fair sex. He had serious interests, however. He dabbled in spiritualism and was a patron of the famous Cagliostro, who cured his asthma and made him gold from base metals, and a real diamond.

Jeanne de la Motte easily obtained the sympathy of Rohan. More important, she also obtained sufficient money from him to enable her to travel to Versailles to pursue her claims at Court. Beyond that, the cardinal could not help her; because Louis de Rohan, for all his fascination and high birth, had an inveterate enemy in the person of Marie Antoinette. The reason why is too long a story to tell. But the cardinal's consuming ambition was to win the favour of the queen and the recognition at Court to which his position entitled him — a strange bond uniting him to the young adventuress.

Jeanne began her campaign at Versailles by making a few useful acquaintances in the Palace, mostly on the back stairs. She soon established a reputation as a *faiseuse d'affaires*, a contact woman, you might call her, about the Court. Her efforts to attract the queen's attention, including a dramatic fainting fit in the royal presence, were completely unsuccessful. But in spite of this she began to boast of the favour of the queen. And what more natural than that she should speak to Her Majesty of the kindness of the cardinal, with such effect as to disabuse Marie Antoinette of her former ill opinion of him, and even to lead her to write to him herself, by way of Madame de la Motte of course. I may add that Jeanne acquired a secretary about this time.

Rohan had no doubt of the genuineness of the letters he received. Jeanne's masterpiece, however, which delivered the cardinal totally into her hands, was the scene in the gardens at Versailles. We know how it was arranged from the evidence of a young woman named Nicole. 'One afternoon in June 1784', she says, 'I was sitting, as I often did, in the gardens of the Palais Royal, when I noticed a tall young man walking up and down in front of me. He stared at me fixedly, and seemed to be measuring my height and examining in detail my figure.' It was in this way that they became acquainted, and a few weeks later he surprised her somewhat by asking if his wife might accompany him on one of his visits. When his wife came — it was Madame de la Motte, of course — she said, according to Nicole, but it sounds too genuine to have been invented, 'Do not be afraid, my dear, of what I am going to tell you. I'm a society woman. I belong to the Court. I have some letters here from the queen herself. She and I are like two fingers on one hand. She has asked me to find someone to undertake a little performance for her. If you were willing to do so, it would be worth fifteen thousand livres to you.'

That was enough for Nicole, on whom, by the way, Madame de la Motte bestowed the title of La Baronne d'Oliva — an anagram of Valois: you can see Mme de la Motte's *idée fixe* emerging. The new Baronne d'Oliva was taken to the house of the la Mottes in Versailles one evening, and dressed up in clothes which exactly copied those of Marie Antoinette in a famous salon portrait by Vigée le Brun. She was a baby-faced blonde, with something of the complexion and carriage of the queen — enough to pass in the dark anyhow. For it was eleven o'clock on a moonless summer night when she was brought by the la Mottes into the gardens at Versailles. There she met a gentleman — she did not know it was the Cardinal de Rohan — to whom, as she had been instructed, she handed a rose, saying, 'You know what this means.' She had a letter to give him also, but in her confusion forgot it, and before anything more could occur someone ran up and said, 'Come away, Madame and Madame la Comtesse d'Artois are approaching.' So she and the la Mottes hurried off. That was the end of Nicole's story. It was enough. The trick had been done.

After the interview in the park with a woman he believed to be the queen, Rohan was wax in the hands of Jeanne, ready to believe anything she told him, even her story of the queen's passion for the diamond necklace.

The time has come to introduce the diamond necklace. It was a very special one. To make it the Court jewellers had collected 579 diamonds of the purest water. They had hoped that Louis XV would buy it for Madame du Barry, but though the old king was infatuated with the du Barry, he was not quite as infatuated as that. Knowing Marie Antoinette's weakness for diamonds, they subsequently pressed her to buy it, but the price frightened her. All this was common knowledge, and it provided the material for Jeanne de la Motte's great coup. She presented Rohan with a letter, which he believed to be from the queen. Marie Antoinette wrote, as he thought, that she wished to buy the necklace but lacked for the moment the necessary funds. It was not unusual, I may say, for the queen to buy jewellery 'on tick'. Would the cardinal cement their new friendship by allowing his credit to be used? Of course he would. On his personal credit Rohan obtained the necklace from the jewellers, brought it to the house of the la Mottes, and there handed it over to a supposed messenger from the queen. Diamonds now began to rain on the market. Jeanne's secretary was arrested with a pocketful. Her husband travelled to London, where he sold large quantities of diamonds roughly hacked from their settings. Jeanne paid her debts in diamonds.

And now she went back to Bar-sur-Aube, this time not to a hovel or a bad hotel but to a mansion. Wagons rolled up, day after day, loaded with pictures, sculptures, bronzes, tapestries, furniture. The la Mottes kept open house in noble style, with dinners, concerts, balls. Their luck lasted for a few months. Then, one evening Jeanne was at a dinner-party when a guest arrived from Paris with the latest news. The Cardinal de Rohan had been arrested by order of the king. With a cry she left the table. She burnt large packets of letters through the night and at four o'clock in the morning was arrested and put in the Bastille. The Cardinal de Rohan was already there and Cagliostro, Nicole, and Jeanne's secretary and her maid were to follow them.

The explanation of this sudden denouement is simple. The jewellers, anxious for their money, had gone to the queen. She saw

in their extraordinary tale some deep-laid plot of Rohan against
her, and informed the king. Astonished and indignant, Louis
ordered the arrest of all concerned. Neither he nor anyone else
knew what it was all about, or realized that a fortuitous combination of circumstances was to drag the Crown in the dust.

Rohan elected to be tried by the *Parlement*, the law court of
Paris, which was notoriously hostile to the Crown. The trial
dragged on for nine months. It was the scandal of a century: the
greatest ecclesiastical prince of France charged with forging the
queen's name to defraud the Court jewellers of diamonds worth
millions! In the dock with him, Cagliostro, the Italian magician,
Jeanne de la Motte from a hovel in Bar-sur-Aube, the so-called
Baronne d'Oliva from the streets of Paris. And mixed up with all
this the name of Marie Antoinette and the tale of a midnight
assignation between a queen and a cardinal in the gardens at
Versailles.

All Paris talked of nothing else. The queen's reputation was not
spared. The cardinal was the hero of the hour. Red on yellow,
cardinal on straw, were the fashionable colours of the year:
though in fact it would be very mistaken to imagine the cardinal as
languishing on a straw bed in a dungeon. On the contrary, he had
a well-furnished suite of rooms in the Bastille, where he gave continual dinner-parties. Even the lesser figures shone in the blaze of
publicity. The demoiselle d'Oliva had a baby in the Bastille and a
considerable number of offers of marriage. Cagliostro really had
nothing to do with the case. Perhaps he had only been called to
throw discredit on the cardinal by his association with such a
strange creature, who, it was rumoured, always slept in an arm-
chair, lived on nothing but cheese, and believed himself to be a
reincarnation of Julius Caesar. Asked, during his examination, if
he had any crime to reproach himself with, he replied, 'One,
alas: I murdered Pompey.' 'I never heard of that murder,' said
the public prosecutor. 'It must have been during my predecessor's
term of office.'

Jeanne de la Motte defended herself like a fury, told one fantastic story after another, and involved the whole affair in such a
tangle of lies that neither the Court at the time, nor anyone since,
has ever been able to disentangle it completely. She accused all
and sundry of a plot against her, feigned madness, tore up her

clothes, and hid under the bed, threw a candlestick at Cagliostro in court, bit her gaoler in the neck, exhibited tireless courage and inexhaustible invention.

Nine months were filled with rumour and scandal, charge and counter-charge. Despite all the efforts of the Crown, the cardinal was acquitted, to the delight of Paris. The king exiled him all the same. Cagliostro was acquitted and carried to his house in triumph by the mob. Little Nicole was dismissed from the case and proceeded to marry one of her suitors. The secretary, who had forged the letters, was banished for life, an extraordinarily light sentence. M. de la Motte was in England and wisely stayed there. From London he had fled to Newcastle-on-Tyne, where the French ambassador tried unsuccessfully to have him kidnapped and taken to France on a coal boat. Jeanne de la Motte herself was left to pay the full penalty of her fantastic, yet up to a point so successful, plot. The sentence of the court condemned 'Jeanne de Valois de Saint Rémi de Luz, wife of Marc Antoine de la Motte, to be flogged, naked, with rods, with a cord round her neck, and branded with a hot iron with the letter V on both shoulders by the public executioner, and afterwards to be led to the prison of the Salpetrière and there kept for life'. Farce had at last turned into tragedy.

So she passes out of history, and all her train with her. Mere curiosity may lead us to learn that she escaped after only nine months, with the aid of a pass hidden in a pot of jam, and provided, it is alleged, by the queen. Chance controlled her fate to the end. She died in 1791 in London, aged thirty-four, by falling, or throwing herself, from a window she had climbed out of to escape arrest for debt. The end was a tragedy not only for Jeanne de la Motte. Beugnot, who opens the story, may end it: 'The central fact in the whole miserable affair', he wrote, 'was that Mme de la Motte had had the audacity to pretend that the Queen of France had given a rendezvous to the Cardinal de Rohan at night in the gardens of Versailles, had spoken to him, offered him a rose, and allowed him to throw himself at her feet, and that the cardinal believed that the queen had done this. That was the crime, against religion, and against royalty ... The revolution already existed in men's minds, when they could treat such an insult to the king, in the person of the queen, with such indifference.'

Marie Antoinette herself had no doubt what the acquittal of the cardinal meant. 'Come and weep with me,' she wrote to her friend, the Duchesse de Polignac. 'Come and console my spirit, my dear Polignac. The verdict which has just been given is a frightful insult. I am bathed in tears, grief and despair.'

The affair of the necklace was the end of her happiness; it has been described as the beginning of the French Revolution — doubtless an exaggeration. Many other and more weighty factors needed to be added before a revolution was possible. Certainly the whole episode of the necklace is irrational and trivial, but if we neglect the irrational and the trivial, the historical pattern that emerges may be prettier, but it will be historically less honest, less true to the world of historical experience, and misleading in the world of contemporary fact. Moreover, to omit the individual and the accidental factors in the interpretation of the past is to be in danger of forgetting the role they play in the present. Perhaps the story of the affair of the diamond necklace may help to safeguard us from at least that among contemporary illusions. The tyranny of history is bad, but the tyranny of an over-rationalized mechanical philosophy of history could be fatal.

# 5

## THE MYTH OF THE FRENCH REVOLUTION

IN consenting to preside at this lecture his Excellency the French
Ambassador has conferred an honour on the new chair and given
a personal pleasure to us all. An ambassador who can win the
trust and the affections of the country to which he is accredited,
without forgetting the interests of the country he represents, and
who can smooth the path of international relations across obstacles
and differences of opinion, without pretending that they do not
exist, is not the commonest of phenomena; and a minister who
holds the balance as justly as Monsieur Massigli does is a subject
for our admiration. When the history of the years since the Second
World War comes to be written, the debt of both our countries to
him will, I believe, prove to be greater than anyone not behind
the scenes of diplomacy can do more than suspect now; and if
one thinks of the problems which the French Union and the
British Commonwealth have faced, and continue to face, everywhere, it will seem difficult to exaggerate the importance of
Anglo-French understanding.

This is not a mere matter of power politics — though why that
balance of power on which the peace of the world and the independence of nations depends should be called mere, I do not
know. Civilization is not to be measured only in terms of factories,
mines, great cities and all the impedimenta of a complex society.
The Pyramids were a wonder of the world like the Grand Canyon
and no more till men found out what was hidden in them. Something more valuable is hidden inside our civilization — possibly
sometimes too well hidden. Its ideas and values come from a long
intellectual and spiritual partnership. I am not forgetting Amsterdam and Geneva, Florence, Naples and the rest — but above all
it has been a partnership between the British and the French
minds, continuous for centuries in peace and never broken by the
centuries of strife. Here, I suggest, is one good reason why our
histories should not be studied in isolation. Increasing interest in

British history in French universities has been a welcome development of recent years, and it has been paralleled by an increasing attention to French history over here. I take the revival of a chair of French history as one sign of this general tendency. It is perhaps also not unconnected with a consciousness that the community of interests, as well as of traditions, between our two nations has not decreased as the problems we both face have grown more acute.

It is interesting to note that the first establishment of a chair of French history in this university occurred at an earlier time when France and Great Britain were also facing great international difficulties. The initiative appears to have come then from the London County Council, which proposed in 1912 the foundation of nine new professorships, including one in French literature and one in French history. The Senate of the University appointed a sub-committee, which approved the proposal and resolved that it was necessary that the professor should have 'a private room in which he would be able to interview advanced students from the various Colleges' and also a special departmental library. Inquiries were made at University College and the London School of Economics as to the possibility of providing these facilities. The School of Economics offered a room twelve feet by ten feet, which the committee inspected and found unsuitable. However, the Provost of University College was not prepared to offer a private room at all. 'The Professors whose departments are provided with departmental libraries', he said, 'do not, as a rule, have separate private rooms; they find that their needs are met by their departmental library.' As the School of Economics held out the hope that in a new building a better room might be found for the new professor, the committee suggested placing the chair there, though the professor was also to have teaching responsibilities at University College. The title of the chair was to be Modern French History and Institutions. Reading between the lines one may suspect that the Board of Studies in History was not entirely happy about this, for it passed a resolution that the teaching of the professor should not be limited to modern times.

An admirable choice was made for the first holder of the chair. Paul Mantoux was a distinguished historian, who had already made a name for himself by his writings on English history, and particularly by his well-known work on the Industrial Revolution of the eighteenth century. He took up his duties in 1913. In 1914 the war called him back to France and his appointment to the secretariat of the League of Nations involved his resignation in 1920. In 1922 the University found a successor in Professor Paul Vaucher, whose unostentatious but extensive learning and innate kindliness endeared him to all, and who is happily still with us in spirit, for after having taught French history to English students, he has more recently, as a professor at the Sorbonne, been occupied in teaching English history to French students. In 1932, however, his ill health led to a division of the duties of the chair. Vaucher remained as part-time professor at the School of Economics, while a Reader was appointed at University College, Arsène Alexandre, whose vivid personality, charm and promise were to be extinguished prematurely and tragically in a German prisoner-of-war camp.

A full-time chair of French history is now revived after an interval of twenty-one years. I hope I am not exhibiting undue prejudice in expressing the belief that there ought to be a chair of French history in this university, which has so many chairs devoted to special fields and countries. If the centre of French studies, which is growing up in this college, were also to be safeguarded by a permanent establishment against any danger of a future lapse, the shade of Jeremy Bentham, whose greatness first achieved recognition among French disciples, would, I believe, bestow a more than utilitarian blessing.

My only qualification for occupying this chair is that for many years I have been studying, writing and talking French history. If I have also committed the almost fatal crime, for an historian, of being more interested in what went on in people's heads than of what went into their pockets, even this has not been entirely useless for an historian of France, where ideas are almost as much a national interest as cricket is with us. The history of France certainly offers ample scope for any historian. For a thousand years France has played a central and often a dominating role in European affairs. Three times at least, under a Frankish conqueror, a Bourbon king and a Corsican emperor, it might be said that French history was European history. Napoleon, of course, was the summing up, if not the conclusion, of the French Revolution, which was not the least important episode in the long story.

Into this tumultuous act were gathered innumerable threads of past history, and out of it led most of those that make up the tangled plot of the modern world. Its interpretation has a contemporary as well as an historical significance, and this, incidentally, is the first justification for my title.

\*

History, said Napoleon, is a myth that men agree to believe. I would rather say that it is this so long as it is something which it is important to them to believe or not. While the past lives it remains a myth, and naturally like all things living, it changes. The history of the French Revolution, whether garbed in the apocalyptic vision of a Carlyle or the profound scholarship of a Lefebvre, has continued to live and to change because it has continued to be bound up with the beliefs and aspirations of mankind.

I am tempted to suggest that in another sense also the French Revolution might be called a myth. At first, I must confess, I thought of entitling this lecture, 'Was there a French Revolution?' However, it seemed that to inaugurate this chair by eliminating the Revolution would be rather awkward; and it would certainly have been tactless to invite our French friends here and begin by abolishing their Revolution for them. I am therefore asking a safer question: 'What was the French Revolution?' We used to think that it began in 1789. Now we know it began at least in 1787. It ended when? In 1815? Thiers and Aulard conclude their histories of the Revolution in 1799, Mathiez and Thompson in 1794, Guérin begins the reaction in 1793, Salvemini ends his history in 1792, and for some it has never ended. To each terminal date corresponds a different interpretation. Worse still follows. The Revolution has ceased to be a revolution and become a series of revolutions – the last Fronde of the nobles and the *parlements*: the revolution of the *tiers état*, the peasant rising, the republican insurrection, the revolt of the *sans-culottes*, the *neuf thermidor* and the various coups d'état under the Directory ending in that of 18 brumaire. The French Revolution is in fact a name we give to a long series of events. What it means depends on the light in which we see the connection between these events. In this sense the French Revolution, if not a myth, is a theory, or rather a number of rival theories.

Does this mean that before we can write it we need a philosophy of history? Certainly that would be one way out of the difficulty. A philosophy of history, like the beam of a searchlight, penetrates the obscurity of the recorded, and even better the unrecorded, past. It gives us the illusion that we are looking back along the path that humanity has followed to arrive at its present uneasy station and that unconscious forces or conscious will have determined that it should tread. But in truth the determination comes from us and is itself determined by the incidence of the light we are directing on the past. Change the angle only slightly and the beam may be lost in fog and mist, or a new set of facts swirl into clear light and an accepted theory die.

On the problem of historical causation de Tocqueville, as might be expected, makes one of the wisest observations:

> I have lived with men of letters, who write history without ever being mixed up with practical affairs, and with politicians, who are only concerned with actual happenings, without ever thinking of describing them. I have always noticed that the former see only general causes, while the latter, living in the midst of the confusion of daily circumstances, willingly imagine that everything can be reduced to a series of separate events, and that the petty strings which they are all the time pulling are those which move the world. It is to be believed that both the former and the latter are mistaken. For my part I hate those absolute systems which derive all the events in history from great first causes, link one to another in a chain of destiny, and, so to speak, eliminate men from history. I find them narrow in their pretended greatness, and false under their air of mathematical truth.[1]

Yet the rule of chance in the great crises of history is one of the most difficult ideas for the human mind to tolerate. In a single separate event what we call chance or accident may be admitted; a universal, world-shaking movement such as the French Revolution seems to force determinism upon us. Historians of the Revolution, particularly of recent times, have increasingly tended to show why all that happened *had* to happen. The historian may not be able to see the strings which move his figures. It may be more interesting for him to pretend to forget them and describe his puppet play as though the actors moved of their own volition. But the really serious historian likes to think that this is make-believe, and prefers to concentrate on the mechanics of the process rather than on the mere twitches of arms and legs which simulate free action. But why should he stop at this? If there is one level of truth in the description of the movements of the puppets, and another in tracing the strings, the real historical causation, it is sometimes held, is to be found in the hidden forces that control them both. These are not to be seen but they may be deduced, as the Greeks detected the vagaries of the inhabitants of Olympus behind the changing destinies of their clients and victims here below. Of course, the new Olympus is infinitely more respectable. The wanton favours and enmities of a pack of uninhibited gods and goddesses no longer bring superhuman success or inhuman punishment. Great impersonal forces have taken their place, or rather a single great impersonal force, which is there operating unseen all the time, though only when there is a great revolution in human destinies, we are told, do we become fully aware of its ceaseless inexorable working, before which one social order passes away and in the predetermined pattern of history, another emerges.

To pass from the general to the particular, in the French Revolution, it is commonly said, the feudal order passed away and the rule of the bourgeoisie took its place. This is, put simply, the myth which has dominated serious research on the history of the French Revolution during the present century. It is often treated as an exemplification of a scientific law derived from the facts of history. If I am calling it a myth, this is in no derogatory sense but in a Platonic way of speaking, which may, of course, be worse. The fact that it has come to be taken for granted is my reason for re-examining it. Simplifying, but then this is essentially a *conte de fées*, the outline of the story is that there was once a social order called feudalism. This was a terrible ogre and lived in a castle; but for centuries a bourgeois Jack the Giant-killer climbed the bean-stalk of economic progress, until finally in the French Revolution he liquidated the old order and put in its place something called alternatively bourgeois society or capitalism. The only divergence from the traditional story is that he did not live happily ever after. I think it would be fair to say that this is the generally accepted myth or theory of the French Revolution, and of course both the factors in it are themselves theories. I propose to discuss them in turn.

The first is feudalism. This is a term that was invented to describe the social organization that prevailed in the Middle Ages. By the time of the French Revolution, as a system of government based on the ownership of land it had long come to an end in France. Not only had the feudal aristocracy ceased to govern the country, it had even ceased to own a large part of the land. A rough estimate is that one-third of the land had passed into the possession of the peasantry, and a fair proportion of the remainder was forest or waste. The so-called feudalism of the eighteenth century consisted in the survival of antiquated dues and services owed to the descendants of the former feudal seigneurs, or to those who had purchased their *seigneuries*. A considerable body of *feudistes* lived out of the continual law-suits that these claims, registered in *terriers*, involved. In the years before 1789 an attempt was made by the possessors of feudal rights — and possibly in particular by their new possessors, though this is a matter that requires investigation — to revive old ones that had long fallen into disuse and to enforce surviving ones more rigorously. In spite of this, they remained a peculiarly functionless survival, the relics of an atrophied organ, which only a very adventurous social biologist could use to justify a classification with some fossil feudal order of the past. In the words of a legal historian, the fief, in the eighteenth century, was 'une forme bizarre de propriété foncière'.[2] The jurists of the time admitted that the 'seigneur utile', that is to say the *tenancier*, was the real proprietor, though his property involved certain obligations, which they described in legal terminology as a 'servitude au profit du seigneur foncier'.[3]

\*

How little the so-called feudal dues deserved their title was to be proved in the course of the attempt to apply the decrees of August 4th–11th, 1789, by which the Constituent Assembly proposed to abolish those dues that were feudal in origin, while at the same time maintaining those payments or services which were of the nature of economic rent. It proved impossible to make the distinction in practice, and after years of legal struggle the attempt

was abandoned and all dues which qualified ownership disappeared. This was just what the Constituent Assembly had feared
and tried to avoid, for to suggest that the members of the Assembly
wanted to abolish dues which many of them had acquired themselves would be a mistake. On the contrary, their disappearance
was an unlooked-for and unwanted by-product of the Revolution.
The night of the Fourth of August was not quite the spontaneous
and generous gesture it has been made to seem. The men of
property who sat in the Constituent Assembly, as Professor
Lefebvre has pointed out, could not approve of confiscatory
methods of dealing with property, especially when some of it was
their own. The countryside took matters into its own hands when
it broke out in the last jacquerie, under the stimulus of economic
distress, the excitement of the drawing up of the *cahiers* and the
election of the *tiers état,* and the general breakdown of authority
resulting from the *révolte nobiliaire.* The unrest in the spring and
summer of 1789 was so widespread that a major military operation
would have been necessary to suppress it. The night of the Fourth
of August was an attempt by throwing overboard some of the dues
to salvage the rest. In the age of Reason, feudal went with such
terms of abuse as Gothic and medieval. If the property rights that
were sacrificed were called feudal, this was at least in part to prevent the episode from becoming a precedent in respect of other property rights. It was necessary to give the dog a bad name in order
to justify his having been hanged. But the peasantry did not draw
such subtle legal distinctions. They simply ceased to pay their
dues, whatever their nature, and no subsequent government had
the strength to make them resume payment. In the words of
Lefebvre, 'they liberated themselves, and the successive Assemblies
only sanctioned what they had accomplished'.[4] If the system of
seigneurial rights can be identified with the medieval social order
called feudal; and if the reluctant acceptance of a *fait accompli* by
the Constituent Assembly can be called abolishing feudalism,
then, I suppose, the first part of the prevailing myth of the Revolution can hold good. The qualifications seem to be so extensive as
to make the statement practically meaningless.

What of the other factor in the theory, the revolt of the bourgeoisie? It is unnecessary nowadays to labour the point that the
Revolution began as an aristocratic rising; the Counter-revolution,

as it subsequently became, in fact preceded the Revolution by at least two years. It has been described as the last Fronde and it marked the ultimate failure of Louis XIV's effort to place the monarchy so far above the privileged classes that they could never again challenge its authority as they had done during his minority. Of set purpose he had excluded the old *noblesse* from positions of authority in the state. Under the *grand monarque* the son of an official of Rouen, Colbert, could become the greatest man in the realm after the king, while only one of the highest nobles was allowed in a ministerial office. Under his weaker successors the Court took its revenge and nobles infiltrated into the government of the state. They monopolized the higher ranks of the Church and the Army, filled the *Conseil d'en haut* and supplied occupants for nearly all the ministries except that of the Controller General. The calling of the Assembly of Notables was a tacit recognition that the king could not govern against the will of the privileged orders, but instead of gaining their support he found that by giving them an organ of self-expression he had merely opened the flood-gates of aristocratic revolt.

The last of the Frondes was in appearance a formidable movement. In reality it was an attempt by a class of parasites to take over the body politic, which they possessed the power to destroy but not to recreate. It was a revolt of the drones, for though nobles might occupy places of influence and power, the one thing the *noblesse* as a class did not do was work. There were, of course, exceptions, but, by and large, the *noblesse de race* had no field of active service to the state except the Army, in which its numbers and courage did not make up for its indiscipline and inefficiency. French society had become etiolated, and if it could still produce fine flowers at the top, it was at the expense of the health of the whole plant. Nobles occupied positions of dignity and remuneration, the Court *noblesse* relied for its finances increasingly on the profits of places and pensions, but nearly all the effective business of the state was done by men a grade lower down. In the embassies one finds that *chargés* or secretaries, emerging from lower social strata, often performed most of the real work of diplomacy. In the *généralités* the duties of the *intendants* — now almost invariably noble even if their nobility was sometimes of rather recent vintage — were increasingly falling into the hands of the *secrétaire de l'inten-*

*dance* and the *subdélégués*, as was shown by the fact that *intendants* themselves sometimes stayed away from their *généralités* for long periods. The ministries in Paris were dependent on the work of their permanent officials. The efficient officers in the Army were largely those whose social origins prevented them from rising to the higher ranks. The legal work of France was carried out not by some thousand proud *parlementaires* but by a host of minor judicial officers. From commerce the *noblesse* was generally excluded under penalty of *dérogeance*; and though it was easy for wealthy *roturiers* to pass into the ranks of the *noblesse*, they could only do so by abandoning their effective functions and *vivant noblement*. Some nobles, or at least *ennoblis*, might be found as exceptions to these statements, but as a broad generalization it may be said that it was all those who did the real work of administering France who formed the *tiers état*. These men were drawn from and constituted an important, perhaps even the greatest, element in the bourgeoisie: and this brings me to the second of my problems, for bourgeois is a term used almost as loosely as feudalism.

In Great Britain we commonly think of the rise of the bourgeoisie as the rise of that class which was primarily concerned with the control of trade, industry and finance, as composed therefore of merchants, bankers, industrialists and capitalists, great and small. The accepted theory of the French Revolution is that it came when the new form of property which such men represented replaced the older form represented by the feudal landowners. Is this a correct analysis? I must begin by premising that if it was a revolt of the 'monied men', to use Burke's term, it was certainly not provoked by economic grievances. The fine eighteenth-century quarters of French provincial towns are standing evidence of the wealth of the men who built them, as well as of the standards of taste that dictated their elegance. However, it is hardly necessary to discuss the reasons they might, or might not, have had for making a revolution until we are quite sure that they made it. Now, in fact, the men who made the Revolution of 1789 were the members of the Constituent Assembly; little of what had been achieved by 1791 was to be lost, and most of what was done subsequently was to be undone. The essential first question to ask, then, is who formed the *tiers état* of 1789?[5]

Were they the representatives of a rising industrial capitalist class? To imagine that this was even possible would be to antedate such industrial revolution as France was to experience by more than half a century. Some kind of clue to their importance in society will be provided if we ask how many manufacturers there were among those elected in 1789. Those who actually sat in the Assembly, either as deputies or *suppléants*, in the *tiers état*, numbered 648. Among these there were just eight who are described as manufacturers or *maîtres de forges*. Perhaps, however, the bourgeois were the merchants? Some 76 of the *tiers* are described as *marchands* or *négociants*. Only about 20 of these came from places of any commercial importance; the remainder should perhaps be regarded primarily as local notables. Very few of them seem to have played any prominent part in the Revolution. The world of finance produced one solitary banker, though one merchant also described himself as a banker. Together, merchants, manufacturers and financiers amount to 85, or 13 per cent of the whole number.[6]

If they were not merchants or manufacturers, then, what were the *tiers état* of 1789? The category of those concerned with trade and industry is easy to identify. The social status or function of the others is apt to be more difficult to distinguish, sometimes for lack of sufficient indication — 'bourgeois vivant noblement' is fairly easy to place, as is even 'citoyen'; but what is the significance of 'bourgeois fils aîné'? Sometimes there appears also that great handicap which the modern historian suffers from as compared with the historian of medieval or ancient times, too much information. How is one to classify a member (of the Convention) described as 'landowner, leather manufacturer, lawyer and professor of mathematics and physics'? My figures are, therefore, all approximate, but I do not think that a variation of a few either way would do much to alter the general picture that emerges of the kind of men who composed the *tiers état* of 1789.

It is usually said that the majority were lawyers. This is undoubtedly true, but it is not as illuminating a statement as might be supposed. True, we can make out an impressive list of well over 400 lawyers in the Constituent Assembly, but this description tells us little about their actual social status or functions. It is as useful as would be a contemporary social classification based on the possession of a university degree.

Fortunately we know something more about most of the

members. Those who are described as lawyers (*avocats* or *notaires*) without any further qualification number 166, just about a quarter and it might be held that this was quite enough for the health of the Assembly. The remainder of the huge legal contingent falls into a different category. It includes members of the *ministère public*, notaries royal, local judges, municipal officers, and above all *lieutenants généraux* of *bailliages* and *sénéchaussées*. It may be observed in passing that there was an extraordinary number of officers of *bailliage* and *sénéchaussée* among those elected, which is perhaps not unconnected with the fact that these areas formed the constituencies. Add to these the various officials of the state services — 25 — and the total of 278 is reached, that is some 43 per cent of the whole membership.

To describe these men simply as lawyers is to ignore one of the essential features of the *ancien régime*. It would be almost as justifiable as a social analysis which classified the Justices of the Peace in England primarily as lawyers, for as late as the eighteenth century administration and justice were inextricably mixed up in most countries. The great majority of the so-called lawyers were in fact juridico-administrative officers, holding *charges* in municipality or *bailliage* or one of the state services. These were nearly always venal posts, which went therefore to those with a sufficient competence to pay the purchase price, unless they were lucky enough to inherit them from a relation. Thus in 1789 the office of notary could cost as much as three or four hundred thousand *livres* in Paris;[7] in the provinces it might be worth much less.

An office or *charge* was an investment, a status and a job. Those who bought them were not spending their money for nothing; they drew in return a commensurate income from fees. How much work they had to do for it must remain a matter of doubt: the number of office-holders is evidence of the financial needs of the Crown, rather than of the administrative needs of the country. One little *bourg* of 3,000 inhabitants in the seventeenth century rejoiced in a *bailli*, a *prévot*, a *lieutenant*, a *procureur fiscal*, six notaries, four *sergents*, twelve *procureurs*, and four *greffiers*.[8] Doubtless they also served the surrounding countryside, but it seems a lot. It is difficult not to suspect that, whatever their fees, they were overpaid for their services. They could reply, of course, that having bought their jobs they were entitled to a return on their investment.

The presence of such a large proportion of venal officers in the Constituent Assembly is at first sight difficult to reconcile with the holocaust of their offices effected by the Assembly itself, apparently with little protest. One can understand that they were ready to sacrifice the privileges of the *noblesse* and the clergy, but that an important part of their own income should have gone the same way appears at first sight to indicate a spirit of self-sacrifice and idealism rarely to be predicated of the average political man. We need not, however, in this case hypothesize any superhuman virtue. The venal offices were abolished, it is true, but not without compensation. Admittedly, the compensation was in *assignats*: but no one as yet knew, or dreamed of, the depths to which the *assignat* was to fall. Those who clung to their paper money long enough doubtless lost it all; but it is permissible to suppose that many rapidly reinvested their compensation. It would be interesting to know to what extent the payment for the venal offices was used for the purchase of the nationalized lands of the Church. Certainly the coincidence by which the venal officers, who formed such an important element in the Constituent Assembly, obtained a large supply of free capital, just at the time when an unprecedented opportunity for its investment in land was opened to them, was a very happy one.

It need not be assumed that there were no other motives, of a more disinterested nature, involved in the treatment of the venal offices. But though the demands of a more efficient administration called for their abolition, the venal officers had no occasion to feel that their posts were contrary to social morality. They were all, in a sense, living on the state; but if they looked higher up the social scale they could see plenty who held places and pensions by favour of the Court, without having had to pay for them, or having to do any work in them at all. In their monopoly of the positions combining the maximum of remuneration with the minimum of duties, the privileged orders had something more valuable than a mere decorative social superiority, and the bourgeois a substantial grievance.

Thiers, who was close to the Revolution and knew many of its participants, held that if the Crown had established some equality in official appointments and given some guarantees, the major source of discontent would have been eliminated.[9] De Tocqueville, a little later, put forward a similar view of the revolution of 1848. 'If many of the conservatives', he wrote, 'only defended the Ministry with the aim of keeping their salaries and jobs, I must say that many of the opposition only appeared to me to be attacking it in order to get jobs for themselves. The truth, a deplorable truth, is that the taste for official jobs and the desire to live on the taxes is not with us the peculiar malady of a particular party, it is the great and permanent infirmity of the nation itself' – 'C'est le mal secret, qui a rongé tous les anciens pouvoirs et qui rongera de même tous les nouveaux.'[10]

De Tocqueville, I think, was mistaken only in supposing that this was peculiarly a cause of revolution in France. I suspect that it has a broader application to other revolutions.

A comparison with England in the eighteenth century is not unilluminating here, if one considers the differing prospects that offered themselves to men of ability, lacking what is in all societies so much more valuable than mere ability – money and family influence – in the England and in the France of the eighteenth century. A Robespierre, a Danton, a Vergniaud, in France before 1789 could not hope to be anything but the kind of petty attorney on whom Burke poured scorn. In England at the same time, Vergniaud would have shone as an orator in the House of Commons, to which his talents would undoubtedly have carried him, even in the company of Fox and Sheridan. It is not difficult to envisage Danton as a future Lord Chancellor. The more modest talents of Robespierre would doubtless have been satisfied with the post of Lord Chief Justice, if he could have reconciled holding such a post with his objections to capital punishment. Fouché might have become Archbishop of Canterbury. Roland would have been a simple under-secretary of state and member of parliament, but the opportunities that such a post provided for mixing in high society and being received at Court would probably have contented that sentimental little salon politician, Madame Roland. Lord Chancellor Eldon and the great international lawyer, Lord Stowell, sons of a Tyneside keelman and an innkeeper, had no better start than any of these; nor did Thurlow, son of a country vicar. A measure of unscrupulousness, combined with eloquence and political ability, brought him to the Woolsack. Similar qualities only brought Danton to the guillotine. In France, if he had ever had sufficient assiduity to accumulate the necessary money, Thurlow might have become president of a *grenier à sel*, perhaps even *avocat au parlement*, hardly more.

The Church under Louis XVI had not a single bishop who was not noble by birth. In England, John Potter, son of a draper, and obtaining his education as servitor at Oxford, could become Archbishop of Canterbury. Isaac Maddox, orphan and apprenticed to a pastrycook, ended up as a bishop, as did Richard Watson, son of a country schoolteacher. The Navy — though not the Army — offered another opening for men of talent to rise to the top. One cannot but ask oneself what would have happened to the Revolution in France if in a similar way so many of those who were to be its leaders had in advance been absorbed into the ranks of power and prestige. Whatever else the *tiers état* of 1789 wanted, they certainly wanted 'la carrière ouverte aux talents'.

Returning to the analysis of the revolutionary bourgeoisie, it may be said that the Revolution did not end with the Constituent Assembly, and that its subsequent developments brought, in the Convention, another set of men into power.[11] An analysis of the membership of the Convention gives results which naturally vary from those for the Constituent Assembly. The financial, mercantile and manufacturing section is even smaller — 83 out of 891, some 9 per cent. Lawyers are present in about the same proportion of one-fourth. Office holders are down from 43 to 25 per cent, though as the venal offices were now a thing of the past, it is unlikely that this figure represents all those who had held such positions under the *ancien régime*. A tiny group of *petits bourgeois* and ordinary soldiers appears, to offset which we have rather more nobles and colonial proprietors. There are more clergy, of course, now that they have no Order of their own. The most notable development is the appearance of a substantial group of what one might call professional men in addition to the lawyers: 32 professors or teachers, some of them also clerics; 58 doctors, surgeons or pharmacists; some lower officers of the Army, the Navy and merchant marine; a few writers and actors. Altogether this category has risen from about 5 per cent to 17 per cent.

Like the *Constituante*, the Convention is still almost exclusively a bourgeois assembly, and in 1792, as in 1789, bourgeois has to be interpreted in the sense of a class of *fonctionnaires* and professional men. Admittedly, its actions were not the same as those of the *Constituante*. Under pressure from the popular movement in Paris, and amid the storm and stress of counter-revolution and war, policies were accepted by a purged Convention which, as is the way of revolutions, after the purgers had themselves been purged, it was to repudiate. These surface storms of the Revolution are not my subject. When they had died down, and under Napoleon it was possible to make some calculation as to who had emerged in triumph, it could be seen that the smaller fry had mostly continued to inhabit the shallows, while the officials and the professional men of the *ancien régime*, mixed with a fair number of former nobles and a few able men from the ranks, had emerged as the governing class of the new regime.

Once again figures tell the story better than words. Of the members of the Constituent Assembly and the Convention, 111 held high office, and 518 lower offices, under Napoleon, and of these over one-third had held office before 1789. Both Assemblies contained many obscure men who subsequently sank back into the obscurity from which they had emerged. They contained more than a few who, republican by principle, refused to accept the Empire and the share in the fruits of office which they might otherwise have had. There were also the liquidations, the method by which revolutions solve the problem of too many people pursuing too few jobs. But in the end it may have been that a fair proportion of those who had given up their venal offices for compensation at the beginning of the Revolution obtained new ones that were free from the stigma of venality at the end. It may at least be suggested as an hypothesis worthy of investigation that the essence of government in France after the Revolution remained where it had been before, in the great and now renewed bureaucratic *cadres*. With Napoleon returned the *Conseil d'État*, to resume the functions of the councils that had formerly surrounded the throne. Since then, assemblies and emperors and kings have come and gone, but the *Conseil d'État* and the *maîtres des requêtes* have remained at the apex of the administrative pyramid and provided the lasting structure of government behind a series of changing regimes.

It may seem that as a result of this interpretation the Revolution is reduced considerably in scope, that everything that survived after 1799 had already been gained by 1791. Essentially this is, I think, true, but how, then, account for eight years of disorder and continuing revolution? One answer that is often given is to attribute it to the struggle against the counter-revolution. I suspect that this is to give too much weight to a movement that was moribund from birth; but the myth of the counter-revolution is not my subject here. The war was, I believe, a more important factor, but that also is another subject.

The Revolution began from above, but it was continued by pressure from below. This did not come from the peasantry, who achieved their objective at an early stage and after that ceased to have any active interest in the Revolution beyond safeguarding their gains. But in the towns the poorer population suffered increasingly from inflation and the shortage of supplies, and constituted, therefore, a source of potential unrest which could be exploited by the political factions. If it had been calculated — which of course it was not — for the perpetuation of a revolutionary situation, the system of inflation could not have been better chosen. But when it came to an end the difference between 1799 and 1791 was far less than that between 1791 and 1789.

If I have put forward the view that the interpretation of the Revolution as the substitution of a capitalist bourgeois order for feudalism is a myth, this is not to suggest that the Revolution itself is mythical and that nothing of significance happened in France at this time. The revolutionaries drew a line at the end of the *ancien régime*, subtracted the negative factors from the past, and added up the sum of what was positive, to be carried forward on the next page. A class of officials and professional men moved up from the minor to the major posts in government and dispossessed the minions of an effete Court: this was what the bourgeois revolution meant. The peasants relieved themselves of their seigneurial dues: this was the meaning of the abolition of feudalism. But even taken together these two developments hardly constitute the abolition of one social order and the substitution of another for it, and if the accepted theory is not quite a myth, it seems singularly like one.

Did the Revolution effect no more fundamental change than this? In French economy it might be considered that it held back rather than encouraged changes which were to come much later and are still very incomplete. Politically it replaced the divine right of the king by the divine right of the people. In theory this was to substitute an absolute power for one limited by its nature, and to eliminate the rights of the people as against a government which was henceforth theoretically themselves. The war dictatorship of the Committee of Public Safety, and the Napoleonic Empire, were the historical if not the logical sequel to the assertion of the sovereignty of the people. But this aspect of the Revolution has perhaps been unduly emphasized of late. Sovereignty remained sovereignty, whether exercised in the name of God or the people, even though the Revolution changed both the possessors and the nature of power in the state.

I implied, earlier in this lecture, that the Revolution was not one but many. One of the greatest of its aspects I have so far neglected. Men have ideas, whatever those historians who have tried to decerebrate history may say, and these ideas are not to be treated merely as the expression of material interests. The explanation of the causation of the Revolution simply in terms of the ideas of the eighteenth century has long been discarded from serious history, but this is not to say that the revolutionaries were mere economic animals to be summed up in terms of the stud book and the bank balance, or reduced to a number of holes punched in an index card. The members of the French revolutionary assemblies had been bred on the ideas of the Enlightenment. Reforms such as the abolition of torture in legal proceedings and many other legal changes, or the removal of the disabilities of Protestants and Jews, are not to be explained in terms of material interests. But here again, though the Revolution may have accelerated some of these reforms, it perhaps put back others. Here also the historian has to admit not only that these reforms were the children of the ideas of the eighteenth century, but that their implementation had already begun before 1789. The reign of Louis XVI was an age of reform, which the Revolution continued. The armies of the Revolution and Napoleon, it has been said, spread the humanitarian ideals of the eighteenth century to the rest of Europe, strange missionaries though they were. There is some truth in this, though if we consider the development of subsequent history we may be tempted to think that the seeds of the Enlightenment, east of the Rhine and south of the Alps and the Pyrenees, fell on very stony ground.

The main point I want to make, however, is that whether we analyse the revolutionary age in terms of social forces or of ideas, it appears more and more clearly as the child of the eighteenth century and only to be understood in terms of the society out of which it emerged. To interpret the Revolution we must look back as well as forward, and forget if possible that 1789 has ever seemed a date from which to begin.

But here I am myself falling into the error of speaking as though there were a single French Revolution, to be summed up in a single formula. This conception, whatever theory it is enshrined in, is the real fallacy behind all the myths of the French Revolution — the idea that there was *a* French Revolution, which you can be for or against. If in some respects the revolutionaries gave expression to the ideas of the Enlightenment, in others they undermined their application; for they stood between the rational and the romantic ages, between the Enlightenment and the religious revival, between a great wave of humanitarian sentiment and the Terror, between the oecumenical ideal and the rise of nationalism, between the idealism of 1789 and the cynicism of the Directory, between the proclamation of universal brotherhood and the wars of Napoleon. They reached the heights of heroism and descended to the depths of civil strife. A whole generation packed with significance for good and evil is summed up in the phrase 'the French Revolution'. We may pick out what we admire or dislike in it and call that the Revolution, but either is a partial verdict. Its significance in the world today is such that we must take all its aspects, for good or for bad, into consideration in our contemporary world-picture. The great school of French historians which has enlarged our knowledge of the revolutionary age has driven farther away the boundaries at which ultimate disagreement begins; but no single historian, and neither contemporaries nor any succeeding generation, has ever grasped the whole of the revolutionary age in a single all-embracing view. Every interpretation of the Revolution must in the nature of things be partial, and every partial view is a myth.

## APPENDIX

The biographical details on which this Appendix is based are derived from:

A. Brette, *Les Constituants. Liste des députés et des suppléants élus à l'Assemblée constituante de 1789* (1897).

A. Kuscinski, *Dictionnaire des Conventionnels* (1920).

A. Robert, E. Bourloton, G. Cougny, *Dictionnaire des parlementaires français* (1891).

A. V. Arnault, A. Jay, etc., *Biographie nouvelle des contemporains* (1820–29).

I have followed Brette for the list of members of the Constituent Assembly, including all deputies and *suppléants* who were elected for the *tiers état* and actually sat in the Assembly, but excluding representatives of the colonies. I have taken the list of those who sat in the Convention from Kuscinski.

Since many of the members fall into more than one category, in order to avoid counting them twice I have adopted an order of priorities:

1. All merchants, manufacturers or bankers are counted as such. The 10 *ouvriers* in the Convention I have also included in this group as the word did not have its modern meaning in the eighteenth century.

2. After the previous category, the possession of an office or *charge*, apart from a few of very minor nature, is given priority over other descriptions. The merely decorative title of *conseiller du roi* is ignored. Where more than one office was held, I have chosen for purposes of classification that which seems likely to have been the most important.

3. The description of *avocat* is adopted for classification only where the deputy does not also fall under one of the previous headings. A large majority in both Assemblies were, of course, lawyers of one kind or another.

4. Similarly I have classified as *propriétaires* or *bourgeois* only those for whom there is no other description.

It must be emphasized that all my figures are approximate and dependent upon the accuracy of the information available as well

|  | Constituent Assembly (*tiers état*) | Convention |
|---|---|---|
| 1. Négociants | 76[1] ⎫ | 58 ⎫ |
| 2. Manufacturers | 8[2] ⎬ 85 | 14 ⎬ 83 |
| 3. Ouvriers | — ⎭ | 10 ⎭ |
| 4. Bankers | 1 | 1 |
| 5. Officers of *bailliages* and *sénéchaussées* | 90[3] ⎫ 185 | 31 ⎫ 92 |
| 6. Other local officers[4] | 95 ⎭ | 61 ⎭ |
| 7. Procureurs | 47 ⎫ | 28 ⎫ |
| 8. Avocats du roi | 12 ⎬ 67 | 45 ⎬ 73 |
| 9. Notaries royal | 8 ⎭ | — |
| 10. Greffiers | 1 ⎫ 278 | 5 ⎫ 227 |
| 11. Officers in state services[5] | 25 ⎭ | 57 ⎭ |
| 12. Officers of provinces or of princes | 7 | 5 |
| 13. Avocats | 159 ⎫ 166 | 233 ⎫ 241 |
| 14. Notaries | 7 ⎭ | 18 ⎭ |
| 15. Army officers[6] | 4 ⎫ | 20 ⎫ |
| 16. Naval officers | — | 6 |
| 17. Captains in merchant marine | — | 4 |
| 18. Professors and teachers (lay and clerical) | 5 ⎬ 31 | 33[7] ⎬ 142 |
| 19. Doctors | 18 | 45 |
| 20. Surgeons and pharmacists | — | 13 |
| 21. Engineers | — ⎭ | 2 |
| 22. Literary men and scientists | 4 | 19[8] ⎭ |
| 23. Clergy | 4 | 46[9] |
| 24. Agriculturalists | 47 | 29 |
| 25. Propriétaires | 14 | 5 |
| 26. Bourgeois | 6 | — |
| 27. Colonial proprietors, officials | 1 | 9 |
| 28. Higher judicial officers | 4 | 7 |
| 29. Nobles | 5 | 23 |
| 30. Commis | — | 4 |
| 31. Soldiers | — | 4 |
| 32. Agricultural worker | — | 1[10] |
| 33. Foreigners | — | 2[11] |
| 34. Not known | — | 63 |
| Total | 648 | 891 |

1. One of these is also described as a banker.

2. Including 4 *maîtres de forges* and 1 *directeur des mines*.

3. Including 68 *lieutenants généraux* or other *lieutenants* of *bailliage* or *sénéchaussée*.

4. The distinction between this and the previous category is rather an arbitrary one.

5. e.g. *subdélégué, receveur, intendant de la marine, directeur des postes, censeur royale, lieutenant des eaux et forêts*, and the like. Since most of the more important officials were stationed in Paris and the elections generally returned local men, it is not to be expected that there would be many of the former in the Assemblies. It is curious to note that out of 891 who sat in the Convention, only some 20 or so were Parisian by birth.

6. Excluding nobles.        7. This figure includes 17 clerical teachers or professors.

8. Composed of 14 writers or journalists, 2 artists, 1 scientist, and 2 connected with the stage.

9. This increase reflects the abolition of the First and Second Orders, as does the smaller increase in the number of nobles.

10. Described as occupied with the 'trauvaux des champs'.

11. Tom Paine and Anacharsis Clootz.

PERCENTAGES[1]

| | | |
|---|---|---|
| Négociants, manufacturers and bankers (1–4) | 13% | 9% |
| Office holders (5–11) | 43% | 25% |
| Lawyers (13–14) | 25% }30% | 27% }44% |
| Other professional men (15–22) | 5% | 17% |

FORMER MEMBERS OF CONSTITUENT ASSEMBLY (*TIERS ÉTAT*) AND CONVENTION HOLDING OFFICE UNDER NAPOLEON

| | Constituent Assembly (*tiers état*) | Convention | Total |
|---|---|---|---|
| Lesser offices | 173 (including 25 Conventionnels) | 370 | 518 |
| Higher offices | 55 (including 9 Conventionnels) | 65 | 111 |

as on the principles of classification adopted. This analysis is only put forward very tentatively, but I think that the results are sufficiently interesting to suggest the desirability of a more thorough examination of the whole question. This would only be possible, however, on the basis of a much more detailed knowledge of the social structure of eighteenth-century France, and particularly of the role and recruitment of the venal officers, than we at present possess. Even from this summary classification they emerge as perhaps the key to the situation. It should be added that since the offices or *charges* were often hereditary, or were bought when sufficient capital had been accumulated, many of those classified as *avocats* might at a later date have acquired them. A thorough investigation would therefore require a study of families as well as of individuals.

Thus 629 out of 1,539 members of both Assemblies held office under Napoleon. Of these at least 139 members of the *tiers état* of the Constituent Assembly and 150 members of the Convention had possessed offices before the Revolution. If the wastage by death and old age, and the rise of a new generation, are taken into consideration, these figures seem remarkably high. A careful examination of the personnel and the reorganization of the administrative services, both of which have hitherto received little attention, might prove very illuminating.

[1] These figures are calculated on the whole membership. If the 63 Conventionnels whose social position remains unknown were excluded, the figures for the Convention would be slightly higher.

# 6

## LOCAL GOVERNMENT DURING THE
## FRENCH REVOLUTION

THE nature and significance of the changes introduced into local government during the course of the French Revolution have hardly been adequately recognized by historians. Stress has been laid on the similarities between the administrative regime of France before the Revolution and the prefectoral system instituted by Napoleon, to the neglect of the intervening period. Most histories of the Revolution contain only a very perfunctory treatment of revolutionary local government before the Napoleonic reorganization, and an adequate modern monograph on the subject does not exist. Even in French there are, to the best of my knowledge, nothing more than a few purely departmental studies, unless we go back to the works of Girardot and Monnet.[1] It seems, therefore, that a short, general survey of the development of local government during this important decade may not be superfluous; a fuller treatment will not be possible until the resources of the departmental archives have been adequately explored.

It is now generally admitted that, as de Tocqueville showed, administrative centralization in France was the work of the *ancien régime*, and not primarily of the Revolution and Napoleon. Already, before the Revolution, the Cour des Aides was complaining, 'On a travaillé à étouffer en France tout esprit municipal, à éteindre si on le pouvait, jusqu'aux sentiments des citoyens; on a pour ainsi dire interdit la Nation entière et on lui a donné des tuteurs.'[2] That this centralization was not as effective in practice as it was complete in theory, is shown by the host of obstacles that confronted a reforming *intendant* such as Turgot. But this does not alter the fact that in France, as it entered the Revolution, centralization had gone so far that though there was local administration there was no local government. The absence of local government was indeed one of the grievances agitated in France during the years leading up to the Revolution. Various writers had put forward schemes for remedying this state of affairs,[3] and the first practical step had been taken in 1779-80, when an edict issued by Necker established provincial assemblies for certain of the *généralités*. In 1787 de Brienne extended this system of provincial assemblies to the whole of France. The capital of every province was to be the seat of a representative body; there was to be a subordinate assembly in each *élection* or *département* (a term borrowed from the fiscal administration), and a municipal assembly in each town or parish. These proposals would have instituted a real system of local government, though the franchise for the election of the local bodies was a very restricted one and their powers were very limited.

In nineteen out of twenty-four *généralités* provincial assemblies were elected, and met for the first time in November 1787. They had little chance to prove their value, however, for the privileged classes, from whom the demand for a freer system of local government had primarily come, were far from satisfied with these concessions, and were pressing for the revival or creation of provincial *états* with much wider powers than the new authorities. The motives of the nobles and lawyers who put forward these demands were largely selfish, but the populace in many towns supported them, under the impression that the setting up of provincial *états* would somehow mean the establishment of popular liberties. The French Revolution, in fact, began with the revolt of 1788 in Dauphiné in support of the demand of the privileged classes for provincial *états*. This struggle was soon to be caught up in the more general revolutionary movement, and the calling of the *États Généraux* transferred public interest to what was happening on the broader stage at Versailles.

The spirit of the *philosophes*, and the interests of the unprivileged middle classes, once these forces had been unleashed in the Constituent Assembly, were too strong and too hostile to privilege to allow of any effective continuance of the movement for provincial assemblies. The unifying spirit of the *tiers état*, and its meaning for the claims of the provinces, were well summed up in the words of Condorcet, 'La vérité et la justice sont les mêmes dans tous les pays et pour tous les hommes. Ce qui est bon dans une province ne saurait être mauvais dans une autre.'[4] It was inevitable that the Assembly should decide against the survival of provincial privileges, and that the provincial *états* should prove stillborn. Mounier, in 1788 the leader of a great popular movement, a year later was merely the representative of what was condemned as a reactionary wing of the Assembly. When he retired to Grenoble after the October Days, and attempted to rally the *états* of Dauphiné against the *États Généraux*, he found that even there the unifying trend was too strong for him, and had to fly to Switzerland to avoid arrest. Stimulated into action by this abortive attempt to arouse opposition in the provinces, the Assembly decreed that the convocation of the provincial *états* should be suspended until further notice.[5] The Assembly, thus, was committed to rejecting the scheme of local government prepared by the king's ministers before the Revolution: it knew what it did not want in respect of local government. Its positive ideas were less clearly defined, but here its hands were forced by the spontaneous action of the people. Everywhere in France during the opening months of the Revolution, and especially after the fall of the Bastille, revolutionary municipalities were being set up by local communities. The Assembly was forced to take notice of this development, and in the course of a discussion on July 23rd, 1789, arising out of the disorders in Paris, Mirabeau seized the opportunity to propose the establishment of a regularly elected municipal government for Paris.[6] A note in the *Ancien Moniteur* adds that it was the first time that this word, *municipalité*, had been used in the Assembly. Mounier, on the other hand, realizing the danger to the scheme of provincial assemblies of which he had made himself the advocate, asked, 'Je demande à M. de Mirabeau s'il a entendu autoriser toutes les villes à se municipaliser à leur manière? Cet objet est du ressort de l'Assemblée nationale, et il serait trop dangereux de créer des États dans l'État, et de multiplier des souverainetés.'[7] This objection, it is to be noted, had not occurred to him in connection with his own scheme for provincial *états*.

The National Assembly soon had to recognize the existence of the new revolutionary municipalities. On the famous night of the fourth of August, when the venality of the old municipal authorities was swept away along with so much else, the officers actually functioning were formally retained in their offices.[8] But the

towns and villages of France did not wait for permission from the
Assembly for their own elected municipalities to function. Conflicts naturally arose between the old authorities and the new. In
many districts an understanding was reached between the existing
town officers and the newly elected council.[9] Elsewhere the
revolutionary committee simply usurped the powers of local
government and presented the central government with a *fait
accompli*.[10] A petition from the town of Fontainebleau to the
Assembly complained that the persistence of the former municipal
officers in attempting to maintain their powers was reducing the
government of the district to anarchy and threatening the security
of the royal palace. The Assembly decided that the commune of
Fontainebleau should be authorized to nominate its own municipal officers, and that the former civil and military officers should
be forbidden to intervene in its administration.[11] Only a week
later the Assembly was appealed to by a municipality which had
drawn up taxation lists and was anxious lest its acts should be
quashed by the sovereign courts. The Assembly again yielded, and
decreed provisionally that the acts of elected municipal and police
authorities should be held valid despite the legal incapacity of their
members.[12] The Assembly really had very little choice in the
matter. In November a deputy declared that if the southern parts
of France thought that they were to be deprived of their elected
municipalities there would be an insurrection.[13] This was one of a
long series of speeches demanding the recognition of the municipal
organization of France, and at the conclusion of the debate the
Assembly decreed that municipalities should be set up in every
'ville, bourg, village ou communauté de campagne',[14] a decision
eventually put into effect by the law on municipalities of December
14th, 1789.

Even this brief summary should make it plain that the establishment of municipalities was not imposed by the Assembly on the
country, but rather by the country on the Assembly. Sieyes, who
took much of the credit for the reorganization of France to himself, later indignantly repudiated the charge of being responsible
for the division of France into 44,000 municipalities,[15] a scheme
which he described as 'l'insigne folie'. 'A l'époque dont nous
parlons', he said, 'les quarante-quatre mille municipalités se
trouvèrent exister tout à coup, non par l'effet d'aucun système

philosophique, mais par une suite inévitable de l'insurrection générale.'[16] Subsequent history has hardly justified his condemnation of the municipalities, which have remained since 1789 the most securely based element in the French system of local government. The influence of Sieyes was undoubtedly great in the reorganization of French institutions, but hardly as great as he himself liked to suppose.[17] It was not Sieyes but Thouret, the more practical jurist, who, acting as the spokesman of the constitutional committee, produced the law on municipalities of December 14th, 1789, and that on local government of December 22nd.[18] The first law suppressed all former local administrations and set up in their place municipal councils and *maires* elected by the 'active citizens'. By the latter the complete structure of *cantons*, *districts* and *départements* was erected above the municipalities. Each *département* had an administration of 36 persons, elected for two years and re-elected by halves; the *district* had an administration of 12; the *canton* had no administration; and the membership of the *municipalité* varied in number from 3 to 21, according to its size. The administration of the *département* elected a Directory of 8 from among its members, and the *district* one of 4. The whole body of administrators met under the title of Council once a year, and between its sessions the Directory carried on the work of local government. In each *département* there was also a *procureur-général-syndic*, and in each *district* a *procureur-syndic*: these were the executive officers. They were the agents of the Councils and were elected for four years; they had no power of their own.

These new bodies were charged with a number of duties, among which the first in order of importance was the division of the quota of local taxation by the *départements* among the *districts*, and by the *districts* among the *municipalités*. They were responsible for the care of the poor and the policing of vagabonds, the inspection of hospitals, almshouses, prisons, and the like, the superintendence of public education, the employment of funds destined for the improvement of agriculture, the protection of all public and communal property, the upkeep of roads and canals, the maintenance of churches, the health services, and the control of the National Guard. This list has an imposing sound. The power of the *départements* and *districts* would have been more effective, however, if it had not been added that the local administrations could take no action affecting the general administration of the country, undertake no new enterprise and raise no funds, without the approval of the central government, which was in fact generally lacking.[19]

Among the new institutions of local government, the municipalities must be regarded as the creation of the people. The *départements* and *districts* were the work of the Assembly, the prime object of which was to meet the need for some intermediate authority other than the old provinces between the central government and the municipalities. Thouret, in his report on behalf of the committee, and in the speeches he subsequently made in the Assembly, ingeniously combined professions of respect for the ancient provincial divisions[20] with a determination to destroy 'l'esprit de province'. 'Si nous mettions des intérêts provinciaux à la place de l'intérêt national,' he said, 'oserions-nous nous dire les représentants de la nation?'[21] The respect paid to provincial traditions amounted in fact to no more than a rejection of various plans for cutting up France on strict geometrical principles, and the substitution instead of an alternative plan for dividing the provinces as far as possible without cutting across existing provincial boundaries. Each province was chopped into pieces separately, except that some of the smaller were united for the purpose, instead of the whole being amalgamated for the process of departmentalizing, but the result on the provinces was much the same.

The laws of December 1789 were the first of a long series on local government. It is not necessary to give here a detailed summary of this legislation. The real significance of constitutional arrangements is to be found not in the texts of laws but in the way in which they are worked. In the first place, however, it is to be asked how they managed to work at all. The answer is that in the main the administrative personnel of the *ancien régime* was taken over with little change by the Revolution,[22] and the same personnel seems to have survived generally in local administration up to the summer of 1793, when the Jacobins introduced considerable changes.[23]

A great deal more detailed research will be required before it is possible to give a reasonably final verdict on the operation of the new system of local government with which France had been endowed by its Assembly, but some important features can be picked out without difficulty. Certain weaknesses at once made their appearance, some of which were perhaps an inevitable consequence of the sudden introduction of government by elected bodies in place of an administrative regime, while others may possibly be attributed to inherent defects in the new institutions. The fundamental fact is that before 1789, as one writer comments, there was not a single truly elected assembly in the country, but only government officials; in 1790 there was no longer a single official, but only elected bodies.[24] It was hardly likely that such a drastic change could be carried through without the appearance of grave difficulties.

The reaction against the *ancien régime* had produced a system in which all power was placed in the hands of committees. 'Tout le monde déliberait, personne n'avait mission d'agir.'[25] The only executive officers of local government were the procureur-syndics, who were charged with putting into effect all the decisions of the local councils, but had no powers of their own at all. This scheme of government by committees may be regarded as the logical consequence of a rigid application of the theory of the separation of powers,[26] combined with the prevailing suspicion of the executive. Sieyes, who was as much responsible as anyone for these tendencies, later reacted violently in the opposite direction, and drew from the failure of the revolutionary system the rather extreme conclusion that no one should ever be elected by those over whom he was to exercise authority.

The executive weakness of the local authorities was not compensated by any strengthening influence from the centre, for there was no effective connection between the *départements* and the central government. On this point long and heated debates had taken place in the Assembly. The constitutional committee began by producing an article declaring, 'Les assemblées administratives étant instituées dans l'ordre du pouvoir exécutif seront les agents de ce pouvoir: dépositaires de l'autorité du roi, comme chef de l'autorité nationale, elles agiront en son nom, et lui seront entièrement subordonnées.'[27] Unexceptionable in theory, this statement raised the most acute practical alarms. Various speakers pointed out that to put it into effect it would be necessary to have an agent of the executive power in each *département*, who would prove to be a new version of the old *intendant*. Lanjuinais declared that it would rob the local assemblies of all effective power. Reubell saw in it a means of subordinating every *département* to the ministers and removing them completely from the influence of the National Assembly. Other speakers echoed these criticisms, and as a result of their attacks the article was withdrawn. A revised version was offered the following day, attenuating the apparent concession to royal power. It declared, 'Les assemblées administratives sont subordonnées au roi, comme chef suprême de la nation et de l'administration générale, et elles ne pourront exercer les fonctions qui leur seront confiées que selon les règles prescrites par la constitution et par les décrets des législatures sanctionnés par le roi.'[28] Even this modified clause could only have been of effect if there had been any willingness to accept the intervention of agents of the Royal Council of Ministers in the local government divisions, and if the necessary administrative machinery had been provided. Neither of these conditions was fulfilled.

The opposition to the presence of a strong executive agent in the local authorities came from both left and right, the former because of memories of the *intendants* and fear of royal power, the latter because of the belief that the first elections might result in the return of advanced revolutionaries, whom the moderate parties would subsequently be unable to displace.[29] But that the Assembly did not intend to leave the *départements* without any settled relations with the central government is shown by an instruction of January 8th, 1790: 'Le principe constitutionnel sur la distribution des pouvoirs administratifs est que l'autorité descende du Roi aux administrations de département, de celles-ci aux administrations de district et de ces dernières aux municipalités.'[30] The principles of hierarchy and centralization could hardly be more clearly expressed; but for lack of any machinery for putting this resolution into practice it remained a pious aspiration.

The absence of central control, at this early stage in the development of local government, was the primary reason for the weakness of the system set up by the Constituent Assembly. There were additional reasons, however. In the second place, the central government, which left the local assemblies unsupported in the field of executive action, in another field deprived them of the most necessary of all powers. The inadequacy of the revolutionary system of local government was most evident in the lack of provision for its finance. The law of December 22nd, 1789, declared that local authorities had no powers of taxation except as fixed by the legislative body. This was doubtless a precautionary measure to check the abuse of their position either by reactionary local authorities or by the new revolutionary municipalities. But as we have said, the law made no provision for financing the many activities that were incumbent on the local authorities. An attempt was made to maintain the communal *octrois*,[31] but in the face of persistent evasion and open opposition this broke down, and they were formally abolished on February 19th, 1791.[32]

It is not surprising to find that by the beginning of 1791 local finances were in a state of collapse. A law of February 6th, 1791, liquidated the debts of the *départements*, re-imposed various burdens on them, and promised that they would be given various revenues to meet these expenses.[33] Little improvement resulted from these promises. One attempt to solve the problem was embodied in a decree of May 14th, 1790, by which the municipalities were given one-sixteenth of the proceeds of the sale of *biens nationaux* (the confiscated Church lands), but out of this sum they had to pay all the expenses involved.[34] Subsequently the free disposition of the sixteenth was taken away from them and it was ordered to be reserved for the extinction of their debts.[35] These decrees were confirmed on November 17th, 1792, and administrative details added,[36] a repetition which suggests that their enforcement left something to be desired. A more serious attempt to cope with the expenses of local authorities took the form of the system by which they were authorized to collect a small supplement to the national taxation for their own purposes.[37] This was fixed at a maximum of four 'sous pour livre'.[38] After the fall of the Terrorist government, however, when the departmental and district budgets were taken over by the central authorities, this addition was incorporated in the total of national taxation.[39] Both as tax-collectors for the central government, and in dealing with their own limited financial responsibilities, the local authorities had failed, as was shown in the report offered to the Convention on this occasion. 'La confection des rôles de 1791 et 1792 ayant été retardée, ceux de 1793 n'étant actuellement en recouvrement que dans une partie de la république, et la contribution de 1794 (vieux style) n'étant pas encore décrétée, il est évident que les corps administratifs ne peuvent faire acquitter leurs dépenses courantes, comme ils n'ont pu faire payer celles de l'année 1793 que sur la partie du trésor public des exercices antérieurs.'[40] The Convention, it is only fair to observe, however, had not only financial motives for its action, for it added, 'Il paraît peu convenable au nouveau système de gouvernement que chacun des districts de la république ait ses fonds particuliers pour les dépenses qui lui sont propres. Un tel régime semble contenir un germe de fédéralisme que l'on ne peut trop soigneusement écarter.'[41] The re-introduction of a measure of local financial autonomy, in the form of the system of *centimes additionels*, which survived the Revolution, did not appear until 1796–8.[42] There is no space here for a fuller account of local finance during the Revolution, but enough has been said to show its weaknesses. The most significant consequence of the inadequate financial arrangements was that the decentralization planned by the revolutionaries at the outset was stultified.

Apart from the absence of co-ordination from Paris, and the inadequacy of local finances, if the local authorities had been working together harmoniously many of their other difficulties might have been overcome. Unfortunately there was here a third source of weakness; profound divisions appeared in their ranks from the very beginning. Even the municipal councils were not united within themselves. One writer on the Revolution in Provence says that the peasants attended the elections on the first day and succeeded in electing the *maire* of their choice. On the following days they returned to the fields and allowed the remaining members of the municipal council to be elected by their bourgeois opponents of the towns.[43]

The final cause for the breakdown of the system established in 1789 is to be found in the rivalry which developed at once between the revolutionary municipalities and the generally more conservative departmental directories. The municipalities felt that the *départements* had come later into the field to rob them of their prerogatives. They derived, says one observer, 'grande vanité de leur plus ancienne création'.[44] This rivalry began in the summer of 1789 and continued until the Committee of Public Safety intervened with a new scheme of local government in December 1793. The essential cause of the conflict was that the departmental directories — elected indirectly, on a higher property qualification, representing a larger area, and limited in membership to those who could afford the time and money for the journey to the *chef-lieu* — were naturally recruited from a wealthier class than were the members of the municipalities. The current accusation against them was that they formed an 'aristocratie d'argent'. The establishment of the *départements* satisfied the well-to-do bourgeoisie, because it took away the authority of the *parlements* and the provincial *états*, and at the same time put them in a position to check the power of the revolutionary communes, which they feared equally.

From August 1789 to August 1790 the municipalities had been practically free from superior control. The resources of the departmental directories for reducing them to obedience were slight. They could nominate two commissioners with the power to inquire into each dispute, but had little power beyond this. However, by the summer of 1790 the departmental directories had managed to assert their authority up to a point, and from then until August 1792 theirs was the stronger influence in the country. This did not end the rivalry between the *départements* and the municipalities, which played an important part in the general history of the Revolution. While the departmental directories, backed by the more conservative country people, accepted the monarchical constitution, the municipalities of the more revolutionary towns were moving in the direction of republicanism. The parties in the Assembly intensified these rivalries by their attempt to use the local authorities as instruments in their political struggle. Roland, while he was Minister of the Interior, had hoped to base the rule of his faction on control of the *départements*.[45] Subsequently the Jacobins took steps to *dérolandiser* the *départements*, and though these were at first inclined to be favourable to the federalist movement, they mostly came quickly to heel after a few local notables had been guillotined.[46]

The municipalities, moreover, had not accepted the control of the *départements* passively. By the end of 1791, as a speaker in the Assembly complained, they were in a state of almost open revolt against the directories.[47] During the first half of 1792 revolutionary communes were being set up in many districts in open defiance of the legally constituted authorities. This process began months before the similar movement in Paris, and in provinces far removed from the centre, but the triumph of the Paris Commune on August 10th, 1792, set the seal on it. On the following day the issue was decided by a decree giving the municipalities charge of police and *sûreté générale*. Finally, by the law of 14 frimaire an II (December 14th, 1793) the Committee of Public Safety put an end to the legal powers of the departmental directories.

Before the significance of the downfall of the *départements* can be adequately appreciated, it is necessary to deal with three important influences which were operating simultaneously in this field of government. The first is the rise and decline of the federalist movement; the second the increasing control exercised over local authorities by the popular societies; and the third the gradual reassertion of a centralizing tendency in French local government.

In the first years of the Revolution there had been, as I have said, a strong current of opinion running in the direction of decentralization and federalism.[48] Among the influences which may be mentioned as contributing towards this tendency was Rousseau's advocacy of a 'république confédérative des petits états', and the revival in the revolutionary period by Calvinist ministers such as Rabaut Saint-Étienne of seventeenth-century Calvinist schemes for dividing France into federal republics, or circles. In the early days of the Revolution some of the leading members of the left wing supported the idea of a federal constitution. The later terrorist, Billaud-Varenne, wrote a book in its favour in 1791.[49] One Terrasson, at the Jacobin club, as late as September 10th, 1792, put forward a proposal for the federal government of France, supporting himself on the authority of Rousseau.[50] Another Jacobin advocate of federalism was Lavicomterie.[51] On the other hand Barbaroux, later one of the leaders of the Girondin faction, was a strong opponent of federalism; indeed among the Girondins Buzot was perhaps the only convinced federalist.[52] The rise of patriotic nationalism, fear of internal enemies and foreign invasion, and the general heightening of revolutionary enthusiasm in the Convention and at Paris, were fatal to any federalist inclination among the more ardent revolutionaries. Brissot and his faction took it up, after they had lost control of the Convention and Paris, not out of conviction but as a measure of self-defence against the Jacobin attack. It did more harm than good to their cause: in the crisis of 1793 the mere suspicion of federalism became equal to a charge of treachery, and it then played an important part in their downfall.

Secondly, we must remember that if we concentrate our attention on the legally constituted authorities we shall miss one of the most powerful influences, and one which for a time became decisive in the field of local government, that of the popular societies or clubs, which exercised an influence over the legal authorities in the *départements* similar to that which the clubs of Paris exerted over the Assembly.[53] As early as September 1792 we meet the complaint, 'Partout des autorités inconnus ont surgi d'elles-mêmes. Les citoyens ne savent plus à qui ils doivent obéir ni de quel droit on les commande, les pouvoirs s'élèvent les uns contre les autres, ce qui donne au règne naissant de la liberté l'apparence du despotisme arbitraire.'[54] Another speaker asserted, 'Partout il existe une lutte entre le peuple et les administrateurs infidèles.'[55] As a result of this debate the Assembly decreed that all administrative, municipal and judicial bodies should be renewed. The result of the elections was not as satisfactory to the Jacobins as a consideration of the conditions prevailing in the autumn of 1792 might have led one to expect. The story continues to be one of increasing antagonism between the clubs and the local authorities, and continually increasing interference by the clubs in the details of local government. The local authorities were inexperienced and often incompetent, and in addition were by no means always sufficiently revolutionary in sentiment. In the absence of any regular means of exercising central control, the revolutionaries fell back on the network of Jacobin clubs with which France was covered. The patriotic ardour of the local authorities was stimulated, though their efficiency was not necessarily increased, by the constant interference of the popular societies, spying on them, denouncing them to Paris, and raising popular disturbances. The Committee of Public Safety and its *commissaires* was led to entrust to the care of the clubs the duties which unwilling or incompetent local authorities had neglected.[56] A decree of October 8th, 1793, called on the clubs to assist in the organization of supplies of horses and military equipment.[57]

Another of November 13th, invited them to nominate citizens worthy of public functions.[58] In many municipalities membership of the Jacobin club and the holding of local office became practically the same thing. Thus at Toulouse, out of 731 members of the club, 103 held some local office; at Metz the number was 61 out of 148.[59] Such membership by officials was, of course, not always voluntary.[60] After the fall of the Committee of Public Safety the Jacobins were accused of greatly enlarging the number of functionaries for the purpose of providing their supporters with remunerative jobs.[61] The results of this policy were in the end not altogether desirable, even from the point of view of the Jacobins themselves. Saint-Just was led to complain of the excessive number of officials in the clubs compared with the number of ordinary citizens, and of the harmful effects this fact produced on public spirit and on the relations between the people and the government.[62] Nor did this policy have the results aimed at in the administrative field. Successful as agents of Jacobin propaganda, less successful but still very influential in the elections, the clubs, their latest historian seems to suggest, were a failure as an addition to the administrative machinery.[63]

It was gradually realized that more regular means of exerting central control over the local authorities were required, and this brings us to the third significant development. In January 1793, Roland had proposed the establishment of national commissaries for the *départements*. His proposal was not followed up immediately, but in March 1793, on the proposal of Danton, the Convention decreed the sending of 83 representatives of the people to the *départements*, nominally to hasten recruiting. In fact their function was to establish revolutionary communes in each municipality.[64] These representatives became the real executive officers of local government, and the *procureurs*, who because of their lack of power had failed to justify their existence, now disappeared.

The establishment of the revolutionary *commissaires* was an emergency measure, but a more systematic and thoroughgoing reorganization of local government was evidently required. This was provided by the famous law of the 14 frimaire an II (December 4th, 1793). After proclaiming that all governmental power receives its impulse from the Convention, it places all other authorities and officials under the immediate control of the Committee of

Public Safety, except in so far as concerns police, which falls into the province of the *Comité de Sûreté Générale*. The supervision of the execution of all 'revolutionary' laws and measures of public safety is entrusted not to the *départements* but to the *districts*, which occupy the key position in the Jacobin system of local government, although the actual application of the laws is placed in the hands of the revolutionary committees of the municipalities. In place of the *procureurs*, *agents nationaux* are appointed by the Convention, and they are required to report every ten days to the two supreme committees. The *départements* are left in charge of the allocation of taxation, the establishment of manufactures, the upkeep of roads and canals, and the superintendence of national property, but their primacy in the system of local government is temporarily ended. All other functions are taken away from them, and in particular the hierarchical system which placed the districts and municipalities under their control is abolished. Finally, the representatives of the people in the *départements* are given the task of supervising the application of the law, and at the same time of purging local bodies of all unreliable elements.[65]

With the rule of the Committee of Public Safety the centralizing tendencies in the Revolution triumphed, and France continued to be governed under these institutions until the downfall of Robespierre brought with it the collapse of the Jacobin *régime*. After Thermidor there was naturally a reversal of the Jacobin system of local government. The law of the 14 frimaire was suppressed.[66] The new law of April 17th, 1795, replaced the *départements* and *districts* in the position they had held before the Jacobins introduced their changes, and at the same time the *procureurs* and the directories were restored. Whereas the Jacobins had opposed the reactionary influence of the *départements*, the Thermidoreans feared the revolutionary tendencies of the municipalities and the Jacobin affiliations of the *districts*. Above all they were alarmed at the political activities of the communes of the large towns. These therefore they suppressed. Paris was put under officials appointed by the government, while the other large towns were divided into separate circumscriptions each with its own authority.

After a period of provisional arrangements the Constitution of the year III settled the new order in France. It suppressed the *districts* altogether, maintained the departmental directories, but without the *conseils généraux*, and treated them in the main as mere agencies of the central government in the general administration of the country. It attempted to substitute for the municipal administration of the commune that of the *canton*, which grouped a number of municipalities together but in areas smaller than the former *districts*. The Directory hoped to make the canton its main organ of local government. Various verdicts have been passed on this attempt to substitute the canton for the commune: some commentators have praised it, while others regard it as a fatal mistake. The chief difficulty of the cantonal organization, one critic points out, was that either the canton was dominated by its *chef-lieu*, or, if it contained several communes of equal importance, there was continual strife between them.[67] On the other hand, another writer suggests that the Directory was successful in making the cantons into living organs of local government, and that Bonaparte suppressed them not because they had failed, but because they had succeeded too well and were becoming too active.[68]

There was certainly a genuine attempt to improve the machinery of local government under the Directory. Steps were taken to deal with some of the main sources of weakness. Local finances were put on a sounder basis. The communes had gradually acquired a certain patrimony. In addition to this by a series of laws the system of *centimes additionnelles* was established, which provided a small but regular source of income.[69] Moreover, the communal budget had a degree of elasticity which contrasted with the rigidity of the departmental budget. The representation of the government in the localities was secured by replacing the *procureurs* with *commissaires* nominated from Paris. These may be regarded as representing a further advance towards the prefectoral system, but unlike Napoleon's prefects they were generally men of the district and were therefore more liable to be under the influence of local sentiment. For the purpose of making these appointments the country was divided unofficially into five groups of *départements*, for each of which one director was in the main responsible.[70] The directors themselves often made their appointments on the recommendation of the deputies from the area concerned. The *république des camarades* was in process of birth. The Directory, of course, only entrusted the local authorities with limited powers.

Two of their most important functions had been taken from them. By a law of October 11th, 1795, police and subsistences were placed exclusively under the control of central bureaux at Paris, Lyons, Marseilles and Bordeaux.[71] By ordering the secondary administrations no longer to correspond directly with the ministers but to follow the administrative hierarchy, the process of re-creating an administrative regime based on the principles of centralization and hierarchy was continued.[72]

The Directory might indeed have solved the problem of local government successfully if it could have secured that support in France as a whole which would have enabled it to work its own institutions with reasonable honesty. Unfortunately it remained throughout a weak and unstable government, struggling constantly against civil war or the threat of civil war, able to rely on the active support of only a small minority in the country, and opposed passively or actively by the majority. It could never develop a genuine system of local government, for it could never trust its subjects with any effective political freedom. The loyalty even of many of its own officials was doubtful. A message from the Directory to the *Cinq Cents* on March 1st, 1797, declared: 'Le Directoire gémit souvent sur l'impuissance où le réduit le défaut de concours d'un grand nombre de fonctionnaires publics qui entravent sa marche au lieu de la seconder, et qui, dédaignant de se couvrir du masque, ont ouvertement refusé de se rallier aux républicains, aux amis de la constitution de l'an III et de prêter le serment solennel qui les y eût enchaînés.'[73] Even when they were loyal the agents of the Directory found themselves opposed in many *départements* by the local administrators, who, however weak their powers, could yet make the situation of the representative of the central government distinctly uncomfortable.[74]

The result was that the electoral machinery never functioned effectively. As early as October 1793 the elections to the municipalities had been suspended on the proposal of Barère, who added suggestively, 'Cette mesure est la plus révolutionnaire que vous puissiez prendre.'[75] In brumaire an IV the Directory, to use the official phrase, 'completed' the elections that had not been concluded in the appointed time. What probably occurred was that in electoral assemblies where the supporters of the Directory were not in a majority they took steps to prevent the majority from finishing the elections, and the Directory subsequently used this as an excuse for filling up the vacant positions with its own supporters. As Dupont de Nemours protested in the course of a debate on December 14th, 1795, 'C'est probablement parce qu'on ne veut pas confier la nomination des administrateurs et des juges aux électeurs qui ont choisi les membres du Corps Législatif.'[76] The existing powers of nominating members of local administrations not proving sufficient, they had to be increased by a law of September 10th, 1797.[77]

Given such conditions it was natural that many of those who were entitled to vote in the local elections, knowing that there was little chance of their vote proving effective, should have abstained. As early as September 1792 it is said that the people of the countryside, tired of the numerous elections, with their religious sentiments offended and their economic interests injured by the policy of the revolutionary governments, were ceasing to take an active interest in politics.[78] This slackening of interest went on progressively and spread from the country to the towns. One example comes from the canton of Châtillon-sur-Chalaronne, where, when the assembly of active citizens met in September 1795, out of 565 entitled to the vote 93 were present. In the same canton the assembly of March 1798 at which 1,544 should have voted only had 135 members when it met, and on the second day when the elections were actually held only 86 were present.[79]

Along with this decline in local interest went, as I have indicated, an open or unavowed increase in central control. But although nomination of the personnel of local administrations from above seems to have been extensive under the Directory, it did not altogether achieve its aim. The Directory may have succeeded in keeping its acknowledged enemies out of official positions; it does not seem to have been able to make the local administrations, which it had rendered subservient to itself, efficient in the execution of their functions. If an unfavourable verdict has generally been returned on its administration the Directory itself set the example. In an often quoted report of the year VII it wrote, 'Le pillage des caisses publiques, les attaques dirigées contre les fonctionnaires publics, l'inertie d'un grand nombre d'entre eux, l'assassinat des républicains, tel est malheureusement l'aspect que présentent plusieurs départements.'[80]

We are forced to conclude that the experiment in local government initiated by the Revolution had failed. The institution of Napoleon's prefects and the practically complete elimination of the electoral system from the local government of France merely drew the logical conclusion to that failure. This is not the place to pass a final verdict on the causes of it, even if one were possible on the evidence at our disposal. But it is worth while remarking that we must probably look for these causes in the sphere of national rather than local politics. None of the successive governments in France from 1789 to 1799 won the lasting support of the people. Probably at no time after the first year could the government have dispensed with the pressure exercised first by the clubs, and later by its own direct representatives. In these conditions free local government could not exist. Moreover, the revolutionaries, in making artificial political units such as the *départements* the basis of their administrative structure, had, perhaps of necessity, deprived their system of local government of those natural roots which might have enabled it to survive a period of political disorder, or stand out against pressure from above. They themselves had laid the foundations of the Napoleonic centralization by providing the essential framework in which Napoleon's *préfets* and *sous-préfets* could operate. The decade that began with a spontaneous outburst of communal liberty ended with the creation of a far more ruthlessly centralized system of local administration than even the *ancien régime* had known. Yet the attempt of the revolutionaries to establish a freer system of local government had not been entirely wasted. Its institutions, or some of them, survived, even if as a mere shadow, and the memory of them remained to provide an inspiration for the next century.

# 7

## THE VENDÉE

THE VENDÉE. By Charles Tilly. Cambridge, Massachusetts:
Harvard University Press, 1964. Pp. xi, 373.

HISTORIANS and sociologists are natural enemies. Their struggle
to establish which is the fitter for survival has brought a mild imita-
tion of the law of the jungle to more than one university. As in
nature, in order to avoid mutual extermination, a delimitation of
territory between the two species has tacitly been adopted — to
the sociologist the present and the static, to the historian the past
and the dynamic. This self-denial has essentially been to the
advantage of neither. Fortunately, it is now showing signs of
breaking down, and Charles Tilly's book is an important contribution to the erosion of this academic frontier. He has invaded strictly
historical territory by taking as his field of study the violent
counter-revolutionary movement which broke out in western
France in 1793, in the hope that sociological techniques will
facilitate the exploration of the nature and origins of a movement
that has hitherto resisted satisfactory historical explanation.

The difficulty for historians has not been the absence of plausible
explanations for the revolt of the Vendée, nor of evidence with
which to support them, but rather the superfluity of explanations
and the attempt to single one prime cause out of so many while
disproving all the others. Perhaps this is because the historian, or
at least the historian who thinks in terms of narrative history, is
apt to see historical development in a linear form. The sociologist,
on the other hand, in analysing a complex system of social
relationships, should be able to see society advancing on a broad
front. The trouble is that all too often, in works of sociology, it does
not advance: it does not move at all. Even Tilly hardly allows
sufficiently for the rapidity of the changes that occurred in the
course of four years of revolution. If there is some lack of a sense of

time, however, there is a compensating gain in sense of space. Tilly joins the many French historians who have turned to social analysis on a local basis as a way of either escaping from, or giving substance to, the broad generalizations that satisfied their predecessors.

He takes for detailed study that part of Anjou south of the Loire known as the Mauges, which became one of the centres of counter-revolution, with, as a control, the contiguous area of the Saumurois, which remained revolutionary in its orientation. These were respectively countries of *bocage* and plain, though this is only the beginning of the differences between them. Tilly uses as the instruments of his analysis two concepts taken from modern sociology — the ideas of urbanization and of the organization of the rural community. I am not quite sure how necessary these concepts are for his results. In any case, they have to be understood in a special sense, which there is not space here to discuss, even if I have grasped them clearly (which I rather doubt). They have served their purpose if they have led Tilly to the discovery of the social facts which are the basis of his analysis of the Vendée. I use the word 'facts' deliberately, because these are what we need most for an understanding of the social background of the Revolution; we have been fed to the teeth with theories. The kind of fact I mean is the demonstration, which by itself demolishes some accepted clichés, that the manly agricultural Saumurois was revolutionary, whereas the counter-revolutionary Mauges was a centre of the linen industry. The description of the Revolution as in part a struggle between town and country, which I have used myself, appears in a different light when we discover the potential hostility between town clothier and rural artisan in a period dominated by the domestic system of manufacture. At the same time we must not jump from one over-simple formula to another. If we are tempted to do so, it will be worth remarking that, whereas Tilly shows that the area of rural textile industry in the Mauges was also a centre of counter-revolutionary activities, according to Paul Bois, the country textile workers in the Sarthe exhibited no similar sympathies. Our confidence in Tilly is enhanced when we find that he does in fact allow for such divergencies. His explanation is that the weavers were caught up in an economic and psychological crisis which made them liable to be drawn easily into violence when other predisposing factors were present.

*

There can be no doubt that there were such factors in the Mauges, and that a major one was the Church. Historians of the *ancien régime* have long been aware of the importance of the rural clergy as agents of the central government, and also of the strong *esprit de clocher* in the countryside. Tilly puts these together and shows the psychological shock that was consequently produced by revolutionary legislation on the Church, which seemed to rob the rural community of its very identity. The reaction in the west was an unexpected one, though it could easily lead us to speculate whether there is a general trend, observable in many times of trouble, for populations caught up in internal social and political stresses, with their customary communal ties disappearing, to get on the move, start marching, go on crusade. In western France at this time, Tilly tells us, religious pilgrimages were being made on an everincreasing scale, until finally the whole Vendée became one huge, armed pilgrimage, surging crazily about the west. Significantly, the Saumurois, with less social tension, remained largely free from the infection.

Another difference between the Mauges and the Saumurois seems to have been the extent of peasant ownership in the latter and of large estates in the former. It is interesting to find that in Tilly's opinion the role of the 'feudal regime' as a focus of revolutionary grievances has been greatly exaggerated, and that in the Mauges, it was not against the nobles but against the 'bourgeois' of the small towns that peasant hatred was directed. I would have liked to know more about the impact of seigneurial rights here and who actually exploited them. It is also a little surprising to find a sociologist using the term 'bourgeois' without qualification, as though it described a clearly defined class whose composition was not in dispute. In fact, his bourgeoisie are the 'group of specialists in administration, co-ordination and communication' (p. 25). If this means, as I assume it does, a class of *fonctionnaires* and professional men, I think it is a fair account of the major element in the revolutionary bourgeoisie of France; but I do not know how to reconcile this view with the Marxist interpretation of the

Revolution, which Tilly seems to accept elsewhere, as a process by which a capitalist class of merchants and entrepreneurs took control of France out of the hands of a feudal regime (p. 161).

However, this is a field which is only now beginning to be opened to systematic historical investigation, and we need not expect perfect consistency. What is more important is the way in which Tilly sees social patterns interacting with political events. He tells us that when the people of the Mauges revolted against the application of conscription in March 1793, this was only the spark that fired an explosive situation. The enemy can be called the bourgeois, but under this label it was the Patriot and the anti-clerical, the revolutionary officials, the stewards and middlemen of the small towns, the lawyers, the men who had bought up the *biens nationaux* that the peasants coveted, the local leadership that had applied the revolutionary legislation and was profiting by it. On a local level the conflicts out of which revolutionary and counter-revolutionary violence grew were social and even personal ones. The struggle over the government in Paris, inaugurated by the calling of the *États Généraux*, politicized them on a national level and, in so doing, generalized them. But to discover the social realities it is necessary to get behind the broad political pattern of Paris and see what was actually happening in the provinces of France. De Tocqueville began this attempt in his classic work, but he has been followed by comparatively few until recently. There is all the more reason to be grateful for Tilly's bold incursion into historical territory.

*

Behind such an attempt there remains the general problem of the relationship of history and sociology. A common complaint of historians is against sociological 'jargon'. A distinction must of course be drawn between a scientific vocabulary, which the study of society needs as much as any other systematic study, and jargon. The object of the former is to assist thought, that of the latter to conceal its absence. It must be admitted that there is often rather too much jargon in sociological writings, and also that the difficulty of a lot of what purports to be scientific terminology is in fact merely the result of an imperfect command of the English language. Fortunately Tilly very seldom resorts to jargon, though even he, when he talks of 'urbanization' in the Mauges, seems to mean, if I have not misunderstood him, no more — at least in the present context — than what economic historians have long known as the domestic system of manufacture.

The apparent inability of sociologists to produce the kind of basic agreed terminology which politics and economics long ago developed is puzzling. The reason may be that political theory grew out of the study of political history, and economics out of economic history, with which it still has close ties. Only recently has the theoretical economist attempted to emancipate himself from, or even dictate to, the historian — so far with rather dubious results. Social history, on the other hand, has too often been what Queen Elizabeth had for breakfast and has been too insignificant to engender a serious social vocabulary. Moreover, the social patterns in different periods and countries are so varied that the same terms can only be used for them all by perverting the historical evidence. When this is combined with an attempt to divide society into a few great social classes, the result is bound to be hopelessly misleading. The virtue of such a study as this of the Vendée should be to demonstrate the futility of such attempts. I believe it also reveals indirectly one of the reasons why they can even seem plausible. This is that, over and above the mosaic of social interests, there is the much simpler pattern of the struggle for political power. For it to be pursued effectively, diverse social interests must be grouped together under a single leadership. Historians, studying the political struggle, naturally see it in its own terms, and, given the traditional acceptance of the primacy of politics, social history tends to have the conditions of the political struggle imposed upon it. This is the ultimate source of that tension between history and sociology which is still far from being resolved.

# 8

## THE FUNDAMENTAL IDEAS OF ROBESPIERRE

IN the next paper,[1] analysing the development and modification of Robespierre's political outlook during the period of the convention and the Committee of Public Safety, I say only as much about his fundamental ideas as is essential for understanding his reaction to the practical problems with which he was then faced. Here it is proposed to study his basic ideas as they were before governmental responsibilities had affected his outlook. This is not a difficult task, for Robespierre was a man of the eighteenth century, which means that his political views were consciously derived from general principles. Some historical figures, in some periods, are aware of the principles behind their specific policies, while with others, in other periods, the basic ideas never become fully conscious. But the only alternative to having such ideas, whether logically consistent and conscious, or merely a muddle of vague sentiments taken for granted, is to follow no coherent policy from one moment to the next. Such perfection of inconsistency is rare. Even if the policy of an individual seems to be capable of reduction to a series of chance decisions, this appearance is normally as illusory as that which results from the undue rationalization of practical politics. In the last resort, the historian who disregards the influence of general principles, or ideas, reduces history not to Machiavellianism but to meaningless intrigue or simple madness.

It is true that political ideas, and particularly those of eighteenth-century France, are often summed up, with an implication of disapproval, as abstract principles, and therefore, it is suggested, of no concern to the historian. But eighteenth-century French thought, in addition to its interest in experimental science and mechanical invention, was overwhelmingly concerned with practical issues of social and political behaviour. Its principles were certainly not abstract in the sense that they were not meant to have practical consequences, or did not have such consequences, for quite clearly they both were meant to and did. It is a mistake, however, to regard these principles as a solid block, to be accepted or rejected as a whole. This must be borne in mind in studying the ideas of Robespierre. Thus the materialist theories of the *philosophes* find no echo in his thought. Throughout his writings and speeches, it has been said, runs a conviction of the supremacy of spiritual values.[2] There are, he held, eternal verities, which are 'des maximes de justice universelles, inaltérables, imprescriptibles, faites pour être appliquées à tous les peuples'.[3] These eternal laws of reason take precedence over conclusions derived from specific experience,[4] as over the critical operations of the individual intellect. 'N'oubliez pas', Robespierre said, 'que votre raison ne doit pas tyranniser la raison universelle.'[5] It is evident, therefore, that when he spoke of reason it was in the older medieval sense, and not of human reasonings as the term was used, for example, by Hobbes. Fundamentally his mind still moved in the tradition of Natural Law thought, ranging back to the later developments of Greek philosophy. Natural Law ideas, of course, only provided a formal receptacle for political thought, into which many different political philosophies have been poured. The first step in the analysis of Robespierre's political thinking, therefore, must be to ask what was his interpretation of these eternal principles. This question is easy to answer. They were the moral principles which all men have in common, — 'Il n'existe', he said, 'pour tous les hommes qu'une même morale, qu'une même conscience,'[6] — and which were closely allied with the fundamental religious ideas of the Supreme Being, Providence and immortality. These were the bases of social morality.[7] There was nothing new in all this. Robespierre belonged to the past, rather than to the future, in holding that the application of fundamental moral principles in government was the only cure for political evils.[8] At bottom this was not very different from saying that the end of politics is the good life.

But what did he mean by 'moral' or by 'good'? Since he was a man of the eighteenth century the answer can hardly be in question. He was a utilitarian. 'Toutes les fonctions publiques', he declared, 'sont d'institution sociale: elles ont pour but l'ordre et le bonheur de la société; il s'ensuit qu'il ne peut exister dans la société aucune fonction qui ne soit utile.'[9] 'Le salut public est la loi suprême.'[10] 'Aux yeux du législateur, tout ce qui est utile au monde et bon dans la pratique, est la vérité.'[11] The aim of legislation must be 'l'accord de l'intérêt privé avec l'intérêt général'.[12] Many similar quotations could be found, but they do not quite settle the question, for there are two angles of approach to utilitarianism: the good may be defined in terms of the useful, or the useful in terms of the good. Robespierre adopted the second formula. In 1784 he had proclaimed his faith that 'la vertu produit le bonheur, comme le soleil produit la lumière, tandis que le malheur sort du crime, comme l'insecte impur nait du sein de la corruption'.[13] Conversely, what is immoral is also impolitic.[14] Utilitarianism, thus interpreted, was consistent with his recognition of the primacy of moral principles. Politics, in fact, was an application of ethics. This attitude of mind produced a disposition to divide governments very simply into two classes, the good and the bad, or, as Robespierre put it, the republic and despotism. 'L'immoralité est la base du despotisme, comme la vertu est l'essence de la République,'[15] and between these opposites there was no compromise.

If good government is based upon ethical principles, we next have to ask where we are to find these principles. Robespierre's answer was that the laws of virtue are written in the heart of man; but this answer was not free from ambiguity. The belief that man as an individual is good by nature has to be distinguished from the belief that the *people* is naturally good. The second formula is the one that we commonly meet in Robespierre.[16] 'C'est dans la vertu et dans la souveraineté du peuple qu'il faut chercher un préservatif contre les vices et le despotisme du gouvernement.'[17] It must be emphasized that the conception of the natural goodness of the individual played little part in his political thinking. The idea of natural man appears only once or twice in the whole of his writings and speeches. To appreciate the historical significance of this omission it must be remembered that the decline of individualistic political theory, of which Locke was the greatest representative, had begun in the heart of the Lockian and individualist eighteenth century, and was closely associated with the development of the idea of the people, or the nation. Robespierre's eulogies were almost invariably directed not to man as such but to the people. His basic political concept, and the true embodiment of the principles of virtue for him, was not man, but the people, whose goodness he never wearied of asserting. 'La moralité qui a disparu dans la plupart des individus', he declared, 'ne se retrouve que dans la masse du peuple et dans l'intérêt général.'[18] He quoted Rousseau in support of this belief in the people, but nowhere provided an adequate theoretic justification for what was at bottom an act of faith.

We now have two of the three basic elements in Robespierre's political creed — that government should be based on ethical principles, and that the people as such is good. One further conception required to be added, and this was the belief that in every community there must be a single sovereign will. He did not feel called upon to prove this assumption any more than the other two. It was one of those ideas — perhaps the most important — which are little discussed when they are most influential, because they are taken for granted. Robespierre adopted it unquestioned from the political premises of the *ancien régime*. Whether it was despotic sovereignty, as on the Continent, or parliamentary sovereignty, as in Great Britain, it was the dominating political concept of the age, only partially held in check by deeply rooted political traditions in England, and against which Montesquieu had asserted the restraints of the rule of law and balance of powers in vain. One distinction among theorists of government is that between the upholders of pure forms of government, in which power is strengthened by being concentrated, and of mixed forms in which it is weakened by being divided. Montesquieu had admired the latter, Robespierre followed the dominant trend of eighteenth-century politics in preferring the former. Unconsciously, he was in the direct line of descent from the royal lawyers who had put into the king's mouth the words employed by Louis XV on March 3rd, 1766, at the famous *séance de la flagellation* of the *Parlement* of Paris, when he proclaimed 'que c'est en ma personne seule que réside la puissance souveraine, ... que c'est de moi seul que mes cours tiennent leur existence et leur autorité, ... que c'est à moi seul qu'appartient le pouvoir législatif sans dépendance et sans partage; ... que l'ordre public tout entier émane de moi.'[19] All that Robespierre did was to substitute the people — or the nation — for the king, and incidentally the polemics of the *Parlements* had already done this before 1789.[20] Robespierre held that the sovereignty of the nation, as that of the king had been declared, was above all constitutional bodies;[21] like the king's it was above the law, for it was the law-maker.[22] The nation's will alone was required to create a constitution.[23] The nation was the highest of judicial tribunals, being the source and interpreter of justice.[24] Sovereignty was equally the basic factor in international relations. Peoples, he said, are 'de grandes sociétés d'hommes libres qui, réglant avec une puissance souveraine et leurs intérêts et leurs actions, ne s'associent, ni s'allient, ne s'identifient que par des conventions réciproques'.[25]

The logical consistency of Robespierre's three fundamental principles seems at first sight unshakable: the end of politics is the embodiment of morality in government, the people is good, the people's will must therefore be sovereign. These principles, however, depend upon an idea which we have not yet discussed, the idea of goodness, or to use the more common term, virtue, in the political sense of the word. Virtue was defined by Robespierre as 'l'amour de la patrie' and the identification of public and private interests.[26] For the origins of this definition we must doubtless look to the influence of the classical historians on Italian students of history and politics in the late medieval and renaissance period. It was made current in eighteenth-century France by the influence of Montesquieu,[27] and its general acceptance may be regarded as a landmark in the development of modern political thought in France, for it implied the end of the identification of the state with the monarch. The theorists of benevolent despotism attempted to perpetuate this identification on a new theoretical basis, but so far as France was concerned without success. During the eighteenth century the impersonal conception of the state had been growing fast. Loyalty was passing into patriotism. The idea of the *patrie* was possibly the dominant, as it was certainly the commonest, idea of all political thinkers in eighteenth-century France. And what was the *patrie*? Once the mainly territorial conception of the community had declined — in the nature of things it could never entirely disappear — the *patrie*, or the state, came to mean primarily the inhabitants, that is, the people. The substitution of the sovereignty of the people for the sovereignty of the monarch was a natural conclusion. Moreover, this was the age of what literary historians call 'pre-romanticism'. Though we must not give to the eighteenth-century term *patrie* a modern connotation, for Robespierre, as for many more, patriotism was not a mere abstract principle, but a passion evoked in terms of romantic ardour. It is possible, indeed, to see in him the beginning, though no more, of a further stage in the evolution of the idea of the state. For the people he most often substituted the term 'nation'; and without suggesting that by nation he understood what the nineteenth and twentieth centuries have understood by the word, it is legitimate to argue that when, as he usually did, he talked of the sovereignty of the nation rather than of the people, he foreshadowed the later development from democracy to nationalism.[28] We need not press this point, however. The significant fact is Robespierre's constant definition of the *patrie* in terms of the sovereignty of the people. 'Qu'est-ce que la patrie', he asked, 'si ce n'est le pays ou l'on est citoyen et membre du souverain?'[29] The republic is any government of free men, who, being free, have a *patrie*, and they are free because in such a government each individual is a member of the sovereign.[30] But the republic is by definition the rule of political virtue. We might say, then, that political virtue prevails where there is a *patrie*, and a *patrie* exists where the sovereignty of the people is recognized. Political virtue and the sovereignty of the people were therefore two terms for the same phenomenon. Robespierre was able to maintain complete theoretical consistency, but only by defining virtue in terms of the sovereignty of the people. This equation was the essential foundation of his whole political system.

The idea of the sovereignty of the people was not further analysed by Robespierre. It included, however, one corollary which should be mentioned in the category of general principles. This was the idea of the political equality of all members of the nation. 'Tout homme', he declared, 'doit concourir à la chose publique ... Les inconvéniens de politique ne doivent pas militer contre les droits sacrés de la nature.'[31] Already in 1784 he had pronounced that in the republic each individual was a member of the sovereign.[32] The close connection in Robespierre's mind between the sovereignty of the nation and equality of rights was shown in his assertion that the Declaration of Rights could be reduced to these two principles.[33] His political theory, in spite of what has been said above, may therefore be regarded as based, in as much as his definition of the people was so based, on the individual. But the force of its individualistic elements depended upon the possibility of giving institutional effect to the equality of rights of all individuals as the constituent factors in sovereignty. There was also an implied assumption of identity between the will of all and the General Will but this is a point to which we must revert later. Only experience could show whether these views were justified or whether they were mere optimistic illusions.

We can now turn from fundamental ideas to the political principles derived from them. Before the general ferment which immediately preceded the Revolution there is no evidence that Robespierre had thought in terms of specific institutions. From his attitude at the time of the agitation against the Lamoignon edicts in 1788, which robbed the *Parlements* of much of their legal powers, we may argue that — like public opinion as a whole — he did not as yet discriminate between the general national interest and the cause of the privileged law-courts.[34] His *Plaidoyer pour le sieur Dupont*, in February 1789, appealed to the king to take up the defence of liberty, and a note explained that he had in mind the policy of Necker. His opinions matured rapidly in the course of 1788–9, and he soon became prominent in the local politics of Arras as the advocate of advanced ideas. His active political career commenced when he joined in the demand for popular representation in the Estates of Arras. He published a pamphlet, *À la nation Artésienne, sur la nécessité de réformer les États d'Artois*, in which he called for the recognition of the electoral principle, as the only rightful basis of a representative body.[35] The Estates of Artois, he said, were a self-chosen oligarchy, recruited by intrigue and favouritism.[36] If talent and virtue were to be, as they should, the only qualifications for membership of a representative assembly, the right of free elections should be given to the people.[37] By the time when the *États Généraux* met the idea of democratic sovereignty was fully matured in his mind, as can be seen in his contributions to the constitutional debates.

Even at this early stage, and before he had much experience of practical politics, it would be a mistake to over-emphasize the abstract character of Robespierre's political thinking. He was condemned, it is true, for his constant relation of policy to principle. Garat wrote, after his fall, of his 'rabâchage éternel' on the rights of man and the sovereignty of the people.[38] But Robespierre was not unconscious of the dependence of positive institutions on circumstances. 'Les avantages et les vices d'une institution', he said, in language that might have been borrowed from Montesquieu, 'dépendent presque toujours de leurs rapports avec les autres parties de la législation, avec les usages, les mœurs d'un pays, et une foule d'autres circonstances locales et particulières.'[39] That he was not a slave to words is shown by his attitude to the monarchy. Republic and monarchy seemed to him vague terms, of little significance in themselves. A republic, in the sense of a state in which the public interest predominated, was not, he believed, incompatible with a monarchy.[40] In 1784 he had declared that England was really a republic,[41] a term which, following general eighteenth-century usage, he was here employing as a synonym for constitutional government. His monarch, of course, would have been very much a rubber stamp, or to use his own term, which aroused murmurs in the Assembly, a mere *commis*.[42] He criticized the scope of the powers which the Constitution of 1791 left to the Crown,[43] but in May 1792, despite his objection to many of its clauses, he declared himself the Defender of the Constitution, and evidently aimed at discrediting his Brissotin opponents by saddling them with the label of republicanism.[44] To support the constitutional monarchy of Louis XVI and at the same time to advocate an advanced democratic policy, however, was to attempt to combine incompatibles. The tide of the revolution was running too strongly against monarchy, and in the last number of the *Défenseur de la Constitution* Robespierre inconspicuously but decisively ranged himself with the republicans.[45]

Even as an upholder of monarchy, of course, he had not intended that it should possess any effective political power. His insistence on the principle of the separation of powers is to be interpreted as an attempt to provide a theoretical justification for a policy aimed at diminishing royal authority and not as the expression of a genuine principle of separation. Earlier in the century, Montesquieu had upheld a real theory of balance of powers in the state, though not a rigid separation. Such a theory was incompatible with the principle of sovereignty, and although the authority of Montesquieu continued to be cited, his ideas on this subject were tacitly ignored, except by the constitutional monarchists. Robespierre argued, rather unrealistically, that while the people could not delegate power, it could delegate functions.[46] He employed the principle of separation as a device for ensuring that the Crown, to which was delegated the executive function, should be excluded from interference with the legislature,[47] in which was embodied the sovereignty of the peoples. His views on government, as they emerged in the early stages of the revolution, can be summed up as the interpretation of the sovereignty of the people in terms of legislative sovereignty.[48] In this way sovereignty was capable of being equated, at least verbally, with another fundamental political conception of the eighteenth century, the rule of law; or to put it the other way round, the rule of law was taken to imply government through the medium of laws made by the sovereign will of the community or its representatives. Recognition of this principle of government was regarded as the essential condition of public liberty; and as no distinction was made between the liberty of the state and liberty for the individual, it was taken for granted that the establishment of popular sovereignty would go hand in hand with the achievement of individual liberties. There was nothing peculiar to Robespierre in this system of ideas, which provides a good illustration of the way in which distinct and even contrary political ideas were fused together in the heat of revolutionary passions to make a conglomerate of doctrine, which would glow with a bright light while the flames of revolution lasted, and which might seem rather dead and inert afterwards. At its heart was an act of faith — the doctrine of the sovereignty of the people. From this it proceeded, as we have suggested, by a series of assumptions. The sovereignty of the people was equated with the sovereignty of the legislative assembly, the inconsistent idea of the separation of powers being translated into the subjection of the executive and judicial functions to the legislative power; the sovereignty of the legislature constituted the eighteenth-century version of the rule of law; where the rule of law prevailed, there, it was held, the republic, that is, a state of political liberty, existed; finally, political liberty, thus interpreted, was the same thing as liberty for the individual member of the community.

During the lifetime of the Constituent Assembly Robespierre

crusaded for the liberties of the individual without any suspicion that popular sovereignty might in any way prove difficult to reconcile with them. He asserted the complete liberty of the press,[49] along with the *droit d'affiche*, the right of petition,[50] and the principle of religious liberty.[51] As a supporter of a democratic system of local government, he won the applause of the right wing in the Constituent Assembly by advocating greater freedom for the districts of Paris, to some of which the royalists looked for support against the more revolutionary municipality;[52] he condemned proposals which put the smaller authorities of local government in a state of dependence on the departmental directories, and these in turn on the minister;[53] and he opposed the influence of royal commissioners in the election of local administrations.[54] That he shared in what are generally called the federalist ideas of the opening phase of the Revolution, which found widespread expression in the *cahiers*, was shown by the title of his first political pamphlet — *À la Nation Artésienne*. Above all, however, from 1789 to 1791 he devoted himself to the cause of a democratic franchise, which appeared to him a necessary condition if the sovereignty of the legislature was to be identified with the sovereignty of the people. In a debate of October 20th, 1789, he upheld the principle of universal male suffrage with four other deputies.[55] 'Je l'ai vu', wrote Dubois-Crancé, 'résister à l'assemblée entière et demander, en homme qui sent sa dignité, que le président la rappelât à l'ordre.'[56] He pursued his campaign, undeterred by isolation and ridicule, through a long series of constitutional debates, in which he defended the rights of excluded classes, such as actors and Jews, to public functions. Appealing from the Assembly to the public, he issued, in April 1791, an as yet undelivered speech in favour of universal suffrage, from which, says Aulard, dated his great popularity.[57] Turning from the general to the particular, he pointed out that the qualifications imposed by the suffrage laws were unworkable in his own province of Artois[58] and in this connection won his point. A decree of February 2nd, 1790, declared that in provinces where there was no direct taxation the qualification should be suspended until the reorganization of the system of taxation.[59] The consistency of his democratic principles was demonstrated most clearly in the debates on the proposal to extend political rights to the coloured population of the West Indies. As well as a fair number of nobles, who had sought in the Indies opportunities for commercial enterprise that were forbidden them in France, the wealthy bourgeoisie had extensive economic interests there, which they were not anxious to sacrifice for the sake of a principle. Thus the logical application of democratic principles in the colonies was not at all to the liking of the majority even of the more revolutionary members of the Assembly. Robespierre's challenge was blunt and uncompromising. 'Dès le moment où dans un de vos décrets vous aurez prononcé le mot esclave', he declared, 'vous aurez prononcé et votre propre déshonneur, et − ' at this point his speech was drowned in mixed murmurs and applause.[60] On another occasion, despairing of obtaining the franchise for all the coloured population, he directed his efforts towards obtaining political rights on equal terms for the free elements in it.[61] The argument on which he relied in all these debates was that if sovereignty resided in the general will of the nation, then all individuals shared the same political rights.[62] A property qualification might be natural to the corrupt and aristocratic constitution of England;[63] in a country which had recognized the sovereignty of the people it would merely be a means of establishing a new aristocracy of wealth and the rule of small groups of intriguers.[64] His democratic principles, it must be emphasized, were not limited to the idea of a middle-class or even a *'petit bourgeois'* franchise. 'J'ai cru', he wrote in 1791, 'que la nation renfermoit aussi la classe laborieuse, et tous sans distinction de fortune.'[65] Indeed, the interest of the poorer members of the community was most like the general interest,[66] and to enable them to share in the exercise of governmental functions, Robespierre argued in favour of payment for public service. As early as the meetings at which the *cahiers* for the *tiers état* of Arras had been drawn up he had proposed, though unsuccessfully, that the artisans who had given up four working days to the discussions should be compensated for their lost time.[67] Later he advocated payment for service on juries[68] and in the National Guard,[69] and carried a measure giving payment for attendance at the Paris *Sections*.[70] There was little likelihood of such views convincing the Constituent Assembly. Though the *marc d'argent* was abandoned, in spite of Robespierre's protests the distinction between active and passive citizens was maintained, and at the end of two years' labour a constitution was produced which has been described as 'fortement antidémocratique'.[71]

Robespierre's liberal principles were so far quite consistent, and the practical problems of their application had not yet appeared. The idea of popular sovereignty contained, however, serious theoretical difficulties, which were not slow in being manifested. In the first place, for the sovereignty of the people to be effective, it was necessary for the people to be conceived as capable of exercising a will, which Robespierre, following Rousseau, called the General Will. He expressly equated it with an individual will. 'La volonté générale gouverne la société', he said, 'comme la volonté particulière gouverne chaque individu isolé.'[72] Some clue to his conception of the General Will may be found in his protest against the division of the National Assembly into a majority and a minority, on the ground that the General Will could not be determined in this way.[73] Robespierre, unlike Saint-Just,[74] avoided any detailed discussion of the nature of the General Will. I am not aware that he ever referred to Rousseau's clearly drawn distinction between the General Will and the will of all, but he can hardly have been ignorant of it. The difficulty was that while a political theorist, like Rousseau, might base his thought on the conception of an ideal will, which should embody the best interests of the community, without necessarily being the actual will of the community or of any element in it, Robespierre, as a practical politician, had to try to give the ideal of the General Will some concrete shape and residence. The attempt to translate an ideal in terms of institutions, thus correlating his political theory and practice, presented from the beginning to the end of his career a problem which he never managed to solve.

A second theoretical difficulty arose out of the necessity of reconciling the principle of popular sovereignty with the existence of a sovereign representative assembly. Eighteenth-century writers on politics, outside the few countries which had effective representative institutions, derived their concrete political conceptions largely from the classical historians and philosophers, and conceived their political ideal in terms of the city-state. In this context the problem of representation did not arise. Locke, with his supreme capacity for avoiding questions he could not, or did not wish, to answer, had simply refused to see that there was any problem at all. 'The society', he had said, 'or, which is all one, the legislative thereof.'[75] The perhaps unduly despised Filmer had pointed out the difficulty presented by representation for the theory of popular sovereignty,[76] but it was hardly faced by any democratic theorist with the exception of Rousseau. Rousseau saw clearly the difference between asserting the sovereignty of the people and attributing that same sovereignty to a representative assembly consisting of a minute fraction of the whole people,[77] and Robespierre followed him closely on this point.[78] Representatives, he agreed, were bound to have personal interests of their own, conflicting with the General Will.[79] It must be remembered that the chief example of representative government that the French had before their eyes was Great Britain, and that while earlier in the century French writers had looked with admiration on British constitutional government, subsequently Whig polemics against George III had revealed the more sordid aspects of British politics.[80] When Robespierre condemned the British parliamentary system as aristocratic and venal he was merely repeating what had become a commonplace. The constitution of Great Britain, he declared, could only have appeared a free one at a time when France herself was sunk in the depths of degradation.[81] Admittedly, what the sovereign people could not do directly it had to delegate,[82] but its delegates were not representatives. 'Le mot de représentant ne peut être appliqué à aucun mandataire du peuple, parce que la volonté ne peut se représenter. Les membres de la législature sont les mandataires à qui le peuple a donné la première puissance; mais, dans le vrai sens, on ne peut pas dire qu'ils le représentent.'[83] Since, however, it was hardly possible to conceive a form of democratic government for France without representation, he turned his attention to the effort to mitigate the inevitable defects of the representative system by emphasizing and safeguarding the responsibility of the representatives to the people. They were to be kept under close popular control and often changed.[84] Frequent elections,[85] direct election,[86] large assemblies to avert selfish intrigues,[87] parliamentary sessions in a great hall before ten or twelve thousand spectators,[88] with the maximum of publicity as a guarantee of public spirit,[89] and the use of the recall,[90] such were his proposals for controlling representatives. In spite of these, he evidently found it difficult to formulate institutions through which the actions of the legislature could be directly controlled by the people, and throughout his treatment of this problem there is a divorce between his actual policy and his theory. At the outset, as a member of the patriot party, despite his views on representation he opposed the idea of *mandats impératifs*. 'La Constitution', he wrote, in a contribution to the controversy over the royal veto, 'ne peut pas être le simple résultat de ces opinions isolées que les Commissaires des Assemblées Bailliagères ont consignées dans des Cahiers informes, rédigés à la hâte ... Vous êtes les Représentans de la Nation, et non de simples porteurs de notes.'[91] Again, in spite of his theoretical belief in government by the direct will of the people, he was always hostile to the idea of the plebiscite. His opposition to the proposal that the people should be allowed to decide the fate of Louis XVI was intelligible on political grounds.[92] He is sometimes said to have demanded a plebiscite in the debate after the flight of the king, but it is not clear that he was requiring anything more than the election of a new Assembly. The *Moniteur* report reads, 'Je propose que l'Assemblée décrète qu'elle consultera le voeu de la nation; qu'elle lève la suspension mise à l'élection des membres de la législature'.[93] Later, he even went so far as to deny to the Primary Assemblies the right of meeting freely, on the ground that this would be equal to creating 'la démocratie pure, une démocratie qui ne sera point tempérée par des lois sages qui peuvent la rendre stable'.[94] Finally, when he came to power with the Committee of Public Safety, it was as a member of the most authoritarian government that the Revolution knew before the advent of Napoleon.[95]

A third difficulty in his theory appeared as it gradually dawned upon Robespierre that in its actual content the will of the people did not always coincide with the dictates of virtue. He saw that herein lay the essential problem of the transition from despotism to a regime of liberty.[96] It was not enough for the people to seize power by force of revolution, they had also to be made fit to wield it. The true revolution would be effected by the march of reason, which was slow.[97] 'Le secret de la liberté est d'éclairer les hommes, comme celui de la tyrannie est de les retenir dans l'ignorance.'[98] He might almost have said, 'We must educate our masters.' Robespierre had a glimpse of the fundamental paradox at the heart of democratic theory, which can only be resolved in terms of a theory of education, but the difficulty of reconciling such an outlook with the principle of the sovereignty of the people, as well as with absolute liberty of opinion, became obvious under the Convention.[99]

In the fourth place comes the problem of the connection between political and economic equality. Robespierre was acutely conscious of their interdependence.[100] While most of the revolutionaries saw the economic or social problem only as it appeared in the conflict of interests between the privileged classes and the rest of society, he realized that it also existed among the unprivileged, or rather that wealth was itself a form of privilege. Nor did he adopt the prevailing *laissez-faire* attitude towards economic questions. Bad laws, he held, were the source of extreme inequalities of wealth,[101] and society, especially the propertied classes, had responsibilities for the economic welfare of the individual. Herein lay, he believed, the justification for political intervention in the sphere of economic life, though the actual measures that he supported were very moderate.[102] Belief in the rights of property was a basic element in eighteenth-century economic and political thought, one of the fundamental motives in the Revolution was the freeing of economic society from the trammels of state control, and Robespierre could not, without breaking drastically with the almost universal opinion of his contemporaries, go any further than he did. Yet in recognizing limitations on state action in the economic field, he was implicitly admitting that there was an area of social life in which the sovereignty of the people, by definition unlimited, was limited, and he was also imperilling his ideal of equality.

The practical difficulties into which these theoretical inconsistencies led Robespierre when, as a member of the Committee of Public Safety, he had to face the responsibilities of government, I discuss subsequently. Three further questions can legitimately be asked, however. What were the sources of Robespierre's ideas? What was their connection with the economic divisions in French society at the end of the eighteenth century? And what is his place in the general development of modern political thinking?

For evidence of the sources of Robespierre's ideas we are limited to his writings and speeches. A list of his books, which does not include Rousseau, provides little clue.[103] He necessarily, like all his contemporaries, drew at large on the great reservoir of eighteenth-century thought, but he only retained what was assimilable with his own democratic faith, and there was much that was not. He referred on two or three occasions to Helvétius and the *philosophes*, but only to condemn them for what he called their atheism, and for their persecution of Rousseau.[104] Mably, who influenced many in the generation before the Revolution, he never mentioned. Montesquieu was the source of his definition of republican virtue.[105] A reference to safeguarding the principles of a government,[106] and the statement that institutions should be related to laws and customs,[107] also recall the author of *l'Esprit des Lois*, whom, however, he cited by name only once or twice.[108] The writer whose name appears and reappears in his writings and speeches is Rousseau. That he was a disciple of Rousseau has generally been recognized, though an alleged meeting between the two is almost certainly suppositious.[109] Of his many references to Rousseau some six are in the form of generalized eulogies, as an example of which we may quote a draft dedication, found among Robespierre's papers. 'Appelé à jouer un rôle au milieu des plus grands événements qui avaient jamais agité le monde; assistant à l'agonie de despotisme et au réveil de la véritable souveraineté ... je veux suivre ta trace vénérée ... heureux si ... je reste constamment fidèle aux inspirations que j'ai puisées dans tes écrits.'[110] On several occasions, as has been said, he referred to Rousseau's criticism of the representative system,[111] and to his idealization of the people.[112] In other places, as for example when he declared that the legislator should separate himself from his work,[113] that nations have only one moment to become free,[114] and that gods are needed to give laws to men,[115] he echoed Rousseau's words.[116] The Rousseauist inspiration of the basic principles that we have been expounding is obvious — the constant relating of political to ethical ends, the definition of utilitarianism in terms of morality, the emotional deism expressed later in the cult of the Supreme Being, faith in the natural goodness of the people, the assertion of the sovereignty of the people and the General Will, emphasis on the idea of equality, suspicion of the rich and powerful, combination of the idea of sovereignty with separation of functions in government, supremacy of the legislative power, hostility to representation — it is unnecessary to do more than enumerate these ideas. Above all, there was a Rousseauist quality in his mind. From Rousseau he derived that tendency to self-justification which marked his speeches. 'Ce disciple de Rousseau', said Mathiez, 'parle comme Saint-Preux.'[117]

In a sense, it is true, the whole generation of 1789 was Rousseauist, but it would be a mistake to argue from their sentimental eloquence a specific indebtedness to the political ideas of their literary master, without a more detailed analysis of their writings and speeches than anyone has yet made. On the whole, it seems reasonable to conclude from the study of Robespierre that in his fundamental ideas he followed the teaching of the *Contrat social* closely. On the other hand it is to be noted that he hardly ever mentioned the social contract or natural rights. Only once did he revert to traditional terminology with the declaration that in breaking the social contract tyranny had restored the rights of nature.[118] It is remarkable also that there is no evidence in Robespierre of any acquaintance with the political writings of Rousseau other than the *Contrat social*. He was quite capable, moreover, of maintaining one view in theory, while following a very different one in practice, as is shown by the contrast between his theoretical views on representation and the direct government of the people, and his actual policy on occasions when this issue was specifically raised. Popular sovereignty in the theory of Rousseau was one thing, and in the practice of Robespierre a very different thing. Even the fundamental ideas which he derived from Rousseau were by no means peculiar to the author of the *Contrat social*. It would be best, perhaps, to say that Robespierre and Rousseau represented, each in his own way, a new attitude to the problems of political life, which was arising towards the end of the eighteenth century, and for the sources of which we must look beyond both.

This brings us to the second question. So far I have discussed Robespierre's ideas without reference to his social background, believing that the study of an individual should begin as far as possible with the analysis of his actual ideas, understood in the light of the social and political conditions of his day, and proceed subsequently to a discussion of their social significance. It is not easy to interpret the basic ideas of Robespierre simply in terms of a class ideology. The existence of such an ideology implies a recognition, either explicit or implied, of the primacy of economic interests. Now Robespierre's economic ideas were distinctly exiguous, rather inconsistent, and with one exception arose in the course of attempts to cope with specific practical problems. The one exception is, of course, the idea of equality: behind the ideal of political equality he was ever conscious of the problem of economic inequality. But this important exception itself presents a difficulty when we come to ask with what class in French society Robespierre's ideas, if they are to be interpreted as a class ideology, can be said to correspond. His views were obviously hostile to the interests of the privileged orders. His bias in favour of equality — which was no mere lip-service, as was shown by such policies as the limitation of property rights, state interference in the control of prices, a graduated scale of direct taxation, and the recognition of social responsibilities to the poor — ran counter to the economic interests and prejudices of the wealthy middle classes. The economic interests of the peasantry he practically never discussed. Industrial wage-earners were not as yet a large or very self-conscious section of society, and Robespierre never showed any awareness of their interests as such. In so far as the poorer population of the towns found leaders it was in the *enragés*, whom he regarded with bitter hostility. Only one possible class remains whose interests Robespierre might be said to express. He is sometimes described as the mouthpiece of the *petite bourgeoisie*. This is more plausible. The tradition of Robespierrist Jacobinism certainly tended to be associated with the ideals and interests of this element in French society during the course of the nineteenth century. But we are not concerned here with the adoption of Robespierrist ideals in 1848 or 1871 or under the Third Republic, but with their inspiration between 1789 and 1794. Now the description of Robespierre's ideas as the ideology of the *petite bourgeoisie* can only be of value for historical interpretation if it is justifiable to transfer nineteenth-century conceptions of classes and the class-struggle to earlier periods.[119] In this connection there are three questions which must be answered. First, what was the extent and nature in 1789 of the class which corresponds to the later idea of the *petite bourgeoisie?* Secondly, if the existence of such a class could be assumed, we should have to discover whether either Robespierre himself, or his following in the Jacobin clubs, from which he undoubtedly drew his main support, could be correctly described as belonging to it. The family of Robespierre, however reduced its circumstances, seems to belong with the professional classes rather than with the shopkeepers and small employers. For the membership of the Jacobin clubs we have indications rather than proof, but they all go in one direction. The subscription to the club of Paris in August 1792 was 36 *livres*, 12 of these being *frais de réception*, not an inconsiderable sum.[120] A list of members early in 1791 gives addresses which are said to be all in the well-to-do quarters of Paris.[121] An analysis of tax assessments covering the whole period from 1789 to 1795 has shown that the members of the Jacobin clubs paid on an average a higher tax than their non-Jacobin fellow-townsmen.[122] There is no doubt that in the opening stages of the Revolution the members of the *Sociétés des Amis de la Constitution* were usually men of good position. Later the membership became more varied, and by 1794 there was no clear class representation in them.[123] The clubs, says Professor Brinton, at this time represented 'a complete cross-section' of the community in which they functioned.[124] On the evidence of the Jacobin clubs, therefore, it is difficult to justify the interpretation of Robespierre as the mouthpiece of the *petite bourgeoisie*. Of course, this is not to deny that further economic analysis, combined with a clear definition of what is meant by the *petite bourgeoisie*, might make a more positive conclusion possible. Moreover, Robespierre could easily have acquired from Rousseau an admiration for the small property-owner and independent craftsman; his economic ideas correspond more closely with their interests than with those of any other section of society; and his most devoted support at the end came from the members of the Paris commune, which a list of its members shows to have been composed largely of craftsmen and shopkeepers.[125] It may be suggested, however, in conclusion, that too much importance should not be attached to all these considerations. The interpretation of schools of thought as the ideologies of social classes involves a tendency to underestimate the flexibility of principles in practice and the extent to which different class interests may utilize the same theoretical principles. There is such a thing as a climate of opinion which pervades an age and provides the intellectual framework on which the most contrary practical policies may be erected. Within the setting that general ideas provide, concrete policies are liable to be determined more by conflicts of interest than by differences of fundamental principle.

It would be a mistake, however, to draw the conclusion that political and social principles are therefore of no importance and that the analysis of them can tell us little of historical significance. Equally it would be a mistake to under-estimate the role of the individuals through whose agency such ideas have become historic forces. As soon as one penetrates into the revolution, says Professor Mornet, 'on se trouve en présence, non seulement de l'action, mais des chefs. Ce sont souvent les idées et les volontés de ces chefs qui importent plus que l'action diffuse des idées impersonnelles. Il faut faire non seulement l'histoire des idées révolutionnaires mais encore celle des idées des révolutionnaires.'[126] Robespierre was undoubtedly one of the most influential of such leaders of the revolution, in thought as well as in action. How far the political and social outlook of Jacobinism was his creation, and how far he was merely the leading exponent of a widespread trend of thought, it would not be possible to say without a close study of the debates and literature of the Jacobin clubs. In either case he remains the chief spokesman of a system of ideas which became a great historic force. Economic and other factors may have denied him success, but history is not only the story of successes. Moreover, in considering historical importance a distinction must be drawn between long-term and short-term significance. From the latter point of view, material interests exercise a more obvious influence than ideas over political action. At the closest level of inspection politics often seems to become a mere network of intrigue. The concentration of attention on short periods and highly specialized topics is therefore apt to be accompanied by a disappearance of significance for ideas of any kind. On the other hand, for the broader tasks of historical interpretation ideas remain of vital importance, and not merely the ideas of the academic theorist but above all ideas in action. Robespierre stands halfway between the pure theorist, who, however, is far less immune from the influence of the actual circumstances of contemporary politics than he himself may imagine, and the man of action, whose response to practical stimuli varies only within limits determined by prevailing trends of thought, even if he himself is no more conscious of these trends than the fishes may be of the great tides in the ocean.

Robespierre's ideas find their broader significance in the current of democratic opinion which developed in England, France and America, towards the end of the eighteenth century. While there were connections across national barriers, and the movement in each country looked back to the same intellectual ancestry, it was not merely imitative in any of the three countries and in fact developed along markedly different lines. This early democratic movement has hardly been adequately studied. Its theoretical and practical sources remain unexplored and its connection with social changes is still speculative. So long as we take care not to generalize from a single example, the study of Robespierre's ideas can be regarded as throwing useful light upon its theoretical content. The basic ideas we have found in him are the classic elements — such as the idea of the law of nature or reason, and the recognition of the ethical basis of society — which had been present in one form or another in the European mind since the time of the Stoics. These were given a new orientation by the impact of the utilitarian outlook which developed during the seventeenth and eighteenth centuries. In addition, the eighteenth century saw the growth of the conception of a nation as the possessor of a corporate political will, which was a result of the transference of the idea of state personality, identified in the early modern period with the monarchy, to the community, or, as Robespierre would say, to the people. At the same time the tendency to shift from the idea of the *patrie* to that of the nation suggests the affiliation, even at this early stage, of democratic with national ideas. From the failure of Robespierre's attempts to apply the principle of democratic sovereignty in practice, as from the failure elsewhere of democratic theories even to approach practical application, we might draw the conclusion that in this movement political theory had out-stripped social forces. The circumstances of revolutionary France, comparable perhaps to those which provoked the rapid and premature development of democratic theory during the Commonwealth in England, to which indeed some of the revolutionaries looked back, provided an opportunity for the attempt to put democratic principles into practice. Robespierre, as the leader of this attempt, played his part in a movement broader in its historic significance than even the Revolution itself, but in his own time the effort to achieve democratic sovereignty led only to the rule of the Committee of Public Safety and ended with the *neuf thermidor*.

There is one final point that it is necessary to make. To Robespierre's importance in the history of the Revolution a century and a half of historical writing bears witness; but what has already been said should be sufficient warning against regarding his ideas as typical for the revolutionaries as a whole. On point after point he stands apart. As practical politicians, the revolutionaries commonly defined the good in terms of utility rather than the reverse. I know of none other than Robespierre who showed any real appreciation of what Rousseau meant by the General Will. There were considerable divergencies of opinion on economic matters, and Robespierre's views were only those of a minority in the revolutionary assemblies. In his critique of the representative theory he was almost alone. Though he was the theorist of the Jacobins *par excellence*, his hold over them rested on something more than his political theories. His Rousseauist eloquence[127] was more potent than the theories he had derived from Jean-Jacques, and his fervid faith in the people was most important of all in establishing him as their champion and the leader of those who, from sentiment or interest, identified themselves with the people, or the people with themselves. Herein, perhaps, as well as in the reaction to the menace of invasion and civil war, lies the explanation of the excesses into which Robespierre and the Jacobins were led. In the words of Garat, "Quand on fait pour Dieu et pour le peuple, on ne croit jamais faire ni trop ni mal."[128] In the end Robespierre's faith was not justified of his generation and the seeds he had sown only bore the harvest of the guillotine. But even in defeat he remains an inestimably greater figure than the Talliens and Fouchés, Frérons and Cambons who overthrew him. He was the first to attempt to give practical effect to one of those ideas that shape the course of a civilization, and since his time, for good or for evil, the sovereignty of the people has remained on the agenda of history.

# 9

## THE POLITICAL IDEAS OF MAXIMILIEN ROBESPIERRE DURING THE PERIOD OF THE CONVENTION

MAXIMILIEN ROBESPIERRE, an obscure and isolated figure in the Constituent Assembly when it met in 1789, by the end of its sessions in 1791 had made a reputation for himself as the leading exponent of democratic ideas. Though the self-denying ordinance which he himself proposed excluded him from the next assembly, he kept himself in the public eye by articles in the press and speeches at the Jacobin Club. He played an important part in the agitation which brought about the fall of the Legislative Assembly in August 1792 and the summoning of a constitutional Convention. The elections of September 1792 were not the triumph for the Jacobins that they had anticipated, but during the course of the next nine months they gradually eliminated their opponents and seized control of the Convention. The Jacobins, and Robespierre himself, whose ascendancy among them had steadily increased, were then faced with the supreme test of all revolutionaries, that of putting their theories into practice. To what extent did Robespierre's democratic principles justify themselves? How far did the necessities of government lead to their abandonment, and what, if anything, did he put in their place? Our attempt to answer these questions will rely mainly on an analysis of his writings and speeches from the meeting of the Convention in 1792 to the *neuf thermidor*. It is more usual, in historical discussions of this nature, for the aims and ideas of politicians to be deduced from their actions. In so far as this procedure is capable of defence it is on the supposition that what a statesman does is the best guide to what he thinks, while what he says may, on the other hand, merely mislead. The prime objection to this method of approach is the implied assumption that acts can stand by themselves and be understood in isolation from the thought which inspired them. In practice, moreover, the historian finds it impossible to maintain this separation: the temptation to deduce the intention from the deed is almost irresistible, although to argue back in this way from the act to the thought is to indulge in an attribution of motives which a rigorous method would exclude. Another result is a tendency to convert into a long-term policy what may have been in fact only a series of separate decisions, taken in response to changing stimuli, without any awareness of their more far-reaching implications. The best source for the study of the ideas of a statesman at any given period, making necessary allowances for conscious or unconscious misrepresentation, is to be found in his own speeches and writings of the same period. This is certainly true in the case of Robespierre, who was fully aware of the principles involved in the great struggle in which he was a protagonist, and who took the greatest pains in the exposition of his own ideas. I am assuming in this article that he meant what he said, and though this point is not discussed here, it is true that his sincerity cannot seriously be challenged.

It has often been taken for granted that Robespierre's political ideas remained unchanged from the beginning to the end of his career. 'Tel nous le voyons à l'Assemblée constituante', wrote Hamel, 'tel nous le retrouverons à la Convention nationale.' [1] Vellay described him as 'prisonnier d'une logique de fer'.[2] We shall see to what extent these views can be substantiated, but it may be said at once that it would be remarkable if Robespierre's principles and policy had remained unaffected by his accession to power, in view of the fact that a radical hostility to all authority had been a salient character of his speeches and writings throughout the earlier stages of the Revolution. He had warned the National Assembly against the mania of over-government;[3] for a long time he clung to the generally accepted principle of separation of powers;[4] he denounced every connection between the legislative and the executive as a source of danger.[5] If a profound suspicion of the powers of government is a hallmark of liberalism, then Robespierre in opposition had been one of the first and most uncompromising of liberals. On the eve of the meeting of the Convention he defined the principal object of constitutional laws as the defence of public liberties against the usurpations of rulers.[6] As late as May 1793 he was still upholding the same point of view,[7] though by this time it was little more than the repetition of a formula which he had outgrown.

As a member of the Convention he rapidly changed his ground, and from a critic became an advocate of authority. During the first few months, while the 'Gironde' was in control, he still appeared mainly as the opposition leader. After the decline of Brissotin influence we find him, by March 1793, recognizing the need to strengthen the government and secure unity of action, even if it involved breaking down the barriers between the Convention and the Executive Council.[8] He followed this up by supporting, although cautiously, Danton's proposal that ministers should be chosen from the members of the Convention.[9] He defended the authority of the newly established Committee of Public Safety, declaring, 'Il est ridicule de vouloir tenir le comité de salut public en lisière.'[10] The completeness of his evolution into a defender of authority was shown by his reply to Billaud-Varennes, who, in August 1793, proposed the creation of a commission to watch over the application of the laws by the Executive Council. Robespierre attacked the proposal as an attempt to degrade the executive power and weaken the Committee of Public Safety under the pretence of aiding it.[11] Again, at the Jacobin Club, in March 1794, when it was proposed that the popular societies should be entrusted with the task of purging public administration, he succeeded in securing the rejection of the proposal on the ground that it would undermine the central authority's control over its own servants,[12] defending his change of attitude on the ground that the ministers had ceased to be the nominees of the king and had become the agents of the Convention.[13]

Robespierre's new policy implied a fundamental change of principle. It involved the tacit abandonment of separation of powers, which but a short while before he had been describing as the chief bulwark of constitutional liberties.[14] At the same time, it must be remembered that separation of powers is one of the most misunderstood of political phrases. It meant one thing for Montesquieu, and quite a different thing for Mably and later eighteenth-century writers. Montesquieu had advocated not the separation but the balance of powers in the state.[15] For Robespierre, following Rousseau,[16] such a balance was in the nature of things inadmissible, for it was incompatible with the sovereignty of the people. It was, he said, either a chimera, or a subterfuge to conceal a conspiracy against the people.[17] In his view, the executive was necessarily subordinate to the legislature, to which it was answerable for its conduct.[18] What he really desired from the beginning was not a separation but a subordination of powers in the state. Hence he condemned the proposal in the Girondin Constitution for the election of the Executive Council by the people, the effect of which, he said, would be to put the legislative and executive powers on the same level and thus establish a dangerous rivalry between them.[19] It is only fair, also, to allow weight to the seriousness of the crisis which faced France in 1793. Practical considerations were evidently beginning to outweigh theoretical in his mind when, in March 1793, he admitted his envy for the promptitude with which the decisions of the British government were carried out.[20] He wrote in a private note that what France needed was 'une volonté une'.[21]

All this was evidence of an abandonment of opposition-mentality which can easily be justified on practical grounds, but Robespierre was not unconscious of the difficulty of reconciling his new policy with his earlier principles. In October 1793 the Committee of Public Safety, probably to safeguard constitutionalism and mark the exceptional nature of its proceedings, declared, 'le gouvernement provisoire de la France est révolutionnaire jusqu'à la paix'.[22] It fell to Robespierre, in a speech of December 25th, 1793, which may be regarded as his constitutional apologia, to explain what they meant by revolutionary government. Its principles, he said, were not to be sought in the works of political writers, but in the laws of necessity and of the welfare of the people. Was this to safeguard himself in advance against any awkward references to the author of the *Contrat social*? It was, in any case, a remarkable statement to come from a prophet of the universal principles of reason and justice. The Revolution, he now argued, was a state of war, in which the literal execution of constitutional principles was not to be looked for, and in which government had to exercise an extraordinary activity and an authority that was not required in normal times.[23]

By government Robespierre here meant not the executive but the Convention.[24] This exaltation of the authority of the legislative body was a second fundamental breach with his earlier political principles. Not only had he been jealous of all authority save that of the General Will of the people, but, unlike the majority of the revolutionaries, he had clearly grasped the teaching of the *Contrat social* on the impossibility of representing the General Will.[25] Sovereignty, according to Rousseau, being an attribute of the General Will, could not be transferred to any representative body. This was the reason for the addition of the term 'inalienable' to the definition of sovereignty in the Constitution of 1791.[26] The exercise of the attributes of sovereignty by representatives, who were inevitably influenced by their own interests or by love of power, and who substituted their personal wills for the will of the sovereign people, was the source, according to Robespierre's earlier view, of the corruption of politics.[27] It opened the gate to what he had described in the Constituent Assembly as 'cette science nouvelle qu'on appelle la tactique des grandes assemblées', which, he said, was but another name for political intrigue.[28] Absolute representative government, such as, he believed, the Constituent Assembly introduced, he denounced as the most insupportable of despotisms.[29] But when the Convention, purged by the Jacobins and disciplined by the Committee of Public Safety, not only claimed, but actually wielded, far more extensive powers, he apparently forgot these objections. The Convention, he said, would always be 'le boulevard de la liberté'.[30] Its majority — he left out of count all those who had been eliminated or had prudently abstained from attendance — was composed of good citizens, from whose discussions the general will emerged, not as the will of a party but as a will renewed by a fresh majority with every fresh deliberation.[31] Thus, to sum up, we may say that the assertion of the right of the purged Convention to almost absolute powers of sovereignty is the outstanding feature in the political theory of Robespierre in the last two years of his life.

It is not possible, however, to accept this statement as by itself an adequate summary of his views, for the Convention, as he knew, was liable to fall under the influence of those whom he regarded as the enemies of the true principles of the Revolution.[32] Therefore it could not provide him with the ultimate source of the strong policy which he now desired. Moreover, he could not abandon what he thought was the true Rousseauist principle of the identification of the General Will with the direct action of the people.

In theory, of course, he was mistaken here, for he envisaged the people as taking specific action, whereas Rousseau had confined the General Will to the function of legislation, but it was more consistent with his own earlier ideas. In the opening stages of the Revolution he had on several occasions constituted himself an apologist for popular violence.[33] 'S'il a été commis quelques désordres ... ', he asked the National Assembly in February 1790, 'pardonnez quelques erreurs en faveur de tant de siècles de servitude et de misère.'[34] 'La nation,' he told the Jacobins early in 1792, 'ne déploie véritablement ses forces que dans les momens d'insurrection.'[35] The mob was one of the instruments by which the Jacobin conquest of power had been achieved, and Robespierre tried to evade the theoretical and practical difficulty involved in the fact that the whole people obviously could not take direct action by arguing that the responsibility for opposing tyranny naturally fell upon that section of the people which was most intimately in contact with it. For this reason, while the struggle with the 'Girondins' was being waged, he demanded the permanence of the Paris Sections, which, as assemblies of the whole people, he said, could not belong to any faction.[36] Paris was 'la citadelle de la liberté':[37] it provided the necessary rallying-point for public opinion. He seems to have regarded the capital as the guardian of the rights of the whole people of France, and argued, in so many words, that the action of Paris was 'comme fondé de procuration tacite pour la société tout entière'.[38] We should not regard this as mere special pleading. The underlying idea is that of the democratic sample, as opposed to the aristocratic idea of representation. What he failed to appreciate was that Paris, and still less the Paris mob, was not, in fact, a true sample of France as a whole.

There was another assumption involved in the appeal to the direct action of the people as the ultimate sanction of authority: it implied a belief that the will of the people was necessarily good. Throughout his career Robespierre accepted without qualification the first principle of Rousseau's ethics — that man is good by nature.[39] But he believed that this natural virtue could only express itself in a democracy, immorality being natural to despotism.[40] And if we ask why man *qua* man should be good, and *qua* privileged classes or despots evil, the answer is that Robespierre, like practically every other political thinker of the eighteenth century, including Rousseau himself, was an utilitarian. No public institution, he said, is justifiable unless it is useful, that is, unless it promotes the happiness of society.[41] Privileged classes, or despots, necessarily sought their own selfish interests; only the whole people could be trusted to seek the interest of the whole. Of course, he followed the lead of Rousseau in reading utility in an ethical context: if an institution were good and just it could not be other than useful. 'Rien n'est utile que ce qui est honnête; cette maxime vraie en morale ne l'est pas moins en politique.'[42] To this optimistic faith he clung to the end. It was his last, as it was almost his first, word in politics. His attempt, on the eve of his fall, to rally the Jacobins, was made in the language he had held from the beginning of his career — 'Il n'est qu'un seul remède à tant de maux, et il consiste dans l'exécution des lois de la nature, qui veulent que tout homme soit juste, et dans la vertu, qui est la base fondamentale de toute société.'[43]

While Robespierre remained in opposition it was easy for him to believe both in the direct action of the people and in the principle of the General Will, because of this assumption that the will of the people was in the nature of things an ethical will. 'Le peuple est juste', he wrote, 'et en général, sa colère, comme celle du ciel, ne frappe que les coupables.'[44] Again, in March 1793, 'Quand la révolution est faite par le despotisme contre le peuple, les mesures révolutionnaires ne sont, entre ses mains, que des instrumens de cruauté et d'oppression: mais dans celles où le peuple renverse le despotisme et l'aristocratie, les mesures révolutionnaires ne sont que des remèdes salutaires et des actes de bienfaisance universelle.'[45] The criticism might be made that in speaking thus he was denying the primacy of moral right, and making the virtue or vice of political action lie, not in the nature of the action itself, but in the identity of the actor. In this defence of direct popular action, moreover, there was a potential practical difficulty. If the action of the people were necessarily the product of an ethical will, there could be no picking or choosing among its various manifestations. It could not be good on one occasion and bad on another. This difficulty did not occur to his mind so long as the force of the mob was an instrument to be used by himself and his own party against the government. When, during the Convention, Robespierre migrated from opposition to government, it was forced upon his notice. He found the threat of popular violence turned against himself, and could only justify his policy by condemning the action of the people.[46] Thus, at the very time when he was helping to create a strong central authority, with governmental powers that he had never before been willing to tolerate, he was also denying the right, not only of the representative assembly, but also of the people acting directly, to the last word in the exercise of these powers. Whither, then, did he look for the ultimate sanction of political authority? We must postpone our attempt to answer this question until we have subjected the change in his attitude to the political action of the people to a detailed examination, for it is the key to the understanding of the development of his ideas during the period of the Convention.

The first point we have to note is that under the Convention popular agitation was raising claims that had not hitherto found political expression. The popular disturbances provoked by the Hébertists and the *enragés* differed in their aims from earlier popular movements because, the peasant revolts apart, in the earlier stages of the Revolution, while hunger or high prices may have stimulated unrest, the objectives of the leaders of popular agitation had always been strictly political. Under the Convention the action of the mob was on occasion directed towards specifically economic ends. Political revolution was threatening to develop into economic revolution. This was something novel and, to Robespierre, undesirable, but it forced him to recognize that political democracy had economic implications. It is curious that although economic difficulties played such a large part in its opening phases, the ideology of the Revolution should have been exclusively political. Robespierre formed no exception to this statement. The Rousseauist sympathy for *les petites gens* which he exhibited in the opening stages of the Revolution did not imply the acceptance of any new economic doctrines.[47] He did not question the view that property, with its necessary inequalities, was the basis of the social order. Economic equality he described as a chimera.[48] The project of a *loi agraire* — as the idea of communism of property was termed in memory of the Gracchi — was a bogey put up to frighten imbeciles by the enemies of liberty.[49]

But he went a stage farther than those who envisaged democracy purely in terms of political institutions, irrespective of the social environment in which they operated. In the Constituent Assembly he had urged that the democratic ideal logically implied the establishment of laws to safeguard political equality in the presence of great inequalities of wealth.[50] While he did not challenge the fundamental right of property, he complained that the rich had restricted the idea unduly, and pretended that only those with property in a narrow sense of the word had political rights.[51] We meet here an echo, conscious or unconscious, of the views of Locke, for whom the term property had a broader connotation than it was allowed later.[52] An important development took place in Robespierre's views when, as a member of the Committee of Public Safety, he had to provide a practical solution for economic problems that he had been able to ignore while he was merely a critic of government. The class division within the *tiers état*, of which he had formerly been vaguely conscious, he was now forced to recognize as one of the determining factors in politics. In his private notes he wrote, 'Les dangers intérieurs viennent des bourgeois; pour vaincre les bourgeois, il faut rallier le peuple.'[53] To interpret this sentence correctly it must be remembered that by bourgeois he meant the wealthy *roturiers*, and by *peuple* he was thinking of a nation of craftsmen and peasants, not a propertyless proletariat.

There had already been other indications which suggested that when Robespierre was faced with the economic demands of the people his response would not be entirely negative. He had formerly spoken in favour of equality of inheritance among the members of a family, on the ground that accumulation of riches led to corruption.[54] Now, he even advocated progressive taxation, though he evidently decided on reflection that this was more than public opinion would stand, for the article of his proposed Declaration of Rights which proclaimed this principle was omitted from the version published in his *Lettres à ses commettans*.[55] In the course of the debate of April 1793 on the draft of a new constitution, he developed his ideas further. He complained that the proposed Declaration of Rights guaranteed the liberty and free use of property but said not a word as to its legitimate character. Your Declaration, he said, is made not for all mankind but for the rich, for hoarders, speculators and tyrants. He proposed to remedy this defect by defining the rights of property more closely, so that the property rights of one man should not prejudice the security, the liberty, the life or the property of others.[56] His proposals were not accepted, but under his influence an article was added recognizing the economic obligations of society to its members.[57] It declared, 'Les secours publics sont une dette sacrée. La société doit la subsistance aux citoyens malheureux, soit en leur procurant du travail, soit en assurant les moyens d'exister à ceux qui sont hors d'état de travailler.'[58] Robespierre thus became a prophet of that principle of the right to subsistence which was to play so prominent a part in later social struggles. By recognizing the economic duties of society towards its members he was taking a step away from the individualistic social philosophy of the period.

But this was only the proclamation of a general principle; in the face of popular agitation, the Committee of Public Safety had to produce practical measures. The position was the more difficult in that advanced thinkers were pledged to the principle of free trade, at least inside France. To go back to regulation would be a reversion to the ways of the *ancien régime*. Robespierre for his part continued to protest his adherence to the principle of freedom of commerce,[59] which as late as March 1794 he was still defending against the extremer popular agitators, on the ground that the result of their onslaught on commerce would be to prevent the provisioning of Paris and the other big towns, and so to reduce the people by hunger to a renewed condition of slavery.[60] Freedom of commerce, however, was only justifiable up to the point at which greed began to abuse it,[61] and he came to believe that this point had been reached and passed. On this ground he joined in the cry against monopolies and hoarding. His argument was that France produced enough for the subsistence of all its inhabitants: famine or scarcity could therefore only be the result of bad laws or corruption.[62] In this way he was led into a modification of the theory of freedom of trade, which, he said, failed to allow for the necessity of discriminating between ordinary articles of commerce and the necessities of life.[63] How could it be pretended, he protested, that regulations on the sale of corn were an attack on the property system?[64] Speculation in the necessities of life was anti-social.[65] Among the conditions which favoured it were secrecy, unrestricted liberty of trade, and the certainty of being immune from punishment.[66] Laws were passed against speculation and hoarding, but the essential measures by which it was attempted to check the rise in the price of necessities were the *maximum*, and a widespread system of requisitioning supplies for the needs of the big cities and the armies. The Committee of Public Safety, in fact, put France on the basis of a war economy. Moderate and inevitable as its measures appear from a modern point of view, they were only accepted with reluctance by the Convention, and under pressure from the mob of Paris.[67] Robespierre took his share in the development of the system of the *maximum*, but it represented the policy of the whole Committee and is not to be regarded as peculiarly his work.

It has been suggested that, in the last stage of the rule of the Committee of Public Safety, Robespierre took a more significant step towards the evolution of a new economic policy. The laws of *ventôse* (February 26th and March 5th, 1794), which decreed the distribution of the property of suspects to those who had none, have been interpreted by Mathiez as an attempt on the part of the Robespierrist faction to create a new social class which should owe everything to the Revolution.[68] There is considerable doubt, however, about Robespierre's connection with this scheme. It was put forward by Saint-Just; Robespierre was absent when the Committee accepted it, and he never made any clear statement in its support.[69] Opposition to the laws of *ventôse* was strong, and no effective means of putting them into practice was ever provided.[70] At best they can hardly be regarded as more than a gesture, and even so there is nothing to associate them particularly with Robespierre. We have no reason to believe that he had any more thought of economic revolution at the end than at the beginning of his political career. Above all, to return to the point which led us into this discussion of his economic policy, he did not for one moment envisage the people's right of direct action as extending to economic objects. Indeed, he took the lead in the counter-offensive of the Convention against Jacques Roux, Varlet and the *enragés*, who were, he believed, undermining the Republic by promoting food-riots.[71] 'Quand le peuple se lève,' he asked rhetorically at the Jacobin Club, 'ne doit-il pas avoir un but digne de lui? mais de chétives marchandises doivent-elles l'occuper? ... Le peuple doit se lever, non pour recueillir du sucre, mais pour terrasser les brigands.'[72]

Robespierre's approval of popular agitation, then, was on the assumption that it was confined to political aims. But his views on the direct action of the people, even thus limited, did not remain unaffected by his accession to a position of authority. Before the Mountain obtained control, he seems to have envisaged the people as intervening at critical moments to cut the knot of some intrigue or frustrate the efforts of a corrupt faction to seize or to retain power in the legislative body.[73] With the Committee of Public Safety firmly in the saddle, the direct intervention of the people in the policy of government seemed both less necessary and less desirable to him. To understand his position we must explain his conception of the nature of popular action. In his view the people resorted to direct action for the purpose of protecting the principles of the Revolution by intimidating its enemies. This was only another way of saying that France was undergoing a revolution, in which intimidation was necessarily a part. Direct popular action, in fact, was another word for terrorism. Robespierre's argument was that the people in normal times ruled by virtue; in time of revolution virtue had to be supplemented by terror,[74] which, as the application of 'prompt, severe and inflexible justice', was an emanation of virtue.[75] In this respect also Robespierre's theoretical views and practical policy were modified under the Convention. Partly as a result of his efforts, the Convention at last succeeded in institutionalizing revolutionary justice. The operation of the Terror by the people, acting for itself, was therefore no longer necessary. The transference of the execution of terroristic justice from the hands of the people to tribunals which, though conceived as 'people's courts', were actually governmental institutions, was an essential element in the policy of the Committee of Public Safety. It has too often been dismissed in a superficial manner, as though all the members of the Committee, and particularly Robespierre, were mere blood-boltered butchers of the type of Jourdon Coupe-tête. The psychology of the Terror is perhaps more easily comprehensible in an age which has seen the reappearance of the phenomenon to which it has given the name of 'Fifth Column' than during the nineteenth century, when the unity of nations was taken for granted. The Committee of Public

Safety had to conduct a war on two fronts, against rebel armies inside France, as well as against foreign invaders. It shared the popular belief in the existence of large numbers of conspirators and brigands, subsidized by the royalists, by Austria, or by Pitt, who were only waiting their opportunity to assassinate honest revolutionaries and join the foreign invader. In these circumstances the Terror seemed to the Jacobins a necessary measure of national and republican defence.[76]

Robespierre accepted the need for the Terror, as did all the other members of the Committee of Public Safety, but irregular executions, indiscriminate massacre, were antipathetic to his legalistic mind. Even at the beginning of the Revolution, although he had been an apologist for popular violence, he had agitated for some means of giving it juridical expression. He found a formula to justify the application of terroristic justice in the distinction which he drew between ordinary crimes and crimes of what he termed *lèse-nation*. In dealing with the former he upheld the principles of impartial justice.[77] Crimes against the nation fell into a category of their own, and as early as October 1789 he was demanding a national tribunal to judge them.[78] We must not exaggerate the novelty of this view. It should be remembered that crimes against the sovereign have normally, in all regimes, been regarded as requiring exceptional treatment. Before 1789 they were prosecuted as *lèse-majesté*. Later generations have called them political offences, but whatever phrase be used the meaning remains the same. They are crimes against the ruling power in the state as such, and in dealing with them the state has rarely either been expected or willing to administer impartial justice. For the *ancien régime* the king was the fount of all justice: he possessed the right of *justice retenue* which entitled him to execute any judicial measure without observing the established forms of law.[79] Robespierre merely substituted the nation for the king. There was no higher tribunal, he declared, than the nation, except that of the eternal reason, and who, he asked, should be the interpreter of its judgments but the majority of the members of society?[80] In such a trial as that of Louis XVI the nation was the injured party, and in this case the nation must be the judge.[81] It followed that crimes against the nation were not within the competence of the ordinary courts. Unless the people were to administer the justice of lynch law, it was necessary to create a people's court which could be entrusted with the task.

It is not necessary for us to describe in detail the stages through which the revolutionaries progressed in their search for a court capable of judging political offences. At the outset the Châtelet was utilized for the purpose, but it devoted most of its time to an inquiry into the October Days, which it pursued in an obviously anti-revolutionary spirit.[82] Robespierre several times demanded its replacement by a truly national tribunal.[83] The High Court set up at Orleans by the Constitution of 1791 was not much more satisfactory to him. Under his inspiration a special tribunal, representing the Sections of Paris, was given the task of judging the 'crimes' of August 10th, 1792.[84] Finally, by a decree of March 10th, 1793, the Revolutionary Tribunal was established. Set up for the purpose of administering political justice, it could not follow the ordinary rules of law. 'Les peuples', Robespierre said, 'ne jugent pas comme les cours judiciaires; ils ne rendent point de sentences; ils lancent la foudre.'[85] Again, he declared, 'La Révolution est la guerre de la liberté contre ses ennemis ... le gouvernement révolutionnaire doit aux bons citoyens toute la protection nationale; il ne doit aux ennemis du peuple que la mort.'[86] His conception of terroristic justice was expounded most fully in connection with the trial of the king. Robespierre saw that only by an assertion of the absolute and unfettered right of the nation to take action and pass condemnation on the king as a political act, could his trial and execution be justified.[87] It was also only by setting up the safety of the nation as the supreme law that he could defend in his own mind the application of the death penalty, which he had hitherto opposed.[88] The trial and execution of the king proved to be the first of a long series of political trials and condemnations, in the course of which all ideas of judicial impartiality vanished. The justice meted out by the Revolutionary Tribunal was indeed the vengeance of the people, and very indiscriminately exercised vengeance. Robespierre cannot be held responsible for the conduct of the trials by Fouquier-Tinville, but it is true that he took a leading part in drawing up decrees which amounted to a virtual abandonment of all ordinary judicial safeguards.[89] On practical grounds an explanation for the institutionalization of the Terror in judicial forms can be given, but at best it must be regarded as an attempt to subsume under the head of justice what properly belonged to the category of civil war. Moreover, it was another breach with his earlier principles, even if he was unconscious of the fact: political justice, when it had been turned into a regular instrument of government, had become a manifestation of the will of the government, not of the people. It represented fear rather than faith in the operation of the will of the people. It was an evasion, not an expression, of the principle of democratic sovereignty.

Once again, then, we find that, in the application of revolutionary justice, as in economic policy, Robespierre as a man of government was very different from Robespierre, the leader of opposition. From both these angles of approach it seems difficult to avoid the conclusion that in practice, if not in theory, he had to a considerable extent abandoned his earlier belief in the direct action of the people and hostility to constituted authority. His attitude of mind will be understood more clearly if we examine his changing views on public opinion. At the outset of the Revolution he had believed that all that was necessary was to release the opinion of the people from the influence of government,[90] and the ideal democratic policy would by that very fact be established. In the early months of 1793 he was still protesting against putting funds into the hands of the Minister of the Interior for the purpose of influencing opinion:[91] this was a means of creating the most monstrous of tyrannies.[92] 'L'autorité publique', he wrote, 'doit laisser à l'opinion publique la liberté de perfectionner les lois et le gouvernement.'[93] He was still optimistic enough, in February 1793, to declare that 'les principes éternels de la justice et de la raison ont fait tant de progrès, ont jeté de si profondes racines, que nous n'avons plus à craindre que l'esprit public rétrograde'.[94] But as difficulties accumulated in the path of the Convention his faith weakened. He did not abandon his belief that the people were good and rational by nature, but he saw now that unfortunately the Revolution had to deal with them, not as they were by nature, but as they came out of the venal and corrupt society of the *ancien régime*. The misfortune of a people which passed rapidly from slavery to liberty, he said, was that it carried over unconsciously the prejudices of the old order into the new.[95] 'Nous avons élevé le temple de la liberté avec des mains encore flétries des fers du despotisme.'[96] How could wise laws and sound social customs be the product of a populace corrupted by despotism?[97] Opinion, he wrote, is queen of the world, but like all queens is flattered and often deceived.[98] What it amounted to was that, although still oppressed with the urgency of establishing democratic institutions, Robespierre ceased to believe that they could be achieved by the simple operation, either directly, or indirectly through representative institutions, of the opinion of the people — that people, which, he now confessed, was 'aussi confiant, aussi léger que généreux, qui a longtems encensé de si ridicules idoles'.[99] The people, he said, quoting Rousseau, necessarily desired the public interest, but they did not always see it, and were easily misled.[100] 'Apprenez', he instructed them, 'à vous défier de vous-mêmes; songez que votre usage est d'apercevoir la vérité deux ans trop tard.'[101] They were liable to fall under the influence of self-interested and venal politicians and journalists, whose insidious propaganda, he said, was more dangerous than the attacks of open counter-revolutionaries. Intriguers, he now realized, packed the Sections, when they sat *en permanence*, to the exclusion of honest working-men.[102] They dominated the clubs, other than the Jacobins.[103] 'La plus belle de toutes les révolutions', he had warned the Jacobins as early as July 1792, 'dégénère, chaque jour, en un honteux système de machiavélisme et d'hypocrisie.'[104] Opinion had started the Revolution: opinion also could stop it.[105]

The conclusion, which Robespierre had reached by June 1792, was that the only way to save liberty was by enlightening public opinion.[106] After the Mountain had obtained power he went much further than this; he accepted the practical necessity for the government to exercise control over the opinions of the people, and abandoned the liberty of the press, which he had formerly defended so often and with such ardour.[107] He described the press as the chief agency of intrigue,[108] and argued that the success of a revolution aimed at reconquering the rights of man might involve the repression of a plot contrived with its aid.[109] In Paris, he said, the people could see for themselves what went on in the Assembly and the clubs: in the *départements* it was known only through reports in journals, which for the most part distorted the truth.[110] 'Proscription des écrivains perfides et contre-révolutionnaires,' he noted, 'propagation de bons écrits.'[111] When the Revolutionary Tribunal was established he said that one of its tasks must be the suppression of all writings — at this there were murmurs and he hurriedly proceeded to add — of all writings which were against the principles of liberty, sovereignty and equality.[112] Suppression, however, was not enough: it was also necessary to enlighten the people.[113] 'Faites des lois populaires,' he declared in the debate provoked by the deputation of the *enragés* to the Convention, 'posez les bases de l'instruction publique, régénérez l'esprit public, épurez les mœurs, si vous ne voulez perpétuer la crise de la révolution.'[114]

During the years 1792 to 1794 Robespierre moved so far from his earlier suspicion of all governmental authority and faith in the unfettered operation of public opinion, that he came to believe in the duty of government not only to control, but also to create, public opinion. For this purpose he became ready to call every agency that could influence opinion into action. National *fêtes*[115] and the theatre[116] were to play their part, along with the dissemination of patriotic pamphlets and journals. 'Il faut répandre de bons écrits avec profusion,' he noted.[117] He himself drew up a decree of the Committee of Public Safety ordering the Committee of Public Instruction to organize national *fêtes*, and to take measures to ensure the fullest publicity for the reports of the Committee of Public Safety to the Convention, and for other documents which were officially published.[118] Those journals which were viewed with a favourable eye received large subsidies to enable them to circulate free copies in the armies and to the popular societies.[119] Robespierre had formerly been profoundly suspicious of proposals for a national system of education.[120] Even at the beginning of 1793 he could still say that at a time when laws were bad and faction prevailed it was merely another weapon put into the hands of government against the people.[121] He abandoned this opposition when, in July 1793, he made himself the advocate of the Le Pelletier report.[122] He was responsible for part of the wording of article 21, proclaiming that education should be brought within the reach of all, in the Jacobin Declaration of Rights, and for the addition, among the benefits which the Constitution guaranteed the French (article 122), of 'une instruction commune'.[123] The state in the eighteenth century lacked, however, much of the machinery which has made its power over opinion so potent in modern times. The two supreme forces on which it could call were those of religion and patriotism, and it is in relation to these that we can see most clearly the influence of power and responsibility upon the development of Robespierre's attitude towards public opinion.

In spite of the propaganda of the *philosophes*, one of the most potent factors in the shaping of public opinion was still religion. At the beginning of the Revolution there had been nothing to distinguish Robespierre's views on the religious question from those of most of the other revolutionaries. He shared the general belief in the justice of appropriating the property of the Church to cope with the financial difficulties of the nation.[124] He supported the establishment of the Civil Constitution of the Clergy,[125] and exhibited the ordinary revolutionary lack of appreciation of the strength of the Church among the people. In one debate he was evidently proceeding to propose the marriage of priests, when he was drowned by uproar in the Assembly.[126] He favoured the election of the clergy on the ordinary civic franchise,[127] on the ground that otherwise it would become a distinct body, capable of setting itself up in opposition to the national will.[128] 'Les ecclésiastiques', he argued, 'ne peuvent être considérés que comme des fonctionnaires publics, salariés par la nation.'[129] He exhibited the usual fear of the political influence of the clergy. On the other hand, he never belonged to the violently anti-clerical faction. When, in March 1791, it had been proposed in the National Assembly to take punitive action in connection with riots in Douai, which the clergy were accused of instigating, Robespierre, amidst applause from the Right and murmurs from the Left, protested that an ecclesiastic was also a citizen, and that no citizen could be penalized for his speeches.[130] He deplored, in November 1791, the publication of a private letter in which he had written with alarm of the influence of the clergy, as giving, he said, the false impression that it was intended as a declaration of war against non-juring priests.[131] On November 29th, 1791, when an essay attacking religion as superstition was being read at the Jacobin Club, Robespierre brought the reading to an end by breaking in with a protest — 'Je crois que la Société ne peut pas entendre cet ouvrage sans danger. Il ne faut pas heurter de front les préjugés religieux, que le peuple adore.'[132] In December 1792 he was declaring that it was not the moment to stir up religious strife.[133]

Finally, at the Jacobins, on November 21st, 1793, he launched a frontal attack on Hébert and his faction. Mathiez claims that the account of his speech in the *Moniteur*[134] gives a false impression that he condemned absolutely the movement of dechristianization, and refers to the account in the *Anti-Fédéraliste* of the 4 frimaire an II (November 24th, 1793), where he is reported as saying that while those attached not to superstition but to divine law should not be disturbed, priests who resist the law must be prosecuted, and all priests should be kept under surveillance. This seems to us hardly sufficient justification for Mathiez's assertion that while Robespierre condemned the war against the idea of divinity, he did not condemn that against Catholicism.[135] Certainly, at the time when he made this speech he was convinced that the power of the priesthood was no longer a danger.[136] 'Il ne reste plus guère dans les esprits que ces dogmes imposans qui prêtent un appui aux idées morales, et la doctrine sublime et touchante de la vertu et de l'égalité que le fils de Marie enseigna jadis à ses concitoyens.'[137] Such dogmas were the ideas of immortality, and of the Supreme Being, which Robespierre believed to be necessary for political virtue.[138] In the words of Levasseur de la Sarthe, he felt that man could not be republican if he were not above all moral,[139] and among the people he believed morality to depend on religion.[140] Holding such views it was natural that he should become the leader of the opposition to the intransigent anti-religious element in the Jacobin Club.[141] The idea of the Supreme Being, he declared, was a continual reminder of justice and hence was republican.[142] 'L'athéisme est aristocratique; l'idée d'un grand Être, qui veille sur l'innocence opprimée, et qui punit le crime triomphant, est toute populaire.'[143] The strength of his convictions, and the hostility they aroused among the more violently anti-religious revolutionaries, was shown in a scene that occurred at the Jacobin Club, when Robespierre spoke of Providence as watching over the Revolution, and striking down the Emperor Leopold, news of whose death had just arrived. The Girondin, Guadet, leapt to the attack, declaring that he saw no sense in the idea that Providence had saved the Revolution, and denouncing it as an attempt to bring the people back under the slavery of superstition. Robespierre retaliated with an outspoken defence of the belief that there was a Providence which presided over the destinies of nations, and in particular guarded the Revolution, and the meeting ended in disorder.[144] The religious bias of his mind was the subject of frequent criticism. A hostile writer, in the *Chronique de Paris* of November 9th, 1792, said of him, 'Il a tous les caractères, non pas d'un chef de religion, mais d'un chef de secte; il s'est fait une réputation d'austérité qui vise à la sainteté, il monte sur des bancs, il parle de Dieu et de la Providence, il se dit l'ami des pauvres et des faibles ... Robespierre est un prêtre et ne sera jamais que cela.'[145] The inspiration of Rousseau is evident in this aspect of his policy. He mingled invocations to Rousseau with denunciations of his persecutors, the infidel *philosophes*.[146] Mathiez is doubtless correct in saying that the social utility of religion concerned Robespierre most, and that his God was primarily a moral law.[147] The same might be said of Rousseau, and Mathiez goes much too far in his alarm lest his hero may be suspected of having had religious sympathies. He describes Robespierre as 'l'adversaire le plus constant et le plus habile de l'Église catholique'.[148] This description is quite unjustifiable. Mathiez attempts to reconcile his opinion with the actual policy of Robespierre by saying that the *philosophe* in him condemned absolutely all religions, but the legislator consented to tolerate them.[149] On the contrary we are bound to say that Robespierre seems to us to have exhibited a constant, and obviously sincere, bias in the direction of religious toleration. We must agree with Aulard, who for his part did not intend it as praise, that in the crisis of the Revolution he was 'vraiment, et autant qu'on pouvait le faire en ce temps-là, le patron et le défenseur des catholiques'.[150]

During the Convention, and even at the height of the Terror, Robespierre remained, so far as circumstances permitted, a defender of religious toleration, and this on grounds both of policy and of principle. A note of autumn 1793 suggests that he favoured the indefinite suspension of the application of the anti-religious republican calendar.[151] He supported the decree authorizing the Committee of Public Safety to protect liberty of religion against the attacks of municipalities, which was presented to the Convention by Barère in the name of the Committee.[152] A letter to a representative on mission, signed by Robespierre and three other members of the Committee, warned against attacks on the objects of Catholic worship. No opportunity, it urged, must be given to the enemies of the Revolution for saying that war was being made on religion itself.[153] Another missive from the Committee, in the hand of Robespierre himself, declared 'Il est des superstitieux de bonne foi ... Ce sont des malades qu'il faut préparer à la guérison en les rassurant, et qu'on rendrait fanatiques par une cure forcée.'[154] When a letter was received from the president of a commune inquiring what measures should be taken against women wearing crosses, Robespierre referred the letter to the *bureau de police*, with the comment that the writer must be either a fool or a rogue.[155] To the Jacobins he said that the man who tried to prevent the celebration of Mass was more of a fanatic than the priest who celebrated it.[156] In 1791 he had declared that nothing should be allowed to restrict the liberty of the theatre: public opinion should be the only censor.[157] In December 1793 he drew up the decree which forbade the performance of the anti-religious play of Léonard Bourdon, *Le tombeau des imposteurs*, 'et toutes celles qui peuvent tendre au même but'.[158] According to a royalist author, cited by Hamel, several priests who had written to Robespierre to know what they should do, were advised by him to remain in their parishes and continue their religious duties as long as they could.[159] On the other hand, he vehemently attacked the atheistic party among the revolutionaries. In fact, of course, the actual ideas of the so-called atheists were not very different from his own deistic principles. By atheism he really meant rationalism and aggressive anti-clericalism,[160] and the political reasons for his antagonism to it bear witness once again to the growth in him of a governmental frame of mind. He was alarmed by the attack on religion above all because it seemed to him a provocation to civil war, and therefore a diversion in favour of the counter-revolution.[161] It was also dangerous to the interests of the Revolution abroad.[162] Were the revolutionary armies, he asked, to renew in Belgium the difficult and bloody struggle they had already had over religion in France?[163]

The example of its religious policy is a warning against the tendency to exaggerate what have been called the totalitarian tendencies of the Committee of Public Safety. The survival of more liberal attitudes of mind is illustrated by the circular, drawn up at a meeting of the Committee attended by Robespierre, which directed local authorities not to persecute the Anabaptists, and ordered that those conscripted for the Army should be allowed to serve as pioneers or in the transport, or even to purchase exemption.[164] The inclination of Robespierre's mind towards religious toleration, and his efforts to limit religious persecution under the Convention, are both beyond dispute. At the same time, to return to the point with which we began our discussion of his religious ideas, he was above all concerned with the influence over opinion that control of religion put into the hands of government. In opposition he had dreaded this power: in office he felt the need to employ it. It was hardly possible for anyone at the time to contemplate leaving religion to itself. Free religion from state control, Robespierre said, and you will witness the growth of a thousand mystical or seditious conventicles.[165] The necessity of an established state religion was generally accepted: the only dispute was over the nature of the religion. Here it must be said that we find it impossible to agree with Aulard that Robespierre, if he had lived, would have returned to Catholicism.[166] His *culte de l'Être Suprême* was patently sincere, and in fact represented in his mind an alternative to Catholicism as a religion of the state. As such, it was not far removed from an attempt to put the last chapter of the *Contrat social* into practice. It was to be a religion without priests: the only priest of the Supreme Being, said Robespierre, is nature itself,[167] whose dogmas are written in the heart of the virtuous man. His religion, like Rousseau's, was a corollary of faith in the natural goodness of man. One feels, writes Jaurès, in the deism of Robespierre, a sort of respect for the conscience of the people; he accommodates himself to their prejudices and seems to put himself on their level.[168] This may be in part the explanation why he did not carry his new authoritarian tendencies so far as to propose to enforce the *culte de l'Être Suprême* by a policy of persecution.[169] If he had gone the whole way with Rousseau, he would have banished, as the last chapter of the *Contrat social* proposed, all who did not believe in God. This principle, he admitted, though it might be theoretically just, was one of those which required to be put forward with discretion.[170] In religion he preferred measures of persuasion and propaganda to those of persecution.[171] Finally, we must repeat that, despite the religiosity that was such a marked feature of Robespierre's mind, Aulard is justified in claiming that, like the other revolutionary cults, the *culte de l'Être Suprême* was inspired partly, if not primarily, by political motives.[172] It was above all an expedient of national and republican defence, and an agency for the inculcation of political virtue.

The religious motive was not the only one, nor perhaps was it the strongest of the emotions to which Robespierre felt it was necessary for the revolutionary government to appeal in its struggle to gain control of public opinion. Religion, as we have said, was regarded as the basis of popular virtue, and it was a commonplace of eighteenth-century political writing that virtue was the quality necessary for the maintenance of republican government. But what was virtue? The classic definition was that of Montesquieu — 'Ce que j'appelle la *vertu* dans la république est l'amour de la patrie, c'est-à-dire l'amour de l'égalité. Ce n'est point une vertu morale ni une vertu chrétienne, c'est la vertu *politique*, et celle-ci est le ressort qui fait mouvoir la gouvernement républicain … J'ai donc appelé *vertu politique* l'amour de la patrie et de l'égalité.'[173] At the opening of the Revolution the leaders of the *tiers état*, being regarded as the possessors of political virtue, were labelled the patriot party. As the need to defend the French Republic against foreign invasion and internal disruption became more pressing, the definition was reversed and republican virtue came increasingly to be attested by demonstrations of patriotism in the narrower sense of the word.[174]

Robespierre's clearest expression of this view was in a speech of June 1794, in which he declared, 'La Montagne n'est autre chose que les hauteurs du patriotisme; un Montagnard n'est autre chose qu'un patriote pur, raisonnable et sublime.'[175] In 1792 he had appealed to patriotic feeling extensively in *Le Défenseur de la Constitution*,[176] and he harped increasingly on this note during the Convention. The growth of the patriotic spirit, even more than the attempt to revive the religious sanction on behalf of the Republic, was significant of the change that was coming over the world of politics: they were both aspects of the re-infusion of emotion into political life. Patriotism, said Robespierre, was a matter of the heart.[177] In glowing invocations to the *patrie* the cold rationalism of the century was discarded. 'Oui,' he proclaimed, 'cette terre délicieuse que nous habitons, et que la nature caresse avec prédilection, est faite pour être le domaine de la liberté et du bonheur; ce peuple sensible et fier est vraiment né pour la gloire et pour la vertu. O ma patrie! ... Je suis français, je suis l'un de tes représentants ... O peuple sublime! reçois le sacrifice de tout mon être; heureux celui qui est né au milieu de toi! plus heureux celui qui peut mourir pour ton bonheur!'[178] Such a specimen of revolutionary oratory may seem a little ridiculous to a generation far removed from the literary conventions of the age, but it was evidence of the new spirit rising in political life.

The significance of his appeal to the spirit of patriotism can best be brought out by a comparison with Robespierre's earlier views on foreign policy. During the period of the Legislative Assembly he had been the leader of the opposition to the bellicose schemes of the Brissotins. His hostility to their plans for war was primarily derived from his haunting fear of military dictatorship.[179] It was also justified by a belief that internal enemies of the Revolution should be eliminated before foreign opposition was provoked.[180] Ensure your own liberty, he was still telling the Jacobins in 1794, before concerning yourself with that of others.[181] 'Faites triompher la liberté au dedans, et nul ennemi étranger n'osera vous attaquer. C'est par les progrès de la philosophie, et par le spectacle du bonheur de la France, que vous étendrez l'empire de notre révolution, et non par la force des armes, et par les calamités de la guerre.'[182] Even after he had accepted the war as inevitable, he continued to disbelieve in the effectiveness of attempts to turn other peoples against their own governments. On this account he deplored the provocative behaviour of French representatives abroad.[183] His most systematic analysis of French foreign policy was contained in a speech of November 1793, in which his chief concern was to reassure the Swiss and Americans, praise the small neutral states, eulogize the Turks as potential allies, denounce the ambitions of the Empress Catherine, and establish the view that the strength of France was necessary to the protection of the liberties of all the smaller states of Europe.[184] Sorel, who could see no good in Robespierre, was unwilling to allow him any credit for what he could hardly deny to be the merits of this speech. 'Toute cette partie,' Sorel declared, 'très classique d'ailleurs, était écrite de l'encre des bureaux.'[185] Beyond what was filched from the traditional foreign policy of France the speech seemed to him nothing but a 'vaine amplification'.[186] But it is too thoroughly in keeping with the general line of Robespierre's thought on international questions for us to deny him the credit for its common sense. In his notebook he had written, 'Les affaires étrangères. Alliance avec les petites puissances',[187] and he was aware that such a policy was incompatible with a revolutionary crusade. As he said, no one loves armed missionaries:[188] those who try to dictate laws with arms in their hands will never be regarded as anything but foreigners and conquerors.[189] He recognized that the peoples of Europe had different customs and dispositions.[190] In an earlier speech against the war he had argued, 'Le gouvernement le plus vicieux trouve un puissant appui dans les préjugés, dans les habitudes, dans l'éducation des peuples ... La plus extravagante idée qui puisse naître dans la tête d'un politique est de croire qu'il suffise à un peuple d'entrer à main armée chez un peuple étranger pour lui faire adopter ses lois et sa constitution.'[191] In line with these views was the hostility which Robespierre clearly, though cautiously, exhibited to the important Cambon decree of December 15th, 1792, imposing revolutionary regimes on all conquered territories.[192] Similarly, he ridiculed, in 1794, those who held that the British people were enlightened and capable of overthrowing their tyrannical governments, stigmatizing such hopes as a mere survival of Brissotin illusions.[193]

After the war had been launched, Robespierre was most of all concerned with its possible reactions inside France. He believed that it could only be reconciled with the interests of the Revolution if it were conducted on truly revolutionary principles, and to ensure this he proposed to add to the Jacobin constitution four articles:

i. Les hommes de tous les pays sont frères et les différents peuples doivent s'entr'aider selon leur pouvoir, comme les citoyens du même état.

ii. Celui qui opprime une nation se déclare l'ennemi de toutes.

iii. Ceux qui font la guerre à un peuple pour arrêter les progrès de la liberté, et anéantir les droits de l'homme, doivent être poursuivis par tous, non comme des ennemis ordinaires, mais comme des assassins et des brigands rebelles.

iv. Les rois, les aristocrates, les tyrans, quels qu'ils soient, sont des esclaves révoltés contre le souverain de la terre, qui est le genre-humain, et contre le législateur de l'Univers, qui est la Nature.[194]

The Convention proved unwilling to go as far as this, and expressed itself in the milder terms of articles 118–21, but Robespierre was right in seeing that the war was, at least in part, of a new kind. The democratic faith of the Revolution in the goodness of the people naturally led to the belief that a war waged by the people could not be fought for selfish gain, but must be one based on principle. This is another way of saying that the Revolution inaugurated the age of ideological warfare, and so revived in a new guise the bitterness of the religious warfare of the past. Once he had accepted the inevitability of the European struggle, and had assumed a share in the responsibility for the conduct of the war, Robespierre abandoned his former pacific language and did what he could to stimulate the new spirit of national and ideological hatred. A revolutionary war, he recognized, could not be waged as an ordinary war against ordinary enemies. It was a people's war for justice and liberty, and the force of a whole people was irresistible. 'Son objet est sublime; sa force est invincible; ses mesures sont sages et grandes; ses attaques promptes et irrésistible.'[195] It followed that those who resisted the will of the people were brigands, assassins, enemies of the human race.[196] The hatred of the revolutionaries was above all concentrated on the English, against whom the war was becoming most like a national struggle.[197] They were, in the words of Robespierre, a corrupt and enslaved people, and the accomplices of their own oppressors.[198] Though he did not go as far as Barère and other revolutionary leaders, and did not consciously use the war as a means of securing or retaining power, there was one significant debate in which Robespierre made a series of efforts to side-track internecine struggles in the Jacobin Club by diverting the discussion to 'the crimes of the English government and the vices of the British constitution'.[199] In the end he came very close to adopting the war ideology for which he had formerly denounced the Brissotins. This patriotic propaganda was the culminating feature in the development of Robespierre's attempt to educate and control public opinion.

In the impressive growth of revolutionary patriotism are to be heard the opening chords of the crescendo of nationalist sentiment which was to dominate the succeeding age. Burke and Rousseau had foreshadowed the new ideas, Sieyes carried the theoretical development of the idea of national sovereignty much farther, but it required the catalytic agency of actual events to precipitate the new ideology. Although, in his *Constitution de Pologne*, Rousseau had approached closely to nationalist ideas, there was a fundamental difference between his theory of the General Will and the revolutionary assertion of national sovereignty. For Rousseau the General Will was primarily an ethical concept: it had an indissolubly individualistic basis. According to Bosanquet, who himself upheld a contrary view, Rousseau appealed to the nation 'regarded as an aggregate of isolated individuals'.[200] His belief in the goodness of human nature was primarily a declaration of faith in the individual.[201] Robespierre, even though he accepted Rousseau as his master, stated his views in very different terms. Morality, he said, had disappeared in most individuals, and was only to be rediscovered in the masses and in the general interest.[202] The age of Lockian individualism, we can see, was drawing to its close, and that of nationalism was taking its place, and among the prophets of the new age not the least was Maximilien Robespierre. The new doctrine of national sovereignty, it may be suggested, is the key to the policy of the Committee of Public Safety, and to that of Robespierre as its member. Propaganda, religion, art, the theatre, education, the patriotic appeal — every force that could influence public opinion was put to the task of creating a strong and united national spirit devoted to the triumph of the French Republic over domestic and foreign enemies.

We can now return to the problem which led us into this long discussion of the changes in Robespierre's views on the action of the people and on the relations of government and public opinion. We asked wherein he found the ultimate source of political authority. His earlier answer had been that he found it in the will of the people, which, as he repeatedly declared, was good and just left to itself,[203] and which — unlike the wills of sections or classes with partial interests — was determined only by the principles of justice and humanity.[204] The people, he had maintained in his *Adresse aux Français* of 1791, was the natural bulwark of liberty, being neither corrupted by luxury, pride and ambition, nor agitated by any of the passions dangerous to equality.[205] The evils of society never came from the people, but always from its rulers.[206] A whole people could not be corrupted,[207] for the people were naturally good. Moreover, the people as a whole could not oppose the public good, for to do so would be to oppose its own interest, which was the general interest.[208] 'Le peuple', he was still writing in September 1792, 'veut toujours le bien public, parce qu'il est le peuple; il n'a pas même besoin de vertu, pour être juste; c'est à lui-même qu'il rend justice.'[209] The effect of democratic institutions, he believed, would be to introduce the principles of morality into government.[210] In the belief that practical politics could be the expression of moral truth, he accurately reflected eighteenth-century optimism, and this faith he never abandoned. His attempt, on the eve of his fall, to rally the Jacobins was made in the language he had used at the outset of his political career — 'Il n'est qu'un seul remède à tant de maux, et il consiste dans l'exécution des lois de la nature, qui veulent que tout homme soit juste, et dans la vertu, qui est la base fondamentale de toute société.'[211]

In the earlier stages of the Revolution, then, it is evident that Robespierre identified the sovereignty of the ideal General Will, which Rousseau had proclaimed, with the actual rule of the popular will. This was the justification for his assertion, in language as absolute as ever Sieyes used, that no power on earth had the right of discussing the principles or censoring the desires of a nation.[212] 'Qu'est-ce que la souveraineté, messieurs?' he asked, and replied, 'C'est le pouvoir qui appartient à la nation de régler sa destinée. La nation a sur elle-même, tous les droits que chaque homme a sur sa personne; et la volonté générale gouverne la société, comme la volonté particulière gouverne chaque individu isolé.'[213] But we have seen that by the time of the Convention he had discovered that the voice of the people did not on all occasions accord with what he regarded as the teaching of virtue. Did it follow that the General Will was corrupted? He could not, any more than Rousseau could, accept this as a possibility. 'Quand l'état, près de sa ruine, ne subsiste plus que par une forme illusoire et vaine,' Rousseau had written, 'que le lien social est rompu dans tous les cœurs, que le plus vil intérêt se pare effrontément du nom sacré du bien public, alors la volonté générale devient muette.' He continued, 'S'ensuit-il de là que la volonté générale soit anéantie ou corrompue?' and replied, 'Non: elle est toujours constante, inaltérable et pure.'[214] Such was also Robespierre's faith, but under pressure of facts, as we have seen, he ceased to think of the General Will as the actual will of the people. He could still fall back upon the conception of it as an ideal will, for almost alone among the revolutionaries he understood that by the General Will Rousseau meant a will which was for the general good, and which was not necessarily the will of a majority.[215]

In theory, and even more plainly in practice, therefore, the General Will, instead of being a synonym, became a substitute for the sovereignty of the people. When the General Will became something that had to be imposed on the people through the machinery of Clubs and Committees and Tribunals, with the aid of all the forces that could be used to influence public opinion, the rule of republican virtue, as Robespierre envisaged it, had become incompatible with the sovereignty of the people, and in effect a justification of minority government. 'Il est peu d'hommes généreux', he complained, just before his fall, 'qui aiment la vertu pour elle-même et qui désirent avec ardeur le bonheur du peuple.'[216] It was this kind of political puritanism, and increasing suspicion of the motives of his colleagues, which led to the fatal breach with most of the other members of the Committee of Public Safety. During a conversation in which he attacked the representative system, it is reported that, asked what he would put in its place, he replied, 'Celui de Lycurge.'[217] Virtue, if it did not emerge spontaneously from below, had to be enforced from above. He still talked in the terms he had always employed of the sovereignty of the people, but evidently for him the term 'people', if it retained any meaning, had come to mean something other than was implied in the normal acceptation of the term. During a speech of April 1791, an interrupter had cried, 'J'entends par *peuple* tous les citoyens.' And so do I, cried Robespierre, 'J'entends par *peuple* la généralité des individus qui composent la société,'[218] and was probably not aware that he was saying anything different. In fact, however, by the people Robespierre had never meant the whole population of the country. At the beginning of the Revolution, in common with most of the patriotic party, he had set up the people in opposition to the privileged classes. The people was the *tiers état*, and even within this he distinguished between the people proper and the wealthy bourgeoisie, the 'aristocratie d'argent'. By the time of the Convention ideological distinctions had entered into his definition of the people. 'Tous les hommes raisonnables et magnanimes sont du parti de la République,' he declared; 'tous les êtres perfides et corrompus sont de la faction de vos tyrans.'[219] In other words, all who did not support the Jacobins were enemies of the state.[220]

> Il y a deux peuples en France [he declared in May 1794], l'un est la masse des citoyens, pure, simple, altérée de la justice et amie de la liberté. C'est ce peuple vertueux qui verse son sang pour fonder la liberté, qui impose aux ennemis de dedans et ébranle les trônes des tyrans. L'autre est ce ramas de factieux et d'intrigants; c'est le peuple babillard, charlatan, artificieux, qui se montre partout, qui abuse de tout, qui s'empare des tribunes, et souvent des fonctions publiques, qui se sert de l'instruction que les avantages de l'ancien régime lui ont donnée, pour tromper l'opinion publique. C'est ce peuple de fripons, d'étrangers, de contre-révolutionnaires hypocrites qui se placent entre le peuple français et ses représentants, pour tromper l'un et calomnier les autres, pour entraver leurs opérations, tourner contre le bien public les lois les plus utiles et les vérités les plus salutaires. Tant que cette race impure existera, la république sera malheureuse et précaire.[221]

It is clear that Robespierre's definition of the people was now strictly limited by his conception of political virtue. The sovereignty of the people was a synonym for the rule of the virtuous. He had, as we have implied, from the beginning inclined to the belief that moral reform should precede political. 'Régénérons les mœurs publiques', he said in 1790, 'sans lesquelles il n'est point de liberté,'[222] and in the speech of May 26th, 1794, he mourned, 'Les lois sont à faire, les maximes du gouvernement à assurer, les mœurs à régénérer.'[223] In his last speech of all he confessed that if the Revolution had been a great outpouring of civic virtue, it had also let loose a mass of corruption.[224] Were the virtuous, in the name of freedom, to stand by while the nation fell under the influence of corrupt intriguers? 'Je vois le monde', he said, 'peuplé de dupes et de fripons.'[225] The bearers of the ideal General Will had ceased to be the whole people and had become a small minority of virtuous republicans and patriots. This minority was, of course, the Robespierrist Jacobins. All reasonable and high-minded men, he declared, belonged to their party, all the false and corrupt to the faction of their opponents.[226] Hence the need for successive purges, leading finally to the great law of proscription of 22 prarial, which, although known in advance to other members of the Committee of Public Safety, is probably to be attributed to the inspiration of Robespierre and Couthon, who intended it to be the instrument of, as they hoped, a final purge.[227] As the circle of those he trusted came to be drawn more and more narrowly, it became impossible to distinguish between what Robespierre called the will of the people and his own will. From an early stage in the Revolution he had identified himself with the people. 'Je ne suis ni le courtisan, ni le modérateur, ni le tribun, ni le défenseur du peuple,' he said, 'je suis peuple moi-même!'[228] His great admirer, Hamel, truly describes him as, at the end, 'retranché dans sa conscience comme dans une forteresse impénétrable'.[229] Critics might well feel that, starting as a tribune of the people, he had become, in the language of Aulard, the high priest of a political orthodoxy, who excommunicated all who swerved even a millimetre from the straight line. Yet he himself, adds Aulard, constantly altered his policy to suit altered conditions. In the presence of such vacillations Aulard characterizes his insistence on political orthodoxy as 'odious hypocrisy'.[230]

Here we might end, but it is too crude an explanation, though a familiar one. Robespierre's ultimate political standpoint can be accounted for on the basis of his theoretical principles and practical circumstances, without bringing in hypotheses about his character. The position he arrived at was the logical consequence of that from which he started, and it was at the same time the birth of a new, and as yet unnamed, political conception. It was not specifically formulated by Robespierre; it was a practical reaction to circumstances; but here was the first appearance of that theory of the *élite* which has been closely associated historically with the rise of the idea of national sovereignty, and which, expounded in diverse forms by different schools of political thought, has played a prominent part in political theory and in practical political developments since the Revolution and up to the present day.

We should be mistaken, however, in concluding that because Robespierre came to this in the end, he had abandoned his democratic ideals, and was willingly or consciously playing the tyrant. On a phrase attributed to Robespierre by the *Moniteur* — 'les comités ne tiennent que de la patrie leurs pouvoirs'[231] — Michelet comments, 'Précisément comme l'empereur Napoléon';[232] but as Hamel has pointed out, the fuller account of the speech in the *Journal des débats* does not give this phrase and is capable of no such interpretation.[233] The truth is, that at the end, as at the beginning of his political career, the creation and preservation of political liberty remained Robespierre's prime aim. After his fear of the monarchy had declined, the establishment of a corrupt oligarchy of wealth, such as ruled England, seemed to him the imminent danger.[234] Subsequently, and especially after the war had broken out, his fears were directed towards the menace of military dictatorship.[235]

> Songez [he wrote in May 1792, in the first number of *Le Défenseur de la Constitution*] à l'ascendant que peuvent usurper, au milieu d'une révolution, ceux qui disposent des forces de l'état; consultez l'expérience des nations, et représentez-vous quelle seroit la puissance d'un chef de parti, habile à capter la bienveillance des soldats, si, le peuple étant épuisé, affamé, fatigué, les plus zélés patriotes égorgés, le roi même désertant encore une fois son poste, au sein des horreurs de la guerre civile, entouré de tous les corps militaires dont on a couvert la surface de l'empire, il se montroit à la France, avec l'air d'un libérateur, et toute la force des partis réunis contre l'égalité.[236]

His last word, in his speech of 8 thermidor, was to warn the Convention against the same menace of military dictatorship. 'Laissez flotter', he said, 'un moment les rênes de la révolution, vous verrez le despotisme militaire s'en emparer.'[237] The prophecy was not false, though the process was to be a more gradual one than he had imagined. Modern research has shown how little he himself was a dictator in the Committee of Public Safety. His last speech was his defence against the charge of personal tyranny, and one which his opponents found it difficult to refute, except by shouting him down. 'Ils m'appellent tyran,' he said. 'Si je l'étais, ils ramperaient à mes pieds, je les gorgerais d'or, je leur assurerais le droit de commettre tous les crimes, et ils seraient reconnaissants.'[238] This was his last word, and history has in this respect vindicated his reputation from the self-interested perversions of the Thermidoreans.

The interest in the career and ideas of Robespierre for the historian, and particularly the historian of political ideas, lies in their value as illustrating the theoretical and practical difficulties involved in the application of the principle of democratic sovereignty. No one at the time of the Revolution went as far as Robespierre in stating what were later to be recognized as the essential conditions of the democratic state. His draft declaration of rights, declares his most authoritative biographer, 'stands out above the flood of revolutionary talk like a beacon ... It illuminates the Revolution, and it explains the greatness of Robespierre.'[239] Universal franchise, equality of rights regardless of race or religion, payment for public service to enable rich and poor alike to hold office, publicity for legislative debates, a national system of education, the use of taxation to smooth out economic inequalities, recognition of the economic responsibilities of society to the individual, the right of national autonomy, religious liberty, local self-government — such were some of the principles for which he stood, and which are now taken for granted in democratic societies. But underlying these were the fundamental ideas of the sovereignty of the people and the rule of the General Will. It was in the course of his attempt to reconcile these basic principles with one another, and with the practical policies that circumstances forced upon him when he attained power as a member of the Committee of Public Safety, that the inconsistencies in Robespierre's political theory emerged. His desperate efforts to maintain consistency bear witness, not to hypocrisy, but to honesty of purpose. If he failed in the effort, he was not to be the last to discover the difficulty of solving the theoretical and practical problems inherent in the principle of popular sovereignty. Conditions in revolutionary France accelerated and intensified the development of contradictions which elsewhere were revealed more slowly, but which gradually came to the front in the course of the next century and a half. To proceed to a further discussion of these problems, however, would be to pass from the field of history to that of contemporary analysis.

# 10

## BRITISH SECRET SERVICE IN FRANCE
### 1784–92

THERE was a general belief in France in 1789, among both royalists and revolutionaries, that the British government was spending money on a large scale for the purpose of stirring up revolution. From Whitehall the Secretary of State for Foreign Affairs, the Marquess of Carmarthen, who succeeded in April 1789 to the title of Duke of Leeds, wrote to the British ambassador at Paris, in July 1789, 'I flatter myself that no one person upon a moment's reflection would give credit to the scandalous reports, respecting this Government having in any shape fomented the disorders either in the Capital or any of the Provinces of France.'[1] He flattered himself too much. When the French ambassador in London, La Luzerne, reported Leeds' expressions of regret that a member of the States General had seen fit to denounce a neighbouring and rival power, by which he obviously meant England, for scattering money among the people during the recent troubles, the ambassador thought that he had 'un air de chagrin affecté'. Though the French ambassador informed Leeds that he regarded the suggestion as quite unreasonable, he wrote to Montmorin, French Minister for Foreign Affairs, that in fact they could not be too watchful, for the conduct of the English would certainly be 'aussi dissimulé qu'intéressé'.[2] Montmorin replied, 'Je m'abstins d'inculper le ministère anglais, parce que je n'ai aucune preuve à sa charge; et il est d'autant plus difficile à en acquérir *que la police n'existe plus.*' Undoubtedly, he added, money had been used widely among the soldiers and the people, from whatever source it had come.[3] He recommended the greatest vigilance to La Luzerne, particularly as there were many French fugitives in London, mostly of evil intention.[4] In October, La Luzerne repeated that in spite of Dorset's protests he was convinced that the British ambassador had employed all means possible to increase the internal troubles in France. He had positive information, he said, that when troops were brought to the neighbourhood of Paris, Dorset assured his Court that this was a mistake and that if the troops were employed they would support the people rather than the king. 'Cet esprit prophétique du duc de Dorset peut assurément faire croire qu'il avoit des données extrêmement positives; et il est difficile d'imaginer comment il eut pû les acquérir s'il ne fut pas lui-même entré dans cette infernale Intrigue.'[5] Among the suspicious characters in London, two whom Montmorin specifically mentioned were Danton and his clerk, Paré.[6] Much has been made of this reference,[7] but apart from Montmorin's suspicions there is no evidence of any kind for the supposition that Danton's presence in London at this time implied any connection with the British government.

Two years later La Luzerne was more cautious in his speculations, writing, in May 1791,

> Quoique assurément je croye à la jalousie et à la malveillance du Ministère anglais et quoique je suis intimement convaincu qu'il employera tous les moyens qui seront en son pouvoir pour perpétuer les troubles de notre intérieur, je ne crois pas cependant qu'il donne aussi ouvertement des secours aux mécontens de notre Gouvernement.[8]

He added a commentary on two notes of denunciation which the French Foreign Minister had sent him on April 24th and 27th.[9]

1. It was alleged that the English agent, Paul Wentworth,[10] was operating in the south of France. La Luzerne commented that Wentworth was believed to be in Holland, though if he were in France he would certainly not be idle.

2. The bankers, Harley and Cameron, it was said, had sent money for the king. La Luzerne observes that it was difficult to know how the informant could have obtained such information, and in any case such kinds of remittances did not pass through the hands of this house but by way of Drummond and Coutts.

3. Field artillery was to be furnished by Wilkinson, many details being given. Anyone, replies La Luzerne, could know that Wilkinson was an ironmaster; but the information provided was too detailed to inspire confidence.

4. Miles Andrews was supplying powder. The answer was that

though he was a powder manufacturer his experiments had not been approved by the British government and he was not employed by them.

5. Brown was to supply 20,000 muskets. La Luzerne observed that Brown had certainly bought several thousand rejected guns at the Tower and had supplied them to the Belgians during their insurrection; he had lost £2,500 in this speculation. Someone who was acquainted with the firm of Brown had assured La Luzerne that he knew of nothing bearing any relation to the facts alleged.

6. The vessel *William*, under Captain Smith, supposed to be sailing for the East Indies, was in fact sailing for Dordrecht with military supplies. La Luzerne characterized this statement as false. Such a subterfuge would in any case have been quite unnecessary, as within the last month three ships laden with arms and munitions had left England for Memel.

7. Harley, Cameron and Van Eck had received a contract engaging the lands of the Prince de Condé for 350,000 livres sterling. This was false, La Luzerne said: he had this assurance from a reliable Frenchman who was a member of the house of Van Eck.

8. Troops were being raised in Ireland. La Luzerne observed that there was at this moment in fact a severe press for sailors, but there was only recruitment for the regiments which were actually in the country.[11]

The French ambassador added that he had been given practically the same information by one Browne-Dignam,[12] and suspected that the informant in Paris might be the same person; if so, he was a man who had spent three years in the hulks for some crime, since then he had been a spy in Holland, and was at the moment unemployed.[13]

Barthélemy, who had been at the French embassy in London for several years, and acted as *chargé* in November–December 1791 after La Luzerne's death, either out of natural Anglophobia, or to curry favour with his masters at Paris, was the author of a series of bitter dispatches on British policy, which were written in a far more hostile tone than those of La Luzerne. He accused the British Cabinet of 'the most perfidious machiavellianism'.[14] The Court of London, he wrote in November 1791, has followed a system of dissimulation 'porté à un point peut-être inconnu jusqu' ici au Cabinet britannique'.[15] What it feared most was the restoration of order in France.[16] The same opinion is reiterated in Barthélemy's *Mémoires*.[17]

Such views found an echo in French journals, both royalist and revolutionary. One example, out of many, is provided by Camille Desmoulins, who wrote:

> On ne peut nier aujourd'hui que Pitt, dans notre révolution de 1789, n'ait voulu acquitter sur Louis XVI, la lettre de change tirée en 1641 par Richelieu sur Charles I ... Pitt avoit encore à prendre sa revanche des secours donnés par Vergennes aux insurgens Anglo-américains ... notre révolution de 1789 avoit été une affaire arrangée entre le ministère britannique et une partie de la minorité de la noblesse.[18]

The refugee journalist Peltier, writing in London in 1795, observed in an introduction to an article reprinted from Richer de Serizi's *Accusateur public*, that it was *de rigueur* to assume that Pitt was the author of the financial crisis of 1788, of the convocation of the States General, the conspiracy of the Duke of Orleans and all the subsequent rebellions. Richer de Serizi himself wrote, 'L'adroit ministre du cabinet de Saint James brûlait d'acquitter sur la tête de *Louis*, les sommes que l'inhumain, mais fameux cardinal de Richelieu avait payées à Hampden.'[19]

The same theme appears in a host of memoirs. According to the unreliable Mme Campan the queen said to her, 'Je ne prononce pas le nom de *Pitt*, que la petite mort ne me passe sur le dos.'[20] Mme Campan herself wrote, 'Cet argent, que répandirent les agens cachés, n'était pas celui du duc d'Orléans: ses finances étaient épuisées alors; c'était celui de l'Angleterre. Le parlement accorda au ministre tous les subsides qu'il demandait, et le dispensait de rendre compte. La destination et l'emploi de ces fonds ne peuvent être mis en problème aujourd'hui.'[21] The Diamond Necklace Cardinal's secretary, the Abbé Georgel, or at least the compiler of his memoirs, was convinced that Pitt had poured out millions to provoke troubles in France.[22] There would be no point in piling up further illustrations of what was an almost universal opinion.

In the early historians of the Revolution there is rather more caution. Thus Lacretelle, after passing in review the arguments of those who accused Pitt and those who absolved him from the charge of fomenting the Revolution, concludes with a verdict of unproven.[23] Thiers, on the other hand, attributes to England from the beginning the sinister design of weakening France by paying revolutionary agitators, while admitting reluctantly that no direct evidence has been revealed in the course of time, which, he optimistically adds, usually reveals everything.[24] Since then many French historians, who as a class naturally suffer from an inability to appreciate the invariable purity of British motives, have repeated the same charge. Among recent writers the more scholarly have refrained from drawing conclusions where there is no evidence, but others have not felt equally inhibited.[25] Indeed, since the condition of a secret service is to be secret, lack of evidence has itself been taken as a sort of proof, the absent documentary support being replaced by what French law-courts cherish, 'une conviction intime' of the guilt of the accused.

The British reply to such charges at the time was an indignant repudiation. Thus in a letter of July 29th, 1789, the British ambassador, Dorset, protested to Montmorin against the unjust suspicion, which had been expressed even in the National Assembly, that the British government had been fomenting disorder in France.[26] Such a protest, by itself, does not prove anything. It is more convincing when we find Dorset writing to Leeds, 'It is unnecessary that I should tell Your Grace how entirely destitute of foundation is this as well as all other reports of the same kind.'[27] Leeds' reply has already been mentioned.[28] On the same day he was writing to the secretary at the Paris embassy, Lord Robert Fitzgerald: 'The French, I find, suspect, or at least wish to have it supposed that we have done by them what they would have done by us in similar circumstances; they are completely wrong in this idea.'[29]

It is difficult to associate any deep-laid plot with such a social butterfly as Dorset, who was chiefly concerned about his own personal safety. By an injudicious attempt to demonstrate his innocence, however, he merely succeeded in increasing suspicion. Michelet attributed Dorset's revelation of the existence of a plot against Brest to the British ambassador's alarm at the discovery of a letter which he had written to Artois.[30] In protesting, on July 26th, 1789, against the rumour that the British government was intending to take advantage of the disorders in France and had even posted a fleet off the French coast for this purpose, Dorset reminded Montmorin of the conversations at the beginning of June in which he warned the French ministry of a conspiracy to seize Brest.[31] The facts seem to be that about the end of May 1789 the British ambassador had been approached by an *abbé*, whose name is not given, for although the emissary offered to reveal his name and address Dorset had declined to hear them.[32] He did, however, agree to a second interview and wrote to London for instructions. Leeds replied to him:

> The very extraordinary proposal which has been made to your Grace, was received in the manner you must have supposed it would be. The circumstance of your Grace having agreed to a second interview with the person who was deputed to you, renders it impossible to give any information upon the subject to the French Court, till after the abbé shall have received your answer expressive of our determination to have no concern in so wicked a project. As soon as there is no danger of the man's being discovered your Grace may perhaps with propriety put the French Court upon their guard in respect to Brest, stating your having received accounts from England of a rumour of such a design being in contemplation. ... At the same time we wish to give our decided opinion against being any way concerned in this business we are equally anxious that no step whatever should be taken which can possibly endanger the safety of those who have thought proper to offer themselves to your Grace upon the subject.[33]

Dorset replied that he would take great care not to expose the individuals involved in the plot, that it was not intended to be put into operation before November at the earliest, and that though the *abbé* promised to return he had seen nothing more of him.[34]

The revelation of the design on Brest brought no advantage to Dorset on any side. Montmorin wrote to La Luzerne, 'Quant à ce que M. le duc de Dorset m'a dit concernant Brest, je ne l'ai regardé que comme une confidence affectée, et qui ne méritoit aucune attention.'[35] On the other hand, those who were involved in the plot believed that the English had betrayed them. A correspondent from Vannes, on August 21st, declared: 'Des lettres particulières assurent qu'on a arrêté le chef du complot contre Brest, et que ce sont les Anglais qui l'ont livré; nous attendons demain la confirmation de cette nouvelle.'[36] A royalist propagandist, writing in 1796, even interpreted the whole affair as a scheme by the British ambassador to increase the hatred for the *noblesse* in France by inventing the report that a group of Breton gentlemen proposed to burn the port of Brest.[37] Dorset might have remembered that there was a French proverb, 'Qui s'excuse, s'accuse', but he was guilty of no more than the naivety of supposing that others would credit him with being as simple as in fact he was.

The idea of British implication in the Brest plot can clearly be eliminated, but in respect to the alleged British instigation of the revolutionary movement in France we have only suspicions on one side and denials on the other, neither a very sound basis for judgment; nor is it quite satisfactory to argue from the general attitude of Pitt and the government to the Revolution, though this is difficult, or impossible, to reconcile with any support of the revolutionaries. As has been said above, lack of evidence, in the matter of secret service, is not a convincing ground of argument. Fortunately, in fact, the evidence is not lacking, it has simply never been looked for, and it is possible to discover from the records the actual nature and scope of British secret service in France in these years. It must be premised, in the first place, that such activities were not pursued for love alone. The first line of inquiry, therefore, is to see how much money was spent on foreign secret service. This is possible after 1782, when an Act dealing with the Civil List laid down specific conditions regulating expenditure upon this object. The relevant clause runs:

> That when it shall be deemed expedient by the Commissioners of his Majesty's Treasury, or the High Treasurer, for the time being, to issue, or in any Manner to direct the Payment of any Sum or Sums of Money from the Civil List Revenues, for foreign Secret Service, the same shall be issued and paid to one of his Majesty's Principal Secretaries of State, or to the first Commissioner of the Admiralty: and the said Secretary or Secretaries of State, or first Commissioner of the

Admiralty, shall, for his Discharge at the Exchequer, within three Years from the issuing the said Money, produce the receipt of his Majesty's Minister, Commissioner or Consul in Foreign Parts, or of any Commander in Chief or other Commander of his Majesty's Navy or Land Forces, to whom the said Money shall have been sent or given, that the same hath been received for the Purpose for which the same hath been issued.[38]

The new procedure was put into practice at once. When the under-secretary to the new Foreign Department asked for payment of a bill for secret service, the reply came from the treasury, on August 9th, 1782, that henceforth payments for this purpose could only be made to the two secretaries of state and the first commissioner of the Admiralty.[39] This condition seems to have been rigidly observed. The production of receipts may have been less systematically followed; at any rate, soon after Grenville, who was a stickler for correctness, became Foreign Secretary, he issued a circular reminding ministers abroad that he was under the obligation to obtain receipts from them for secret service payments and produce them at the exchequer within three years.[40]

The details of expenditure on foreign secret service between 1784 and 1792 provide an important indication of the scope of the service. They may be derived from a considerable variety of sources, including Parliamentary Papers, Civil List Accounts, Treasury Warrants and Order Books, Audit Office Accounts and Discharges, Foreign Office registers and so on. In 1786 the annual charge on the Civil List for foreign secret service was estimated at £25,000,[41] and the normal expenditure over the period 1784–92 did not differ greatly from this estimate, as a summary of the figures obtainable from a considerable number of different sources will make clear.

*Foreign Secret Service Accounts*

*1784*

| | | |
|---|---|---|
| Carmarthen (F.O.) | £19,700 | + fees £1,026 0s. 6d. |
| Sydney (H.O.) | £5,965 0s. 6d. | + fees £315 0s. 6d. |
| Total | £27,006 1s. 8d.[42] | |
| Civil List: | £27,006 1s. 8d.[43] | |

*1785*

| | | |
|---|---|---|
| Carmarthen (F.O.) | £29,300 | + fees £1,524 3s. 6d. |
| Sydney (H.O.) | £1,000 | + fees £54 7s. 0d. |
| Total | £31,878 10s. 6d.[44] | |
| Civil List: | £31,878 10s. 6d.[45] | |

*1786*

| | | |
|---|---|---|
| Carmarthen (F.O.) | £23,000 | + fees £1,200 14s. 0d. |
| Sydney (H.O.) | £1,499 14s. 7d. | + fees £77 8s. 0d.[46] |
| Total | £25,727 16s. 7d.[47] | |
| Civil List: | £25,727 16s. 7d.[48] | |

*1787*

| | | |
|---|---|---|
| Carmarthen (F.O.) | £89,100 | + fees £4,736 16s. 0d.[49] |
| ibid. | £89,100[50] | |
| Sydney (H.O.) | £4,000 | + fees £211 5s. 0d.[51] |
| Civil List: | £39,884 1s. 0d.[52] | |
| ibid. | £98,050 1s. 0d.[53] | |

of which sum £58,166 was repaid to the Civil List in 1788,[54] leaving £39,884 1s. 0d.

*1788*

| | | |
|---|---|---|
| Carmarthen (F.O.) | £19,438 15s. 0d. | + fees £1,015 6s. 6d. |
| making | £20,454 1s. 6d. | |
| ibid. ('to be replaced') | | |
| | £182,000 | + fees £9,342 13s. 0d. |
| making | £191,342 13s. 0d. | |
| Total to Carmarthen | £211,796 14s. 6d.[55] | |

In T. 53/59 the sum paid to Carmarthen was £19,438 15s. 0d. with additional sums of £91,000, £45,000 and £46,000, making £182,000. These figures are without the fees. In F.O. 366/426, *Government Offices, Treasury 1788–1792*, Carmarthen's foreign secret service for 1788 amounts to £17,688 15s. 0d.: the detailed payments here correspond to those in T. 53/59, except that one entry, for £1,750, is missing. The addition of this sum would bring the total into correspondence with the sums given in T. 53/59 and T. 38/168. The three large sums amounting to £182,000 are not given in this entry book.

| | |
|---|---|
| Sydney (H.O.) | £1,000 + fees £54 6s. 6d.[56] |
| Total for both offices | £212,851 1s. 0d.[57] |

Civil List: £212,851 1s. 0d.
  repayment £191,342 13s. 0d.[58]

sanctioned by Parliament on June 9th, 1789.[59] The sum remaining was thus £21,508 8s. 0d.

Civil List: £21,508 8s. 0d.[60]

*1789*
Leeds (Carmarthen)
  (F.O.) £29,550 + fees £1,549 15s. 0d.[61]
Sydney (H.O.) £1,000 + fees £54 6s. 6d.[62]
Total £32,154 1s. 6d.[63]
Civil List: £32,154 1s. 6d.[64]

*1790*
Leeds (F.O.) £21,900 + fees £1,555 4s. 6d.[65]
Grenville (H.O.) £3,000 + fees £165 16s. 0d.[66]

Another register gives Grenville's expenditure on foreign secret service, February 1790–February 1791, as £3,460 3s. 0d.[67] His Audit Office roll, February–December 1790, is for £3,165 16s. 0d.[68]

Grenville's account from the Audit Office for foreign secret service as Principal Secretary of State for the Home Department, from February 24th, 1790, to his removal to the other Principal Secretaryship on June 8th, 1791, was £3,780. It is to be presumed that this money all passed through the hands of one of the undersecretaries, Evan Nepean, to whom it is also put down in the Audit Office account.[69] The total foreign secret service expenditure of the two offices in 1790 thus amounts to £26,221 0s. 6d., including fees, and this is the figure which appears in the Civil List accounts.[70]

Civil List: £26,221 10s. 6d.[71]

*1791*
  Leeds (at F.O. to June 8th, 1791) £8,945 9s. 6d.[72]
  Leeds (F.O.) £8,500.[73]
  Grenville (H.O. to June 8th, F.O. June 8th–December)
    £13,299 4s. 3d.[74]
  Total for Leeds and Grenville £22,244 4s. 9d.[75]

Other figures given elsewhere for Grenville are

£13,100,[76] £13,299 4s. 3d.[77]
Grenville (H.O. January–June 8th 1791) £1,579 19s;[78]
(F.O. June 8th–December 1791) £11,850;[79]
(F.O. June 8th 1791–February 1792)
£10,896 5s. 3d.[80]

Grenville's expenditure on foreign secret service at the Home Office, from June 1789–June 1791, is given as £5,040 2s. 0d.,[81] whereas the total reached by adding together the separate figures for 1790 and 1791 is £4,745 15s. 0d.;[82] but these entries may include some payments made in January–February 1791. No payments for foreign secret service to Dundas at the Home Office June 8th–December 1791 have been found.

    Civil List:         £22,244 4s. 9d.[83]

*1792*
    Grenville (F.O.) £10,323 2s. 0d.[84]

Sums attributed to Grenville in other registers are

£9,800,[85] £9,794 9s. 0d.[86] and £8,500[87]
Dundas (H.O.) £4,675 10s. 10d.[88]
Total for both offices £14,998 12s. 10d.[89]
Civil List:        £14,998 12s. 10d.[90]

Minor discrepancies in these figures, some of which are to be explained by the omission or inclusion of the fees and charges of the treasury, are nowhere significant enough to justify a minute examination. On the whole the other sources confirm the figures given in the report of 1798–9 admirably. The Home Office expenditure on foreign secret service over the nine years averages some £2,600 a year, while, deducting the amounts that were repaid to the Civil List for 1787 and 1788, the Foreign Office expenditure averages about £24,000 a year. The additional expenditure in 1787 and 1788 is the feature which naturally calls for explanation. I have examined this in detail in a book on the mission of Sir James Harris to The Hague. Here all that is necessary is to say that the former represents aid to the Orangist party in the United Provinces, and the latter a loan to the Zealand Chamber of the East India Company.

The Admiralty remains to be considered in this connection, but though the first commissioner had the right of expending money for the purpose of foreign secret service, no entries have been found anywhere recording such expenditure for this period. Admiralty payments to Mrs Wolters and the Hakes, who will be mentioned below, are described as pensions in February 1785.[91] It is true that a number of naval officers were engaged on intelligence in France, but in all cases where there is evidence about payments to them the source is Nepean, under-secretary for the Home Department.[92]

The figures for foreign secret service are thus compatible only with activity on a small scale, and it must be remembered that this money covered expenditure for secret service in all countries, so that the amount available for use in France would be still smaller. In addition, it is to be noted that the organization of the secretaries' offices was rudimentary; their staff consisted of two under-secretaries in each office, twelve clerks for Home and ten for Foreign, and a handful of miscellaneous officials — the gazette writer, gazette printer, secretary of the Latin Language, keeper of the State Papers, interpreter of Oriental Languages, collector and transmitter of State Papers, embellisher, decypherers, and deputies for such of these as held their offices as sinecures.[93] Moreover, secret service was not a matter within the province of any officials under the rank of the Principal Secretary of State and his two under-secretaries. Indeed, for the greater part of these years, in fact up to 1789, there was only one under-secretary, Fraser, at the Foreign Office, the reason whereof appearing in a letter of Carmarthen to Pitt, who had wanted him to appoint Ryder as under-secretary.

One of the two Under-secretaries is usually the confidential friend of the Secretary of State and the other generally a person of character and discretion taken from the Office itself and this arrangement appears in every respect a very proper one. The moment poor Fraser's health rendered his return to the Office doubtful the propriety of restoring the old number of Under-secretaries occurred to me, as indeed the only reason for not having done it before was my regard for Fraser, and the advantage he derived from being sole under-secretary was of such considerable importance to him and his family, as to make me unwilling to make any change in his situation in the Office.[94]

The smallness of the sums spent on foreign secret service, and the fact that in London all such business had to pass through the over-burdened hands of the under-secretaries, might lead us to suppose that it could not have been on a large scale; but only a study of the actual operations of the departments concerned can take the subject out of the realm of speculation. I propose to begin with the Foreign Office, as the most logical centre for the operation of what foreign secret service there was. With a single exception Foreign Office espionage in France was conducted indirectly through its ministers abroad. The exception is the so-called Rotterdam agency. As I have dealt with this elsewhere, all that need be said here is that the active operations of Mrs Wolters and the Hakes from Rotterdam came to an end with the arrival of Sir James Harris at The Hague. In January 1785 the under-secretary of the Foreign Office wrote to Harris that it was proposed to discontinue payments for Mrs Wolters' alleged correspondents, though the principals would continue to receive pensions; any further intelligence they had to provide should go through the hands of Harris.[95] Letters of intelligence continued to be sent by Hake until June 1785,[96] but Harris thought them of no value and after this they came to an end.

Apart from the Hake-Wolters correspondence, which is of no significance after the conclusion of the War of American Independence, most intelligence relating to France for the period 1784–92 seems to have come in not directly but by way of the ministers abroad. The Paris embassy is the obvious source for investigation in the first place. The instructions of Dorset, when he was sent out in 1784, directed him to use his utmost endeavours to discover any French plans for action in the East Indies, the terms of treaties, in existence or projected, between France and other European states, and whether any foreign ships of war were in French ports.[97] Reports of suspected expeditions to the East Indies, of the state and disposition of the French fleet, and of the defences of the French coast, were in fact the points on which intelligence was almost exclusively concentrated. The agents employed by the British embassy to secure this information were neither numerous nor very effective.

The first one we meet is named de St Marc. A letter of February 25th, 1785, from Grenville to Carmarthen indicates that his first approach had probably been made to Pitt and in London. It continues by outlining

the terms on which M. de St. M. proposed to be employed and on which Mr. Pitt imagined that it might be worth while to try him for a short time. They were that he was in the first instance to receive 100 guineas for the information which he is to give *here*, and if it appeared satisfactory 100 gs. more.

That he was to be employed at Paris to give intelligence to Mr. Hailes at an allowance of 60 gs. a month for three months and at the end of that time of 250 gs. if Govt. was satisfied with his services.

He states that it will be in his power to give copies of all material dispatches sent by the French Court to India, and also to furnish correct accounts of the number and distribution of the ships at Rochefort.[98]

Carmarthen wrote to Hailes on March 2nd, 1785, passing on these suggestions and informing him that he would receive a visit from de St Marc, adding that he was already known to the Duke of Dorset. In order that their relations might be kept secret he suggested that 'our friend Lady Margaret Fordyce' might permit them to meet *chez elle*.[99] On March 17th, Hailes informed Carmarthen that de St Marc had arrived in Paris and had asked for money to finance a journey to Brest and Rochefort.[100] On May 12th and 19th, Hailes forwarded information provided by de St Marc about these ports, with more on June 2nd and 9th.[101] On July 7th the agent was pressing for payment of his 'conditional gratification'.[102] Carmarthen replied, 'You may quiet Mr. St. M.'s fears as his allowance is to go on for three months more, and if we are satisfied at that period, then to be continued.'[103] The next report on his activities was less satisfactory. Hailes wrote, on August 11th,

I have only seen St. Marc once within these three weeks, that is to say, since I gave him the last hundred guineas. He is either afraid, or indolent, or unwilling. He has a very pretty Englishwoman with him that he calls his wife, but I rather suspect from her appearance that she is his concubine, and I think the style in which he lives is hardly warranted by his frequent complaints of distress, and his precarious existence. I cannot help doubting his having been to Rochefort as he pretended. I really do not think he shows any activity, and I find him uninformed upon the most common topics in public affairs.

Carmarthen replied,

There is great reason to suspect Mr St. M. is no spy at all, or a double one, in either of which cases I think the sooner we are rid of him the better.[104]

Finally, on September 1st, Hailes forwarded some scraps of naval information, saying that they were all the agent had afforded him for the last hundred guineas and proposing to pay him off.[105]

One other agent of the Paris embassy is identified by name. Hailes sent to Carmarthen, on October 9th, 1787, a note on the proposed disposition of troops on the Atlantic and Channel coasts, charts of the coast of Normandy, and a manuscript volume entitled *Reconnaissance Militaire de la Normandie*, explanatory of the charts, all 'executed with the most minute exactness'.[106] A private letter of the same date explained that the source of this intelligence was an artillery captain 'resident at Versailles, and in immediate relations with the principal secretaries of the War and Marine departments'. His name, it appeared subsequently, was de la Fond. Hailes promised him £250 and suggested taking him into regular pay.[107] Carmarthen said that the information was well worth the sum promised and suggested that more be invited with the promise of further payments.[108] On October 18th, Hailes forwarded further material from the same source,[109] and on October 25th enclosed a receipt from de la Fond for 6,000 livres, adding that he was

certainly the most intelligent person I have met with in his line ... I shall beg leave to recommend him as a golden key to the ports of this country ... I have directed him to come to me from Versailles every Wednesday, and to meet me in the

Thuilleries; I have chosen that day as it comes between the ordinary arrival and departure of the messenger.[110]

Dorset, in a dispatch of the same date, was characteristically cautious:

M. de la Fond seems a very intelligent fellow and may be of use, but I have always disliked having anything to do with this sort of gentry especially in such a watchful country as this.[111]

On December 6th, 1787, Hailes sent a memorial on French plans in India by M. de Brasseur, former *intendant* of the Île de France, which, he said, had been procured by de la Fond, for which he had been promised 'something permanent or considerable'.[112] Here, however, information on this agent comes to an end.

There were evidently also a few other spies who are not mentioned by name. In March 1785 Dorset wrote that he had advanced £200 for intelligence respecting Toulon, and hoped to be able to provide similar information about the naval forces at Brest for a smaller sum.[113] In May 1786 he expressed his regret that an informant he was expecting from Brest had not arrived,[114] and a month later wrote, 'the person who promised to provide me intelligence from Brest has *levanted*'.[115] The British government was particularly interested in the new port which the French were building at Cherbourg, and which was destined not to be completed for many years. Eden, who had been sent out for the commercial negotiations, was called on for assistance in this connection. Carmarthen wrote to him,

Although Government is already in possession of many particulars respecting the nature and progress of the works at Cherbourg, I shall very thankfully receive any additional information you may be able to collect respecting that object.[116]

The embassy at Paris also occasionally forwarded information on the French ports from British naval officers; these, however, will be dealt with subsequently under a different heading.

Dorset's temporary successor, Lord Robert Fitzgerald, only appears as being involved in one matter of espionage. On April 9th, 1790, he forwarded to Carmarthen an anonymous offer of information.[117] Carmarthen warned him to be discreet,[118] and Fitzgerald replied,

> I judged it best not to hazard expense to Government for information which, in the present state of affairs in this country, could not be of very great importance to us.[119]

The Revolution, indeed, appeared to have eliminated all present danger from France, and neither the papers of Fitzgerald, nor those of his successor Gower, provide any material for our subject.

After Paris, the next obvious object for investigation is the activities of the British minister at the neighbouring capital of Brussels, which so often afforded a view-point whence events in France could be observed. This minister was Lord Torrington, by all accounts a perfect nincompoop. However, up to 1784 he was apparently receiving as large a sum as £1,000 a year for secret service expenditure.[120] His quarter's accounts, from January to March 1785, consist of three entries — 'Chev. fl. £105', his correspondents £157 10s., and Torrington's own expenses £70.[121] It is easy to see that there is no surplus out of £1,000 a year for any other expenses, and the one agent mentioned here practically monopolized Torrington's secret service allowance. The 'Chev. fl.' was the Chevalier Floyd.[122] He claimed that his employment had been authorized by Fox,[123] but also, in 1785, that he had been in the service for eight years, which would date his first employment from about 1777.[124] Whatever his service may have been during the American war, in 1784 Carmarthen had come to the conclusion that Floyd was 'not a person in whom an *unlimited* confidence should be reposed'.[125] When Sir James Harris passed through Brussels on the way to take up his appointment at The Hague, in December 1784, he conveyed a message to Torrington from the Foreign Secretary to the effect that his secret service allowance was to be drastically reduced.[126] In a woeful letter Torrington wrote back to Carmarthen that it only amounted to £1,000 a year, 'N.B. Purchasing copies of papers excepted', and sprang to the defence of Floyd. 'In respect to the Chevalier — *I can assure your lordship! (whatsoever you may have heard to the contrary)* He is *Invaluable* — In our *Line* — whosoever knows and has seen him work with me, will allow he richly earns, his £400 pr. annum.'[127] Floyd wrote in his own defence to Carmarthen, 'Ainsi donc le fruit de plus de huit ans de sollicitudes et d'argent que j'ai dépensé est donc perdu.'[128] He asked that at least the expenses of the current quarter, and £250 owing to him, should be paid.[129] Carmarthen replied, 'J'ignore entièrement, Monsieur, aucune demande que voux pourriez avoir sur le Gouvernement, aiant seulement été employé par My lord Torrington qui n'a pas manqué de recevoir les sommes specifiés dans les differens comptes qu'il a envoyé ici.'[130] Floyd's claim for current expenses was apparently allowed, for Torrington wrote to Carmarthen in April,

> I certainly! had misunderstood your Lordship's meaning, respecting the Secret Service Money. I am very glad to find I was so Mistaken: In consequence! I send your Lordship enclosed — the Expenses incurred Last Quarter. Concerning the Chev. Floyd — that affair is over. Sorry I am to find! his Secret Intelligence has not proved so correct as Government expected.[131]

It was probably to Floyd that Carmarthen referred in a letter of April 26, 1785, to Hailes, in which he said that de St Marc seemed 'as perfectly useless as C f d, who by not having answered my letter of the 5th is I hope either dead or run away'.[132] Torrington had already answered Carmarthen, 'The chev. fl. is now gone and *his* expenses are at an end.'[133]

Torrington continued to forward news bulletins from Paris and other places,[134] but I have not been able to identify their author. An unsigned letter from London, of November 23, 1789, may represent an attempt by Floyd to recover his position as an informant. It refers to the interruption of the correspondence from Brussels by the opening of letters at Ghent by the Patriots. The writer says that in these circumstances he has ventured to come to London to offer his services.[135] Whether the overture was from Floyd or not, he certainly made such a proposal later, for in a draft of September 1791 the Foreign Office regrets its inability to accept the offer.[136] The unfortunate Floyd must now have been in serious financial straits, for he wrote to Pitt asking for aid from the address of the King's Bench Prison.[137] In March 1793, a pathetic begging letter came from his wife at Boulogne.[138] Finally, in 1793-4 Floyd is found writing several times to Pitt and giving extracts from letters from Paris.[139] He seems never to have been re-employed and this is really the end of him, so far as the records go.

Torrington left Brussels in July 1789, and though Colonel Gardiner, who had a confidential mission to Brussels from 1789 to 1792, provided the government with intelligence about developments in the Austrian Netherlands, I have found no trace of any information concerning France in his papers. Brussels only becomes again an important centre for the collection of such information after the withdrawal of the British ambassador from Paris in August 1792.

Also in the Netherlands, but at Liège, the activities of that curious individual, William Augustus Miles, need to be mentioned, for the edition of his *Correspondence* does not quite tell the whole story.[140] Miles, a gentleman of modest but independent means, who had achieved some reputation as a publicist, settled, in 1783, in the bishopric of Liège, whence he wrote to the marquess of Buckingham offering to communicate information to the Government. Pitt, to whom the offer was transmitted, apparently accepted it, though there do not appear to have been any immediate results.[141] Miles's *Correspondence* states that in 1787 he was entrusted with a confidential mission at Liège by Carmarthen.[142] The nature of this mysterious mission is not revealed, but it is natural to assume that it had some political content. It proves, however, to have been a private rather than public commission. Miles was asked to deliver a letter to the Prince Bishop of Liège and, in connection with this, to bring back a young boy, Lord Gormanston, to England.[143] As this affair clearly does not fall into the category of foreign secret service, the whole complicated story need only be outlined briefly. The young Lord Gormanston succeeded to the title as twelfth viscount on the death of his father in December 1786.[144] It is to be presumed that he was taken to Liège by his uncle, Mr Preston, to be brought up in his father's religion. Mr Preston was protected by the Prince Bishop of Liège, 'full of apprehension for the safety of the child's soul which would be endangered, he said, by his return to England, where he would be forced to change his religion'.[145] After a good deal of fruitless negotiation, by the summer of 1788 Miles was proposing to resort to kidnapping. He informed Carmarthen that 'three men of determined resolution set off this morning at three o'clock'.[146] Apparently their resolution was not enough, for a month later Miles was writing that he had two other schemes for securing possession of the youthful peer.[147] In September he proposed 'to set off this evening or early to-morrow incog. for Liège whence I hope to return with Lord Gormanston in a few days'.[148] Poor Miles, in this as in other matters, was incurably optimistic and incurably unsuccessful.

Of slightly greater interest are Miles's relations at Liège with a democratic journalist named Lebrun, editor of the *Journal Général de l'Europe*.[149] Lebrun's agitation against the Prince Bishop led to his expulsion from Liège, but he continued to edit his paper from the neighbouring town of Hervé, in Austrian territory. His activities there, however, aroused the hostility of the States of Brabant and police were sent to arrest him. He escaped in a destitute condition and Miles supplied him with twenty guineas, as he informed Carmarthen,

> which money I humbly hope your Lordship will not think ill applied when I inform you that the editor Monsieur Le Brun has for these twelve months past availed himself of every opportunity to speak of his Majesty's Government and of the English nation in the highest terms of panegyric — that of all the foreign editors he is the only one who has not made it a point to decry the British Government. In the commencement of his paper he fell into the common error that we were ruined by our taxes, and must infallibly become bankrupts. This is the language of all the editors, who from the *defined policy* of France are all Frenchmen. I took the trouble to write this man a very civil letter explaining to him his mistake and a few well timed attentions effectually won him to the British interest. The pecuniary trifle that I sent him has fixed him for ever, and as he means to return again he will not fail to do justice to his Majesty's councils. I do not mean to make a charge of this to Government. I shall feel myself amply recompensed by having my conduct on this occasion honoured with your Lordship's approbation.[150]

Later in the year Miles made use of Lebrun in his attempt to seize Lord Gormanston by a *coup de main*. A curious letter of September

10th, 1787, from the journalist thanks 'Monsieur' (presumably Miles) and Lord Torrington for their recommendation of him and his journal to Pitt, whom he praises in the most fulsome language.[151] But Miles was, as usual, too optimistic in thinking that he had won Lebrun for ever. The episode would hardly be worth mentioning were it not that this same Lebrun was to be the foreign minister of France who declared war on Great Britain in 1793.

It is clear that Miles's relations with Lebrun were purely personal and unofficial. His ventures into the field of secret service proper were not very momentous. An account which he sent in to Carmarthen in March 1789[152] enumerates them:

> 1787 Oct. 1. An excursion to the Frontier of the principality of Liège on the side of Givet to watch the motions of the French army, at that time said to be under orders to march into Holland . . . £15 15s. 0d.

> 1787 (expense for paper, postage and a journey to London and back)

> August. Expenses incurred on a journey to the frontier of Liège and that neighbourhood on the side of Givet and Maubeuge on being informed that magazines were forming, and that it was apprehended the encampments at St. Omers were intended to facilitate the march of a French army into the United Provinces . . . . . . £35 15s. 0d.

> September. A journey to Cologne for the purpose of examining if any magazines were forming on the Rhine as was reported . . . . . £20 10s. 0d.

> 1789 January (a journey through Flanders)  £50 0s. 0d.
> March Expenses of going to London
> Journey to Frankfurt  + £44 2s. 0d.

The total claim of Miles under the heading of secret service from September 25th, 1787, to March 25th, 1789, was £487, and there is no reason to believe that any of his journeys, except perhaps his return to London and subsequent departure for Frankfurt, were commissioned by the British government or were other than private ventures. He also dabbled in the domestic politics of

Liège, even to the point of sending Carmarthen a plan for a revolution in the bishopric, which he urged would be advantageous to British interests. 'It is not necessary', he wrote, 'that Government should espouse their cause openly. My credit and influence will be found equal to prepare the way for this change.' As an inducement to this adventure he added that 'the moment a commotion ensues I am promised to have Lord Gormanston delivered to me.'[153] He brought the offer to London in person, but the British ministers were not revolution-mongers, and he was told they could not go to such lengths.[154]

The great aim of Miles was to secure official recognition as *chargé* or Resident at Liège,[155] and he evidently thought that he had some promise from Carmarthen to this effect.[156] After many disappointments, at last, in March 1789, he was instructed to proceed to Frankfurt, with, if not an official position, at least an official allowance of £250 a year.[157] There he immediately renewed his requests for an official appointment[158] and continued to bombard influential acquaintances in England, including the Marquess of Buckingham and the East India merchant Richard Neave, with letters of political information.[159] By December 1789 he was tired of waiting for recognition and returned to England,[160] to find himself in the bad books of the Foreign Secretary.[161] He reappears in this study, occupying a slightly more important role, in 1790, but for the period up to 1789 it may be concluded that the suspicions which have led to his being regarded as an important secret agent of the British government are not founded on fact.

One further British representative in the neighbourhood of France remains to be mentioned. The consul at Nice, writing in 1780 to the British minister at Turin, said that he was permitted to lay out a sum not exceeding £30 annually on procuring intelligence about Toulon.[162] No other source of intelligence concerning France appears in Foreign Office papers of the period. The impression given by the financial aspects of the foreign secret service of the Foreign Office between 1784 and 1792 is thus confirmed by a detailed study of its operations in France.

The second of the persons entitled, after 1782, to draw money for foreign secret service was the Principal Secretary of State for the Home Department. The expenditure of the Home Office in this respect was naturally far smaller than that of the Foreign Office.[163] It seems in all cases to have passed through the hands of one of the under-secretaries, that able professional administrator Evan Nepean, and, like the intelligence received by the Foreign Office, with very few exceptions to have been directed to one object — intelligence about the situation and distribution of the French Navy. The names of some eight informants, mostly British naval officers, appear in the records as employed at various times by Nepean to procure information about the French Navy. One of the most active of these agents was Richard Oakes, who, before Nepean's time, was sending information about the movements of Dutch ships to Philip Stephens, secretary to the Board of Admiralty,[164] and in a letter of 1782 refers to himself as a merchant.[165] In 1782 his reports were sent to Orde and Nepean at the Home Office.[166]

A letter of November 1782 sent observations he had made at Paris directly to Pitt, saying that he had made them at the request of Nepean and Stephens.[167] Some indication of the nature of his activities is provided by a letter to Nepean, in which Oakes gave information about the Dutch fleet, adding that he had informed Stephens of the opportunity of landing his informant, who had resided in Amsterdam twelve years, knew the American envoy Adams from infancy, and had lived at Philadelphia with Franklin; he was also one of the finest draftsmen we had. Oakes himself offered to go to Ostend, 'from which place I can with safety transmit the Needful'.[168] With the conclusion of peace Oakes drops out of the records, to reappear, when there was a prospect of further war with France, in 1787, sending reports from Brussels of French ships sailing for the East Indies.[169] The year 1790 finds him at Paris, obtaining information about the French attitude on the question of the application of their alliance with Spain from a M. Royer 'on his return from the duc d'O's'.[170]

Another agent whom Nepean inherited was Dalrymple, recommended to Government in a letter of January 1781 as one who had lived for many years as a merchant at Cadiz, 'who I may venture to say will more accurately relate what will affect the Spanish trade and navy than any other man in Europe'.[171] In 1785 one Dalrymple sent information to Carmarthen from Paris that sixty persons had been taken from the prison of the Bicêtre and sent to Brest, to be put aboard de la Perouse's squadron sailing to New Zealand, where they were to be left to form a settlement.[172] It is not clear if this was the same agent, and certainly the Major-general Dalrymple who sent intelligence relating to expeditions to the Indies and to the state of the French Navy in 1787 and 1788 was not.[173] Writing to Pitt in October 1789, Nepean said that

> Major-general Dalrymple has returned from Paris where he was on a visit to his brother-in-law Count Dillon. He reported that Dillon had received orders to prepare to embark on foreign service. It was currently reported and indeed understood by the Count that the five Regiments were to be employed with him in the East Indies.[174]

Among the naval officers employed on intelligence service was the Jerseyman Philip d'Auvergne, later adopted by the last prince de Bouillon as his heir. A statement of his services which he drew up for Windham at a later date says that when travelling in France for his health in 1784 he took notes on the provinces bordering the Channel, which he forwarded to Lord Howe at the Admiralty.[175] In 1787 and 1788, in command of the frigate *Narcissus*, he reconnoitred the French coasts between St Malo and Le Havre and reported to Howe and Chatham on the works at Cherbourg.[176] In 1792 he made a tour in the French maritime provinces to obtain information about the French Navy, in the course of which he established contacts in the chief French ports;[177] and in this year begin the services which were to make him the chief organizer, at first under Nepean, of British agents in France; but his major activities come after the end of the period with which this study is concerned.

In March 1785 intelligence about ships at Toulon was sent by Captain Phillips from Nice,[178] but there is no indication whether this was merely incidental information or if he was in the employment of any government department. Captain Dumaresq provided intelligence in November 1787 and June 1788.[179] Between November 1787 and June 1788 he sent reports to Nepean of ships and troops preparing to sail from Brest to the East Indies.[180] In February 1790 he wrote from Jersey, where he had just arrived from St Malo, about the Spanish fleet.[181] He wrote from St Malo again in May, and in June reported a journey to Spain to collect information.[182] In September he was again at St Malo and describing mutinous conditions in the French fleet at Brest.[183] In October 1790 he wrote that wishing to investigate the truth of reports he had received, he 'packed some goods and set off for Morlaix', evidently posing as a travelling merchant.[184] Another naval officer, Lieutenant Monke, sent reports about Gravelines and Dunkirk in September 1787, and about Marseilles and Toulon in October.[185] Monke's report on his visit to Toulon runs,

> By stratagem, got into Toulon at 4 in the morning by following the Mail and while the officers were at dinner, and frenchifying his person as much as possible and finding himself out of the sight of everybody he made the following observations.

There follows a detailed account of the ships at Toulon.[186]

Another note of October 1787 is addressed to Nepean, and a slip of paper says 'Intelligence received from Lieut. Monke between the 18 September 1787 and the 7 September 1788. Twice in Flanders. Twice at Toulon.'[187] In September 1788 there is a further report on the ships at Toulon from the same agent. It is forwarded by Hailes from Paris to Fraser, the under-secretary at the Foreign Office, but says that Monke is to receive the financial assistance he needs from Nepean at the Home Office.[188] Monke sent another account of the French naval forces at Toulon through the Paris embassy in February 1789 and again referred to his payment being derived from Nepean.[189] Another intelligence report about Toulon, forwarded by the Paris embassy in September 1788, came from Captain Henry Warre,[190] and doubtless there were other agents providing similar information whose records have not survived.

The Admiralty itself was accustomed, as we have seen in the case of d'Auvergne and the *Narcissus*, to send out small scouting vessels to keep watch on Continental ports. Thus in 1790, when there was concern both about the situation in the Baltic and the possible development of a conflict with Spain, scouting vessels were sent out in both directions, as well as to the coast of France. The sloops *Zebra* and *Fury* were posted off Cadiz and Ferrol, with orders, if a Spanish squadron put to sea, immediately to dispatch a cutter to England with the news; the *Hound* sloop was sent to watch the movements of the Swedish fleet in the Baltic; and Captain Pole in the *Melampus* was posted off Brest to obtain information of the number and fitness of French ships there, reporting by cutter to England, and then to watch for any squadron leaving the port.[191]

All these orders came direct from the Admiralty, but in another similar operation Nepean and the Home Office were concerned. In May–June 1790, Nepean gave instructions to Richard Oakes for the purchase of a cutter, the *Alert*, to be used for obtaining information off Ferrol.[192] Oakes wrote to Nepean, 'This vessel may with a great degree of safety [be] employed to look into any of the ports of France or Spain, as she will in course pass for a smuggling vessel.'[193] A report from Mr Morris, the master of the *Alert*, quoted information from sailors of a Spanish ship whom he had enticed on board, explaining, 'I had hoisted French colours and kept but one or two hands on deck, making my language a mixture of French and Portuguese.'[194]

Thus far Nepean's intelligence seems to have been exclusively concerned with naval matters. With one other contact, however, he goes beyond this field. This was a Corsican named Masseria. When France bought its rebellious possession of Corsica from the Republic of Genoa and commenced the task of subjugating the island, Great Britain, in spite of protests against its passivity, took no overt action. A complaint many years later by George III against money being taken from the Civil List to aid the Orangists in the United Provinces — 'I now reluctantly consent to it from the fatal experience of having fed the Corsican cause, and Ministry never having, as they had promised, found means of its being refunded to me, which made me consequently appear afterwards in an extravagant light to Parliament'[195] — leads one to suspect that secret assistance may have been sent to the Corsicans. Certainly, after the defeat of Paoli, he and those who fled with him were given British pensions.[196] A regiment was raised from them for British service and among its members was Masseria. A note of September 1789 describes him as 'Mr. Masseria who served as a lieutenant in the Corps of Corsicans at Gibraltar during the late war, and has since been appointed a lieut. in the 60th Regt. but is now on half-pay'.[197] According to the historian of the conquest

of Corsica, Paoli sent Masseria to Paris as his representative in
1789.[198] This is not quite the whole story.

Possibly after consultation with Paoli, though there is no
evidence for this, in September 1789 Masseria himself proposed to
the British Government that he should go to Versailles,

> where I am sure of being well received by some in the Assem-
> bly who are great enthusiasts in the Corsican cause, and who
> have read my pamphlet. I shall take a Passport from the
> National Assembly for my own security in my passage to
> Corsica, where I shall go very soon, and use my best endea-
> vours to unite the inhabitants, and advise them to recall
> General de Paoli, when I think it is a proper time. In the
> meanwhile, I will affect to act with the same spirit that ani-
> mates the French at this moment.[199]

That this proposal was taken seriously is shown by a note on the
back of the letter, 'Read by the King, Mr. Pitt, Duke of Leeds,
Lord Chatham, Duke of Richmond'. It was followed up by
further correspondence in October and November, in the course
of which a suggestion for bringing Corsica under British rule
emerged.[200] Masseria wrote that civil war was likely in France,
and that the minister the marquis Latour-Dupin was so em-
barrassed at home that he was ready to comply with all the
demands of the Corsican patriots. 'What a favourable opportunity will then be offered to the Corsicans to prove their attach-
ment to the English, and to the English themselves to increase
their power and influence in the Mediterranean.'[201]

There are other signs of British interest in Corsica at this time.
A report on conditions in the island which bears the name of
Gaspari was sent by Joseph Brame, consul at Genoa.[202] Suspicions of Russian intrigues in the Mediterranean, which did not
diminish British interest in Corsica, are reflected in anonymous
intelligence of December 1789.

> On a tout lieu de croire que le cabinet de France avoit con-
> venu d'admettre dans quelque port de l'isle de Corse les
> flottes de quelqu'autre Puissance, et peut-être de lui céder
> l'isle en entier.[203] A cette cause on peut attribuer la grande
> repugnance que le Ministère français temoigna lorsque fut

question de sanctionner le décret de l'Assemblée qui declaroit ce pays une Province de la royaume[204] ... Dans ce cas la Grande Bretagne ne verait-elle pas son intérêt à insister que la Corse demeurat dans un état d'indépendance ... [205]

Early in 1790 Masseria himself sent to Nepean a copy of the decree incorporating Corsica in France and described the French efforts to win over the Corsican patriots.[206] Meanwhile Paoli had announced the intention of the Corsican exiles, who had been subsisting on British pensions in Tuscany, to return to their native land.[207] He himself, in May 1790, asked for an audience of the king before his departure for Paris, where, he said, his supporters were pressing him to appear, in order to dissipate suspicion.[208] In dissipating French suspicion, Paoli succeeded in arousing English. Masseria felt obliged to write a memorandum from Florence defending him from the charge of ingratitude.[209]

Masseria found himself in difficulties for similar reasons. In October 1790 he wrote from Florence,

Having been obliged to leave Leghorn by order of the Governor, as suspected to be attached to the principles of the National Assembly of France; but not having the honour of being in any way known to his Lordship, or anything to show to him to prove that I am in His Majesty's service, he declines to take any part in this affair till he receives some lines from you.[210]

Masseria added the news that he had received letters from Ajaccio saying that he was to be elected colonel of the National Militia there, consisting of some 1,600 men, and that the inhabitants had taken his advice to compel the French commandant of the Citadel to admit a daily guard.

Before I left England I informed you, Sir, that Ajaccio was the most eligible place in Corsica for the English, as having a very spacious and good harbour, a fine citadel regularly built, and a large and rich country round it. What a favourable moment it would be, now that I may think myself master of the said citadel, if there was to be a war, I leave it to you to consider.[211]

With this letter the correspondence with Masseria ceased until August 1793, after which it began to produce positive results.

Altogether the activity of Nepean in the field of foreign secret service, if unexpected, is on a very restricted scale. The interesting question to ask is why the under-secretary at the Home Office should have undertaken such responsibilities at all, and the answer is to be found in one aspect of the important, but curiously neglected, administrative revolution of 1782. It is well known that for the division of the offices of the two Principal Secretaries of State into the northern and the southern department was then substituted a division into Home and Foreign. This change, as Anson puts it, 'took place with singularly little noise or notice'.[212] Apart from a circular letter by Fox, as the new Foreign Minister, to British ministers abroad,[213] no contemporary reference to it has been found, though it involved a fundamental administrative reform. Now, before 1782, the two Principal Secretaries of State had exercised considerable influence in naval matters, but, as the Mediterranean and France fell within the scope of the Secretary of State for the southern department, he was naturally much the more important of the two in this respect.[214] There is ample reason for believing that in 1782 the southern department became the new Home Department and the northern the Foreign. Thus the clerks in the northern department reappear in the list of the Secretary of State for Foreign Affairs, and those of the southern department continued to serve under the Secretary of State for the Home Department. Again, Fraser, who had been under-secretary to the northern department, continued to fill the same post in the Foreign Department. Colonies, which had been attached to the southern department up to 1768, was united to the Home Department in 1782.[215] It is almost impossible not to draw the conclusion that Nepean at the Home Department was dealing with naval espionage in France and the correspondence with Masseria because by tradition the southern department had dealt with such matters.

To return to the main issue, it may be suggested that substantial evidence has been adduced for holding that neither of the secretaries of state engaged in anything more than normal, but sporadic, espionage in France between 1789 and 1792. Since so much detailed information has survived, it would hardly be reasonable to suppose that if there were any deeper laid and more far-reaching secret activities, their records would have disappeared completely, leaving no traces in the financial accounts or in official and unofficial correspondence. For the sake of completeness, however, it may be as well to deal briefly with one secret negotiation which is well known but has sometimes been misinterpreted. This was the Miles and Elliot mission of 1790, for which Pitt was directly responsible.[216]

The British Government, involved at this time in the dispute over Nootka Sound with Spain, was anxious that the Family Compact between Spain and France should not be brought into operation. To prevent this, Pitt was even prepared to negotiate unofficially, behind the back of the king of France and his government, with the leaders of the National Assembly. The nature of such a negotiation amply explains the secrecy with which it was covered. The instructions, which Pitt wrote out in his own hand for Hugh Elliot, were returned by the latter to the Foreign Office and have disappeared.[217] From scattered letters, however, the aim and nature of the mission can be discovered. Although his role was an unofficial one, Elliot was in contact with Lord Gower at the embassy, and Gower, in a dispatch of October 22nd, 1790, wrote that 'the popular party' had signified to him through Elliot 'their earnest desire to use their influence with the Court of Madrid in order to bring it to accede to the just demands of His Majesty'.[218] A few days later he reported that 'The opportunities which Mr. Elliot has had of conversing with members of the Comité Diplomatique, and which from my situation it was not in my power to have, have enabled him to convince them of the pacific intentions of His Majesty.'[219] Pitt expressed his pleasure at Elliot's success 'in opening a confidential intercourse with the leaders of what appears to be the Ruling Party in France', while warning him that 'no ostensible intercourse can be admitted but through the medium of accredited Ministers'. The persons with whom Elliot was in contact were to be given no assurances 'which go farther than that this Country means to persevere in the neutrality which it has hitherto scrupulously observed with respect to the internal dissentions of France'.[220]

In submitting to the king the letters received from Gower and Elliot, Pitt gave a rather disingenuous account of Elliot's mission.

The latter went lately to Paris, principally from curiosity, but before his departure he mentioned to Mr. Pitt, that he had formerly happened to be in habits of intimacy with M. de Mirabeau, and might probably be able to learn something from him respecting the views of the prevailing Party in France on the subject of the discussion with Spain. Mr. Pitt recommended to him to be very cautious not to commit any body by his conversation but to endeavour to find out whether there was any chance of making any of the leading persons see in a just light the nature of the dispute between this Country and Spain, and of thereby preventing or delaying any hostile measures which might be taken by France.[221]

The king replied that he could not object to this measure — though he was not sanguine that it would succeed — so long as it was confined to the sole object of preserving peace, 'but no encouragement must be given to forwarding the internal views of the democratical Party'.[222]

I have only found a few letters from Elliot to Pitt, but these help to fill in the picture. One, undated, runs,

The sentiments expressed in my conversation with the deputation of the Diplomatick Committee were such as I thought best suited to my audience, and the particular purpose I had in view, but were not to be taken as literally *mine*. The speech I made was in every sense a *French* speech, and therefore the terms *Glorious revolution* and others of a similar nature are applicable to *their* notions and not to my own opinion.[223]

On October 26th, he reported a satisfactory interview with representatives of the diplomatic committee of the National Assembly, and he added his own opinion that the existing government of France was 'bent upon cultivating the most unbounded friendship with Great Britain'. A cryptic sentence says, 'what has taken place in my more intimate conversations with individuals, cannot be committed to paper.' However, his postscript is a safeguard against supposing the existence of any hidden manœuvres which do not appear in these letters — 'I must observe that there is no such thing as a private negotiation to be carried on here. Everything like a secret is avoided as dangerous, and likely to expose those concerned to the *Lanterne*.'[224] The diplomatic committee, after receiving the report of the conference with Elliot, decided to wait on Montmorin to urge the desirability of a *rapprochement* with England and the avoidance of war. They asked Elliot to return to England to explain their sentiments, a move in which Montmorin concurred. Elliot did this, and on November 6th, when he was on the point of returning to Paris, he heard that Spain had yielded to British pressure. He wrote to Pitt that therefore he had written letters to the vicomte de Noailles and to Mirabeau. His first object was to keep the door open for further communications if they were expedient.

> The Second, to treat Burke and his book with that degree of levity, which I believe the best means of preventing Government here, from being harassed with formal applications from the French Court, for the prosecution of the author, as a libeller either of the present Government of France, or indeed of the persons of the Sovereigns themselves. You will also be pleased to observe, that I have fully expressed to Mirabeau, our resolution to take no share in the internal divisions in France, and have, I hope, fulfilled the whole of your idea upon that delicate subject.[225]

Elliot's mission achieved its object all the more easily, perhaps, because internal forces in France would almost certainly have produced the same result without any British attempt at intervention.

Miles, sent for the same object as Elliot, was less fortunate or less discreet. Indeed, it is possible that Elliot was sent because of doubts in Pitt's mind of the reliability of Miles as an emissary, for Miles had been dispatched earlier, in July 1790. He was instructed to have no communication, either directly or indirectly, with the British ambassador.[226] In Paris he met Lafayette, Mirabeau, Pétion and others, and became a member of the Jacobin Club and the Société de 1789.[227] He announced in October that his mission was likely to succeed,[228] but he was not content to stop at this and went on to urge the case for an Anglo-French alliance.[229] He claimed later that he and Elliot,

> were the only two who did not humour the erroneous wishes of our Court by assuring Ministers that a counter-revolution

was on the point of being declared. On the contrary, we respectively wrote — not in concert, for we were ignorant of each other's letters at the time — that the Revolution would not be interrupted in its march, that any attempt to stay it would only enrage an immense population.[230]

It is true that Miles's observations in France during the Revolution are marked by considerable insight and correctness, but governments prefer informants who tell them what they want to believe, rather than those who tell them the truth, and Miles's suggestion of an Anglo-French alliance would certainly not be to the taste of Pitt and his colleagues, nor did it indicate a very modest sense of his own importance. A querulous letter to Pitt on December 10th, 1790,[231] was followed by a complaint to Lord Buckingham, 'Two months have elapsed since I despatched my first letter to Mr. Rose on the subject of my mission. I have not received any answer.'[232] If he ever received one it has not survived. He hung on in Paris until April 1791, when he returned to England.[233]

It might be suggested that the alleged English plots in France during the opening stages of the Revolution can be regarded as disposed of, and replaced by a positive account of the actual secret proceedings of the British government. To complete the picture, however, it is desirable to offer some explanation for the widespread belief in France at the time in the existence of this legendary British plot. If Pitt's agents were not busy sowing the seeds of revolution in France, how are we to account for the general conviction that they were? It is not possible to deny that some Englishmen did engage in seditious activities in France in the early stages of the Revolution. If they were not Pitt's agents, who were they? Forth, Smith, Clarke, Rotundo, Moreton, Grieve, Shée — these are some of the names. A pathetic set of nonentities, it is true, and not all even English, though they were all described as such. Little is known about this underworld of agitators, though I believe that it may be possible to unearth a great deal more than has been discovered up to the present. One thing is clear, however: they practically all emerged from the shadows of the half-world of the Palais Royal, and some of them, at least, belonged to that mercenary army which the author of *Les Liaisons Dangereuses* had enlisted under the moth-eaten banner of Orleans. The history of

the part played by the Orleanist movement in the Revolution has
never been written, nor is this the place to write it; but it is easy
to see how Orleanist agitators could come to be identified as
English agents. Orleans's reputation for Anglomania, among
other unnatural vices, provided the link, in the popular imagina-
tion, between the Orleanist faction and the British government.
The source of his agents, as of his money, was seen as England.

> Oh, le bon peuple que ces Anglais! .. Le duc leur a promis
> tout ce qu'ils ont voulu, et ma foi, ce n'est pas trop; des gens
> si obligeants qui nous donnent tout d'un coup 15 millions, et
> qui n'exigent, pour l'intérêt, que la cession de nos colonies ...
> L'ami Pitt et l'ami Fox ... ne se contentent pas de nous donner
> des guinées, ils prévoient tout. Ils savent qu'il nous faut des
> agents et des agents habiles.[234]

Out of a host of possible illustrations I will only give one other:

> Qui pourroit douter maintenant des cabales odieuses du
> héros du Palais-Royal? Ne sait-on pas qu'il est le bas valet
> et l'espion du très-petit ambassadeur d'Angleterre, petit et
> très-petit agent du présomptueux Pitt, et que les sommes
> énormes distribuées par Capet [Philippe] venoient en grande
> partie de Londres par les ministres, jaloux de notre révolution
> afin de la faire tourner à leur gré, et mettre le royaume dans
> une extremité telle qu'ils fussent venus nous dicter les lois en
> vainqueurs.[235]

When, after the October days, the French Court sent Orleans
to England to get him out of the way, this confirmed popular
suspicions.

> Le vertueux prince Philippe! l'âme de boue la plus pro-
> noncée de son parti ... gagna l'Angleterre, source où il a
> puisé ses principes et ses moyens.[236]

An early *Père Duchêne* pictured him passing his days and nights in
England 'dans des orgies délicieuses avec le Prince de Galles et
tous les Lords Anglais'.[237]

The French Court had its own suspicions of Orleans; he was
given ironical instructions, 'Le premier objet des recherches de
M. le duc d'Orléans sera de découvrir si et jusqu'à quel point la

Cour de Londres a cherché à fomenter nos troubles; quels moyens et quels agents elle a employés.'[238] All the time the duke was in England La Luzerne was watching him carefully and reporting his movements to the French government. He came to the conclusion that Orleans was not being used by the king of England or Pitt against the king of France.[239] He was obviously despised by English society[240] and La Luzerne wrote that he seemed to be paying no attention to political questions.[241] 'Le vin, les chevaux, le jeu, les filles et Made de Buffon paroissent occuper uniquement ce Prince';[242] he was completely discredited and was drunk every evening.[243]

Whereas the role of Pitt's agents and English gold among the causes of the Revolution is undoubtedly a myth, however, the Orleanist faction certainly existed, though its size and coherence have been exaggerated. The possibility of a definite verdict on this point must await further research, but it may be said that the manœuvres of Orleans and his supporters are hardly sufficient to account for the torrent of democratic agitators, many of them from foreign countries, which poured into the muddy waters of the Palais Royal in 1789. Where did they come from, these shady characters, most of whose names are not even down among the *dramatis personae* of respectable history, and who are often described as Orleanists or as English agents? Taking the French Revolution out of the unnatural isolation in which it is commonly treated, and replacing it in its European background, it can be seen as the last and greatest of a series of revolutions. The end of the eighteenth century could be called, quite as justly as the age of enlightened despotism, the age of the democratic revolutions. The American revolution, the agitation for parliamentary reform in England, the unrest in Ireland, the revolt against the *Petit Conseil* in Geneva, the anti-Orangist revolution in the United Provinces, the Vonkist movement in the Austrian Netherlands and the troubles in Liège, all precede the French Revolution. Except in America these movements all failed, and in 1788–9 a flotsam and jetsam of democratic politicians and journalists gathered in Paris. This, I suspect, was the reality behind the mythical agents of Pitt, and perhaps also behind the possibly exaggerated Orleanist conspiracy.

In conclusion, it must be pointed out that this study has as its terminal date the year 1792, but for that year some material has had to be omitted, as belonging rather with what came after than with what went before. The British secret service did not continue to operate on such a restricted scale; the gold of Pitt was not permanently a negligible force. For the years which were to follow the outbreak of war, the error has not lain, as for the preceding years, in inventing non-existent plots and agents, but in ignoring or underestimating the scope of the underground war against France, which, starting from small beginnings in 1793, was to develop rapidly and grow to proportions which entitle it to be considered one of the major aspects of the struggle.

# 11

## THE BEGINNING OF THE CHANNEL ISLES
## CORRESPONDENCE
### 1789–94[1]

WHENEVER Great Britain was at war with France — or for that matter at peace — the Channel Isles was the natural centre for the collection of information about French naval preparations in the ports of the west. This activity continued on its normal small scale in the years before 1789,[2] and the outbreak of the French Revolution made no difference in this respect. The usual flow of information came in to Evan Nepean, under secretary at the Home Office, which, as I have explained above,[3] had inherited a responsibility for naval espionage from the former southern department. It seems also to have carried over, at least for a time, a vague responsibility for matters of defence. It is interesting to note that when Grenville became Foreign Secretary, in April 1791, Pitt was anxious to replace him in the Home Office by the country's chief military expert, Cornwallis. Dundas was only appointed Home Secretary on the understanding that he would make way when Cornwallis returned from India.[4] However, this should not be taken as implying any belief in the imminence of war. The confidence of the British government that it would not become involved in hostilities with revolutionary France is well known. It is reflected in the failure to take any steps to improve military and naval intelligence.

The first move towards increased activity came not from Whitehall but from Jersey, and as late as December 20th, 1792, when Philippe Fall, the lieutenant-governor, wrote to Nepean, 'If, in the present appearance of things on the Continent, you should think my position such as might be useful to Government, I wish much to have particular instructions how far I could venture with the people I might employ on secret service.'[5] Nepean replied, on December 25th, that he wished particularly to know of any naval preparations at Brest and Bordeaux. At the latter port, he said, it was alleged that many ships were collected 'ready to fall upon our Trade in case any hostility between the two Countries should take place.'[6] A fuller letter which followed on January 13th, 1793, said,

> I understand that the French are equipping at L'Orient, Rochefort etc. and if you can find a fit Person, I mean a person conversant with shipping, it will be extremely desirable that you should send him to those places as soon as possible. It is very material that he should bring intelligence of the *Names* of the ships which have sailed and of those remaining in these ports with their conditions — viz. whether they are manned and fit for sea, Building, Equipping, or lying up as Hulks, and as I am in possession of a list of the whole Navy of France, I can from a reference to it at once ascertain their force. I mention this that the memory of the Person or persons you send may be as little stretched as possible ... P.S. What is doing at Cherbourg?[7]

Evidently Fall accepted this authorization, for he produced, in the same month, a report from an agent sent to cover the coast from St Malo to Cherbourg.[8] A little later there was one at Brest, of whom Fall said, 'His plea for travelling is to recover debts owed him in most of the sea-port towns along the Coast of Brittany.'[9]

Whitehall was also making efforts to secure naval information through a Mr Martin at Paris, who was to send agents to Toulon, Brest and the other chief ports. Contact with him was apparently effected by way of a royalist 'Baron de Giliet'[10] [*recte* Gilliers], to whom John King, the other under-secretary at the Home Office, sent £200 for Martin. King added that the name that would be used by an agent sent from Jersey to establish contact at Granville was James Jacques Alexander.[11] The other end of this affair appears in a letter of February 18th, 1793, from Nepean to Fall:

> A Gentleman is now employed on the Continent from whom some letters of a nature extremely important are expected. They are intended to be sent by a Person, who is to assume the character of a dealer in Merchandise, who means to be at Granville very shortly, and will occasionally resort to the

house of a Mrs. Adam to whom the enclosed letter is addressed, and it is very material that you should find a very confidential person to meet him at that place, under the character of a Smuggler in Tobacco etc. in order that as soon as he can be sure of his man, he may receive the communications from him, and bring them to you that they may be forwarded to me ... She [Mrs. Adam] is totally ignorant of the plan and looks forward only to some smuggling concern ... [He must] carry with him from Jersey ... something contraband ... the exportation of which must be winked at though it will not of course amount to any great quantity, but at the same time enough to ensure him a favourable reception.

The person you may send must assume the name of *James Alexander* ... [and the other person] shall state himself to be a friend and an acquaintance of a *Mr. Martin* of Paris.[12]

Because of the absence of a regular packet service to the Channel Isles this letter took a month to reach Fall,[13] and when he put the plan into operation it had little success. On April 30th he had to write to Nepean,

I hear [by a ship from Cherbourg] the disagreeable report that two Jerseymen had been brought to that town, which by description of them, I have every reason to suppose, are, the person I had sent to Granville with your letters, and the boatman which was to bring him back ... The person I had sent to Brest so long ago as the middle of January, was stopt in consequence of the declaration of war, and is now confined at Dinan.[14]

It is little wonder that Nepean wrote, 'We have been out of luck with our Intelligence.'[15] Meanwhile, however, Gilliers, forwarding a letter of general information dated March 4th, 1793, from 'Martin', reported that the latter was coming to England with all his papers and information. A note adds that 'Mr Jarjaye (keeper of the plan of fortifications etc.) ... was desired by the last post to get out of France with his Plans and Papers as soon as possible. M. Pitt authorized me to have him written to for this purpose.'[16] The implication seems to be that 'Mr Martin' was Rénier de Jarjayes, a well-known counter-revolutionary.[17]

Besides these efforts from Jersey, there were also attempts to secure intelligence by agents dispatched from the other islands. The lieutenant-governor of Guernsey was instructed, 'If you could find a trusty man to send to the Coast, I should not have any objection to pay one or two Hundred Pounds to him if he did his Business properly ... The objects are the Preparations upon the Coast opposite to you and the State of the Fleet at Brest.'[18] On April 10th he reported to Nepean that he had sent the Chevalier du Laurens to obtain information in Brittany.[19] From Alderney, Peter le Mesurier was writing to Nepean, on March 1st, 'My French smuggler on whom I much depend is expected to-morrow, or as soon as the weather will permit, when I hope to have further intelligence of their ships.'[20] Successful or not, these seem rather amateurish as well as small-scale efforts, but only by assembling such trivial details can the rather insignificant nature of the whole proceedings be demonstrated. Not that the collection of information about the movements of French warships was to remain insignificant when war had broken out, but such espionage, of major importance for naval strategy, is not the subject of this paper. At first, moreover, the outbreak of war with France evidently had a disrupting effect on even such minor espionage as was being conducted. One of the well-established agents, Captain Dumaresq,[21] who was still sending back information from France in January 1793,[22] now lost his *modus operandi*, for he wrote that the war had involved him in the loss of supplies of goods to Morlaix, etc., for which he had not been paid.[23]

About this time, Nepean obtained an assistant in this branch of his work, more or less fortuitously, as a result of the passage, in January 1793, of the Aliens Act. What happened can best be explained in the words of young Huskisson, who had been a protégé of the Gowers at the Paris embassy, and early in 1793 was at dinner with them, the party including Pitt and Dundas. The conversation, wrote Huskisson,

> gave rise to the accidental circumstance which has called me to my present situation. A lady of France having made an application to Lord Gower in the morning, with respect to the manner of conforming to the Aliens Bill, the question was referred to Messrs. Dundas and Pitt. The former said that

they were in want of a person who could speak the language, and direct the execution of that Bill according to the views of Government, which were, to shew every possible civility and respect to all Foreigners, whose conduct in this Country had not given rise to any suspicion, and especially to save to the ladies the trouble of appearing at the public offices. M. Dundas gave several hints that he wished me to accept of the Post.[24]

Huskisson, who had considerable facility both with the French language and the ladies, yielded to the hints. His new position, in which he served directly under Nepean, for whom he rapidly acquired the greatest admiration and affection, proved to have a broader scope than he had imagined. It provided, as his successor Wickham was to observe, 'singular facilities and advantages' for obtaining foreign intelligence.[25]

After the French declaration of war the efforts of the Home Office to obtain information by way of the Channel Isles were promoted more energetically, and consideration also began to be given to the possibility of military co-operation with the royalists. The British government moved very cautiously, for it was still influenced by its pre-war anxiety not to be committed to taking sides in the struggle in France. Also, it could not seriously make use of the counter-revolutionary movements in France until it had some positive information to go on. How little was known of them is shown by the first British steps towards intervention. According to a rumour flying round Europe the leader of the royalist army in the west was one Gaston. Nothing of a positive nature was known, but legendary feats were attributed to him. The source of the Gaston myth may have been the reports of the republican representatives on mission, which, read at the Convention, led Europe to suppose that he was the chief royalist general, commanding a formidable army.[26] When the rumour reached the émigrés they clutched at the hope it offered. The duc d'Harcourt, representative of the princes, learnt in May 1793, in Jersey, that a mysterious M. Gaston was in command of an army of 200,000 men in the Vendée, and was invited to send emissaries to him.[27] Gilliers told the British government in July 1793, 'Gaston a besoin de secours'.[28] Nepean had heard of Gaston from some other source, before this. He wrote to the acting consul at Ostend, Gideon Duncan, in May, saying that it was desired to hire a ship 'to go upon the coasts of France, and learn what Gaston, who was at the head of the royalists of La Vendée was doing, and what assistance we could give him'. He asked Duncan to hire an American schooner, but the consul recommended the *Lydia*, owned by John Kirkpatrick & Co., which was chartered on May 16th, 1793, at £150 a month. The supercargo, a Milanese named Madeny, was to be the only person on board who knew the real object of the voyage. 'For a cover the *Lydia* was cleared out for Lisbon, and to call at Nantz, by way of looking for freight; whatever information she could pick up she was to deliver to the Government of Jersey or Guernsey, and all the English men of war had notice of her, that she might not be molested.' Arriving at Nantes, the *Lydia* at once found herself under an embargo with all other ships in the port. She subsequently conveniently forgot the mission she had been hired for and engaged in trade between France and America and Hamburg, until she was seized in the Channel, with a cargo from Holland to Bordeaux, by a British warship. Duncan thought there had been collusion between Kirkpatrick, Madeny and the captain, and Nepean evidently got no information for his money.[29]

The government of the Dutch Republic also had the idea of sending an agent to try to establish contact with Gaston. Their man was Colonel or Baron d'Angély, who received his mission on May 28th, 1793, from the Stadtholder.[30] D'Angély was a French adventurer who had served in the Russian army, in the American campaign, and in the Maillebois legion at the time of the Patriot struggle in the Dutch Republic, and had made a sideline of supplying information.[31] A report to the French Directory in 1798, with partially correct intelligence, was to describe him at that time as the most dangerous of English spies in the North.[32] He had emigrated to Holland in 1791 and there became an agent of the Pensionary van de Spiegel,[33] who was doubtless responsible for his mission to Gaston. D'Angély also offered to collect information for the allied British government. In a memorandum to Dundas he explained that he was sent on behalf of Holland and proposed to land at La Rochelle, whence a gentleman of that district named de Loynes had offered to conduct him

233

to Gaston.[34] It was probably for d'Angély in the first place that a declaration of the British attitude towards Gaston was drawn up, with corrections in the hand of Dundas and a translation into French, presumably by Huskisson. This explains that it is impossible to come to Gaston's assistance till the real extent of his power is known. It puts forward as their common aims the overthrow of the existing rulers of France and the restoration of peace and order, and entreats Gaston 'to believe that England is not attached to any party of which the pretensions might operate as obstacles to the attainment of these desirable ends'.[35] This letter for Gaston was dispatched to Rochefort on June 13th, to be delivered 'by the person going in the Danish ship' (*i.e.* d'Angély) with a covering note by Dundas saying that he had 'no objection to give it any authenticity that is desired'.[36] Despite this letter, d'Angély evidently regarded himself as operating primarily on behalf of the Dutch for on his return he reported to that government, though the *greffier* Nagel sent a copy of d'Angély's memoir to Great Britain in October. It contains a long, interesting, and pretty fair account of the state of the royalist forces, and a letter dated August 10th or 11th at Chantonnay from their leaders. Along with it is the curt announcement, 'le général Gaston est mort depuis longtemps'.[37] He had been, d'Angély said in his memoir, a *garçon perruquier*, 'plein de zéle, de courage et doué de quelques talens pour la guerre', who had joined a local rising at the head of several hundred peasants.[38] He seems to have been captured and shot at Saint-Gervais on April 15th, 1793.[39] This was the end of the Gaston legend, at least for the British government.

Meanwhile other attempts had been made to establish contact with the royalists.[40] Colonel Craig, appointed commander-in-chief in Jersey in January 1793, sent the chevalier de Tinténiac on a mission which succeeded in establishing a definite correspondence with the royalist leaders, who replied with a detailed statement of their needs in a letter from Châtillon on August 18th.[41] At the same time a rather mysterious negotiation was being conducted at St Malo. In June 1793, a Mr Hammelin held discussions there with Corbin, municipal officer, Pellé, commissaire de la marine, and various other officials. The subject was the surrender of the town to the English, though the negotiators declared that they were not willing to act if it were to be taken over by the princes.[42] Craig wrote to Nepean in August that he was negotiating with caution, not knowing the views of the ministers.[43] They were slow to formulate them, but in October a letter was sent to the royalist armies suggesting a possible combined action to seize St Malo.[44] Nothing came of this, but the negotiation set on foot with the army of the Vendée by Tinténiac proved more fruitful. It is sufficient to say, of an often-told story, that eventually the army of the Vendée set out north and attacked Granville, which it failed to capture, in November 1794. When a small expedition under Lord Moira belatedly reached the French coast on December 2nd the Vendéans had already turned back.[45] A pathetic appeal for help from their remnants, conveyed by de la Robrie from the isle of Noirmoutier on December 4th, 1793, reached the British government on January 1st, 1794.[46]

Military co-operation evidently presented great difficulties, and there was the further practical problem for the British government of knowing which of the various royalists faction was most likely to rally support in France. The British ministers were anxious not to commit themselves to the cause of the 'pure' royalists, which was dominant in the emigration, for they suspected that this would be to sacrifice the hope of effective support inside France. Unfortunately the marquis du Dresnay, who had been sent to Jersey to organize a corps of émigrés, as the representative of the Bourbon princes naturally aimed at furthering their interests.[47] On June 8th, 1793, Colonel Craig was informed,

> If the nature of the instructions given by the Duke of Harcourt to Mr. du Dresnay had been known, I can assure that Government would not have provided the means of sending him and his companions to Jersey — the Duke's instructions certainly carry an insinuation that this country has acknowledged the Regent of France, and consented to cooperate with him in the particulars therein mentioned, which is by no means the case.[48]

There were also differences of opinion among those who were conducting the embryo correspondence from the Channel Isles, as well as with the royalists. The lieutenant-governor of Jersey, Fall, instructed to consult with the military commander,[49] reported that Craig seemed unwilling to co-operate,[50] and then, in a letter of August 10th to Nepean, launched into a full-scale indictment of him. After explaining that he had arranged for an agent to be conveyed to France, Fall went on,

> Colonel Craig ... had, by some means or other, intimation of this boat being on the point of sailing; the Master's house was watched day and night by troopers, and when he got under way (at a remote little cove from the Town) a scout immediately set off to acquaint Col. Craig of this man's departure, on which information the Colonel despatched the two Cutters and Lugger in the service of Government, to intercept my boat, which one of them overtook, and notwithstanding the Master produced my Pass, requiring all His Majesty's cruisers not to molest her, as she was employed by me on secret service, the Commander of the Cutter said he had peremptory orders to seize her: the Master and Crew were made prisoners, and, with their boat, publicly brought into the Town harbour, and my Pass taken from them. This public transaction exposed my people to very injurious suspicions throughout the Island. I represented to Col. Craig that I was acting, as he well knew, in consequence of your instructions. He answered that no boats should sail without his approbation and consent, and that, besides, he had heard a very bad character of the man I employed, and believed him to be a great Rascal, and a suspicious person ... What has a good deal surprised me since, and which I cannot help mentioning, is that the Master of my boat ... he [Col. Craig] immediately employed in the same secret service I did, and I understand that, ever since, with the assistance of this man the Colonel has been successful in procuring intelligence.[51]

The Fall–Craig team clearly could not be allowed to continue, and in October 1793 an opportunity was taken to send Craig as lieutenant-governor to Guernsey, where he only stayed two months.[52] Lord Balcarres replaced him in the more important military command at Jersey,[53] and naturally also took charge of the still rudimentary correspondence with France.

Soon after taking over Balcarres sent to Dundas an account of two agents he was using in the correspondence with Brittany,

Bertin and Prigent[54] — 'le fameux Prigent', as the republican administrators of St Malo called the latter when he was captured at the end of 1794. Prigent was to be the chief as well as the most controversial figure in the conduct of the Correspondence for the next fifteen years. He appears first in Craig's letters in April 1793, in a reference to a 'clever young man' whom he had sent to St Malo.[55] Subsequently we learn that the clever young man is called P.,[56] then 'Mons. Pritgens, whom you have hitherto known by the name of P– only'.[57] Under Balcarres, Prigent must have been used extensively, for in 1798 he received £500 as compensation for his services at this time.[58] His success did not endear him to all the royalists in Jersey. One émigré wrote in January 1794 of 'Prejan qui est devenu un grand monsieur'.[59] On the other hand the comte de Puisaye, who for a time was to be the chief, though far from undisputed, leader of the royalists of the west, in the eyes of the British government, with some exaggeration attributed the opening of all their communications with Great Britain to Prigent, and praised his zeal, perseverance, enterprise and courage, in unqualified terms.[60] Prigent was born at St Malo about 1768[61] and described himself as '*né négociant*'.[62] He gives an account of his early career which can on the whole be confirmed from other sources. In the conspiracy of de la Rouerie, says Puisaye, Prigent was given command of a company to attack St Malo. After the failure of this rising he lived a more or less clandestine existence, making many trips to take refugees to the Channel Isles. Thus when Craig wanted a man with local knowledge to open correspondence with the mainland, Prigent was an obvious choice,[63] and he became so essential to the growing Correspondence that he was able to write, in October 1794, with not a little pride, that the Correspondence from Guernsey was being suppressed, and there was only to remain that from Jersey, organized by Balcarres, 'us', and the prince de Bouillon.[64]

This brings us at last to the man who for many years was to be the head of the Channel Isles Correspondence. Philippe d'Auvergne, known as prince or duc de Bouillon, was a naval officer from Jersey, whose life would seem to belong to fiction rather than history were it not so well documented.[65] Only a bare outline can be given here. Beginning his naval career under the patronage of Lord Howe, he served in Russian, Arctic and

American waters. In 1779, as first lieutenant in the *Arethusa*, he was wrecked off Ushant and made a prisoner of war in France. Here his name was brought by the minister of the Marine, de Sartine, to the notice of the duc de Bouillon, whose family name was also d'Auvergne and whose line was likely to become extinct unless he could find an heir.[66] After being exchanged, d'Auvergne returned to service in the *Lark* to the Cape and the *Rattlesnake* to Trinidad, where his cutter was lost and he was marooned with a small party for a year.[67] In 1784 he brought back from India dispatches announcing the end of the war there, and a message from the Nabob of Arcot, and was promoted post captain.[68] In London he now met the duc de Bouillon, travelling incognito and still looking for an heir.[69] Bouillon invited him to France and according to d'Auvergne concluded a formal act of adoption in 1784.[70] After travels, during 1786, in France and Germany, and election as a fellow of the Royal Society, d'Auvergne was appointed in April 1787 to the *Narcissus* to watch the French Channel ports.[71] In some correspondence of this time, his friend J. T. Townshend, son of Lord Sydney, the Home Secretary, made the suggestion that he could have a baronetcy if he would give up the prospect of succeeding to the title and estates of the prince de Bouillon and accepting employment in France.[72] Nothing came of this proposal. In 1790 d'Auvergne visited the duc de Bouillon at Navarre. He was formally adopted as his heir by the duke (to succeed a son who was incapable of continuing the line and unlikely to live long), given the title to an appanage in Auvergne, and invested with the sword of Turenne.[73] When the duc de Bouillon died in December 1792, d'Auvergne inherited some £2,450 from him, which he later spent in making Mont Orgueil Castle in Jersey into a residence for himself.[74] The situation in France in 1792 did not permit his entry into his ducal inheritance, but henceforth he adopted the title of prince de Bouillon.

Bouillon, as we may now call him, resigned his command of the *Narcissus* in January 1790 on the ground of ill health,[75] but after the outbreak of war he was posted to the *Nonsuch*, in command of a gunboat flotilla defending the Channel Isles.[76] In this capacity he was naturally also used for communications with France.[77] A letter from the royalist leader Puisaye to one of the agents of the Correspondence, on September 29th, 1794, says ' ... que desormais vos opérations soient aussi secrettes qu'elles ont été publiques jusqu'ici; que personne à l'exception de Lord Balcara et du prince de Bouillon ne connaisse les jours de votre départ et de votre retour'.[78] Incidentally, this letter suggests that the Correspondence was still somewhat rudimentary in its organization and indiscreet in its conduct.

When, in the summer of 1794, it was decided that Balcarres was to leave Jersey, Bouillon aspired to succeed to the control of the growing Correspondence. During the summer and autumn of 1794 he bombarded influential friends with requests for the appointment. The first such letter I have found is one of August to Windham, a leading advocate of the cause of the French royalists and just appointed secretary at war.[79] In October Puisaye wrote to Windham asking that Bouillon be charged with the entire Correspondence with the royalists of the west.[80] Bouillon also wrote to Nepean, referring to 'our old and tried friendship',[81] to his chief, Dundas,[82] and again to Windham, stressing his intimate acquaintance with the French country, language and inhabitants.[83] The chief danger to his ambitions came from the lieutenant-governor, Fall, who also aspired to conduct the Correspondence[84] and continued to send out agents on his own responsibility.[85] Although Fall remained a nuisance and his activities were the subject of later complaints, Bouillon succeeded in his application. Lord Chatham wrote to him that he had

> most strongly represented to Mr. Pitt and Mr. Dundas the infinite benefit that would result, from the communication with the Continent being exclusively lodged in your hands ... and also that any pecuniary assistance to the French residing in the Islands, should be entrusted to your disposal. I am happy to say that they have fully concurred with me.[86]

Balcarres left the island on October 15th,[87] and on November 1st Bouillon was able to tell Prigent that he had received orders from the minister granting what he wanted.[88] At the same time a less pleasant charge was made by the withdrawal of the *Nonsuch* and the substitution of the *Bravo*,[89] which Bouillon later described as 'a Vessel that can scarcely be called one, from its absolute Nullity for every kind of service',[90] or more succinctly as 'a floating target'.[91]

The arrangements of the British government at Whitehall underwent a general reorganization at this time. Dundas left the Home Department for a new office of secretary of state for war in July 1794, taking with him Nepean and Huskisson and their embryo intelligence service. The Home Department now ceased to play much part in foreign secret service. Under Portland its expenditure in this line sank to some £2,000 to £3,000 a year, while that of the new secretary for war was in 1795 over £80,000. There was still, of course, a secretary *at* war, as distinct from the secretary *for* war. The former office had normally no connection with intelligence, but Windham, as secretary at war, was a passionate advocate of the cause of the French royalists and this made him a natural contact with them. He was also responsible for the corps of émigrés that were now being raised, in which function he was assisted by that curious individual Emperor J. A. Woodford, inspector of foreign forces.[92]

Bouillon, though his previous connections had been closer with Dundas and Nepean, shared in the beginning the more optimistic views of Windham, to whom he wrote

> on the advantages of decided and active operations in the Provinces of Brittany and Normandy on the part of the Allied Powers, depends its salvation, that of Europe I mean, and Dominion of its Colonies, for the West India islands may be invaded, but will never be conquered elsewhere than in the Maritime Provinces of France, and it is there that the Olive of Peace must be found.[93]

These hopes were fairly widely shared in 1794, and in the closing months of the year there was much activity. This was connected with the arrival in Great Britain of a royalist leader, the comte de Puisaye, who was able to win the confidence of the British government. Puisaye left Brittany early in September under the conduct of Prigent.[94] It was Prigent who represented him in an interview on September 22nd[95] with Pitt, who wrote to Chatham after the interview, 'Prigent's general accounts are that the Royalists are in great force, and the Republicans in very little ... I rather suspect exaggerations in his account.'[96] The Correspondence now took on a much larger scope, though in the last months of 1794 it suffered considerable delays from bad weather. A severe blow followed when, on the night of December 30th–31st, 1794, Prigent was captured by the republicans. He gave a very full account of the whole set-up, and lavish assurances of his republican sympathies, to his captors.[97] He was released at the Pacification of La Mabilais, April 20th, 1795, and resumed his employment in the Correspondence with the support of Puisaye, who continued to have implicit faith in him, but very much against the wishes of Bouillon.[98]

The opening phase of the Channel Isles Correspondence was now over. From 1794 to the Peace of Amiens it was to be a large-scale enterprise, with a host of agents and continual traffic between Brittany and the Channel Isles, which has left a massive documentation in French and British archives. The representatives on mission wrote to the Committee of Public Safety from Brest, on January 1st, 1795, that 'la fréquentation des bateaux de Jersey avec la France, est presque aussi commune qu'en temps de paix'.[99] But it may be held that the best possibility of effective co-operation with the royalists of the west to overthrow the Republic had already been lost in 1793. Possibly even then it was only a faint hope.

The government of Pitt has been severely criticized for its failure to come to the assistance of the royalists in time. Since the minds of Pitt and his colleagues were firmly set on peace, and they were anxious not to be involved in the plans of the counter-revolutionaries, they could hardly have intervened before war had been forced on them by the act of French Convention in 1793. Up to this point the activities of British intelligence agents in the French ports had been on a very small scale, though sufficient to provide what was wanted, information of the movement of French ships. The actual situation in French was largely hidden from Pitt and Dundas, but they distrusted the agitation of the émigrés and did not share the hopes of Windham and Burke. When positive information was obtained — and d'Angély's report was only the first of many — it seemed to confirm this distrust. They were probably right in suspecting that the royalists of the west were doomed to failure. Many reasons, of varying validity, have been offered for this failure, but it can only be adequately understood in the light of an analysis of the internal situation in Brittany, Normandy and the Vendée, and perhaps in particular of the relations of town and country, such as has hardly yet been made, in spite of the mass of writing on the royalist revolts. The British ministry was not aware of the strength of republicanism even in the west, but it appreciated from the very beginning the difficulties of co-operation with the royalists. A minute, I think in the hand of Nepean, stressing the need for the Correspondence to be carried on through a centralized direction in Jersey, adds the disillusioned note:

> This point is very material but long experience of these people [the royalists] has shown that it is impracticable — They have intrigues to carry on amongst themselves and with Monsieur [the comte de Provence] and those about him, which are the true objects of their journeys here: and the bringing intelligence is only a pretext to cover this.[100]

For their part, of course, the royalists had extensive, and by no means unjustified, suspicions of the aims of Pitt and Dundas, though they knew they had a firm advocate in Windham. The division in the government did not make for an effective policy; and as has been seen, in Jersey itself there was a struggle for control of the Correspondence. Even after Bouillon had obtained this he was not free from rivalries and jealous attacks. At Whitehall Windham and the Portland Whigs pushed the claims of the royalists of the West against the more sceptical Dundas, Huskisson and Nepean, while Grenville and Wickham were developing a connection with a different royalist organization in Paris. As failure followed failure, disappointment bred disillusionment and Bouillon came to feel, not without cause, that he was ploughing the sea. But history is not only the story of success, and in 1794 he might with reason have thought that he had attained the key position in the developing struggle with revolutionary France.

# 12

## CARLYLE'S *FRENCH REVOLUTION**

THERE are many different histories of the French Revolution and Carlyle's is a very special one of his own. It is worth considering, for it fixed in the British mind a picture of the Revolution which has remained to this day. Carlyle is an historian whom it is difficult to place in the development of historical thought. He is neither the descendant of Gibbon nor the ancestor of the Oxford History of England. The examiners of a modern doctoral thesis, confronted with a history on Carlyle's pattern, would greet the phenomenon with consternation; while Gibbon, if he could have read it, might have recanted his faith that the days of the Goths and Vandals could not come back again. Carlyle was, indeed, in some sense the historian of a new Gothic age. His *French Revolution* should have been illustrated by Doré or by Delacroix, perhaps best of all by the Géricault of the guillotined head or the 'Raft of the Medusa'. He is the word-painter of a society in shipwreck. Tempest-tossed he cast an anguished eye on the world. Driven to despair by his smug contemporaries, who could not see the waves beating or hear the winds roaring, he bravely faced the hurricane's blast in a Chelsea drawing-room. So thin-skinned that he devised a double-tegumented sound-proof room for protection from the infringement of the world on his ego, still he could not exclude the howling outside. A worshipper of strength, he had the sensitiveness of the weak. We may easily sympathize with the fate of the bright, clever Jane Carlyle, yoked unequally with him, yet feel that there was some truth in what Geraldine Jewsbury, who loved Jane, said — 'His was the soft heart and hers the hard one.'[1]

Neurasthenic Carlyle undoubtedly was, yet not lacking in determination, as was shown on one disastrous day when Mill, deathly pale and almost speechless, came to him. 'Gracious Providence,' cried out Jane, 'he has gone off with Mrs Taylor;' but the news

* This is a revised version of a paper first printed in a privately produced journal called *Montjoie*, which only survived for two numbers and has probably been seen by very few.

Mill brought was of a blow struck by chance, not choice. The first part of the manuscript of the *French Revolution*, lent by Carlyle to Mill, had gone up, appropriately, in fire and smoke. Carlyle turned to Jane after Mill had left them and said, 'Well, Mill, poor fellow, is terribly cut up: we must endeavour to hide from him how very serious this business is to us.' It was a disaster, for after repeated failures the *French Revolution* was, as he wrote, his 'last throw'. That night, wild dreams tormented him, of his dead father and sister, alive again, 'yet all defaced with the sleepy stagnancy, swollen hebetude of the grave, and again dying in some strange rude country.' But his Journal, the next day, registered that he was fixed not to 'quit the game'. 'I have written to Fraser to buy me a "Biographie Universelle" (a kind of increasing the stake) and fresh paper.'[2]

The blow was a harder one than it would have been to many writers. Even allowing for his self-dramatization, it is clear that Carlyle composed like a soul in torment. On September 1st, 1834, he had written to his mother that he was that day to commence writing.[3] Three weeks later he told his brother, 'The best news is that I have actually *begun* that "French Revolution", and after two weeks of blotching and boring have produced — two clean pages!'[4] Two years later he was still struggling with it — 'A hundred pages more, and this cursed book is flung out of me.'[5] It was finished on January 12th, 1837 — 'a wild savage book, itself a kind of French Revolution, which perhaps, if Providence have so ordered, the world had better not accept when offered it.'[6] The world did accept it. Was it not curious, Mrs Carlyle observed in one of her acid comments, that her husband's writings were adequately appreciated only by women and mad people.[7] This was really not quite true, certainly not of the *French Revolution*. Thackeray, Dickens, Southey, Emerson, Mill sang its praises, and the public read the book, better still, bought it.

Wordsworth wrote three sonnets against historians of the French Revolution in whose works

> History can appear
> As the cool Advocate of foul device;
> Reckless audacity extol and jeer
> At consciences perplexed.

But the poet belonged to an earlier age of more stable values —
the age, in fact, of the Revolution itself. Wordsworth was no
longer the man who had thought it bliss to be alive and very
heaven to be young when the French were making their new
constitution and a young Englishman could be the companion of
the republicans of Blois and the lover of Annette; but it is to the
early Wordsworth and his contemporaries that we should turn to
understand the age of the Revolution. The spirit of an age is such
a volatile thing that it escapes us even as we take the cork out of
the bottle, but at least a vintage of the right years should be
chosen for sampling. Carlyle's *French Revolution* was bottled in '37
not in '92. It was written in the decade of rioting and reform,
Chartism and cholera, when the hand-loom weavers were starving
and the factory population, beginning to teem in the cities, was
at the mercy of boom and slump. What Carlyle called 'the condition of the people question' was much in men's minds; it penetrated into literature with *Oliver Twist* and *Sybil*; and the 'people',
which to eighteenth-century democrats had been the solid
middle classes, was now metamorphosed into a ragged and rebellious proletariat.

Respectable society, or such part of it as could divert its gaze
from the pleasing spectacle of its own prosperity, was becoming
uneasily aware that it was enjoying a picnic in the crater of a
volcano, and one which, far from being extinct, was showing signs
of subterranean activity. As they peered down through the cracks
in the social structure, the early Victorians saw a sinister red
smoke rising. Carlyle could smell the sulphurous fumes at a dinner-
party and hear the boiling and bubbling in Regent Street.

> The world (he wrote in 1835) looks often quite spectral to
> me; sometimes as in Regent Street the other night (my nerves
> being all shattered), quite hideous, discordant, almost in-
> fernal. I had been at Mrs. Austin's, heard Sydney Smith for
> the first time guffawing, other persons prating, jargoning.
> To me through these thin cobwebs Death and Eternity sate
> glaring. Coming homewards along Regent Street, through
> street-walkers, through — Ach Gott! unspeakable pity
> swallowed up unspeakable abhorrence of it and of myself.[8]

Froude thought that Carlyle was looking at early-Victorian

England with eyes that were clouded by imaginings of revolutionary France. It would perhaps be truer to suggest that he envisaged the Terror in terms of the fears of the England of his own day. 'The whole frame of society is rotten', he wrote in 1830, 'and must go for fuel wood — and where is the new frame to come from? I know not, and no man knows.'[9] There spoke the nineteenth century, for the eighteenth did know. If it proposed to have 'fires out of the Grand Duke's wood', it had a theory to justify the fires: it knew where it was going. In the nineteenth century doubt was creeping in, and most of all with those, like Carlyle, who were more in tune with the future than the past. He condemned the eighteenth century as the age of doubt, but in fact those dogmatic, positive spirits of the French Enlightenment and the Revolution had a faith which he had lost. In Carlyle emotions took the place of principles. Essentially he was a disillusioned Scottish radical. From his mother and father, and early years in Annandale, he had imbibed radicalism, along with Presbyterianism; but neither faith survived, though the mental habits they had bred in him lasted.

My object is not to sketch Carlyle's mental development, but to deal with a greater theme. The French Revolution was a cataclysm of European, and ultimately of world-wide proportions, whereas Carlyle was at worst only a domestic disaster. His early radicalism needed to be mentioned because it helped him to discover the people — 'hunger-stricken vagabonds, poor naked wretches'. Many such there doubtless were in eighteenth-century France, but Carlyle was mistaken in thinking that it was *their* revolution. That every known leader of the Revolution was bourgeois has long been realized. Robespierre, Marat, Danton were not the scrapings of the gutter but respectable professional men. The rank and file of the revolutionary mobs, or the *armée révolutionnaire* of the Terror, came from lower social strata, but still largely from the small masters of the faubourgs, the shopkeepers, craftsmen, not from the homeless vagabonds or criminal underworld. That they suffered from economic grievances is true, as it is that these could mostly be summed up in the single fact of the scarcity and high price of bread, on which so large a proportion of the income of the poorer population of France was spent. But the *menu peuple* — those whom we might now call, roughly, the lower middle classes — suffered from scarcity as much as, and possibly more than, the *journaliers* or the poorer peasants.

Carlyle's failure to realize that the Revolution was from beginning to end essentially directed by the middle classes, and that even the mobs which constituted its fighting force should be envisaged largely in terms of the small masters and craftsmen of eighteenth-century France and not the urban proletariat of nineteenth-century England, is comprehensible if it is appreciated that he was writing in terms of the social revolution feared by his contemporaries; whereas, apart from the peasant revolt of 1789 and its sequel, the first great French Revolution was concerned with changing the political rather than the social structure of the country.

If Carlyle's interpretation of social forces was wild and wide rather than deep, however, this was not all loss. The absence from his work of a modern social analysis may even be counted an advantage in so far as it saved him from the mistake of attempting to interpret the Revolution in terms of an ideology derived from a later social situation. His explanation of the Revolution was in fact a much simpler one, derived in the first place from the Old Testament Calvinism of his upbringing. The Revolution was God's revenge on a society that had abandoned His law to seek after the flesh-pots. The people, wild and formless, were the agents of divine justice,[10] and the punishment itself was a proof of the crime.

This is an interpretation of history which all too easily turns, as it did later with Carlyle, into the glorification of success: the historian, looking for divine justice, justifies the gods against Cato and applauds the winning side. Even more dangerous ways of thought were to emerge in the later writings, but up to the *French Revolution* Carlyle was modestly content to condemn the losers without always applauding those who won. His view of human history, applied to the French Revolution, involved a damning judgment on the *ancien régime*. As a radical he despised its social and political structure, as a Presbyterian its immorality and irreligion.

A third and later element in his intellectual make-up was added to the pattern on which his verdict was composed. Goethe had taught him that there were alternating periods of *Unglauben* and

*Glauben*. From Saint-Simon he imbibed the theory that history progressed by an alternation of critical and organic ages.[11] The eighteenth century had been one of the former; its task had been to eliminate the lumber of the past and it was completed, appropriately, by a revolution of destruction. Against this conception of the Revolution as a gigantic cleaning-out of the Augean stables of monarchy, royalist historians have protested by lauding the Bourbon monarchy, without winning many scholarly laurels in the process. By insisting that there was nothing that needed alteration in the *ancien régime* they have helped to conceal the fact that the eighteenth century in France, already before 1789, was an age of extensive social changes and of reforms which grew out of the supposedly merely critical philosophy of the age. The destructive aspect of the Revolution, being so much the more dramatic, tended to obscure its positive achievements. Carlyle himself passed in silence over the reforming movements both before and after 1789. The theories on which it was based he did not know and would have condemned if he had known — 'Theories of Government! Such have been, and will be; in ages of decadence.'[12]

Carlyle's view of the destructive genius of the eighteenth century fitted in with his severe moral disapproval of the French nation, in which that genius had found its fullest expression. His knowledge of France was indeed not extensive, but he had paid a visit in 1824 to 'the Temple of Frivolity and Dissipation', in the course of which he grew daily, for some fourteen days, 'more and more contemptuous of Paris, and the manière d'être of its people', who, he discovered, spent their lives in cafés and theatres and on the streets.[13] A French historian has supposed that Carlyle thought the Revolution great because in it he saw one of the Latin nations, which he so despised, turning against itself and destroying its own civilization.[14]

This brings me to a fourth factor in Carlyle's interpretation of the Revolution. He admired the genius of the German *Sturm und Drang* as much as he scorned the spirit of the French writers of the *siècle des lumières*. He had studied the German literature of the Romantic period perhaps more thoroughly than any other man of his time, had translated *Wilhelm Meister*, written a life of Schiller and an unpublished history of German literature; he corresponded with Goethe, read Fichte and became increasingly obsessed with the idea of the Hero and contemptuous of parliamentary institutions:

> One thing an elected Assembly of Twelve Hundred is fit for: Destroying. Which indeed is but a more decided exercise of its natural talent for Doing Nothing. Do nothing, only keep agitating, debating; and things will destroy themselves ... With endless debating, we get the *Rights of Man* written down and promulgated: true paper basis of all paper Constitutions. Neglecting, cry the opponents, to declare the Duties of Man! Forgetting, answer we, to ascertain the *Mights* of Man ... In such manner labour the National Deputies; perfecting their theory of Irregular Verbs.[15]

For Carlyle, the Revolution suffered from the fact that it seemed to have a surplus of assemblies and a deficiency of heroes, but whenever he comes across a possible candidate for the role, Carlyle's tone lightens and his heart is for a moment lifted up:

> Royal Mirabeau! Conspicuous among all parties, raised above and beyond them all, this man rises more and more. As we often say, he has an *eye*, he is a reality; while others are formulas and eye-*glasses*.[16]

Or again, the epitaph on Danton, in whom Carlyle was perhaps the first to appreciate the element of greatness:

> So passes, like a gigantic mass, of valour, ostentation, fury, affection and wild revolutionary force and manhood, this Danton, to his unknown home. He was of Arcis-sur-Aube; born of 'good farmer-people' there. He had many sins; but one worst sin he had not, that of cant. No hollow Formalist, deceptive and self-deceptive, *ghastly* to the natural sense, was this; but a very Man; with all his dross he was a Man; fiery-real, from the great fire-bosom of Nature herself.[17]

No other heroes materialize, and even these two, to use Carlylean language, are but spectral, though Mirabeau's last appearance is also a fine one:

> It was he who shook old France from its basis; and, as if with his single hand, had held it toppling there, still unfallen.

What things depended on that one man! He is as a ship suddenly shivered on sunk rocks: much swims on the waste waters, far from help.[18]

Radical pamphleteer, Old Testament prophet, Saint-Simonian sociologist, German romanticist, Fichtean philosopher of Might and Right, Carlyle was to compose his history of the Revolution as each of these in turn, or all at once; but separately or taken together they did not make up a coherent historical philosophy. This was perhaps as well, for it allowed their defects at least in part to cancel one another out. There was still room in the wide gaps between his prejudices for history to take root and grow. Aulard judged him one of the most impartial in intention, and even perhaps in achievement, among the historians of the Revolution.[19]

Whatever his incipient ideologies, Carlyle was not unconscious of the need for facts. He did his best to acquire the raw material: he asked his brother, who was passing through Paris, for a piano-score of the *Ça ira*, and inquired of him if the tree of liberty planted in 1790 in the rue du Faubourg St Antoine were still there.[20] He had the advantage that he wrote at a time when a considerable body of source material for the history of the Revolution had recently come into print. He drew heavily on the *Moniteur*, the *Choix des Rapports*, so far as it had been published, the *Histoire parlementaire* of Buchez and Roux, and on the twenty-volume miscellany attributed to *Deux amis de la Liberté* but in fact compiled by a series of journalists. It is evidence of his shrewdness of judgment that he realized that only the first seven volumes of the last work, up to early 1792, possessed any real historical value.[21] He made use also of the earlier histories of the Revolution by Lacretelle, Toulongeon and others, though he judged them of little value.[22] From them he could at least learn that not everything in the Revolution was evil, for they were the work of men who had lived through it and to some extent compromised with it, who therefore could not denounce it from alpha to omega without repudiating their past lives.

The more recent historians, Thiers and Mignet, make no appearance among his references. He had read Thiers, but dismissed him with 'Dig where you will you come to water';[23] his work was superficial and full of errors;[24] Mignet was more honest, but his history lacked life and colour and its ideas were mere logical abstractions.[25] Would it be fair to suggest that Carlyle was not anxious to lavish praise on dangerous rivals in the same field? He himself would doubtless have said that he preferred to dig his ore direct from the native rock, and not receive it pounded up and sieved by his own race of historians, for which he had such contempt.

His most important source was 'that ravelled immeasurable mass of threads and thrums, which we name Memoirs', out of which, he said, the 'magic web' of Universal History is woven.[26] Now Memoirs constitute one of the most dangerous forms of historical material. Their authors are usually concerned to present a picture of themselves which will correspond to that which was hoped for rather than that which actually was. They are, however, not so misleading on this account as might be supposed: the one thing that their writers invariably do is to give themselves away. The danger lay rather in the general historical information which was drawn from them by Carlyle, not unconscious of the 'indolent falsehood of these *Histoires* and *Mémoires*'[27] but accepting what they said none the less, except on the few occasions when the lie was too whopping even for him to swallow.

His reliance on Memoirs is partly responsible for the episodic character of his history,[28] as it is for the innumerable anecdotes, which he liked to throw out in passing with a knowing air, in an allusive style calculated to whet rather than satisfy the reader's appetite. There was plenty of such picturesque material in the Memoirs, since to provide it had, indeed, been the chief object of their compilers, who often were not those whose names appeared on the title page. For example, the memoirs of Besenval, on which Carlyle draws heavily, are a collection of often scandalous anecdotes compiled by Ségur and disavowed by Besenval's family; those of Weber were largely drawn up by Lally-Tolendal. Carlyle was in no position to discriminate between what was true and false, and if he had been, presented with a good story it would have been too much to expect him to inquire into its authenticity. Legends which he accepts are such as the cup of aristocrats' blood drunk by Mlle de Sombreuil to save the life of her father, though there are fewer of such gross fabrications than Dr Gooch suggests.[29]

When his account of the sinking of the *Vengeur* was challenged by a naval officer who had been present at the battle, Carlyle accepted the correction, though he only won thereby a French denunciation in verse,

> Détracteur orgueilleux de notre vieille gloire,
> Digne héritier de Burke, Basile d'outre-mer.[30]

A more serious consequence of his dependence on memoir-writers is a tendency to explain great events by petty personal motives, as when Choiseul is dismissed by Louis XV because he 'would discern in the Dubarry nothing but a wonderfully dizened Scarlet-woman'; or the Seven Years War is fought 'that a Harlot might take revenge for an epigram'. Such conclusions are no more than the logical corollary of Carlyle's belief that 'biography is the only history', to which we owe also the brilliant, if not always reliable, character vignettes which decorate almost every chapter. There is, of course, far more in Carlyle's *French Revolution* than this. His remarkably detailed knowledge is revealed so often merely in passing, by a single adjective or noun, that it escapes notice on a rapid view, and only on a close examination can one see that what look like broad sweeps of colour are in fact made up of a mosaic of minute separate details. The later episodes in the history are the more impressionistic. After the death of Robespierre, when the oncoming tide of revolution broke in a final great wave of blood and foam, Carlyle's interest visibly recedes.

> It all stands pretty fair in my head [he wrote] nor do I mean to investigate much more about it, but to splash down what I know in large masses of colours, that it may look like a smoke-and-flame conflagration in the distance, which it is.[31]

He has on occasion rather a cavalier attitude to mere facts. 'England has cast out the Embassy: England declares war ... Spain declares war,' he writes. Then he observes that this is wrong: France declared war first on them — 'a point of immense Parliamentary and Journalistic influence in those days, but which has become of no influence whatever in these'.[32]

One is tempted to think of Carlyle as a great pageant-master. He is at his best in the dramatic scenes of terror and death, when the guillotine is reaping its harvest. Aulard describes his history as the epic of *sans-culottisme*.[33] Nor does he fail to see something of what was behind the Terror.

> That the French Nation has believed, for several years now, in the possibility, nay certainty and near advent, of a universal Millennium, or reign of Freedom, Equality, Fraternity wherein man should be the brother of man, and sorrow and sin flee away. Not bread to eat, nor soap to wash with; and the reign of Perfect Felicity ready to arrive, due always since the Bastille fell! ... Bright was our Hope then, as sunlight; red-angry is our Hope grown now, as consuming fire. But, O Heavens, what enchantment is it, or devilish legerdemain, of such effect that Perfect Felicity, always within arm's length, could never be laid hold of ... Tremble, ye traitors; dread a People which calls itself patient, long-suffering; but which cannot always submit to have its pocket picked, in this way — of a Millennium![34]

And when the disappointed multitude took its revenge — for it did not occur to Carlyle that possibly the Terror was the work of the few and not of the many — he could not condemn them severely:

> It was not the Dumb Millions that suffered here; it was the Speaking Thousands, and Hundreds and Units; who shrieked and published, and made the world ring with their wail, as they could and should: that is their grand peculiarity.[35]

He was charged with indifference to the suffering by a royalist who had lived through it.[36] Michelet thought he was deeply marked with the national sin of England — 'le satanique esprit d'orgueil' — and added in a note to his edition of 1837, 'La Révolution est pour lui le cimetière d'Hamlet; il prend, il pèse les crânes avec un sourire amer où paraît trop souvent une pitié dérisoire: ceci est un crâne de fou, cela un crâne de bouffon ... le mot qui manque, c'est celui du cœur: "Ah! pauvre Yorick!" — Dieu me garde de manier si froidement les os de mes ennemis.'[37] Yet Carlyle's death scenes are not lacking in pathos, as witness his epitaphs on the massacred Swiss Guard, on Danton, even on the dying Robespierre:

> He had on the sky-blue coat he had got made for the Feast

of the *Être Suprême*' — O Reader, can thy hard heart hold out against that?[38]

There is more kinship between Michelet and Carlyle than the French historian admits. Taine even describes Carlyle as 'un Michelet anglais'.[39] The suggestion that he took his inspiration from Carlyle was indignantly repudiated by Michelet, calling him a 'fantaisiste' and his book an 'ouvrage pitoyable'.[40] Despite this repudiation Aulard thought the resemblances between them, both in form and method, striking: 'C'est presque la même manière de voir, d'évoquer, de peindre, d'émouvoir, d'étonner. On dirait le même lyrisme, et surtout si on se reporte au texte anglais, trop souvent intraduisible, le même procédé de style, presque la même façon de couper ou disloquer la phrase, les mêmes figures littéraires, surtout l'exclamation ou l'apostrophe.'[41]

Like Michelet, Carlyle writes of the men and women of the Revolution as if they were his contemporaries: that is the greatest vice and virtue of his history. One is tempted to think that he was an historian against his will and despised his own task.

> Alas, what mountains of dead ashes, wreck and burnt bones, does assiduous Pedantry dig up from the Past Time, and name it History, and Philosophy of History; till, as we say, the human soul sinks wearied and bewildered; till the Past time seems all one infinite incredible grey void, without sun, stars, hearth-fires, or candle-light; dim offensive dust-whirl-winds filling universal Nature; and over your Historical Library it is as if all the Titans had written for themselves: *Dry Rubbish shot here.*[42]

After this one can see his heroes as a kind of compensation for what he had failed to be himself. He might have written with Michelet, 'J'ai passé à côté du monde et j'ai pris l'histoire pour la vie.'

Such regrets resulted in his later writings in too much wish-fulfilment and too little history, but in the *French Revolution* Carlyle's prejudices were not yet obsessions. With all its defects, the work has some of the qualities of a great history, more capable of being appreciated, perhaps, in an age of wars and revolutions, when its portrayal of passions let loose strikes home, than in quieter times. Economic and social analysis, the complicated problems of foreign policy, constitutional struggles, administrative and legal developments, local government, he touches on slightly or not at all. The ideas which flash through the Revolution, intermittently throwing light on the confused struggle, like the beams of a light-house sweeping round and then disappearing, do not penetrate the darkness in Carlyle. His Revolution is a vortex in an intellectual void.

When all this is said, however, the very deficiencies of his approach bring with them certain compensating advantages. History has been written most often from above. France does this or England does that. Ministers and Secretaries of State form and carry out their plans, and history becomes a pattern of calculated policies and foregone conclusions. This is not the way in which things really happen, especially in time of revolution. His assemblage of *Memoirs*, if they misled Carlyle on many points of detail, enabled him to see the Revolution not in terms of the actions of a few dominating men, but as the field in which innumerable lesser lives crossed and tangled, in which each successive phase was the product of a host of individual destinies. 'History', he believed, 'is the essence of innumerable biographies.'[43] We are far here from the textbook enumeration of causes and results and are plunged instead into the confusion of actual life. Aided by the conditions of contemporary England, Carlyle was able to see the Revolution and to write its history in terms that were hardly to be envisaged by another historian for a century or more. It was for him what it has become again in our own day, a history of sans-culottism.[44] To pick out any one of the many facets of the Revolution and to insist that this *was* the Revolution is patently unhistorical. Yet there is a sense in which sans-culottism was that which was most revolutionary in the Revolution, and this, Carlyle, unlike so many of the far sounder historians who followed him, did see.

# 13

## HISTORIANS OF THE FRENCH REVOLUTION

THROUGHOUT the nineteenth century the French Revolution was contemporary politics in France, and each history of it, almost in the nature of things, also a political manifesto. Mme de Staël, Mignet, Thiers, Lamartine, Michelet, Louis Blanc, Taine, even Tocqueville, with many lesser writers, framed their verdict on the regime they lived under in the form of a history of the Revolution, selecting out of its vast repertoire the themes and facts appropriate to their tacit or explicit argument. Some of these histories are still worth reading for their literary qualities, but a literary genius has usually something better to write than history and when he does write it one usually wishes that he had not. If the great nineteenth-century historians of the French Revolution survive it is for their intellectual powers, especially in social and political analysis, and their insight into the way in which things happen, rather than for the validity of their account of what actually did happen. On the personalities, motives and actions of individuals they are apt to be all at sea and to produce fancy pictures which are irreconcilable both with what contemporaries thought when the men were alive and with the verdicts of more scholarly investigation subsequently. It would only be a slight exaggeration to say that what were written as contributions to the history of the French Revolution are now of greater value as source material for the history of the nineteenth century.

*

As one comes to the historical writing of the last years of the century, however, it becomes more difficult to pass such judgments and, curiously, this is not the result of the increasing stature of historians, for we lose the great names that decorate its earlier years. The historian who comes to dominate the history of the Revolution is Aulard, and from an intellectual or literary point of view Aulard is not pre-eminent. The secret of what he did for the

history of the Revolution is to be found in the first three of the
ten commandments which he was accustomed to give to his
students at the beginning of each academic year: 1. Always go to
the sources; 2. Say nothing which you do not know from an
original source; 3. Write nothing without giving your references.
With these principles he transformed revolutionary historiography. When he retired, in 1922, after nearly forty years of
teaching the history of the Revolution at the Sorbonne, Aulard
could boast, with pardonable exaggeration, that no one would dare
to write on the Revolution, even to attack it, without quoting his
authorities and giving his sources. Under his inspiration revolutionary historiography belatedly began to emulate the achievements of the *École des Chartes* in the publication of historical texts;
and if Aulard's own editorial methods leave something to be
desired, quantity was at the time perhaps more important than
quality. The library of documentary material on the history of the
Revolution that has been published since Aulard has played an
important part in stimulating a flood of monographic literature. It
has also made the dependence of the history of the Revolution on
the memoirs or pseudo-memoirs which formerly distorted it a
thing of the past. On the other hand, since the sources printed
were to begin with mainly official documents, the result was
naturally to promote a kind of official history, seeing policies and
their results from the point of view of those who dictated them —
the revolutionary Assemblies, Jacobin Club, Commune of Paris,
Committee of Public Safety. For the same reason it was also
mainly political history.

A new trend was started by the socialist leader Jaurès. In his
*Histoire Socialiste* he developed, what Tocqueville and Taine had
already pointed at, a sociological interpretation of the Revolution.
For Jaurès the belief that the Revolution was mainly a political
one was a bourgeois illusion: on the contrary it was also, and even
primarily, a great social revolution. Believing that the essence of
history lies in the play of economic interests and social forces, he
escaped from the purely political interpretation and at the same
time from the rather bellicose nationalism that was a feature of the
historiography of the Third Republic. Although inspired partly
by Marxism, Jaurès's ideas were not confined in any narrow
dogmatic formula. Aulard himself expressed admiration for the

historical impartiality of the great socialist politician. By founding the *Commission de l'Histoire Économique de la Révolution* Jaurès also stimulated the addition of many volumes of economic texts to the big political series.

Among historians who followed these were Marcel Marion and Philippe Sagnac; but it was above all Albert Mathiez who continued the work that Jaurès had started, though with less moderation and with a more dogmatic devotion to the materialist conception of history. Even the anti-clerical movement was for Mathiez primarily an expression of economic interests. The conflict of the so-called Girondins and the Jacobins he saw equally as a class struggle, though without confirming his view by an analysis of the social composition of the two factions. He tended to interpret the policy of the Jacobin Mountain in ana-chronistically socialist terms. Thermidor became for him a bourgeois revolt against a socialist government, and the subse-quent period was a mire of corruption, in describing which he seems to be indirectly indicting the bourgeois Third Republic. On the other hand, from the experience of economic controls in the First World War Mathiez came to a better understanding of such measures of the Committee of Public Safety as the maximum on prices. With a perseverance worthy of a better cause he con-ducted a vendetta against Aulard — one-sided, for the older historian never replied to it. Moreover, since such an intense spirit had to have a hero and a villain, he cast Danton, who had been built up as the safe bourgeois patriot with no dangerous ideas about equality, for the latter role and Robespierre, the incarnation of the Jacobin Terror, for the former. This may read like an indictment of Mathiez's work, but it would be unfair not to recognize that his interpretation is at bottom fairer to the op-ponents of the Revolution and broader in its scope than was that of Aulard. Danton may not have been the corrupt and vulgar demagogue that Mathiez portrayed: after him he can never be put on the same pedestal again. Robespierre may not have been a model of all virtue and all statesmanship: his name will not easily be ousted from the central place in the history of the Revo-lution where Mathiez firmly set it.

Ideologically Mathiez remained for a time the farthest left among important historians of the Revolution. This is odd, for revolutionary historiography has up to recent times faithfully followed the progress of political opinion. There have, indeed, been Communist historians of quality in France. If, apart from an occasional obeisance, the result of their researches is more recognizable as sound history than as Communist ideology, we shall not complain, though we may speculate about the reason why, and how far it is to be attributed to the dominance of the sources. Mention should perhaps be made of a history by M. Guérin, which is Trotskyite in its inspiration. For M. Guérin, the French Revolution is an embryo proletarian revolution and Robespierre the social democrat who frustrated it. He bitterly attacks all previous historians of the Revolution. Jaurès 'has not broken the umbilical cord which binds him to bourgeois democracy', Mathiez, like Aulard, is a 'functionary of the Third Republic', and Lefebvre has not disengaged himself from 'the cocoon of bourgeois democracy'. Guérin's history has the stimulating quality that extreme perverseness can sometimes give, and it is not without significance as showing the way in which extremes meet, for in its attack on the main line of revolutionary development this left-wing history meets and joins forces with the historians of the right.

\*

As Guérin makes use of the Thermidorian and counter-revolutionary attacks on Robespierre to support his case, so Gaxotte brings in the material of Mathiez to support an otherwise traditional critique of the Revolution. To account for the Revolution he falls back on the work of Cochin, who himself derived from Taine; but where Taine had seen the Revolution as the result of popular passions, Cochin, with experience of the politics of the Third Republic, explained it in terms of a political machine which set the mob in operation. His work has had a justifiable influence: contemporary historians are less willing than their predecessors to see the mob as a *deus ex machina* and attribute all the great *journées* of the Revolution to spontaneous combustion; but Cochin's thesis attributing the Revolution to the intrigues of a conspiratorial faction has not had much success. Cochin at least went to the sources. Gaxotte, like most other right-wing historians, relied mainly on the work of others and has been content with able popularization.

Madelin, on the other hand, who writes in a clear narrative style, accepts the necessity for the Revolution up to August 1789. After that it falls under the influence of ambitious adventurers, from whose rule France is rescued by Napoleon. Madelin's Revolution is indeed a mere unfortunate prologue to the heroic age of the Empire: his history is a reminder that there is a Bonapartist as well as a royalist right in France. Perhaps the slighter volumes of Lenotre, especially the series entitled *Vieilles Maisons, vieux papiers*, should be mentioned. Lenotre gives rather scanty clues to his sources, but now and then one can come across the material he must have used in the archives, and whenever one does his facts seem correct. His brilliant little vignettes are frankly royalist in sympathy and do not pretend to any depth, but they provide a fascinating *marginalia* to the real history of the Revolution.

During the last generation the historical study of the Revolution has come to be increasingly dominated by the magisterial figure of Georges Lefebvre. Ideologically Lefebvre is in the succession to Jaurès and Mathiez and well to the left; but this is to say very little, for ideology is becoming less a determining factor in historical writing on the Revolution. One sign of this is to be found in the history of the Church during the Revolution. On this ancient battlefield, littered with the corpses of clerical and anti-clerical historians, today Catholic historians like Laflon and Latreille can meet a strong anti-clerical like Lefebvre and at least come far closer on a basis of the recognition of the same facts than would have formerly seemed possible. Lefebvre, for all the strength of his convictions, has himself played a leading part in freeing revolutionary historiography from the dominance of political passions. Such monographs as his massive study of the peasants of the Nord, or the masterly piece of historical detection on the Great Fear of 1789, are evidence that there is a depth of research at which ideological bias becomes almost irrelevant. In the brilliant short study translated as *The Coming of the French Revolution* and in the general history of the revolutionary period in the *Peuples et Civilisations* series, Lefebvre goes farther. By his analysis of the successive phases from the aristocratic revolt of 1787–8 to the Jacobin revolution of August 10th, 1792, and the unsuccessful risings of Hébertists and *enragés*, he has made it impossible henceforth to treat the Revolution as a single entity to be approved or condemned *en bloc*. Another important lesson that Lefebvre has taught is that the problems of revolutionary historiography are not to be dealt with by preconceived formulas; he has shown how, by the critical collection and marshalling of an army of facts, in the hands of a master, new and unsuspected territory is won, and in the process of discovering how things happened we gain insight into why they happened.

\*

A school of distinguished historians is continuing the work of Lefebvre. Among them may be mentioned M. Godechot for his studies of institutional history, M. Labrousse for his brilliant analysis of economic conditions in France before the Revolution, and the author of the authoritative life of Carnot, M. Marcel Reinhard, in whom the chair of Aulard and Lefebvre found a worthy successor. Many other historians of the past and present generation deserve to be mentioned, but their very number would turn this essay into a catalogue. How far the exploration of the sources has progressed in the last generation may be seen by a comparison of the first and second editions of the invaluable *Manuel pratique pour l'étude de la Révolution française* by Pierre Caron; and it will be realized that I am confining myself to French historians and therefore say nothing of important American and British contributions.

The flood of revolutionary history is still running at full spate. It will be fitting to conclude by indicating some of the new channels it is showing signs of digging for itself. First, there is a growing appreciation of the vast resources of the departmental archives, although we are still only at the beginning of the writing of the history of provincial France during the Revolution. The biggest gap in the history of the Revolution is, paradoxically, the history of the counter-revolution. Long ago it was pointed out that by writing the history of one side in the struggle without that of the other, the policies of the revolutionaries were reduced on occasion to the appearance of maniacal gestures in the air, like the actions of a duellist if those of his opponent were rubbed out of the picture. There is a kind of French equivalent of Whig history, in which the course of French history is seen as a majestic sweep from

revolution to revolution and a counter-revolution is an undesirable
excrescence not to be permitted on the historical portrait. Failure,
however, is not a reason for deleting any chapter from the story.
A more thorough study of the counter-revolution is above all
necessary for an understanding of the ideological elements in the
European struggle that the Revolution initiated; and then it may
be appreciated that the Revolution in France was only the greatest, but not the first, of a series of democratic revolts which
signalize the second half of the eighteenth century as the opening
of a new age in the history of the western world. To grasp adequately the nature and significance of the war of ideas, methods of
exact scholarship, which are unfortunately too often lacking in the
field of the history of ideas, are needed. Mornet's work on the
intellectual origins of the Revolution in France, and Balden-
sperger's on the ideas of the emigration, represent only a beginning in this task.

*

There are signs, however, that some of the most fruitful research
in the near future will take a new line. The history of the Revolution, like most other history, has largely been written from above.
Even in Mathiez we learn far more about the policies and decrees
of assemblies and committees than of the people who were putting
them into operation, of those in whose daily life they were something more than pieces of paper, and of what they meant in
practice. It is surprising that with all the research that has been
devoted to the Revolution we do not really know who the revolutionaries were. General histories still talk about *noblesse*, bourgeois, workers, peasants, but these categories are totally inadequate
for an understanding of the real social structure of France. So
long as historians were content to write primarily political history
this rather artificial, juridical pattern of classes passed muster.
Economic historians for a time were able to make use of the simple
classification of aristocracy, bourgeoisie, proletariat, with the
peasants thrown in for make-weight, so long as economic history
was simply another way of writing political history in different
terms. Now that detailed research has begun to reveal the real
complexities of French eighteenth-century society, a much more
realistic and empirical analysis will be required.

This monument of research that has been, and will be, erected to ten years in the life of a single nation is — it must be our final word — no mere mausoleum over the dead. 'Alas, what mountains of dead ashes, wreck and burnt bones, does assiduous Pedantry dig up from the Past Time, and name it History': Carlyle's condemnation need not be feared. The effect of the new lines of research that are developing will be to impose a need for putting the Revolution back into its setting in French and even world history, from which it has sometimes been unnaturally isolated. The Revolution also cannot be understood apart from the society out of which it emerged: one of the less happy results of the concentration of so much attention on the Revolution has been the comparative neglect of the years from 1715 to 1789, which are still largely given over to historical myths, at least in the more general histories in this country. The period after 1794 has also been neglected and seen as an illogical contradiction of what went before, instead of its historical sequel. Spreading out from the history of the Revolution one can envisage a reshaping of modern French history which will transcend the arbitrary political cleavages of the past, and indeed throw new light on the whole history of the modern world. The interpretation of revolutionary history and its general setting is likely, therefore, to undergo considerable change in the next fifty years; but the new history will be built on, and has indeed been made possible by, the work of the great school of French historians, from Aulard to Lefebvre, who in the last half-century have laid foundations too solid to be shaken.

# 14

## POLITICAL VERSUS SOCIAL
## INTERPRETATIONS OF
## THE FRENCH REVOLUTION

HISTORIANS have become increasingly interested of recent years in problems of social structure. Their researches in this field have often produced results which seem to run counter to accepted interpretations. They have in consequence sometimes found themselves talking at cross-purposes with more orthodox historians and frustrated by mutual incomprehension. The explanation of this failure of understanding is not necessarily the same for all periods. It is a reasonable supposition that in some cases it may result from the application of classifications relevant to one type of society to other societies in which they are quite inappropriate. Thus there is an obvious danger of confusion resulting from the use of such terms as *caste, ordre, classe* in the study of seventeenth-century Europe. For the period of the French Revolution, to which I am devoting this paper, however, this kind of misunderstanding either does not exist, or has largely been overcome. The history of the Revolution can be written without dependence upon any of these terms; and when they are used, as in the phrase 'privileged orders', there is, it seems to me, little disagreement as to their meaning. This is not to say there is no conflict of opinion on the nature and significance of social factors in the revolutionary period, but I believe that here we have to look for a different explanation.

There has recently appeared an example of the conflict of views on the history of this period which provides an admirable illustration of its nature and causes. A short book which I wrote on *The Social Interpretation of the French Revolution*, as I anticipated, has aroused considerable opposition, sometimes not untouched with emotion. Its most thorough and fundamental *critique* so far is undoubtedly that published in the *Revue Historique* by my friend

Godechot, who writes in the leading French historical journal with the authority of one of the most distinguished French historians of the Revolution, and who has moreover devoted his whole academic life to the study of the period between 1789 and 1815.[1] The first thing that strikes one about his review is the almost total breakdown in understanding between author and reviewer. I will begin with a single point, which can be separated from the general argument. This is the question of *partage* of the common lands during the Revolution.

M. Godechot points out my error in this matter with the aid of an appeal to the authority of Marc Bloch. Now we have only to look at the chapter to which he refers to discover that Marc Bloch says precisely the opposite of what he supposes.[2] There are other major issues on which what I myself have said is read by my reviewer in quite the contrary sense of what I supposed I was saying.[3] My object in drawing attention to these apparent misunderstandings is not to complain of them, or even just to keep the record straight; but rather to attempt to explore the reasons for them, as well as for broader differences of interpretation, because I believe that they are relevant to the problem of the writing of social history.

If an historian of the highest competence reads into what appear to be quite simple statements something very different from their plain intention, it would be fair to suppose the explanation to lie in a deep-seated difference of presuppositions, which has the effect of changing the meaning of one set of historical judgments by translating them into a different world of historical thought. An examination of this particular failure in communication may therefore be of value as a contribution to the search for an explanation for the present lack of mutual comprehension among historians, not only of the French Revolution but of other periods.

Initially, the difference of opinion may seem little more than a matter of terminology, and it may appear, as for example it does to M. Godechot, as a lot of fuss about nothing. What I thought was a vagueness and uncertainty about the meaning of the terms commonly used for social description in eighteenth-century history seemed to me to present a serious problem to historians; but for M. Godechot there is no difficulty. The words that we use in describing French society in the eighteenth century, he says, 'doivent être parfaitement connus de tous les candidats à la licence, s'ils ont quelque prétention au succès ... Alfred Cobban enfonce des portes ouvertes.'[4] This is doubtless true, if one is thinking of the kind of dictionary definition that can be given in two lines. On the other hand, if we wish to go a little deeper into the understanding of past societies we are hardly likely to be satisfied to remain on the level of the kind of history that any undergraduate knows.

Let us take some of these terms, to see if they are in fact perfectly understood. We all know, says M. Godechot, what *officier* means. But do we know the role of the *officiers* in French society, their functions and relative status, how these had been changing, and in what direction, during the course of the eighteenth century? There is a whole book to be written on this subject as a sequel to M. Mousnier's great work, and no inconsiderable or unimportant one. Again, M. Godechot gives *manufacturier* and *ouvrier* as examples of terms which are perfectly well understood. On the contrary, it seems to me that they tell us practically nothing about the social position at the time of the Revolution of an individual thus described, except that he is in some way connected with manufacture. He may have been a wealthy employer or a poverty-stricken wage-earner: without further information we cannot possibly tell. This, I assume, is what M. Soboul has in mind when he explains that, 'Il est ainsi le plus souvent impossible, dans les documents de l'époque, de faire le départ entre le compagnon, le petit artisan, l'entrepreneur.'[5]

In respect of the world of commerce, some interesting pages of Brunot discuss the complicated, overlapping and changing meanings of such terms as *commerçant, négociant, marchand, trafiquand, merchand en grand, grossier, marchand magazinier, regrattier, détailleur*.[6] The social terminology of agriculture was at least as imprecise as that of industry and commerce. Without knowing the details of each specific case nobody could possibly guess the social and economic position of someone described as a *fermier*. A *cultivateur*, despite M. Godechot's confidence in the complete undergraduate comprehension of the word, might be, during the Revolution, a wealthy proprietor or a poor smallholder. We thought we at least knew the meaning of *métayer*, until Paul Bois showed that in the Sarthe a *métayer* was one of the richer peasants.[7]

The first cause of misunderstanding will now be obvious. It consists in the belief that the imprecise language of contemporary usage is adequate for the purposes of social history. Here I can only echo the warning of M. Mousnier against the use of contemporary terms without careful examination and criticism. The variety of meaning to be found in practically every single social term is useful historical evidence. The very vagueness and overlapping of contemporary descriptions is significant. But this does not justify us in using them for the purpose of historical analysis without an attempt to differentiate between their various meanings and to discover the social realities behind them. Where they can be, and normally are used, is in ordinary narrative and descriptive history, concerned to trace the main sequence of events on the great stage of national politics. In this kind of history social analysis is an unnecessary complication, irrelevant to the task the historian has set himself.

The fact is that there is more than one kind of history, and we are here dealing with two different *genres*. One of these accepts the social terms of the past as adequate for its purpose, while the other tries to analyse them and break them down into what are believed to be more realistic elements. This opposition appears even more plainly if we turn from the more specific social terms to broader ones, such as the 'régime féodal'. A certain measure of agreement has been reached here. M. Godechot declares himself in perfect agreement that 'le régime féodal en France, à la fin du XVIIIᵉ siècle n'avait guère de rapports avec ce qu'il était au XIIIᵉ.' But he continues, 'Est-ce une raison pour en déduire qu'il avait disparu?' and his answer, to our surprise, is no. The significant point is the reason he gives for this answer: 'Aux yeux des contemporains il était très vivant.' This cannot mean that contemporaries knew what feudalism was in the thirteenth century and by comparing this with their own conditions concluded that it was still alive. It can only mean that since they used the word to describe the contemporary situation we need not inquire further. Indeed this is what M. Godechot himself says: 'Qu'il soit peu justifié d'identifier les droits seigneuriaux et les dîmes avec le régime féodal, c'est certain. Mais peu importe, puisque les contemporains le jugeaient ainsi.'

Herein, evidently, is to be detected the difference between

narrative history, which accepts the contemporary social vocabulary at its face value, and analytical history, which subjects it to critical treatment. But this is not the whole explanation. Why is it that many historians can still use words like bourgeois or *paysan*, can even, with M. Godechot, talk of 'l'alliance, en 1789, et surtout de mai à septembre, entre la bourgeoisie et la paysannerie' as though these were meaningful phrases, whereas to others, like myself, it has seemed necessary to abandon them? Since it would be very wrong to try to claim that in such a major difference of view between reputable and serious historians either side is just totally and stupidly at fault, the only reasonable conclusion that I can see is that we are in fact starting from different premises, writing different kinds of history, and therefore inevitably reaching different conclusions. I believe, in fact, that a study of some of the major points at issue will demonstrate that this is so.

Let us begin with the statement already quoted that there was a peasant-bourgeois alliance, particularly from May to September 1789. Now clearly M. Godechot would not assert this unless it were a fact commonly accepted by historians. On the other hand, the evidence of conflict between the interests of the wealthier but non-noble social elements in the towns and the rural population is overwhelming.[8]

The reader will already have noticed a second point of difference to add to that arising from differing attitudes towards contemporary social terminology. M. Godechot's belief in a peasant-bourgeois alliance is specifically referred to the period of May to September 1789. He appears to be willing to recognize that before and after these months there may have been a conflict. On the other hand, my own emphasis was on the long-range opposition of interests between town and country: this does not exclude the possibility of temporary and partial alliances between them. One kind of history, thus, is concerned primarily with the blow-by-blow account of the political struggle, while the other analyses a social situation which changes more slowly and normally not from day to day or month to month.

When we look at the apparently contradictory facts of M. Godechot's history and of mine, a third difference also appears. The conflict between urban and rural interests is revealed in the *cahiers* and in the elections to the *États Généraux*, but the conflict

did not stop there. Sporadic outbreaks of violence in the countryside built up to a widespread movement during the spring and
summer of 1789. There is ample evidence that the attacks of the
peasant population were not confined to the property and rights
of the privileged orders. Thus it hardly seems correct, from my
point of view, to speak of the peasant-bourgeois alliance, even from
May to September, or to say, 'C'est seulement après l'abolition
de celle-ci [the abolition of the feudal regime on August 4th] ...
que les paysans se sont retournés contre les citadins.' Furthermore,
to repress the outbreak, in both town and country, the Assemblée
Nationale called on the *milices bourgeoises*, which did indeed take
very effective action, sometimes in the form of punitive expeditions into the countryside. The disturbances were put down, and
those who were seized as guilty of the attacks were punished, often
ruthlessly, by forces recruited from or by, and certainly representing, the better-off population of the towns — those who presumably are meant by the loose designation 'bourgeois'. How are these
facts reconciled with the supposed peasant-bourgeois alliance?

The answer is that they are not: they exist on a different plane.
The conflict between urban and peasant interests appears all over
France in studies of local history: the alliance is demonstrated for
M. Godechot by the vote of the Tiers in the Constituent Assembly,
on August 4th, abolishing feudalism. But over and above the social
struggle scattered up and down the provinces of France, there was
a general struggle between revolutionaries and counter-revolutionaries for the government of France. This, it seems to me, is the
justification for M. Godechot's view. It was a struggle for power
in the central government. Such struggles involve almost inevitably an alignment of forces on one side or the other. You were
either *for* the Revolution or *against* it, and probably in 1789 most
of those who did not belong to the privileged orders (as well as
some of those who did) were *for* it, whether they could be described
as *paysannerie* or bourgeoisie. In this sense M. Godechot is correct
in saying that they were in alliance.

The third point to be noted is, therefore, the difference between
history written in terms of the overriding political struggle and that
concerned with the basic social conditions. One cannot for a
moment question the importance of political history. Indeed, in
discussing the 'social interpretation' of the Revolution I specifically

recognized that the Revolution was, in large measure, a political struggle, waged for the government of France.[9] The nature of a political struggle is to divide a nation into two sides. There is no incompatibility between accepting the existence of this simple political dichotomy and finding underneath the political struggle a much more complex social and economic nexus. The error does not lie in seeing in the Revolution a political struggle for power, but in taking the political division as the basis for social history. This, I believe, is the chief cause of the present misunderstanding, which is evident also in other historical periods, between historians brought up to see historical conflicts in terms of the struggle for political power, and those who are more concerned to study the social patterns and conflicts which political history naturally leaves on one side.

It is not difficult to provide further examples of the transfer of political categories into social ones. Thus it is obviously difficult for orthodox historians of the Revolution to believe that the so-called Girondins and the Montagnards could come from the same social strata. Their political opposition, it seems, must be assumed to reflect a difference in their social origins, even if there is no present evidence of this.[10] Again, the concentration on political issues naturally produces a political vocabulary. M. Godechot rightly sees that the term *aristocratie* is, according to me, a political one. When the revolutionaries denounced aristocrats they did not necessarily mean nobles by this description. A noble might be a patriot, in which case he would not be an aristocrat, whereas a *roturier*, or even a peasant, might be, and sometimes was, denounced as an aristocrat. Similarly, as M. Soboul has shown, the *sans-culottes* of the Year II were identified, not by belonging to any specific social category, but by their political beliefs.

But when it is suggested that I also include *artisans* and *paysans* and all their sub-divisions among political categories, this, of course, is absurd. The suggestion once again indicates a basic opposition between two different approaches to history. The responsibility for the misunderstanding must be mine, for failing to allow for the strength of commitment to the political interpretation of the Revolution in recent historiography. As I have said, one result of this is that the terms used to describe the major elements in the revolutionary struggle, while they possess social overtones, are essentially political. It is what one would expect if the Revolution was the product, as M. Labrousse said long ago, of a conjuncture of political and economic factors. This is true of terms like the *régime féodal*, the bourgeoisie, aristocrats, *sansculottes*. But there is no reason to suggest that *artisans* or *paysans* are political terms, nor do I do so. The suggestion itself is indicative of the breakdown in communication and of a failure to appreciate the objection to the use of large omnibus terms, such as 'bourgeois', in social history. Their defect is that they obscure significant social differences and stand in the way of a more adequate social analysis. It has truly been observed that the use of the word 'bourgeois' has the effect of lumping together social categories at the very point where their differences become sociologically significant.[11]

To sum up, the historical thought of the school of historians of the French Revolution represented by M. Godechot is conditioned by its primary concern with the political struggle for power. In so far as it takes notice of social divisions, it superimposes the established political categories on them, and assumes that the broad, general terms of the political struggle are valid for the purpose of social analysis. This is in effect to identify social and political interests and tacitly to exclude the possibility that they might be in opposition, or even irrelevant, to one another.

The contradiction in interpretations of the Revolution now seems to be explained, but an explanation is still needed for the present predominance of political history. It is all the more remarkable in that the dominance of the political interpretation is very largely a development of the last twenty years. From the time of Jaurès up to the Second World War the economic and social history of eighteenth-century France and the Revolution was far from being neglected. It is in the last twenty years that there has been a fundamental change in historiographical direction, which cannot but reflect a change in the basic outlook of the leading historians of the Revolutionary period. Such a change has indeed taken place. Up to the end of the 1930s all serious historians of the Revolution were influenced by Marxism, even when they did not dogmatically follow a rigorous Marxist interpretation. Since the Second World War its influence has largely been replaced by that of Marxism–Leninism. This has resulted in a major reorientation of historical thinking, because it has shifted the emphasis from economic development and the facts of the social situation to the political struggle for power.

M. Godechot seems to regard the suggestion that historians have been subjected to these influences as an attack upon them, as though it were wrong for an historian to possess a coherent social philosophy. I would not have drawn as heavily as I have done upon the works of Marxist or semi-Marxist historians if I had not recognized the value of their researches. Our differences of opinion lie on a different level of thought, which M. Godechot, perhaps, does not appreciate. If he did, I think he could hardly have written, if I follow him correctly, of Mousnier, Palmer, Ciampini, as well as myself, that our criticisms seem 'plus fondées sur un parti pris politique que sur un réel effort pour faire avancer cette histoire'. Obviously there is another failure in communication here, but again for the same reason. There is a great difference between attributing an opposition in historical interpretations to the holding of different social philosophies, and attributing it to a 'parti pris politique'. The latter, I cannot help feeling, is once more the result of the tendency to see history and the writing of history in exclusively political terms.

Finally, in his description of the end of the Revolution, as of the beginning, M. Godechot gives a political interpretation. How did the Revolution leave France? The wealthier classes, he agrees, still kept their predominance and had even strengthened it; though, he adds, if it was still the rich who ruled, it was 'pas les mêmes riches!' The important point is that, 'Les nobles, tout en conservant une partie de leur fortune, ont été peu à peu écartés du pouvoir politique.'

On the political plane this verdict is quite clear. But as soon as we move from the sphere of political power to that of social relationships a fog of confusion descends. Having said that, after the Revolution, 'Les riches ont à peu près maintenus leurs positions et les ont même consolidées', he goes on to assert that 'l'ascension sociale a été facilitée et accélérée: la révolution économique, qui a permis l'élévation du niveau de vie des diverses classes sociales, a été finalement facilitée par la Révolution.' The meaning here is not very clear. Can M. Godechot really mean that though France after the Revolution was still ruled by the rich, and even more effectively than before, it was now easier to climb into their ranks and this was the great achievement of the Revolution? And does he also mean, as he seems to say, that as well as a political revolution it was also an economic revolution, which raised the standard of life of all social classes? This latter statement is very difficult to reconcile with the facts of the social and economic condition of the French people after the Revolution. Lefebvre, for example, more realistically, had spoken of the 'terrible condition' into which the working population was precipitated in the early decades of the nineteenth century.[12] The only explanation of the contradiction that I can see is that Lefebvre was thinking of economic conditions, whereas M. Godechot is once again unconsciously transferring his political interpretation of the Revolution into the social and economic field.

The consistency of the interpretation of revolutionary history of which he is one of the most distinguished exponents is undeniable; nor would I deny its validity within its own sphere. I have said myself that the French Revolution was 'primarily a political revolution, a struggle for the possession of power and over the conditions in which power was to be exercised. Essentially the revolution was the overthrow of the old political system of the monarchy and the creation of a new one in the shape of the Napoleonic state.'[13] The account of such a struggle is naturally a political narrative; the social terms to be used can be those that contemporaries used; the relevant social affiliations and oppositions are those that relate to the political struggles; national politics provides the basic divisions from which social classifications are deduced; political groupings and party labels are identified with social distinctions; changes in the balance of political power are taken to be equivalent to changes in social structure. The result is, inevitably, the kind of history which is irreconcilable with any serious social analysis.

The antithesis could not be demonstrated more clearly than it is by M. Godechot in the four pages which sum up admirably the political interpretation of the Revolution. For a social interpretation we have to turn to other historians — Jaurès, Sée, Bourgin, Mathiez, Lefebvre up to the 1940s, Labrousse,[14] among others; and among more recent ones, Paul Bois, Saint-Jacob, Tilly,

George V. Taylor, Reinhard and so on. Their work has not yet penetrated the fortresses of orthodox political history. Nevertheless progress is being made. 'Peut-être', writes M. Godechot, 'les travaux qui sont en chantier nous amèneront-ils à réviser nos conclusions.' I believe they will; indeed, I wrote my book under the impression that they should have done so already.

# THE FRENCH REVOLUTION: ORTHODOX AND UNORTHODOX INTERPRETATIONS
## A REVIEW OF REVIEWS

ANY attempt at historical revision, especially one which questions the conclusions of a great and powerful school of historians as my book on *The Social Interpretation of the French Revolution* did, is likely to provoke a reaction. It has also met, here and there, with some approval. If I say little of those who have agreed with my views, it is not through lack of appreciation, but because I feel that there has been some misunderstanding of what I wrote by my critics, and for this my own lack of clarity may be responsible. So I must try again. A review of reviews is also to me a novel and therefore an interesting literary exercise.

The main lines of criticism of my *Social Interpretation* are represented by three distinguished authorities on the history of the Revolution, from England, France and America respectively. For Professor Goodwin,[1] in a short and kindly but devastating review, the main ideas I criticized were Aunt Sallies, old-fashioned textbook clichés long abandoned by serious historians and set up by me anew only to be able to knock them down. Professor Godechot[2] did not see them in this light at all. On the contrary, he was indignant at my 'conclusions paradoxales'. Thirdly, Professor Crane Brinton[3] envisaged the situation in more personal terms. 'There is the compulsion — no weaker term will do — on the historian,' he wrote, 'and particularly on the young scholar seeking to establish himself, to be original ... The creative historian, like the creative artist, has in our time to produce something new as "interpretation". He has, in short, to be a revisionist.'

Flattering as it is to find myself classified with young scholars seeking to establish themselves, this third point of view, since it is primarily a judgment of the historian's motives, is naturally the most difficult to discuss. It presents all historians, and not only the younger ones, with a problem. If they are to forswear writing anything new, what are they to write — endless textbooks to summarize time and again what has already been said a host of times before? When research is indulged in, presumably it is only allowable if it takes the form of the accumulation of detail to confirm an already accepted interpretation or to fill out the gaps in an agreed narrative. Since this would obviously make nonsense of historical study, perhaps it would be fairer to assume that Professor Brinton does not mean what he says, that he really objects not to true originality but only to the craving for a false originality which sets up Aunt Sallies to knock down, or produces paradoxes for the sake of making an impression. This, in effect, amounts to a repetition of the criticisms of Goodwin and Godechot. These are important contributions to the discussion because they set out clearly views on which they believe there is general agreement among historians, though as to the nature of these generally agreed views they obviously disagree.

Since I have discussed the criticisms of Professor Godechot above, I would like to take those of Professor Goodwin as the primary basis of my discussion here. Godechot contented himself with a reassertion of the validity of the views I opposed. On the other hand, Goodwin argues that my *Social Interpretation* was largely misdirected because it was concerned with attacking 'a series of historical clichés'. He calls them 'accepted' views in inverted commas, by which I think he intends to convey that they are *not* accepted, at any rate by serious historians, today. This is a sophisticated approach. It demolishes at a single blow both orthodox historians like Professor Godechot and revisionists like myself. We are left fighting a mock battle over superannuated platitudes; but before abandoning such a pointless struggle I would like to examine the supposed Aunt Sallies, abandoned clichés or straw men, to quote another reviewer, to make sure that they really are such. The clamour of 'Aunt Sally', 'cliché', 'straw man', or sometimes 'old hat', 'old chestnut', has been raised so often against me by learned reviewers in scholarly journals that, doubtless like many of their readers, I have almost been persuaded myself by sheer force of repetition. I am only encouraged to persist when I find that an historian who has made major and original contributions to the precise subject under debate, Professor George V. Taylor, can refer to 'the theory that the Revolution was the triumph of capitalism over feudalism' as 'what Cobban rightly calls "the established theory of the French Revolution" '.[4]

This is the greatest and all-embracing of my Aunt Sallies, but like a Russian wooden doll it contains within it a series of smaller models of itself. Goodwin reveals the first of these as 'the view that the revolution was precipitated by a "bourgeois" assault on seigneurial dues and agrarian "feudalism" '. There must be a slip of the pen here because everyone knows that the Revolution was 'precipitated' by the financial crisis of the royal government and the conflict with the privileged orders that this brought about. What I criticized was the view that there was in fact a bourgeois attack on feudalism, or more specifically on seigneurial dues and obligations, not that this precipitated the Revolution. Presumably it is the former view which Goodwin regards as a cliché which need no longer be taken seriously.

Godechot's reactions when he read my interpretation of the famous vote of the *tiers état* on the night of the fourth of August were entirely different. He burst out with 'Ici nous sommes en plein paradoxe. Que les députés du Tiers à la Constituante aient voté à la quasi-unanimité l'abolition de la féodalité, seraient la preuve de leur opposition.' Professor Soboul, though he admitted that the deputies of the *tiers état* regarded seigneurial dues as legitimate property, the abolition of which would be dangerous for the whole bourgeois order, added, 'Il est cependant nécessaire de souligner nettement que l'objectif fondamental du mouvement paysan coincidait avec les buts de la révolution bourgeoise: la destruction des rapports féodaux de production.'[5] Again, Godechot writes, 'Le caractère le plus spécifique de la Révolution est d'avoir abattu le régime "féodal".' Many other examples of the 'bourgeois versus feudalism' interpretation could be given to show that it is far from dead. Nor, though I disagree with this view, do I think it should be written off as a mere hackneyed cliché.

I need not repeat the arguments against it, or the various modifications which have been introduced in the hope of preserving it, except for one interesting recent shift in its formulation. This has been best put by Professor R. R. Palmer. Leaving the 'bourgeois' out of the picture for the moment, he asks what the eighteenth century meant when it attacked feudalism. His answer is: 'When the French, and other Europeans, in the eighteenth century made "feudalism" a term of reproach they did not mean by it merely the seigneurial dues. They meant the confusion and fragmentation of public authority, the overlapping of jurisdictions, the blurring of public and private spheres, the obstacles in the way of rational government, and above all the protected, privileged, special status of favoured elements in society, notably the nobles, ecclesiastics, or others, many of whom, rightly or wrongly, justified their power by harking back to the Middle Ages.'[6]

This is an interesting point of view. It would be even more interesting if it were the result of an historical examination of the use of the term feudalism in the eighteenth century rather than a simple assertion. I do not mean that Palmer is necessarily wrong in saying that when the men of the eighteenth century denounced feudalism they meant by this the whole decaying *ancien régime*. Perhaps they did, but it would be nice to be given the evidence for it.[7] The problem may turn out to be a little more complicated than Palmer supposes. For example, he obviously includes all seigneurial dues in the feudal category. Yet the National Assembly seriously debated which seigneurial dues were derived from personal servitude and *were* feudal, and which were *not* derived in this way and therefore were *not* feudal.

It is possible to go farther than Palmer in expanding the idea of the revolt against feudalism. This has been done by Professor Gilbert Shapiro in an article which is primarily directed against one by Mrs Elizabeth Eisenstein.[8] In the course of this he has invented a two-headed monster called 'Cobban and Eisenstein', which must have astonished Mrs Eisenstein as much as it did me and certainly makes any analysis of his contribution very difficult. There are a few relevant points, however, which can be lifted out of it. On feudalism he says, 'What we need is not a historically justifiable definition of feudalism for the eighteenth century.' This, at least, is frank. What we need, according to Shapiro, is simply to know what Marxist historians mean by the term. There follows a list of the vices of the *ancien régime* similar to that given by Palmer, and the conclusion is that 'What is important in the Marxist view' is that they 'functioned inappropriately for the demands of

278

the "capitalist" (read "modern") world'. We seem to be back almost where we started, with the 'bourgeois versus feudalism' theory still stuck up to frighten off intruders, though now in the rags and tatters of the scarecrow rather than the imposing academic array it was once decked in.

Shapiro next proceeds to a summary of the social and economic significance of the Revolution, practically amounting to the next Aunt Sally which, according to Goodwin, I have set up in order to be able to knock it down. This is the belief that the Revolution 'marked a significant stage in the development of economic individualism'. In treating it as a mere superannuated cliché Goodwin is again unfair to many notable historians who have specifically upheld this interpretation of the Revolution. Lefebvre certainly did, and within the last few years Soboul has written, 'Le fait essentiel est que l'ancien système économique et social fut détruit et que la Révolution française proclama sans aucune restriction la liberté d'entreprise et de profit, déblayant ainsi la voie devant le capitalisme.'[9] Godechot seems to put forward the same view of the Revolution, though in more guarded language, when he writes, 'La révolution économique qui a permis l'élévation du niveau de vie des diverses classes sociales, a été finalement facilitée par la Révolution.' With greater or less emphasis on the word *finalement*, this seems to be in accord with the current Marxist view, which is now commonly expressed in more qualified terms than it used to be, though without changing the essential meaning.

To take what I assume to be an unimpeachable source, Samuel Bernstein, in *Science and Society*, writes, 'Marxist historians have never regarded the Revolution as a *deus ex machina* that replaced feudalism by bourgeois society. [It seems to me that, Marxist or not, many historians *have* written as though it were.] They have merely been saying that the Revolution created the conditions for the subsequent development of that society.'[10] He goes much farther in modifying the traditional Marxist interpretation of the Revolution when he continues, 'The situation of most Frenchmen had not been seriously altered. Thus there was greater continuity socially than might be believed ... Capitalism had not been accelerated during the revolutionary decade.' Professor George Rudé comes even closer to my view. He specifically picks out for agreement the judgment that the French Revolution 'probably retarded capitalist economic development in France'.[11] When he proceeds, immediately after this, to add 'And these in fact are precisely the sort of things that Marxist and neo-Marxist historians (Lefebvre and Soboul among them) have been saying for 30 years', I cannot but express astonishment and incredulity.

This does, however, seem to be the new Marxist line, in which, although in a somewhat different context, they are echoing Goodwin: we said it all along. J. Kaplow, for example, after a review which consists of a series of anguished rhetorical questions, ends, 'What Cobban has succeeded in showing is that the Revolution was not made by, and did not bring to power, an industrial bourgeoisie. The question is: who ever said that it did?'[12] This question, at least, has an answer: I thought that he did. He prefaced a book on Elbeuf during the Revolution with the justification that it 'provides an opportunity to study a budding industrial bourgeoisie, the very class that was to profit so greatly from the Revolution in action',[13] and in the introduction to a collection of essays he wrote, 'the existence of such a class [the industrialists owning the means of production and operating within a capitalist model] was a result rather than a cause of the French Revolution.'[14]

Obviously, in relation to the interpretation of the French Revolution Marxist historiography is in a state of flux, in which contradictory opinions can be expressed at the same time, but it may fairly be said that the idea that the Revolution 'marked a significant stage in the development of economic individualism' is still far from being the Aunt Sally that Goodwin suggests.

This brings me to the third of the clichés that I am supposed to have attacked — the assumption that the Revolution 'resulted from the social and political frustrations of a vague and undifferentiated middle class'. This time, in suggesting that it is an old-fashioned cliché not worth powder and shot, Goodwin is hardly fair to himself. In the introduction to Volume VIII of the *New Cambridge Modern History* he gave 'middle-class resentment against social and political inequality' as one of the reasons why 'France came to be the real crucible of the Western revolutionary movement'.[15] This is, I admit, rather a cliché, but as a general statement I have no criticism to make of it. Goodwin is also right in saying that historians recognize that the 'middle class', standing between the privileged orders and the people, was differentiated internally; it included militant revolutionary, passive and even counter-revolutionary elements. Similarly, I do not suppose as Goodwin suggests, that serious historians hold the view that 'the social and economic structure of the peasantry was monolithic'.

Presumably I did not make my argument in this matter clear: it is not that the use of such terms as bourgeois, middle-class or peasantry is incorrect, but simply that the terms are liable to stand in the way of the assimilation of the results of modern historical research into general history. In the same volume of the *New Cambridge Modern History* R. R. Palmer puts the point very well. ' "Aristocrat", "bourgeois", "peasant", "working-man",' he writes, 'are the names of abstract categories, not so much empty as over-full.'[16] They are in fact the categories inherited by Marx from the French historians and economists of the early nineteenth century, who themselves were adapting to new conditions the *ancien régime* division of society into orders. If they have become, to use Palmer's term, 'over-full', this is not because they never had any value, but because historical research has revealed divisions within the broad categories which are sometimes much more significant than any unity they may possess.

An example of the tendency of historians to cling to the broad categories they have inherited is provided by the term 'rural bourgeoisie'. I questioned the utility of this concept in my Wiles lectures. Goodwin, who discovers so many other clichés that I have attacked unnecessarily, springs to the defence of this one. It was not, he says, 'an ideological concept, but a reality of the countryside'. I would not suggest that because a concept is ideological, therefore it cannot correspond to any reality. My argument was simply that if it does so we should be able to identify it with a reasonable degree of precision.

Lefebvre provides us with ample information as to its composition. According to him the rural bourgeoisie included *grands fermiers* (i.e. the stewards and rent collectors of great landlords), *fermiers* (in the sense of tenant farmers), *laboureurs* (the peasant proprietors with the larger holdings), *rentiers* (in this context I presume he must mean those letting their land and not actually working it themselves), merchants, notaries, doctors, surgeons, officers of local courts and such individuals as the local post-master, all these latter living in the small towns or bourgs.[17]

Undoubtedly such people existed and were the better-off inhabitants of the small towns and villages. It is also true for the most part that they profited from the Revolution, and that they frequently tended to promote and support it. All this is not in question. My criticism in this case also is directed against the use of an omnibus term. What I question is the value of identifying all the various social elements enumerated by Lefebvre under the heading of rural bourgeoisie as a single social entity. It is once more the problem of the 'over-full' category.

The trouble with 'rural bourgeoisie' is that, like the terms 'bourgeois' and 'peasant', it is a hindrance rather than an aid to historical understanding, and for the same reason. It brings together disparate and hostile interests and so forms a barrier to realistic social analysis. Thus, the conflict of venal officers and mercantile interests in eighteenth-century French towns is notorious; the stewards, or rent and dues collectors of the greater landlords, were on terms of bitter enmity with the peasant proprietors and tenant farmers; the larger tenant farmers had to face intense resentment from those who were only *laboureurs*; the bourgeois owners of land and seigneurial dues were hated by the peasants; the lawyers, other professional men and property-owners of the small towns often only obtained local offices early in the Revolution after a bitter struggle with representatives of the *laboureurs*; they were faced with their continuing resentment and opposition, and the disposition of the *biens nationaux* intensified this enmity. This whole area of social conflict is brushed under the carpet and concealed by the use of the term 'rural bourgeoisie'.

All this, it seems to me, provides a model illustration of the difficulties involved in the attempt to make the results of more recent research fit into a framework of categories established at an earlier stage of historical investigation.

It must be admitted that to challenge in this way the well established broad categories of orthodox history is bound to be disturbing. One can sympathize with reviewers for whom the removal of the familiar landmarks seems to leave only a trackless desert. Faced with this situation, Palmer provided me with a way out. He concluded that my view must be 'that the French Revolution after its first few months was essentially a political conflict, without much social meaning. That is, it was mainly a struggle for power among the men involved in the Revolution ... a contest without significant issues.'[18]

This was not an unfair conclusion: I can see some grounds for it in what I have written, and it would not, I think, be an unreasonable position to adopt, though it is not in fact the position I do adopt. Although I have criticized the tendency to use the political terms of revolutionary history as equivalent to social categories, this was not intended to deny the importance of political history. It must be recognized that a good deal of what has happened in history does in fact take the form of a political struggle for power. Also history must move forward in time; narrative is its essential character. The factor in history which moves forward more patently than any other is the political one. Governments and their policies change more rapidly and continuously than any other collective human activity. Government also exercises the most obvious and direct effect on the life of civilized society. Perhaps this is why there has recently been something of a swing back in historical writing in the direction of political history. The more closely religious and other conflicts over ideas are studied, the more clearly the naked struggle for power appears beneath the thin veil of ideological decency. This tendency, as I pointed out, is evident in recent Marxist writing on the French Revolution, in which the most important new contributions have concentrated on the struggle for power and the factional divisions and alliances which it produced, overriding, at least partially, social and class distinctions.

Even in a book devoted to an attempt to analyse the social aspects of the Revolution, I felt bound to say that it was 'primarily a political revolution, a struggle for the possession of power and over the conditions in which power was to be exercised. Essentially the Revolution was the overthrow of the old political system of the monarchy and the creation of a new one in the shape of the Napoleonic state.'[19] In fact, however, though an historian may legitimately concentrate his attention on social or political history, and in particular needs to discriminate between these categories, the suggestion of a rigid antithesis between social and political has never been historically valid. The sentence just quoted has been rather unfairly treated by being taken out of its context. In it I was endeavouring to redress the balance of a book devoted almost exclusively to social and economic questions; but I immediately added that, 'Behind the political regime there is always the social structure, which is in a sense more fundamental and is certainly more difficult to change.' For the sake of clarity we still need to make a distinction between political, social and economic factors, but it increasingly becomes necessary to see them also as complementary factors in a complex historical situation.

What I wrote on this subject has obviously puzzled another of my reviewers, Professor Brinton. His conclusion was that I must be attacking, 'in the new fashionable manner', the economic interpretation of history. This is an extraordinary assumption, because the chief criticism I made of the current neo-Marxist approaches to the Revolution was that it has laid undue stress on *political* conflicts and categories and that the *economic* history of the Revolution has recently in consequence been neglected.[20]

Perhaps Brinton did not notice the distinction I was making between Marxism and neo-Marxism. As regards the former, my criticism was not against it *qua* economics, but *qua* general sociological theory. He seems to be most seriously worried because I criticize the established interpretation of the Revolution partly on the ground that it derives its categories from a general sociological theory. He rightly sees that I am critical of any attempt to derive history from, or make it agree with, such a theory. But it appears to puzzle him that I am not exactly in the opposite camp either. 'Cobban himself', he says, 'does not quite fit either the Heraclitan or the Parmenidean box.' I take it that what troubles him is the fact that, though I believe history and sociology to be disciplines which can contribute much to one another, as I have just said, I do not believe that history can be deduced from general sociological theory. I hold, on the contrary, that the historian or sociologist who wishes to reach conclusions of value in the field of social history will not do so unless he is prepared to do the necessary historical research. The sociologist who has a general theory, and still more the historian who is prepared to accept some such theory at second-hand and apply it, say, to any or all revolutions for the sake of establishing a uniform pattern, may escape this necessity, but what he produces will, I suspect, contribute little of value either to sociology or to history.

Marx's *Das Kapital* was valuable because Marx had studied the conditions of the English industrial revolution: for the same reason it does not have much relevance to the French Revolution of 1789. There is very little to quarrel with, and much to admire, in Lefebvre's *Paysans du Nord, La Grande Peur*, and all his other detailed studies. The subtle and penetrating analysis in such works is the product of long and profound research. I knew and admired Lefebvre greatly and have borne frequent witness in print to his eminence as an historian. Shapiro, in a piece entitled, for no reason I can comprehend, 'The Many Lives of Georges Lefebvre', declares, 'Cobban ... presents Lefebvre's views as if he were a simple-minded Marxist.' Apart from straight quotations from Lefebvre, I have in fact only one statement on this point, where I say that Lefebvre 'seems to have come to believe, in his later years, that Marxism could provide both a theoretical basis for his researches and a conclusion he could draw from them'.[21] 'Simple-minded' is the last adjective I would dream of applying to him. As for his Marxism, Shapiro himself writes 'Lefebvre was certainly a Marxist.' In fact, of course, I have tried to show that Lefebvre was far more than a simple Marxist and that from his researches conclusions can be drawn which take us far beyond any orthodox Marxist interpretation of the Revolution.

I have sometimes ventured to suggest that on important points I was just repeating what Lefebvre himself had said. But alas, even this is not allowed. For example, I put forward the view, many years ago, that the venal *officiers* and the professional men, especially lawyers (social categories which frequently overlapped), provided the Revolution all through with a large proportion of its leadership, its ideas and its impetus, while the mercantile and industrial sector played a minor and generally passive role. In this respect I thought I was supported by the views of Lefebvre. Goodwin denies this. Lefebvre, he says, 'did not ... specifically commit himself, as is here claimed, to the view long championed by the author that the real middle-class revolutionaries were the holders of venal offices and the members of the liberal professions'. To be precise, what I wrote was, 'That the *officiers* and the men of the liberal professions prepared and directed the Revolution, and that the business men were not its prime movers, was the sounder view of Lefebvre.'[22] The relevant passage, to which I provided a specific reference so it really should not have been too much trouble to check it, comes in the 1951 edition of Lefebvre's masterly volume on *La Révolution française*. After giving a long list of reforms, he continues, 'Ce n'est pas à dire, pourtant, que ces réformes aient suscité l'enthousiasme au point de s'être inscrites au premier plan dans l'esprit de la bourgeoisie, en sorte que les hommes d'affaires auraient été les premiers moteurs de la Révolution. Bien plus efficaces furent le règne de la loi et l'égalité des droits, qui en appelaient à la dignité autant qu'aux intérêts. C'est la vieille bourgeoisie d'Ancien Régime, celle des officiers et des hommes de loi qui, relativement indépendante et disposant d'un certain loisir, professionellement attachée, autant par intérêt que par sa culture, à faire prévaloir la loi sur la violence et l'arbitraire, fut à cet égard l'institutrice de l'opinion.'[23] What I wrote seemed to me, and still seems to me, a fairly close paraphrase of this.

Elsewhere, it is true, Lefebvre made statements which are difficult to reconcile with this one. Curiously enough, it seems to have occurred only to one reviewer, Professor Leo Gershoy, that the thought of a great historian like Lefebvre is not necessarily all turned out of one single mould, pulped into an homogenized mass.[24] I have not made a careful chronological analysis of Lefebvre's writings, but my impression is that most of the more rigid ideological formulations came from his later years. This impression may be mistaken, but there can be no mistake in the belief that the great French school of social history, of which he was one of the founders, is solidly based not on ideological presuppositions but on thorough historical research. It is continued in the work of such French historians as Tudesq, Saint-Jacob, Adeline Daumard, Leroy-Ladurie, Paul Bois, who give us real social history for the same reason that it was given us in the *Paysans du Nord*: their conclusions follow from the evidence instead of preceding it.

Paradoxically, it is the very extent of historical research undermining the orthodox theory of the Revolution which presents what on the surface looks like the most difficult problem, with which this review of reviews may appropriately end. Given the research that has already been conducted on the social history of the Revolution, it may reasonably be asked why it has not already made a more effective impact on orthodox history. My explanation would be that most orthodox history is general history. Indeed it can hardly be regarded as orthodox until it is enshrined in general histories and textbooks. There is naturally a time-lag before this occurs. It is a gradual process. Moreover in a general history, even when unorthodox interpretations do appear, it is only here and there as part of a broad picture most of which is necessarily 'agreed' history. They can be found, for example, in my *History of Modern France* or in Norman Hampson's excellent *Social History of the French Revolution*. The champions of orthodoxy did not take fright at such books, apparently because they did not notice what was happening in them. The outburst of alarm and indignation only came when I isolated specific views in my lecture on 'The Myth of the French Revolution' and in my *Social Interpretation*. Presented in stark nudity they then seemed shocking, but there was no other way, I believe, of making a direct impact on the rigid orthodoxy into which the general history of the Revolution had been hardening. Judging by the reviews, in particular those I have been discussing here, the impact has been made. Without undue optimism, I believe it can now be said that the social significance of the Revolution is no longer a subject for *ex cathedra* statements but is once again entered in its own right on the historical agenda as a subject for free debate.

# NOTES

## THE STATE OF REVOLUTIONARY HISTORIOGRAPHY

1. Harvey Mitchell, *The Underground War against Revolutionary France* (1965), gives an account of the relations between William Wickham and the royalists from 1794 to 1800. W. R. Fryer, *Republic or Restoration in France, 1794–7?* (1965), based on a much scantier documentation, concentrates on D'André. Jacqueline Chaumié, *Le réseau d'Antraigues et la Contre-Révolution* (1791–3) (1965), is well documented but puts more faith in such a great mystifier as d'Antraigues than he deserves.
2. e.g. A. Soboul (ed.), *Babeuf et les problèmes du babouvisme* (1963); C. Mazauric, *Babeuf et la conspiration pour l'Egalité* (1962); and a work on Babeuf in Russian by V. M. Daline.
3. R. R. Palmer, *The Age of the Democratic Revolution. A Political History of Europe and America, 1760–1800*, ii. *The Struggle* (1964); J. Godechot, *France and the Atlantic Revolution of the Eighteenth Century, 1770–1799* (1965).
4. Joan MacDonald, *Rousseau and the French Revolution* (1965).
5. A. Cobban, *In Search of Humanity: the Role of the Enlightenment in Modern History* (1960); Peter Gay, *The Party of Humanity* (1964).
6. Y. Coustau, *La vente des biens nationaux dans le Gers* (1962).
7. J. Kaplow, *Elbeuf during the Revolutionary Period* (1964).
8. R. Cobb, *Terreur et subsistances, 1793–1795* (1965).
9. G. Rudé, *The Crowd in the French Revolution* (1959); *The Crowd in History: a Study of Popular Disturbances in France and England 1730–1848* (1964).
10. A. Soboul, *Les Sans-culottes parisiens en l'an II* (1958); see also, *Précis d'histoire de la Révolution française* (1962).
11. R. Cobb, *Les armées révolutionnaires* (1961–3).
12. G. Lefebvre, *Etudes orléanaises*, 2 vols. (1962–3); *Cherbourg à la fin de l'Ancien Régime et au début de la Révolution* (1965).
13. Olwen H. Hufton, *Bayeux in the late eighteenth century* (1967).
14. M. Faucheux, *L'insurrection vendéenne de 1793, aspects économiques et sociaux* (1964); C. Tilly, *The Vendée. A Sociological Analysis of the Counter-revolution of 1793* (1964).
15. Norman Hampson, *A Social History of the French Revolution* (1963).
16. J. Egret, *La Pré-Révolution française (1787–1788)* (1962).
17. E. Bernardin, *Jean-Marie Roland et le ministère de l'Intérieur (1792–1793)* (1964).
18. J. F. Bosher, *The Single Duty Project: a study of the movement for a French Customs Union in the eighteenth century* (1964).
19. e.g. P. de Saint Jacob, *Les Paysans de la Bourgogne du Nord au Dernier Siècle de l'Ancien Régime* (1960); Paul Bois, *Paysans de l'Ouest. Des structures économiques et sociales aux options politiques depuis l'époque révolutionnaire dans la Sarthe* (1960); A.-J. Tudesq, *Les Grands Notables en France (1840–1849)* (1964); Adeline Daumard, *La bourgeoisie parisienne de 1815 à 1848* (1963).

The books referred to in this paper represent only a select bibliography of those published since 1960.

## THE ENLIGHTENMENT AND THE FRENCH REVOLUTION

1. Hippolyte Taine, *Les Origines de la France contemporaine: L'ancien régime* ([1875] 14th ed.; Paris, 1885), pp. 221–2.
2. Ibid. p. 521.
3. A. Aulard, *Taine, historien de la révolution française* (Paris, 1907), p. viii.
4. A. de Barruel, *Mémoires pour servir à l'histoire du jacobinisme* (Hambourg, 1803).
5. A. de Lamartine, *Histoire des constituants* (Paris, 1855).
6. Michelet, *Histoire de la révolution française* (Paris, 1877), I.59–60.
7. Ibid. p. xliv. Preface of 1847.
8. Louis Blanc, *Histoire de la révolution française* (Paris, 1847), I.9.
9. A. de Tocqueville, *L'ancien régime et la révolution* (Paris, 1856).
10. J. Godechot, *Les Révolutions (1770–1777)* (Paris, 1963), p. 284.
11. A. N. Whitehead, *Adventures of Ideas* (New York, 1933).
12. Cf. E. Carcassonne, *Montesquieu et le problème de la constitution française au XVIIIᵉ siècle* (Paris, 1927).
13. This is discussed by Dr Joan Macdonald in her book, *Rousseau and the French Revolution, 1762–1791* (London, 1965); cf. Alfred Cobban, *Rousseau and the Modern State* (2nd ed.; London, 1964), pp. 280–2.
14. Mallet du Pan, *Mémoires* (Paris, 1851), 126n.
15. e.g. Peter Gay, *The Party of Humanity* (New York, 1964); Arthur Wilson, 'The Development and Scope of Diderot's Political Thought', *Studies on Voltaire and the Eighteenth Century*, Vol. XXVII, ed. T. Besterman (Geneva, 1963).
16. Alfred Cobban, *The Social Interpretation of the French Revolution* (Cambridge, 1964), pp. 82–3.
17. Dr J. Q. C. Mackrell has studied this in his London Ph.D. thesis and forthcoming book, 'The Attack on "Feudalism" in Eighteenth-Century France'.
18. Cobban, *Social Interpretation*, pp. 39–40.
19. *What Is the Third Estate?*, ed. S. E. Finer (London, 1963), pp. 124, 128.
20. Alfred Cobban, 'An Age of Revolutionary Wars: An Historical Parallel', *Review of Politics*, XIII (1951), 131–41.
21. Cobban, *Rousseau and the Modern State*, pp. 71–81.
22. Ibid. p. 69; cf. R. Derathé, *J.-J. Rousseau et la science politique de son temps* (Paris, 1950), pp. 238, 369; Appendix III, pp. 410–13.
23. F. L. Ford, 'The Revolutionary-Napoleonic Era: How Much of a Watershed?' *American Historical Review*, LXIX (1963), 18–29.
24. Ibid. p. 29.

## HISTORIANS AND THE CAUSES OF THE FRENCH REVOLUTION

1. E.g. J. Godechot, *La Grande Nation* (1956); and the article of R. R. Palmer in the *Political Science Quarterly*: 'The World Revolution of the West' (March 1954).

## THE *PARLEMENTS* OF FRANCE IN THE EIGHTEENTH CENTURY

1. On the organization and powers of the *parlements* see H. Carré, *La fin des Parlements (1788–1790)* (1912), pp. 1–19; A. Esmein, *Cours élémentaire d'histoire du droit*

*français* (15th ed., 1925), pp. 373–402; M. Marion, *Dictionnaire des institutions de la France aux xvii<sup>e</sup> et xviii<sup>e</sup> siècles* (1923), art. 'Parlements'.

2. C. Loyseau, *Traité des seigneuries*, ch. v, s. 62, *Œuvres* (ed. of 1701).
3. A. Le Moy, *Le Parlement de Bretagne et le pouvoir royal au xviii<sup>e</sup> siècle* (1909), pp. 16–17.
4. A. Floquet, *Histoire du Parlement de Normandie* (1840–42), vii. 329.
5. L. Wolff, *Le Parlement de Provence au xviii<sup>e</sup> siècle* (1920), p. 19.
6. Le Moy, loc. cit.
7. Carré, p. 79.
8. Wolff, p. 40.
9. C. Desmaze, *Le Parlement de Paris* (2nd ed., 1860), p. 99.
10. P. N. Ardascheff, *Les intendants de province sous Louis XVI* (1909), pp. 10–14.
11. On the venality of the *parlements* see Marion, *Dictionnaire*, art. 'Paulette'; Esmein, pp. 394–7; E. Perrot, *Les institutions publiques et privées de l'ancienne France jusqu'en 1789* (1935), p. 409; Carré, loc. cit.
12. Arthur Young, *Travels in France* (ed. M. Betham-Edwards, 1913), pp. 320–2.
13. Ardascheff, p. xiv.
14. For a description of a *lit de justice*, so named from the throne of four cushions of blue velvet sown with *fleur de lys* on which the king sat, see Saint-Simon, *Mémoires* (ed. A. de Boislisle, 1879–1928), xxxv. 218–37.
15. *Chronique de la régence et du règne de Louis XV (1718–1763)*, i. 460.
16. G. Pagès, *La monarchie d'ancien régime* (1928), p. 176.
17. *Lettres Persanes*, No. XCIII.
18. H. Leclerq, *Histoire de la régence* (1922), i. 97–126; Saint-Simon, xxix, 12–27; J. G. Flammermont, ed., *Remontrances du parlement de Paris au xviii<sup>e</sup> siècle* (1888–1898), i. 1–30.
19. On eighteenth-century Jansenism see A. Gazier, *Histoire générale du mouvement janséniste* (1922).
20. Jourdan, Isambert and Crusy (generally cited as Isambert), *Recueil général des anciennes lois français* (1822–33), xxi. 366. This decree was quashed by the king the next day.
21. Cf. F. Rocquain, *L'esprit révolutionnaire avant la Révolution* (1878), livres V and VI.
22. M. Marion, *Machault d'Arnouville* (1891).
23. F. Funck-Brentano, *Les lettres de cachet* (1926), ch. xxii.
24. Carré, pp. 20 ff.
25. F. Delbecke, *L'action politique et sociale des avocats au xviii<sup>e</sup> siècle* (1927), pp. 221–4.
26. Marion, *Dictionnaire*, art. 'Censure'; Rocquain, *passim*.
27. Cf. F. Piétri, *La réforme de l'état au xviii<sup>e</sup> siècle* (1935).
28. A. Aulard, *Histoire politique de la révolution française* (4th ed., 1909), p. 16.
29. Saint-Simon, xxxvi. 308; cf. also xxv. 246 ff., 331; xxvii. 104; xxxi. 250; xxxv. 18.
30. R. Bickart, *Les parlements et la notion de la souveraineté nationale au xviii<sup>e</sup> siècle* (1932), pp. 13–22.
31. *Mémoires des intendants sur l'état des généralités*, tome i, *Mémoire sur la généralité de Paris* (ed. A. M. de Boislisle, 1881), pp. 173–4.
32. E. Carcassonne, *Montesquieu et le problème de la constitution française au xviii<sup>e</sup> siècle* (1927), pp. 6–7; Bickart, pp. 115–42; W. F. Church, *Constitutional Thought in sixteenth-century France* (1941), pp. 23–32, 144.
33. Bickart, pp. 333–42, 89–96.
34. Le Paige, *Lettres historiques sur les fonctions essentielles du Parlement* (1753), I, 96.
35. *De l'esprit des lois*, liv. II, ch. iv; cf. Bickart, pp. 101–11.
36. Flammermont, *Remontrances*, i. 522.

37. *Remontrances* of the *parlement* of Rennes, May 2nd, 1788. Le Moy, p. 538.
38. e.g. d'Aiguillon in Brittany, Fitz-James at Toulouse, d'Harcourt at Grenoble, Dupré de Saint-Maur at Bordeaux.
39. On Choiseul and the *parlements*, see P. Sagnac, *La fin de l'ancien régime et la révolution américaine, 1763–1789* (1941), pp. 123–6.
40. Cf. J. Flammermont, *Le Chancelier Maupeou et les parlements* (1883).
41. M. Marion, *Histoire financière de la France depuis 1715*, tome I, *1715–1789* (1914), i. 248–79.
42. *Œuvres complètes*, ed. of 1879; *Dictionnaire philosophique*, iv. 178, art. 'Parlement de France'. In 1771 the article concluded at the first sentence given above. The remainder was added by Voltaire, who had plunged into the fray on the side of Maupeou, in 1775.
43. D. Dakin, *Turgot and the Ancien Régime in France* (1939).
44. Carcassonne, pp. 463–6; Bickart, pp. 249–50.
45. Mably, *Œuvres complètes* (1792), iii. 499.
46. Marion, *Hist. financière*, i. 337.
47. Isambert, xxviii. 534–67.
48. Carcassonne, p. 567.
49. On the role of the *parlements* in the critical years 1787–9, see especially Carré, op. cit.; L. Meyniel, *Un facteur de la révolution française. La querelle des impôts au parlement de Paris en 1787–1788* (1907); M. B. Garrett, *The Estates General of 1789* (1935); E. Glasson, *Le Parlement de Paris* (1901), ii. 443–94.
50. For protests by ministers against their publication, cf. Rocquain, p. 242; Floquet, vii. 62.
51. Gazier, ii. 68.
52. A. Mathiez, *La révolution française* (1928), i. 8.
53. *Histoire de l'assemblée constituante* (1828), i. intro., p.c.
54. Garrett, pp. 157, 159.
55. C. E. Labrousse, *La Crise de l'économie française à la fin de l'ancien régime et au début de la révolution* (1944).
56. *Mémoires biographiques, littéraires et politiques de Mirabeau* (1834), iv. 483.

## THE MYTH OF THE FRENCH REVOLUTION

1. A. de Tocqueville, *Souvenirs*, ed. L. Monnier (1942), p. 72.
2. E. Perrot, *Les Institutions publiques et privées de l'ancienne France jusqu'en 1789* (1935), p. 532.
3. Ibid., p. 533.
4. G. Lefebvre, *The Coming of the French Revolution*, trans. R. R. Palmer (1947), p. 213.
5. The analysis of the *tiers état* of the Constituent Assembly and of the Convention, on which the subsequent remarks are based, is given in the Appendix.
6. It might be suggested that the members of the assemblies, even if they did not belong to these classes, represented them or were influenced in their policies by them. To discuss this suggestion adequately would require much more space than I have here and a good deal of research. All I can say here is that this view is at present no more than an hypothesis, to substantiate which would require a careful historical examination of the relevant facts.
7. M. Marion, *Dictionnaire des institutions de la France au XVIIᵉ et XVIIIᵉ siècle* (1923), p. 401.
8. A. Babeau, *Le village sous l'ancien régime* (5th ed., 1915), p. 218.
9. 'Si ... le roi eût spontanément établi une certaine égalité dans les charges, et

donné quelques garanties, tout eût été apaisé pour longtemps' (*Histoire de la Révolution française*, Ch. 1).

10. De Tocqueville, op. cit., p. 47.
11. I have not here taken the membership of the Legislative Assembly into consideration.

## LOCAL GOVERNMENT DURING THE FRENCH REVOLUTION

1. The only two general accounts of local government during the Revolution with which I am acquainted are: Baron de Girardot, *Des administrations départementales, électives et collectives* (1857); E. Monnet, *Histoire de l'administration provinciale, départementale et communale en France* (1885), cc. ii–vi.
2. Remonstrance of the Cour des Aides, May 6th, 1775; quoted in P. E. Cardilhac, *Les Projets de régionalisme administratif* (1921), p. 30.
3. e.g. d'Argenson, *Considérations sur le Gouvernement Ancien et Présent de la France* (1785); Necker, *Mémoire sur l'établissement des administrations provinciales, donné au roi* (1785); Dupont de Nemours, *Des administrations provinciales, mémoire présenté au Roi, par M. Turgot* (1788).
4. Condorcet, *Essai sur la constitution et les fonctions des Assemblées provinciales, 1788*; *Œuvres* (1847–9), viii. 658.
5. October 26th, 1789. *Réimpression de l'ancien Moniteur* (Paris, 1840–5; cited hereafter as *Anc. mon.*), ii. 91–3.
6. The history of local government in Paris is excluded from this study, as the capital received separate treatment throughout the Revolution.
7. *Anc. mon.* i. 191.
8. Ibid. i. 288, 332–3.
9. e.g. at Périgord. Cf. G. Bussière, *La Révolution en Périgord* (1903), p. 177.
10. e.g. at a commune in the Gévaudan; *Anc. mon.* ii. 231.
11. October 15th, 1789; *Anc. mon.* ii. 65.
12. October 23rd, 1789; *Anc. mon.* ii. 85–6.
13. Speech of the comte de Virieu, November 12, 1789, ibid. ii. 182.
14. Ibid.
15. Clermont-Tonnerre had written, 'L'adoption du système de M. l'abbé Sieyes a livré la France aux municipalités, énervé le pouvoir en le partageant; il a changé la monarchie en une multitude de petites portions détachées, qui ont leurs intérêts, leurs préventions, leur régime, n'obéissent à personne, et qui regardent ce qui reste du pouvoir exécutif plutôt comme un ennemi commun que comme un centre de réunion.' *Anc. mon.* x. 134–6.
16. *Anc. mon.* x. 135.
17. Mignet relates that he asked Sieyes if he were not the principal author of the division of France into *départements*. 'Le principal! me répondit-il vivement et avec un juste orgueil; mieux que cela, le seul!' *Notice historique sur la vie et les travaux de M. le comte Sieyès* (1836).
18. The text of the essential clauses in these laws is given in L. Cahen et R. Guyot: *L'œuvre législative de la Révolution* (1913), pp. 148–60.
19. Cahen et Guyot, op. cit. p. 158, section iii, arts. 5 and 6.
20. e.g. 'On a respecté, autant qu'il a été possible, les anciennes limites.' *Anc. mon.* i. 527. 'Ces affections d'unité provinciale qu'on croit si dangereux de blesser, ne sont pas même offensées par le plan du comité.' Ibid. ii. 157.
21. November 3rd, 1789; *Anc. mon.* ii. 126. Cf. Reubell in a speech of November 18th,

1789: 'En divisant les provinces, vous vous êtes proposé de détruire l'esprit de province'. *Anc. mon.* ii. 196. Duquesnoy, on November 4th, 1789: 'La division de la France ... doit avoir pour but de fondre lcs esprits et les mœurs, de manière qu'il n'y ait en France que des Français, et non des Provençaux, des Normands, etc.' *Anc. mon.* ii. 132.

22. Thus the *employés* of the departmental directory in the Meurthe were drawn from the *Intendance* and the *Chambre des Comptes*. Bovier-la-pierre, *Les employés de préfecture et de sous-préfecture* (1912), p. 169.

23. J. Jaurès, *Histoire socialiste* (1901), i. 420.

24. A. Métin, *La Révolution et l'autonomie locale* (1904), p. 19.

25. Monnet, op. cit. p. 163.

26. It should be remembered that this was not the theory of Montesquieu, who upheld the idea of a *balance*, but not of an absolute separation of powers in the state.

27. *Anc. mon.* ii. 223.

28. November 24th, 1789; *Anc. mon.* ii. 231.

29. Girardot, op. cit. p. 60.

30. Quoted in E. Coüard: *L'administration départementale de Seine-et-Oise, 1790–1913* (1913), p. 14.

31. The rights of *octroi* of local authorities were specifically maintained by a law of March 9th, 1790; *Anc. mon.* iii. 570.

32. Ibid. vii. 431.

33. Ibid. 318.

34. Cahen et Guyot, op. cit. pp. 405–6, sec. 11.

35. *Anc. mon.* ix. 323.

36. Ibid. xiv. 507–8.

37. February 6th, 1791; *Anc. mon.* vii. 318.

38. March 17th, 1791; *Anc. mon.* vii. 647.

39. Ibid. xxi. 687.

40. September 5th, 1794; *Anc. mon.* xxi. 686.

41. Ibid.

42. Cf. n. 69, below.

43. J. Viguier, *Les débuts de la Révolution en Provence* (1895), p. 85.

44. Ibid. p. 140.

45. L. de Cardenal, *La province pendant la révolution* (1929), p. 166.

46. Ibid. p. 178.

47. Quoted in Monnet, op. cit. p. 183.

48. This is not to be confused with the *Fédération* of 1790, the tendency of which was rather centralizing than decentralizing.

49. *L'Acéphocratie ou le gouvernement fédératif démontré le meilleur de tous pour un gran empire* (Paris, 1791).

50. A. Aulard, *Histoire politique de la Révolution française* (4th ed. 1909), p. 263.

51. *La République sans impôts* (Paris, 1792).

52. Aulard, op. cit. pp. 264, n. 3, 401–2.

53. Cf. on this topic Cardenal, op. cit.

54. Monnet, op. cit. p. 199.

55. September 22nd, 1792; *Anc. mon.* xiv. 14.

56. In a letter to the popular society of Périgueux dealing with the maximum on wood and coal, the commissaire for the Dordogne says: 'Inutiles efforts, aucune réponse, aucun avis ne m'a été fourni. Une dernière mesure, un dernier devoir me reste à remplir pour m'acquitter entièrement sur ce point intéressant, c'est de tourner mes regards vers les nourrices-nées de la Révolution, les sociétés populaires.' Cardenal, op. cit. p. 474.

57. Decree of October 8th, 1792, Article xvii; *Anc. mon.* xviii. 77.
58. P. Mautouchet, *Le gouvernement révolutionnaire* (1912), pp. 204–6.
59. Crane Brinton, *The Jacobins* (1930), p. 121.
60. Ibid.
61. *Anc. mon.* xxiv. 398.
62. 'Il y a dans ces Sociétés trop de fonctionnaires, trop peu de citoyens.' *Anc. mon.* xix. 688.
63. Brinton, op. cit. p. 135.
64. Cahen et Guyot, op. cit. p. 68.
65. Ibid. pp. 83–92.
66. Ibid. pp. 174–5.
67. L. Dubreuil, *L'idée régionaliste sous la Révolution* (1919), p. 57.
68. A. Métin, *La Révolution et l'autonomie locale* (1904), p. 27.
69. e.g. July 13th, 1796, December 15th, 1797, December 1st, 1798.
70. G. Robison, *Revellière-Lépeaux, citoyen-directeur, 1753–1824* (1938), pp. 119–21.
71. Cahen et Guyot, op. cit. p. 177.
72. Monnet, op. cit. p. 259.
73. Quoted in Monnet, op. cit. p. 260.
74. Cf. the repeated attempts of the commissaire for the Côtes-du-Nord to have his resignation accepted, and the difficulty of the Directory, when eventually he obtained relief from his onerous task, in obtaining a successor. L. Dubreuil, *La Révolution dans le département des Côtes-du-Nord* (1909), pp. 208, 222.
75. *Anc. mon.* xviii. 275.
76. Ibid. xxvi. 453.
77. Ibid. xxviii. 809–11.
78. Dubreuil, op. cit. p. 116.
79. E. Dubois, *Châtillon-sur-Chalaronne et son district pendant la Révolution française* (1926), p. 190.
80. Monnet, op. cit. p. 278.

## THE FUNDAMENTAL IDEAS OF ROBESPIERRE

1. See p. 158.
2. J. M. Thompson, *Robespierre* (1935), ii. 169.
3. *Adresse de Maximilien Robespierre aux Français* (1791), p. 2.
4. *Discours et rapports de Robespierre*, ed. C. Vellay (1908), pp. 10–11 (Constituante, February 5th, 1791).
5. *Lettres à ses commettans*, 2nd series, p. 52 (January 10th, 1793). Dates of publication for this and for the *Défenseur de la Constitution* are those established by G. Laurent in his edition of the *Défenseur*, pp. xiv–xxvi.
6. *Discours et rapports*, p. 45 (Constituante, May 16th, 1791).
7. Cf. pp. 176–7.
8. *Discours et rapports*, pp. 305, 352 (Convention, December 5th, 1793, May 7th, 1794); *Réimpression de l'ancien Moniteur* (1858–63) (cited hereafter as *Anc. mon.*), xxi. 240 (Jacobins, July 9th, 1794).
9. *Anc. mon.* iv. 504 (Constituante, May 31st, 1790).
10. Ibid. v. 464 (Constituante, August 23rd, 1790).
11. *Discours et rapports*, p. 361 (Convention, May 7th, 1794).
12. *Lettres à ses commettans*, 2nd series, p. 50 (January 10th, 1793).
13. *Œuvres complètes*, ed. E. Déprez et E. Lesueur (1912–13), i. 31 (*Discours sur les peines infamantes*, 1784).
14. *Discours et rapports*, p. 329 (Convention, February 5th, 1794).

15. Ibid. p. 354 (Convention, May 7th, 1794).
16. *Le Défenseur de la Constitution*, ed. G. Laurent (1939), pp. 115–16 (June 7th, 1792), and in many other places.
17. *Discours et rapports*, p. 260 (Convention, May 10th, 1793).
18. *Le Point du Jour*, no. 329, x. 455 (June 11th, 1790).
19. *Remontrances du parlement de Paris au XVIIIe siècle*, ed. J. Flammermont (1888–98), ii. 557–8.
20. Cf. J. Bickart, *Les Parlements et la notion de souveraineté nationale au 18e siècle* (1932).
21. *Anc. mon.* ix. 555 (Constituante, August 31st, 1791).
22. *Défenseur*, p. 144 (June 15th–17th, 1792).
23. *Le Point du Jour*, no. 84, iii. 39 (September 20th, 1789).
24. *Lettres à ses commettans*, 1st series, p. 197 (November 15th, 1792).
25. *Discours sur la pétition du peuple Avignonois*, 1790, p. 8.
26. *Œuvres*, i. 24; *Défenseur*, p. 251 (Jacobins, July 5th, 1792); *Lettres à ses commettans*, 1st series, p. 6 (September 30th, 1792).
27. *De l'esprit des lois: avertissement*.
28. Cf. pp. 180–84.
29. *Discours et rapports*, p. 328 (Convention, February 5th, 1794); cf. *Œuvres*, i. 23; *Journal des États Généraux*, v. 149 (Constituante, October 22nd, 1789).
30. *Œuvres*, i. 23–4, *Anc. mon.* ii. 81 (Constituante, October 22nd, 1789); A. Aulard, *La Société des Jacobins: recueil de documents pour l'histoire du Club des Jacobins de Paris* (1889–97), iii. 12 (July 13th, 1791); *Discours et rapports*, p. 328 (Convention, February 5th, 1794).
31. *Journal des États Généraux*, v. 149 (Constituante, October 22nd, 1789).
32. *Œuvres*, i. 23.
33. *Adresse aux Français* (1791), p. 5.
34. Thompson, *Robespierre*, i. 41.
35. *À la Nation Artésienne, sur la nécessité de réformer les États d'Artois* (1789), p. 5.
36. Ibid. pp. 10–11.
37. Ibid. p. 12.
38. D. J. Garat, *Mémoire sur la Révolution* (1794), p. 50.
39. *Discours et rapports*, p. 3 (Constituante, February 5th, 1791).
40. *Adresse aux Français* (1791), pp. 8, 15; Aulard, *Société des Jacobins*, iii. 12 (July 13th, 1791); *Défenseur*, p. 9 (May 17th–18th, 1792).
41. *Œuvres*, i. 26 (*Discours sur les peines infamantes*, 1784).
42. *Anc. mon.* iv. 397 (Constituante, May 18th, 1790).
43. Ibid. ix. 564 (Constituante, September 1st, 1791).
44. *Défenseur*, pp. 11–12 (May 17th–18th, 1792).
45. Ibid. p. 359 (August 20th, 1792).
46. *Anc. mon.* ix. 362 (Constituante, August 10th, 1791).
47. Cf. p. 159.
48. It might be pointed out that the theory of Locke could be summarized in precisely the same terms.
49. *Discours et rapports*, pp. 22–42 (Constituante, May 11th, 1791); *Journal des États Généraux*, iii. 96 (Constituante, August 24th, 1789), vii. 668 (Constituante, March 19th, 1791), ix. 462, 471 (Constituante, August 22nd–23rd, 1791).
50. *Anc. mon.* viii. 353–4 (Constituante, May 9th, 1791).
51. Cf. p. 179.
52. *Anc. mon.* iv. 282 (Constituante, May 3rd, 1790).
53. Ibid. vii. 532 (Constituante, March 3rd, 1791).
54. *Le Point du Jour*, no. 257, viii. 233–6 (March 30th, 1790); cf. *Anc. mon.* iii. 734 (Constituante, March 28th, 1790). To provide local authorities with the means

of effective action he also argued that a proportion of the revenue should be left at their free disposal. *Discours et rapports*, p. 263 (Convention, May 10th, 1793).

55. A. Aulard, *Histoire politique de la Révolution française* (4th edn. 1909), pp. 63-4 (Constituante, October 20th, 1789).

56. Cited in L. Jacob, *Robespierre vu par ses contemporains* (1938), p. 83.

57. Aulard, *Histoire politique*, pp. 99-100.

58. *Le Point du Jour*, no. 196, vi. 184-5 (January 26th, 1790); cf. *Anc. mon.* iii. 227 (Constituante, January 25th, 1790).

59. *Procès-verbal de l'Assemblée nationale*, no. 190, pp. 10-11 (February 2nd, 1790). An attempt was made to maintain the property qualification, however, by excluding from the franchise 'dans les Villes, ceux qui n'ayant ni propriétés, ni facultés connues, n'auront d'ailleurs ni profession, ni métier; et dans les Campagnes, ceux qui n'auront aucune propriété foncière, ou qui ne tiendront pas une Ferme ou une Métairie de trente livres de bail'.

60. *Anc. mon.* viii. 395 (Constituante, May 13th, 1791).

61. Ibid. viii. 381-2 (Constituante, May 12th, 1791).

62. Ibid. ii. 81 (Constituante, October 22nd, 1789).

63. *Discours et rapports*, p. 13 (Constituante, February 5th, 1791).

64. Ibid. pp. 90-1, 103 (Constituante, August 11th, 1791); *Correspondance de Maximilien et Augustin Robespierre*, ed. G. Michon (1926), p. 58 (November 1789).

65. *Adresse aux Français* (1791), p. 5.

66. *Discours et rapports*, p. 97 (Constituante, August 11th, 1791).

67. G. Walter, *Robespierre: la montée vers le pouvoir* (1936), pp. 114-15.

68. *Discours et rapports*, p. 21 (Constituante, February 5th, 1791).

69. *Discours sur l'organisation des gardes nationales* (1790), pp. 29-31; *Anc. mon.* viii. 238-9, 245 (Constituante, April 27th, 1791).

70. *Anc. mon.* xvii. 683 (Convention, September 17th, 1793).

71. M. Deslandres, *Histoire constitutionelle de la France de 1789 à 1870* (1932-7), i. 83.

72. *Lettres à ses commettans*, 2nd series, p. 6 (January 5th, 1793). Cf. *Dire de M. de Robespierre contre le veto royal* (1789), p. 1; 'Tout homme a, par sa nature, la faculté de se gouverner par sa volonté; les hommes réunis en Corps politique, c'est-à-dire, une Nation, a par conséquent le même droit.'

73. *Discours et rapports*, pp. 242-3 (Convention, December 28th, 1792).

74. e.g. 'La volonté générale, proprement dite et dans la langue de la liberté, se forme de la majorité des volontés particulières.' *Œuvres complètes de Saint-Just*, ed. C. Vellay (1908), i. 428.

75. Locke, *Second Treatise on Government*, section 89.

76. Filmer, *Patriarcha*, ch. iii. par. 14.

77. *Du contrat social*, liv. iii, ch. 15.

78. *Anc. mon.* ix. 362 (Constituante, August 10th, 1791); *Discours et rapports*, pp. 134 (Jacobins, January 2nd and 11th, 1792), 264 (Convention, May 10th, 1793); *Défenseur*, pp. 142, 147 (June 15th-17th, 1792).

79. *Lettres à ses commettans*, 2nd series, pp. 30-31 (January 5th, 1793).

80. G. Bonno, *La Constitution britannique devant l'opinion française de Montesquieu à Bonaparte* (1932), pp. 140-42.

81. *Discours et rapports*, p. 14 (Constituante, February 5th, 1791).

82. Ibid. p. 327 (Convention, February 5th, 1794).

83. *Anc. mon.* xvi. 668 (Convention, June 16th, 1793).

84. *Journal des États Généraux*, iii. 409 (Constituante, September 12th, 1789); *Défenseur*, p. 360 (August 20th, 1792); *Lettres à ses commettans*, 2nd series, p. 6 (January 5th, 1793); *Discours et rapports*, p. 264 (Jacobins, May 10th, 1793).

85. *Journal des États Généraux*, iii. 409 (Constituante, September 12th, 1789).

86. *Défenseur*, p. 358 (August 20th, 1792); *Lettres à ses commettans*, 1st series, p. 19 (September 30th, 1792).
87. *Journal des États Généraux*, vi. 43 (Constituante, November 18th, 1789). He appealed also for an increase in the size of the departmental assemblies, ibid. 51–2 (Constituante, November 19th, 1789).
88. *Discours sur les moyens de sauver l'État et la liberté* (1792), pp. 28–9 (Jacobins, February 10th, 1792).
89. *Discours et rapports*, p. 269 (Convention, May 10th, 1793).
90. Ibid. p. 265 (Convention, May 10th, 1793).
91. *Dire contre le veto royal* (1789), p. 4.
92. *Anc. mon.* xiv. 877–8 (Convention, December 28th, 1792).
93. Ibid. ix. 126 (Constituante, July 14th, 1791).
94. Ibid. xvi. 653 (Convention, June 14th, 1793).
95. Cf. p. 160.
96. *Défenseur*, p. 115 (June 7th, 1792).
97. *Discours et rapports*, p. 122 (Jacobins, January 2nd and 11th, 1792); *Défenseur*, p. 250 (Jacobins, March 26th, 1792).
98. *Lettres à ses commettans*, 1st series, p. 242 (November 22nd, 1792).
99. Cf. pp. 173–4.
100. *Œuvres*, i. 241 (*L'homme champêtre*, 1786); *Anc. mon.* viii. 56 (Constituante, April 5th, 1791); *Discours et rapports*, pp. 95 (Constituante, August 11th, 1791), 246 (Convention, April 24th, 1793).
101. *Discours et rapports*, p. 95 (Constituante, August 11th, 1791).
102. Cf. pp. 166–8.
103. Thompson, *Robespierre*, i. 181.
104. *Défenseur*, p. 37 (Jacobins, April 27th, 1792); Aulard, *Société des Jacobins*, iv. 550 (December, 5th, 1792); *Discours et rapports*, pp. 364–5 (Convention, May 7th, 1794).
105. *Œuvres*, 1. 24 (*Discours sur les peines infamantes*, 1794); *Défenseur*, p. 305 (July 25th, 1792); *Lettres à ses commettans*, 1st series, p. 6 (September 30th, 1792).
106. *Discours et rapports*, p. 328–9 (Convention, February 5th, 1794).
107. Ibid. p. 3 (Constituante, February 5th, 1791).
108. e.g. *Œuvres*, i. 24; *Défenseur*, p. 305 (July 25th, 1792).
109. Walter, *Robespierre: la montée vers le pouvoir*, p. 35.
110. *Œuvres*, i. 212 (*Dédicace à Jean-Jacques Rousseau*); cf. *Discours sur les moyens de sauver l'État et la liberté*, p. 35 (Jacobins, February 10th, 1791); *Discours et rapports*, pp. 101–2 (Constituante, August 11th, 1791), 165 (Jacobins, April 27th, 1792), 365 (Convention, May 7th, 1794); *Défenseur*, pp. 122–3 (June 7th, 1792).
111. *Discours et rapports*, pp. 134 (Jacobins, January 2nd and 11th, 1792), 264 (Convention, May 10th, 1793); *Défenseur*, pp. 142, 147 (June 15th–17th, 1792).
112. e.g. *Défenseur*, p. 34 (Jacobins, April 27th, 1792).
113. *Anc. mon.* viii. 77 (Constituante, April 7th, 1791).
114. Ibid. iii. 438 (Constituante, February 22nd, 1790).
115. *Lettres à ses commettans*, 1st series, p. 13 (September 30th, 1792).
116. Cf. also *Anc. mon.* ix. 362 (Constituante, August 10th, 1791); *Défenseur*, p. 299 (July 25th, 1792); Aulard, *Société des Jacobins*, vi. 134 (May 15th, 1794).
117. A. Mathiez, *La corruption parlementaire sous la Terreur* (1927), p. 323.
118. Here, moreover, Robespierre's object is clearly to make out a case for the trial and punishment of the king. If the government becomes a tyranny, he says, the nation re-enters into the rights of nature, and can judge the king not according to constitutional laws, but by the laws of nature. The first of these is the right of self-protection, and the second is the duty of aiding those who are oppressed,

which may involve punishing their oppressors. *Lettres à ses commettans*, 1st series, p. 198 (November 15th, 1792).

119. Cf. M. Lhéritier, *La Révolution à Bordeaux dans l'histoire de la Révolution française: la fin de l'ancien régime* (1942), p. 7.

120. G. Walter, *Histoire des Jacobins* (1946), p. 40.

121. Ibid. pp. 102–3.

122. C. Crane Brinton, *The Jacobins* (1930), pp. 52–5.

123. Ibid. pp. 68–72.

124. Ibid. p. 70.

125. P. Sainte-Claire Deville, *La Commune de l'an II* (1946), pp. 361–78.

120. D. Mornet, *Les origines intellectuelles de la révolution française (1715–1787)* (1933), p. 4.

127. Cf. Aulard, *Les Grands Orateurs de la Révolution* (1914), p. 289.

128. Garat, op. cit. p. 51.

## THE POLITICAL IDEAS OF MAXIMILIEN ROBESPIERRE DURING THE PERIOD OF THE CONVENTION

1. E. Hamel, *Histoire de Robespierre* (1865), i. 175.

2. *Discours et rapports de Robespierre*, ed. C. Vellay (1908), p. iii.

3. *Réimpression de l'ancien Moniteur*, 1840–5 (cited hereafter as *Anc. mon.*), vi. 631 (Constituent Assembly, December 14th, 1790).

4. *Discours et rapports*, p. 262 (Convention, May 10th, 1793); *Œuvres complètes de Robespierre*, tome iv: *Le Défenseur de la Constitution*, ed. G. Laurent (1939), p. 321 (Jacobins, July 29th, 1792). Cf. Notes, *infra*, n. 14. Where the reference is not to the reprint of a speech in the *Défenseur*, the date of publication is given for this, and for the *Lettres à ses commettans*, as established by G. Laurent, pp. xiv–xxvi.

5. *Anc. mon.* viii. 90 (Constituante, April 9th, 1791); ix. 407 (Constituante, August 15th, 1791); *Défenseur*, pp. 37 (Jacobins, April 27th, 1792), 332 (Jacobins, July 29th, 1792).

6. *Lettres à ses commettans*, 1st ser. p. 10 (September 30th, 1792); cf. ibid. second series, p. 53 (January 10th, 1793).

7. *Discours et rapports*, pp. 257, 260, 263 (Convention, May 10th, 1793).

8. *Anc. mon.* xv. 674 (Convention, March 10th, 1793).

9. Ibid. xv. 687 (Convention, March 11th, 1793).

10. *Journal des débats*, no. 457, July 26th, 1793, p. 3 (Jacobins, July 24th, 1793).

11. *Anc. mon.* xvii. 527 (Convention, August 29th, 1793).

12. A. Aulard, *La Société des Jacobins: recueil de documents pour l'histoire du Club des Jacobins de Paris*, 1889–97, v. 693–4 (Jacobins, March 16th, 1794).

13. *Anc. mon.* xviii. 592 (Convention, December 4th, 1793).

14. *Défenseur*, pp. 37 (Jacobins, April 27th, 1792), 93 (May 31st, 1792), 321 (Jacobins, July 29th, 1792).

15. Cf. 'Voici donc la constitution fondamentale du gouvernement dont nous parlons. Le corps législatif y étant composé de deux parties, l'une enchaînera l'autre par sa faculté naturelle d'empêcher. Toutes les deux seront liées par la puissance exécutive, qui le sera elle-même par la législative' (*De l'esprit des lois*, liv. xi, ch. vi).

16. *Du Contrat social*, livre ii. ch. 2.

17. *Discours et rapports*, pp. 260–1 (Convention, May 10th, 1793).

18. Ibid. p. 265 (ibid.).

19. *Anc. mon.* xvi. 655 (Convention, June 15th, 1793).

20. Ibid. xv. 674–5 (Convention, March 10th, 1793).

21. S. A. Berville et J. F. Barrière, *Papiers inédits trouvés chez Robespierre, Saint-Just, Payan, etc., supprimés ou omis par Courtois, précédés du rapport de ce député* (1828; cited hereafter as Courtois), no. xliv, ii. 15.
22. *Procès-Verbal de la Convention Nationale*, xxii. 210.
23. *Discours et rapports*, pp. 311–12 (Convention, December 25th, 1793).
24. If Robespierre had followed Rousseau's terminology consistently he would have confined the word government to the executive power. Cf. 'Qu'est-ce donc que le Gouvernement? Un corps intermédiaire établi entre les sujets et le souverain pour leur mutuelle correspondance, chargé de l'exécution des lois et du maintien de la liberté tant civile que politique ... J'appelle donc *Gouvernement* ou suprême administration l'exercice légitime de la puissance exécutive' (*Du contrat social*, livre iii, ch. 1).
25. *Du contrat social*, livre iii, ch. 15; cf. *Discours et rapports*, pp. 134 (Jacobins, January 2nd and 11th, 1792), 260, 264 (Convention, May 10th, 1793); *Anc. mon.* ix. 362 (Constituante, August 10th, 1791); xvi. 668 (Convention, June 16th, 1793); *Lettres à ses commettans*, second series, pp. 30–1 (January 5th, 1793); *Défenseur*, pp. 121 (June 7th, 1792), 142, 146–7 (June 15th–17th, 1792), 328 (Jacobins, July 29th, 1792).
26. According to A. Vermorel, *Œuvres de Robespierre* (1886), p. 56, this proposal was made by Robespierre. Vermorel gives no sources, however, and *Anc. mon.* ix. 362–3 (Constituante, August 10th, 1791) attributes it to Pétion.
27. *Lettres à ses commettans*, 2nd ser., pp. 30–1 (January 5th, 1793), 52–3 (January 10th, 1793), *Défenseur*, pp. 121 (June 7th, 1792), 257 (July 14th, 1792), 320 (Jacobins, July 29th, 1792); *Discours et rapports*, pp. 163 (Jacobins, April 27th, 1792), 257, 260 (Convention, May 10th, 1793).
28. *Anc. mon.* viii. 419 (Constituante, May 16th, 1791).
29. *Lettres à ses commettans*, 1st ser. p. 12 (September 30th, 1792); *Défenseur*, pp. 146–7 (June 15th–17th, 1792); *Anc. mon.* ix. 362 (Constituante, August 10th, 1791).
30. Aulard, *Société des Jacobins*, v. 87 (Jacobins, March 13th, 1793). Robespierre evidently liked this phrase, for two months later he also described the Jacobin Club as 'le boulevard de la liberté'. Ibid. v. 179 (Jacobins, May 8th, 1793).
31. *Discours et rapports*, p. 242 (Convention, December 28th, 1792).
32. *Anc. mon.* xvi. 104–5 (Convention, April 10th, 1793).
33. e.g. Le Hodey, *Journal des États Généraux*, vi. 443 (Constituante, December 13th, 1789); vii. 417 (Constituante, January 16th, 1790); viii. 469–74 (Constituante, February 22nd, 1790); *Le Point du Jour*, vii. 12 (Constituante, February 9th, 1790).
34. *Le Point du Jour*, vii. 151 (Constituante, February 22nd, 1790).
35. Robespierre, *Troisième discours sur la guerre*, January 26th, 1792, p. 28.
36. *Anc. mon.* xv. 75 (Convention, January 6th, 1793).
37. P. J. B. Buchez et P. C. Roux, *Histoire parlementaire de la révolution française*, 1834–8, xxviii. 197 (Jacobins, June 12th, 1793); Aulard, *Société des Jacobins*, v. 277 (Jacobins, June 28th, 1793).
38. *Discours et rapports*, pp. 198–9 (Convention, November 5th, 1792); Aulard, *Société des Jacobins*, v. 254 (June 14th, 1793). Robespierre added, however, that the action of Paris was endorsed by delegates coming from all parts of France.
39. Cf. his poem *L'homme champêtre*, *Œuvres complètes*, ed. E. Déprez et E. Lesueur (1912–13), i. 241; *Défenseur*, p. 111 (June 7th, 1792); *Lettres à ses commettans*, 2nd ser. p. 49 (January 10th, 1793).
40. *Discours et rapports*, pp. 328 (Convention, February 5th, 1794), 354 (Convention, May 7th, 1794).
41. *Journal des États Généraux*, xii. 24 (Constituante, May 31st, 1790).

42. *Œuvres*, i. 31; cf. *Discours et rapports*, pp. 45 (Constituante, May 16th, 1791), 92 (Constituante, August 11th, 1791).
43. *Anc. mon.* xxi. 240 (Jacobins, July 9th, 1794).
44. *Défenseur*, p. 24 (May 19th, 1792).
45. *Lettres à ses commettans*, 2nd ser. p. 380 (early March, 1793).
46. Cf. Notes 71, 72.
47. Robespierre, however, always believed that the laws should tend to diminish economic inequality. *Anc. mon.* viii. 56 (Constituante, April 5th, 1791).
48. *Discours et rapports*, p. 246 (Convention, April 24th, 1793).
49. *Défenseur*, pp. 116–17 (June 7th, 1792); *Discours sur l'influence de la calomnie sur la révolution* (Jacobins, October 28th, 1792), p. 19.
50. *Discours sur l'organisation des gardes nationales* (1790), p. 30; *Anc. mon.* viii. 56 (Constituante, April 5th, 1791).
51. *Discours et rapports*, p. 95 (Constituante, August 11th, 1791).
52. 'Every man has a "property" in his own "person". This nobody has any right to but himself. The "labour" of his body and the "work" of his hands, we may say, are properly his.' Locke, *Second Treatise on Government*, sec. 27.
53. Courtois, no. xliv, ii. 15.
54. *Anc. mon.* viii. 56 (Constituante, April 5th, 1791).
55. *Discours et rapports*, pp. 248, 251, 254 n. (Convention, April 24th, 1793).
56. *Anc. mon.* xvi. 213 (ibid.).
57. A. Mathiez, *Girondins et Montagnards* (1930), p. 100.
58. L. Cahen et R. Guyot, *L'œuvre législative de la Révolution* (1913), pp. 72–3.
59. *Anc. mon.* xiv. 637 (Convention, December 2nd, 1792).
60. Aulard, *Société des Jacobins*, v. 694 (Jacobins, March 16th, 1794). This opinion had a great deal of truth in it. The attempt to extract supplies of food by force from a reluctant peasantry, without providing what it regarded as an adequate economic return, was not likely to prove successful.
61. *Anc. mon.* xiv. 636 (Convention, December 2nd, 1792).
62. Ibid.
63. Ibid.
64. Ibid.
65. *Lettres à ses commettans*, 1st ser. pp. 395–6 (December 13th, 1792).
66. Ibid. p. 401 (ibid.).
67. Cf. A. Mathiez, *La vie chère et le mouvement social sous la terreur* (1927), p. 369.
68. Mathiez, *Girondins et Montagnards*, pp. 110, 204.
69. R. R. Palmer, *Twelve who ruled: the Committee of Public Safety during the Terror* (1941), p. 284.
70. G. Lefebvre, R. Guyot et P. Sagnac, *La révolution française* (1930), p. 247.
71. Aulard, *Société des Jacobins*, iv. 557 (Jacobins, December 7th, 1792); v. 43–4 (Jacobins, February 25th, 1793); v. 277–8 (Jacobins, June 28th, 1793), 330 (Jacobins August 5th, 1793).
72. Ibid. v. 44–5 (Jacobins, February 25th, 1793).
73. Buchez et Roux, xxvii. 243, 244 (Jacobins, May 26th, 1793).
74. *Discours et rapports*, p. 332 (Convention, February 5th, 1794).
75. Ibid. It has been pointed out that the word *terreur* is employed in an active rather than in a passive sense, and would be better translated by 'intimidation' than terror. J. M. Thompson, *Robespierre* (1935), ii. 140 n.
76. Statistical investigation has shown that there was a close connection between the incidence of the Terror and the fear of civil war and invasion. The victims of the Terror of 1793–4 came to an overwhelming extent from the *départements* which were affected by one or the other. On one calculation 70 per cent of the victims of

death sentences came from five *départements* and another 19 per cent from eight more, leaving 11 per cent for the remaining 74. D. Greer, *The incidence of the Terror during the French Revolution* (1935), p. 147 (Table III).

77. Cf. *Discours ... le jour de l'installation du tribunal criminel du département de Paris,* pp. 4–5 (Jacobins, February 5th, 1792); *Anc. mon.* vii. 287 (February 2nd, 1791); E. Seligman, *La justice en France pendant la Révolution (1789–1792)* (2nd edn., 1913), pp. 97, 294, 315, 443–4.

78. *Anc. mon.* vi. 211 (Constituante, October 25th, 1790); *Journal des États Généraux,* v. 120 (Constituante, October 21st, 1789).

79. A. Esmein, *Cours élémentaire d'histoire du droit français* (2nd ed. 1895), pp. 440–1. The exercise of *justice retenue* was, however, rarely arbitrary, and in some respects had come to be subject to rules as precise as those of ordinary justice. J. Declareuil, *Histoire générale du droit français des origines à 1789* (1925), p. 664.

80. *Lettres à ses commettans,* 1st ser. p. 197 (November 15th, 1792).

81. Ibid. pp. 196–7.

82. Seligman, op. cit. pp. 275–9; cf. *Anc. mon.* v. 464–5 (Constituante, August 23rd, 1790).

83. Ibid.

84. E. Seligman, *La justice en France pendant la Révolution (1791–1793)* (1913), pp. 194–201.

85. *Discours et rapports,* p. 214 (Convention, December 3rd, 1792).

86. *Anc. mon.* xix. 51 (*Rapport sur les principes du gouvernement révolutionnaire,* Convention, December 25th, 1793).

87. *Discours et rapports,* p. 215 (Convention, December 31d, 1792).

88. This was not the end of the intellectual difficulties in which the trial of Louis XVI involved Robespierre. Having justified the condemnation of the king on the ground of the right of sovereignty inherent in the people, it was awkward to have to combat the Girondin proposal that the sentence should be confirmed by the voice of the people expressed through their primary assemblies. He was reduced to arguments which in other connections he himself had discredited. The nation as a whole, he said, could not act as a court of law. Hence its place had to be taken by the Convention, which offered 'l'image la plus parfaite de la représentation nationale', *Lettres à ses commettans,* 1st ser. p. 212 (November 15th, 1792). From a practical point of view his opposition to an appeal to the primary assemblies of the people was understandable, but on Robespierre's own principles it was difficult to justify. Cf. ibid. pp. 217–18 (ibid.); *Discours et rapports,* pp. 66–71 (Constituante, May 30th, 1791), 230–6 (Convention, December 28th, 1792); *Anc. mon.* ii. 32 (Constituante, October 10th, 1789, note by editor); viii. 546–7 (Constituante, May 30th, 1791); xv. 265 (Convention, January 21st, 1793).

89. e.g. on October 24th, 1793, he demanded the revocation of the decree requiring the publication of the charges on which arrests were made. Must we, he added, for the sake of individual liberty, by the use of subtle forms allow public liberty to perish? *Anc. mon.* xviii. 215–16 (Convention, October 24th, 1793).

90. *Discours et rapports,* pp. 30, 31, 35–40 (Jacobins, May 11th, 1791); cf. ibid. p. 263 (Convention, May 10th, 1793); *Lettres à ses commettans,* 2nd ser. p. 52 (January 10th, 1793).

91. *Lettres à ses commettans,* 2nd ser. p. 56 (January 10th, 1793).

92. Ibid. p. 54.

93. Ibid. p. 52.

94. Aulard, *Société des Jacobins,* v. 27 (Jacobins, February 15th, 1793).

95. *Discours et rapports,* p. 106 (Constituante, August 11th, 1791); *Défenseur,* p. 115 (June 7th, 1792).

96. *Lettres à ses commettans,* 1st ser. p. 16 (September 30th, 1792); cf. *Discours ... sur l'influence de la calomnie sur la révolution,* p. 4 (Jacobins, October 28th, 1792).
97. *Discours ... sur l'influence de la calomnie,* pp. 4, 16 (Jacobins, October 28th, 1792).
98. *Lettres à ses commettans,* 1st ser. p. 241 (November 22nd, 1792).
99. Ibid. p. 112 (October 30th, 1792).
100. *Discours et rapports,* p. 134 (Jacobins, January 2nd and 11th, 1792); ibid, p. 235 (Convention, December 28th, 1792); *Lettres à ses commettans,* 2nd ser. p. 285 (February 15th–20th, 1792).
101. *Lettres à ses commettans,* 1st ser. p. 112 (October 30th, 1792).
102. *Anc. mon.* xvii. 683 (Convention, September 17th, 1793); xv. 75 (Convention, January 6th, 1793).
103. Ibid. xix. 87 (Jacobins, December 26th, 1793).
104. *Défenseur,* pp. 257 (Jacobins, July 11th, 1792), 320 (Jacobins, July 29th, 1792).
105. *Discours ... sur l'influence de la calomnie,* p. 2 (Jacobins, October 28th, 1792).
106. Buchez et Roux, xv. 226 (Jacobins, June 13th, 1792).
107. e.g. *Défenseur,* p. 146 (June 15th–17th, 1792); *Discours et rapports,* p. 22 (Constituante, August 24th, 1789), 23 ff. (Jacobins, May 11th, 1791); cf. Aulard, *Société des Jacobins,* ii. 396–411; *Journal des États Généraux,* iii. 96 (Constituante, August 24th, 1789); *Anc. mon.* vii. 501 (Constituante, February 28th, 1791); ix. 462 (Constituante, August 22nd, 1791); ix. 471 (Constituante, August 23rd, 1791).
108. Aulard, *Société des Jacobins,* v. 68 (Jacobins, March 6th, 1793); cf. ibid. v. 350 (Jacobins, August 14th, 1793).
109. *Anc. mon.* xvi. 183 (Convention, April 19th, 1793).
110. Buchez et Roux, xix. 85 (Convention, September 25th, 1792); xxviii. 457–8 (Jacobins, August 11th, 1793), 465 (Jacobins, August 14th, 1793); *Discours ... sur l'institution d'une nouvelle garde par la convention nationale,* p. 13 (Jacobins, October 24th, 1792).
111. Courtois, no. xliii, ii. 15; cf. ibid. ii. 13.
112. *Anc. mon.* xv. 688 (Convention, March 11th, 1793); cf. Aulard, *Société des Jacobins,* vi. 188 (Jacobins, June 24th, 1794).
113. Courtois, no. XLIII, ii. 13.
114. *Anc. mon.* xvi. 748 (Convention, June 25th, 1793).
115. The holding of civic fêtes was a spontaneous development in the Revolution, not the artificial product of a theory, as is often assumed. Cf. A. Mathiez, *Les Origines des cultes révolutionnaires (1782–1792)* (1904), p. 77.
116. *Discours sur les moyens de sauver l'état et la liberté,* pp. 35–6 (Jacobins, February 10th, 1792); *Discours et rapports,* p. 247 ff. (Convention, April 24th, 1793).
117. Courtois, no. XLIII, ii. 14. Cf. Mathiez, *Robespierre terroriste* (1921), p. 69.
118. A. Aulard, *Recueil des actes du Comité de salut public,* 1889–1918, xiii, 411–12 (May 10th, 1794). From the record of Robespierre's presence at a meeting of the Committee, his agreement with any particular decree of the same date cannot safely be argued. The only decrees with which he can be identified with certainty, in the absence of other evidence, are those in his own hand, and these are few.
119. Robespierre himself drew up the decree ordering 50,000 copies of the act of accusation against the Girondins to be printed and sent to all popular societies, municipalities, &c., Aulard, *Actes du Comité de salut public,* vii. 583 (October 23rd, 1793). Camille Desmoulins alleged that 205,000 livres were given to Hébert for the dissemination of the *Père Duchesne* between June and October 1793. (*Le Vieux Cordelier,* ed. H. Calvet (1936), no. v. pp. 170–1); cf. Aulard, *Actes du Comité de salut public,* viii. 388–9 (November 13th, 1793).
120. *Discours sur les moyens de sauver l'état,* p. 35 (Jacobins, February 10th, 1792).
121. *Lettres à ses commettans,* 2nd ser., pp. 51, 54, 58–60 (January 10th, 1793).

122. *Anc. mon.* xvii. 134 (Convention, July 13th, 1793).
123. *Procès-verbaux du comité d'instruction publique de la Convention nationale*, ed. M. J. Guillaume (1891), i. 420, 504, n. 2.
124. *Journal des États Généraux*, vii. 441 (Constituante, January 18th, 1790). A letter to this effect, written by Robespierre, in December 1789, to the *Affiches d'Artois*, is cited in G. Walter, *Robespierre: la montée vers le pouvoir (1789–1791)* (1936), p. 243.
125. *Anc. mon.* iv. 504 (Constituante, May 31st, 1790); x. 453 (Constituante, June 9th, 1790).
126. Ibid.
127. *Le Point du Jour*, x. 311 (Constituante, May 31st, 1790); x. 453 (Constituante, June 9th, 1790).
128. *Anc. mon.* iv. 586 (Constituante, June 9th, 1790).
129. *Le Point du Jour*, xi. 206 (Constituante, June 24th, 1790).
130. *Anc. mon.* vii. 668 (Constituante, March 19th, 1791).
131. *Correspondance de Maximilien et Augustin Robespierre*, ed. G. Michon (1926), pp. 127–9 (November 4th, 1791).
132. *Journal des débats*, no. 103, p. 2.
133. *Lettres à ses commettans*, 1st ser. p. 344–5 (December 6th, 1792).
134. *Anc. mon.* xviii. 507–9 (Jacobins, November 21st, 1793).
135. A. Mathiez, *La Révolution et l'église* (1910), p. 124.
136. *Anc. mon.* xviii. 507 (Jacobins, November 21st, 1793).
137. *Lettres à ses commettans*, 1st ser. p. 340 (December 6th, 1792).
138. *Discours et rapports*, pp. 359–60 (Convention, May 7th, 1794), 425 (Convention, July 26th, 1794).
139. R. Levasseur (de la Sarthe), *Mémoires*, ed. A. Roche (1830–32), ii. 193.
140. *Lettres à ses commettans*, 1st. ser. p. 341 (December 6th, 1792).
141. A. Mathiez, *Les Origines des cultes révolutionnaires*, p. 107.
142. *Discours et rapports*, p. 361 (Convention, May 7th, 1794).
143. *Anc. mon.* xviii. 508 (Jacobins, November 21st, 1793); cf. *Discours et rapports*, pp. 360–62 (Convention, May 7th, 1794).
144. Aulard, *Société des Jacobins*, iv. 699–701 (Jacobins, March 26th, 1792); Buchez et Roux, xiii. 442–9.
145. L. Jacob, *Robespierre vu par ses contemporains* (1938), p. 126.
146. Aulard, *Société des Jacobins*, iv. 550 (Jacobins, December 5th, 1792); *Défenseur*, pp. 37 (Jacobins, April 27th, 1792), 68 (May 24th–25th, 1792); *Discours et rapports*, pp. 364–5 (Convention, May 7th, 1794). In December 1792, the bust of Helvetius in the Jacobin Club was destroyed on the proposition of Robespierre (Aulard, loc. cit.).
147. Mathiez, *La Révolution et l'église*, p. 70.
148. Mathiez, *Girondins et Montagnards*, p. 235.
149. Mathiez, *La Révolution et l'église*, p. 143, n. 1; in the same sense, M. Dommanget, *Robespierre et les cultes* (*Annales historiques de la Révolution française* (1924), i. 193–216).
150. Aulard, *Le culte de la raison et le culte de l'être suprême (1793–1794)* (3rd edn., 1909), p. 240.
151. Mathiez, *Robespierre terroriste*, p. 62.
152. *Anc. mon.* xviii. 603–5 (Convention, December 5th, 1793); Buchez et Roux, xxx. 321–4 (ibid.).
153. Aulard, *Actes du Comité de salut public*, viii. 59 (October 27th, 1793).
154. *Correspondance*, p. 214 (November 1793); cf. ibid. p. 225 (December 10th, 1793).
155. A. Ording, *Le Bureau de police du comité de salut* (1930), p. 81.
156. Vermorel, pp. 119–20 (Jacobins, November 21st, 1793); cf. *Anc. mon.* xviii. 507 (ibid.).

157. *Anc. mon.* vii. 119 (Constituante, January 13th, 1791).
158. Aulard, *Actes du Comité de salut public*, ix. 582 (December 22nd, 1793).
159. Hamel, iii. 491.
160. Thompson, *Robespierre*, ii. 176–7.
161. *Discours et rapports*, pp. 338, 341 (Convention, February 5th, 1794); cf. ibid. pp. 359–61 (Convention, May 7th, 1794); *Anc. mon.* xviii. 604–5 (Convention, December 5th, 1793), 691 (Jacobins, December 16th, 1793).
162. *Lettres à ses commettans*, 2nd ser., p. 257 (February 5th, 1793).
163. Ibid. p. 263 (ibid.).
164. Aulard, *Actes du Comité de salut public*, vi. 25 (August 19th, 1793).
165. *Lettres à ses commettans*, 1st ser., p. 346 (December 6th, 1792).
166. Aulard, *Les orateurs de la Révolution: la législative et la convention* (1906–7), ii. 378.
167. *Discours et rapports*, p. 368 (Convention, May 7th, 1794).
168. J. Jaurès, *Histoire socialiste (1789–1900)*, iii. *la Convention*, n.d., i. 244.
169. Aulard, *Société des Jacobins*, vi. 134 (Jacobins, May 15th, 1794).
170. Ibid.
171. Aulard's allegation — 'C'est pour n'avoir pas pensé sur Dieu comme Robespierre que ces infortunés [Chaumette, Hébert, Clootz, &c.] furent traînés à l'échafaud' — is quite unjustified. Aulard, *Le culte de la raison*, p. 244.
172. Ibid. pp. vii–viii.
173. Montesquieu, *De l'esprit des lois*, avertissement; cf. Robespierre, *Lettres à ses commettans*, 1st ser. p. 6 (September 30th, 1792).
174. *Défenseur*, p. 251 (Jacobins, March 26th, 1792).
175. *Anc. mon.* xx. 716 (Convention, June 11th, 1794).
176. *Défenseur*, pp. 9, 19, 26 (May 19th, 1792), 331 (Jacobins, July 29th, 1792).
177. *Discours et rapports*, p. 391 (Convention, July 26th, 1794).
178. Ibid. pp. 350–51 (Convention, May 7th, 1794).
179. *Troisième discours sur la guerre*, p. 23 (Jacobins, January 26th, 1792).
180. *Lettres à ses commettans*, 2nd ser. pp. 197–8 (January 30th, 1793); *Discours ... sur le parti que l'Assemblée Nationale doit prendre relativement à la proposition de guerre*, pp. 3, 25 (Jacobins, December 18th, 1791).
181. Aulard, *Société des Jacobins*, v. 633 (Jacobins, January 30th, 1794).
182. *Anc. mon.* xvi. 107 (Convention, April 10th, 1793); cf. *Défenseur*, pp. 250 (Jacobins, March 26th, 1792), 331 (Jacobins, July 29th, 1792).
183. *Discours et rapports*, p. 285 (Convention, November 18th, 1793).
184. Ibid. pp. 275–300 (loc. cit.).
185. A. Sorel, *L'Europe et la Révolution française* (17th edn., 1922), iii. 529; cf. F. Masson, *Le département des affaires étrangères pendant la Révolution, 1789–1804* (1877), p. 295, where Robespierre's speech is described as naïve and full of empty phrases.
186. Sorel, iii. 530.
187. Courtois, no. XLIV, ii, 16.
188. *Discours et rapports*, p. 122 (Jacobins, January 2nd and 11th, 1792).
189. *Lettres à ses commettans*, 2nd ser. p. 259 (February 5th, 1793).
190. Ibid. p. 258 (February 5th, 1793).
191. *Discours et rapports*, p. 122 (Jacobins, January 2nd and 11th, 1792).
192. *Lettres à ses commettans*, 2nd ser. p. 261 ff. (February 5th, 1793); *Anc. mon.* xiv. 755–6 (Convention, December 15th, 1792); cf. G. Michon, *Robespierre et la guerre révolutionnaire, 1791–1792* (1937), p. 131.
193. Aulard, *Société des Jacobins*, v. 633 (Jacobins, January 30th, 1794).
194. *Anc. mon.* xvi. 214 (Convention, April 24th, 1793).
195. *Défenseur*, pp. 225–6 (July 5th, 1792).
196. *Lettres à ses commettans*, 1st ser. p. 60 (October 20th, 1793).

197. Cf. Robespierre's speech in support of the proposal for the arrest of all the English in France and the seizure of their property, *Anc. mon.* xviii. 88 (Convention, October 9th, 1793); Aulard, *Société des Jacobins*, v. 634 (Jacobins, January 30th, 1794).

198. *Anc. mon.* xix. 373 (Jacobins, January 30th, 1794).

199. Ibid. pp. 198–200 (Jacobins, January 10th, 1794).

200. B. Bosanquet, *Philosophical Theory of the State* (3rd edn., 1920), p. 109.

201. On this point cf. Cobban, *Rousseau and the Modern State* (1934), pp. 41–4, 133–5, 239–53.

202. *Le Point du Jour*, x. 455 (Constituante, June 9th, 1790).

203. *Discours et rapports*, pp. 96–7 (Constituante, August 11th, 1791), 163 (Jacobins, April 27th, 1792), 257 (Convention, May 10th, 1793); *Défenseur*, pp. 115–16 (June 7th, 1792), 124 (ibid.), 325 (Jacobins, July 29th, 1792).

204. *Discours et rapports*, p. 134 (Jacobins, January 2nd and 11th, 1792).

205. *Adresse aux Français* (1791), p. 6.

206. *Discours et rapports*, p. 256 (Convention, May 10th, 1793).

207. *Défenseur*, pp. 115 (June 7th, 1792), 325 (Jacobins, July 29th, 1792).

208. *Discours sur l'organisation des gardes nationales* (1790), p. 24.

209. *Lettres à ses commettans*, 2nd ser., p. 30 (January 5th, 1792); cf. Rousseau, 'L'intérêt personnel … augmente à mesure que l'association devient plus étroite … preuve invincible que la volonté la plus générale est aussi toujours la plus juste.' (*Économie politique, Political Writings of Rousseau*, ed. C. E. Vaughan [1915], i. 243.)

210. *Discours et rapports*, p. 352 (Convention, May 7th, 1794); cf. ibid. p. 15 (Constituante, February 5th, 1791).

211. *Anc. mon.* xxi. 240 (Jacobins, July 9th, 1794).

212. *Journal des États Généraux*, iv. 367 (Constituante, October 5th, 1789).

213. *Lettres à ses commettans*, 2nd ser., p. 6 (January 5th, 1793).

214. *Du Contrat social*, iv. 1.

215. Even Saint-Just could write, 'La volonté générale … se forme de la majorité des volontés particulières.' *Discours sur la constitution à donner à la France*, April 24th, 1793. *Œuvres complètes de Saint-Just*, ed. C. Vellay (1908), i. 428.

216. *Anc. mon.* xxi. 239 (Jacobins, July 9th, 1794).

217. Jacob, p. 80.

218. *Anc. mon.* viii. 239 (Constituante, April 27th, 1791).

219. *Discours et rapports*, p. 306 (Convention, December 5th, 1793).

220. Cf. ibid. p. 333 (Convention, February 5th, 1794).

221. *Anc. mon.* xx. 589 (Convention, May 26th, 1794); cf. ibid. xx. 731 (Jacobins, June 11th, 1794), 'Il existe encore deux partis dans la république: d'un côté, le patriotisme et la probité; de l'autre, l'esprit contre-révolutionnaire, la friponnerie et l'improbité.'

222. *Discours sur l'organisation des gardes nationales* (1790), p. 67. The difficulty of providing a date for some of Robespierre's speeches is well illustrated by this one, which was written in 1790, printed in January 1791, and delivered in April 1791. Thompson, *Robespierre*, i. 128.

223. *Anc. mon.* xx. 588 (Convention, May 26th, 1794).

224. *Discours et rapports*, p. 414 (Convention, July 26th, 1794).

225. Ibid. p. 391 (ibid.).

226. Ibid. p. 306 (Convention, December 5th, 1793).

227. Ording, pp. 178, 180. It is remarkable that even in the crisis of the Revolution Robespierre clung to legal methods. His inactivity in the decisive days of Thermidor has equally been attributed to scruples of legality. Hamel, iii. 781, 785; cf. Aulard, *Histoire politique de la Révolution française* (4th edn., 1909), p. 499. Mathiez,

*Robespierre à la Commune le 9 thermidor (Ann. hist. de la Rév. fran.*, 1924, i. pp. 289–314), rejects this view and argues that Robespierre's reluctance to appeal to force was due to a miscalculation of the political situation, which led him to believe that he could regain his influence over the Convention peacefully.

228. *Défenseur*, p. 39 (Jacobins, April 27th, 1792).
229. Hamel, iii. 617.
230. Aulard, *Orateurs de la législative et de la convention*, ii. 357.
231. *Anc. mon.* xx. 96 (Convention, March 31st, 1794).
232. Michelet, *Histoire de la Révolution*, vii. 172 (edn. of 1899).
233. Hamel, iii. 477–8, n. 2. (*Journal des débats*, no. 558, p. 185.)
234. *Discours et rapports*, pp. 84–5 (Constituante, July 14th, 1791).
235. *Défenseur*, pp. 53–4 (May 24th–25th, 1792), 60 (ibid.), 98 (May 31st, 1792), 142 (June 15th–17th, 1792); *Discours et rapports*, p. 131 (Jacobins, January 2nd and 11th, 1793); cf. Michon, *Robespierre et la guerre révolutionnaire*, pp. 73–4.
236. *Défenseur*, pp. 26–7 (May 19th, 1792); cf. *Troisième discours sur la guerre* (Jacobins, January 26th, 1792), pp. 19 ff.
237. *Discours et rapports*, p. 423 (Convention, July 26th, 1794).
238. Ibid. p. 396 (ibid.).
239. Thompson, *Robespierre*, ii. 46.

## BRITISH SECRET SERVICE IN FRANCE 1784–92

1. British Mus. Add. MSS. 28064, fo. 186, Carmarthen to Dorset, July 31st, 1789.
2. Arch. Aff. Étran., Correspondance Politique Angleterre 570, fos. 180–82, La Luzerne to Montmorin, 31 juillet 1789.
3. Ibid. vol. 570, fo. 201, Montmorin to La Luzerne, 3 août 1789.
4. Ibid. vol. 570, fo. 224, loc. cit., 10 août 1789.
5. A.A.E., C.P. Angleterre 570, fo. 230, La Luzerne to Montmorin, 14 octobre 1789.
6. Ibid. vol. 571, fo. 203, La Luzerne to Montmorin, 26 novembre 1789.
7. e.g. by P. Gaxotte, *La Révolution française* (s.d.), i. 217.
8. A.A.E., C.P. Angleterre 577, fo. 238, La Luzerne to Montmorin, 13 mai 1791.
9. These notes are in C.P. Angleterre, supplément 29, fo. 113, and M. D. France et divers états (1744–92) 517, fo. 240.
10. Wentworth was employed for unofficial negotiations during the American War. Cf. *The Correspondence of King George the Third*, ed. Sir J. W. Fortescue (1927–8), iii.-v. *passim*. There is no evidence that he was working for the British government in 1791.
11. A.A.E., C.P. Angleterre 577, fos. 244–7, La Luzerne, 13 mai 1791.
12. An anonymous memoir of 1796–7 declares that Browne-Dignam was Irish, that he had been released from his fetters by the Duke of Richmond in 1781 to serve as a spy in Holland, had subsequently offered intelligence to both La Luzerne and Barthélemy and had put forward a proposal for burning the ships at Portsmouth. It adds, 'Ce scélérat était un agent de Pitt.' Browne-Dignam was possibly the same as the 'Mr Browne' who offered information about French ships sailing for India to the British ambassador at Paris in April 1791. Gower, like La Luzerne, doubted the value of his information and suspected that Browne was a spy in the pay of Montmorin. (F.O. 27/36, Gower to Leeds, April 22 1791). If the identification is correct he was presumably employed by neither country, but merely trying to turn a dishonest penny by offering vamped-up information to both.
13. A.A.E., C.P. Angleterre 577, fos. 239–40, La Luzerne to Montmorin, 13 mai 1791.

14. e.g. A.A.E., C.P. Angleterre, 578, fos. 182, 229–30, 311; 579, fos. 34, 130, 142, 238. Dispatches of Barthélemy 26 août, 9 sept., 30 sept., 14 oct., 4 nov., 11 nov., 2 déc 1791.
15. Ibid. vol. 579, fo. 142, Barthélemy to de Lessart, 11 novembre 1791.
16. Ibid. vol. 579, fo. 238, loc. cit., 2 décembre 1791.
17. Barthélemy, *Mémoires*, ed. J. de Dampierre (1914), p. 66.
18. *Fragment de l'histoire secrète de la Révolution, sur la faction d'Orléans, le Comité Anglo-Prussien et les six premiers mois de la République*, par Camille Desmoulins, pp. 5–6 (Brit. Mus. F 255–6).
19. *L'Accusateur public*, nos. 6, 7 and 8, reprinted in M. Peltier, *Paris pendant l'année 1795* (1795).
20. Mme Campan, *Mémoires sur la vie privée de Marie-Antoinette* (1822), ii. 188.
21. Ibid. ii. 388.
22. Abbé Georgel, *Mémoires* (1817), ii. 458–60.
23. J. C. D. de Lacretelle, *Histoire de l'assemblée constituante* (1821), ii. 177–80.
24. Thiers, *Histoire de la Révolution française* (4th ed., 1834), i. 239–43.
25. e.g. P. Gaxotte, *La Révolution française* (s.d.); E. Dard, *Le Général Chloderos de Laclos* (1936); O. Havard, *Histoire de la Révolution dans les ports de guerre* (1913).
26. F.O. 27/32, Dorset to Montmorin, July 26th, 1789.
27. *Despatches from Paris 1784–1790*, ed. O. Browning (1910), ii. 251. Dorset to Leeds, July 27th, 1789.
28. Cf. *supra*.
29. Brit. Mus. Add. MSS. 28064, fo. 194, Leeds to Fitzgerald, July 31st, 1789.
30. Michelet, *Histoire de la Révolution française* (1847), liv. ii. ch. iii, pp. 187–9.
31. F.O. 27/32, Dorset to Montmorin, July 26th, 1789. Dorset reported the sending of this note in a dispatch to Leeds of July 27th, 1789 (Browning, *Despatches from Paris*, ii. 250). A description of the Brest affair, which assumes that it was in fact an English plot, is given in Havard, op. cit. ii. 52 ff.
32. Ibid. Dorset to Leeds, August 6th, 1789.
33. Brit. Mus. Add. MSS. 28064, fo. 114, Leeds to Dorset, June 3rd, 1789.
34. Ibid. fo. 124, Dorset to Leeds, June 11th, 1789.
35. A.A.E., C.P. Angleterre 570, fo. 293, Montmorin to La Luzerne, 24 août 1789.
36. Brit. Mus. Add. MSS. 41170, fos. 87–90, Lemalliaude de Kerhamos to comte de Trauvent, Vannes, 21 août 1789.
37. Galart de Montjoie (pseud. of Ventre de La Touloubre), *Histoire de la conjuration de Louis-Philippe-Joseph d'Orléans* (1796), iii. 22–5.
38. 22 Geo. III. 82, xxv.
39. F.O. 27/4, George Rose to William Fraser, August 9th, 1782.
40. Brit. Mus. Add. MSS. 34441, fo. 236, circular from Grenville to Auckland, etc., January 17th, 1792.
41. *Report from the Committee on Accounts relating to His Majesty's Civil List*, March 15th, 1802, p. 208.
42. T. 38/168, *Payments on account of His Majesty's Civil List, 1783–88.*
43. *Journals of the House of Commons*, xli (1786), 645; *Accounts and Papers*, 1798–9, xlviii. no 962 (1). *An Account of the Charges incurred and paid for Secret Service Money for the last Twenty-five years, distinguishing each year, and what Sums have been made good by Parliament.*
44. T. 38/168.
45. *Journals*, xli (1786), 645; *Accounts and Papers*, xlviii, no. 962 (1).
46. T. 38/168. The figures for Sydney's expenditure are confirmed by T. 53/58, *Warrants relating to money, 1785–7*, and T. 60/27, *Miscellanea—Order Books, General, 1786–9.*

47. T. 38/168.
48. *Journals*, xli (1786), 597; *Accounts and Papers*, xlviii, no. 962 (1); *Report from the Committee on Accounts, 15 March 1802*, pp. 208–9.
49. T. 38/168.
50. T. 60/27; T. 53/59, *Warrants relating to money, 1787–90.*
51. T. 38/168. The same figures are given in T. 53/58 and T. 60/27.
52. *Journals*, xlvi (1791), 597; *Report from the Committee on Accounts, 15 March 1802,* pp. 208–9.
53. *Accounts and Papers*, xlviii, no. 962 (1).
54. Ibid. xxxiv (1790–1), no. 738.
55. T. 38/168.
56. Ibid. This figure is confirmed in T. 60/27 and T. 53/59.
57. Ibid.
58. *Accounts and Papers*, xlviii, no. 962 (1).
59. *Parliamentary Register*, xxvi. 477.
60. *Journals*, xlvi (1791), 597; *Report from the Committee on Accounts, 15 March 1802,* pp. 208–9.
61. T. 38/169, *Payments on account of His Majesty's Civil List, 1788–93.* This figure is confirmed in T. 53/59 and T. 60/27. F.O. 366/426 gives only £26,050, one entry of £3,500 being omitted.
62. T. 38/169. This figure is confirmed in T. 53/59 and T. 60/27.
63. Ibid.
64. *Journals*, xlvi (1791), p. 597; *Accounts and Papers*, xlvi, no. 962 (1); *Report from the Committee on Accounts, 15 March 1802,* pp. 208–9.
65. T. 38/169. In T. 60/28, *Miscellanea— Order Books, General 1789–94,* the figure is £20,900, and in F.O. 366/426, £22,900. This last sum is produced by an additional entry of £1,000 in December 1790.
66. T. 38/169; the same figure is given in T. 60/28.
67. F.O. 83/6, *Treasury Correspondence, 1788–1808.*
68. A.O. 1/2121, roll 5.
69. A.O. 1/2121; A.O. 3/949.
70. *Accounts and Papers*, xlviii. no. 962 (1).
71. *Journals*, xlvi (1791), 597. In *Report from the Committee on Account, 15 March 1802,* pp. 208–9, the figure is £22,221 10s. 6d. Presumably this is a mistake.
72. T. 38/169.
73. T. 60/28.
74. T. 38/169.
75. Ibid.
76. T. 60/28.
77. A.O. 1/2121.
78. F.O. 83/6.
79. F.O. 366/426.
80. F.O. 83/6.
81. Ibid.
82. T. 38/169; T. 60/28; F.O. 83/6.
83. *Accounts and Papers*, xlviii, no. 962 (1); *Report from the Committee on Accounts, 15 March 1802,* pp. 208–9.
84. T. 38/169.
85. F.O. 366/426.
86. A.O. 1/2121.
87. T. 60/28.
88. T. 38/169. The same sum for foreign secret service money issued to Dundas

appears in A.O. 1/2122 roll 6. In T. 60/28 the figure given for the period May–December 1792 is £4,433 11s. 4d.

89. T. 38/169.
90. *Accounts and Papers*, xlviii, no. 962 (1); *Report from the Committee on Accounts, 15 March 1802*, pp. 208-9.
91. Cf. F.O. 37/6, Harris to Fraser, February 25th, 1785.
92. Cf. *infra*.
93. *Court and City Register*, 1790.
94. Brit. Mus. Add. MSS. 28064, fo. 180, Leeds to Pitt, July 29th, 1789. A copy of this letter is in P.R.O., G.D. 30/8/151.
95. F.O. 37/6, to Sir James Harris, January 4th, 1785.
96. F.O. 27/6 contains the last series of these advices, from January 3rd–June 24th, 1785.
97. L. G. Wickham Legg, *British Diplomatic Instructions 1689–1789* (1934), p. 306. Instructions for … Duke of Dorset, January 9th, 1784.
98. Brit. Mus. Add. MSS. 28060, fo. 273.
99. Brit. Mus. Eg. MSS. 3499, Carmarthen to Hailes, March 2nd, 1785.
100. F.O. 27/16, printed in Browning, *Despatches from Paris*, i. 46–7.
101. Brit. Mus. Eg. MSS. 3499.
102. Ibid., Hailes to Carmarthen, July 7th, 1785.
103. Ibid. Carmarthen to Hailes, July 15th, 1785.
104. Brit. Mus. Eg. MSS, 3499, Hailes to Carmarthen, August 11th, 1785; Carmarthen to Hailes, August 26th, 1785.
105. Ibid., Hailes to Carmarthen, September 1st, 1785.
106. Browning, *Despatches from Paris*, ii. 249, Hailes to Carmarthen, October 9th, 1787.
107. Brit. Mus. Add. MSS. 28062, fos. 370–1, Hailes to Carmarthen, October 9th, 1787.
108. Ibid. fo. 374, Carmarthen to Hailes, October 15th, 1787.
109. Ibid. fo. 380, Hailes to Carmarthen, October 18th, 1787.
110. Ibid. fos. 395-9, Hailes to Carmarthen, October 25th, 1787.
111. Ibid. fos. 406–7, Dorset to Carmarthen, October 25th, 1787.
112. Ibid. fos. 468–9, Hailes to Carmarthen, December 6th, 1787.
113. F.O. 27/16, Dorset to Carmarthen, March 3rd, 1785. Printed in Browning, *Despatches from Paris*, i. 45.
114. Browning, op. cit. i. 113.
115. Brit. Mus. Add. MSS. 28061, fo. 136, Dorset to Carmarthen, June 8th, 1786.
116. Ibid. fo. 162, Carmarthen to Eden, June 23rd, 1786.
117. Brit. Mus. Add. MSS. 28065, fo. 267.
118. Ibid. fo. 277, Leeds to Fitzgerald, April 16th, 1790.
119. Ibid. fos. 319-21, Fitzgerald to Leeds, April 30th, 1790.
120. Brit. Mus. Eg. MSS. 3501, Torrington to Carmarthen, December 3rd, 1789.
121. Brit. Mus. Add. MSS. 28060, fo. 317, money laid out for Government by Lord Torrington between January 1st and March 31st, 1785.
122. He described himself later as English, despite his language — he wrote in French — and subscribed himself *le chev. Wil Floyd* (P.R.O. 30/8/136, Floyd to Pitt, September 8th, 1791).
123. Brit. Mus. Add. MSS. 28060, fos. 297-9, Floyd to Carmarthen, 15 mars 1785.
124. Ibid. fo. 269, Floyd to Carmarthen, 25 février 1785.
125. Brit. Mus. Eg. MSS. 3501, Leeds to Torrington, July 6th, 1784.
126. Brit. Mus. Add. MSS. 28060, fos. 191–2, Harris to Carmarthen, December 2nd, 1784.

127. Brit. Mus. Eg. MSS. 3501, Torrington to Carmarthen, December 3rd, 1784.
128. Brit. Mus. Add. MSS. 28060, fo. 269, Floyd to Carmarthen, 25 février 1785.
129. Ibid. cf. fos. 267–8, Floyd to Carmarthen, 19 février 1785.
130. Ibid. 28060, fo. 285, Carmarthen to Floyd, March 5th, 1785.
131. Ibid. fos. 313–17, Torrington to Carmarthen, April 13th, 1785.
132. Brit. Mus. Eg. MSS. 3499, Hailes to Carmarthen, August 26th, 1785.
133. Brit. Mus. Add. MSS. 28060, fos. 351–2, Torrington to Carmarthen, June 23rd, 1785.
134. Cf. F.O. 26/11 ff.
135. F.O. 26/13, 23 novembre 1789.
136. F.O. 26/17.
137. A curious letter among the papers of the Directory at the *Archives nationales*, A.F. III 58 *Relations extérieures, Angleterre* (a copy in A.F. III 69, dossier 280, pl. 2), may be mentioned here. It is addressed, without signature, to the *Ministre des Relations extérieures*, and dated *le 19 fructidor an IV* (September 5th, 1796). The author says that at the request of the maréchal de Castries (Ministre de la Marine, 1780–7), who thought the English obtained information from his bureau, he had made certain inquiries. The establishment by which the English obtained intelligence from France was founded, the writer says, by Lord Chatam [*sic*] in 1758. (This date would be more consistent with the Wolters-Hake agency at Rotterdam than with the career of Floyd as we know it.) The letter continues, 'La seule personne d'Angleterre de qui je pouvais apprendre quelque chose et même tout sur ce sujet (les Lords de l'Amirauté n'en connaissant pas la marche eux mêmes) avait été à la tête de cette correspondance 14 années de suite. Elle venait de quitter cette place, l'ayant vendue 2,000 livres sterling. Le Lord Howe qui entrait à l'Amirauté [this was in 1784 and 14 years earlier would bring us to 1770, which is too late for the beginning of the Wolters agency, and too early for Floyd] ne voulut reconnaître ni le droit du vendeur ni sela de l'acquéreur.' (But it was Carmarthen and not Howe who dealt with Floyd, who, so far as can be seen, had no relations with the Admiralty.) 'Mon ami qui avait touché 1200 livres sterling se trouva dans l'embarras, il fur arrêté pour dettes, mis en la prison du Banc du Roy.' (If he was not Floyd, there is at least a coincidence here.) 'C'est là que je négociai l'affaire.' (The ensuing description of the presents and persuasion by which he obtained the information he was seeking may be omitted) ... 'A la fin entre la poire et la pomme il se déboutonna. Il me prouva qu'ils n'avaient jamais reçu d'intelligences par la voie des Bureaux de Versailles, qu'ils n'en avaient reçu d'extraordinaires que deux fois, par Mr. Fitzherbert (aujourd'hui Lord St. Helens) leur ambassadeur à Bruxelles, que cet établissement était toujours entretenu, mais moins étendu et moins couteux pendant la paix. Que toutes leurs intelligences avaient toujours été datées de Toulon, de Rochelle, de Brest, de St. Malo et du Havre, qu'elles leur parvenaient par la Hollande, par Amsterdam et Rotterdam, qu'à ce dernier endroit les dépêches y étaient transcrites littéralement, et que seulement les copies leur en étaient envoyées.' (All this describes the Wolters-Hake correspondence very well. The writer adds that his informant only knew the persons in Holland, one of whom was a lady: this might easily be Mme Wolters. He continues that the Admiralty thus never sent a force out without knowing the situation of the French fleet.) 'Que lui seul avait eu cette partie pour en faire les traductions et les extraits qui étaient envoyés aux Amiraux et Commandans, qu'il y avait travaillé comme un esclave pendant toute la guerre renfermé dans son Bureau nuit et jour.' (The implication is that the informant was a clerk in the Admiralty, who had wanted to sell his post in 1784, and therefore not Floyd.) 'Je fus aisément persuadé de la vérité de tout ceci

par l'expérience que j'en avais. Il m'était facile de pénétrer que l'on ne peut pas retirer d'intelligences assez efficaces par la voie des Bureaux soit de Versailles ou de Londres. On n'y connaît pas assez exactement le mouvement des Ports. Il faut donc voir dessus les lieux mêmes.' (The letter concludes with the suggestion that the Directory might perhaps 'découvrir les fils de cette correspondence par ses agens en Hollande'.)

138. F.O. 26/18, 10 mars 1792.
139. P.R.O., G.D. 30/8/136, Floyd to Pitt, 20 juin, 11 octobre, 28 octobre 1793, 10 novembre 1794.
140. *The Correspondence of William Augustus Miles on the French Revolution 1789–1817*, ed. C. P. Miles (1890).
141. Ibid. i. 17, 19.
142. Ibid. i. 25.
143. F.O. 26/9, Carmarthen to Miles, May 31st, 1787.
144. *The Complete Peerage*, vi. 25.
145. F.O. 26/9, Miles to Carmarthen, June 7th, 1787.
146. Brit. Mus. Eg. MSS. 3503.
147. F.O. 26/11, Miles to Carmarthen, August 22nd, 1788.
148. F.P. 26/13, September 22nd, 1788 (misplaced). Lord Gormanston remained attached to his paternal religion and played a part as a Catholic peer in the movement for Catholic emancipation.
149. S. Tassier, *Les démocrates belges de 1789* (1930), pp. 71 ff.
150. F.O. 26/9, June 20th, 1787.
151. P.R.O., G.D. 30/8/151, Le Brun, 10 septembre 1787.
152. F.O. 26/12, Miles to Carmarthen, March 26th, 1789.
153. F.O. 26/25 (unsigned, undated and misplaced).
154. Miles, *Correspondence*, i. 29–30.
155. F.O. 26/10, Miles to Carmarthen, June 3rd, 1788.
156. *Hist. MSS. Comm.*, *Twelfth Report, Appendix, Part ix*, 1891, p. 354, Miles to [Carmarthen], February 15th, 1787.
157. F.O. 26/12, Miles to Carmarthen, March 1789; cf. Miles, *Correspondence*, i. 33.
158. Ibid. Miles to Fraser, April 26th, 1789.
159. F.O. 26/12 and 13.
160. F.O. 26/13, December 23rd, 1789.
161. F.O. 26/14, Miles to Leeds, February 15th, 1790, cf. Brit. Mus. Add. MSS. 28065, fo. 213, Miles to Leeds, March 19th, 1790; ibid. fo. 299, April 21st, 1790.
162. F.O. 57/1, John Birkbeck to Lord Mountstewart, January 6th, 1780; by 1782 the sum had become £50.
163. Cf. *supra*.
164. Adm. 1/5118, Richard Oakes to Philip Stephens, May 13th, 15th, 20th, 1781.
165. H.O. 42/1, Richard Oakes to Orde, May 24th, 27th, 1782.
166. Ibid. Oakes to Nepean, May 24th, 1782, etc.
167. P.R.O., G.D. 30/8/164, Richard Oakes to Pitt, November 27th, 1782.
168. F.O. 95/5, Richard Oakes to Nepean, May 22nd, 1782.
169. F.O. 26/26, Oakes, September 4th, September 5th, October 6th, 1787; P.R.O., G.D. 30/8/334, September 25th–October 5th, 1787.
170. W.O. 1/395, May 7th, June 10th, June 17th, 1790.
171. F.O. 97/246, Barrington to My Lord [    ], January 31st, 1781.
172. Brit. Mus. Eg. 3501, Dalrymple to Carmarthen, June 8th, 1785.
173. F.O. 95/2, Dalrymple, 1787, 1788.
174. P.R.O., 30/8/163, Nepean to Pitt, October 19th, 1789.
175. W.O. 1/924, Philip d'Auvergne (Prince de Bouillon) to Windham (s.d.).

176. Windsor Archives, Geo. III cal. 6340, 6439, Lord Howe to George III, October 29th, 1787, May 30th, 1788. I must acknowledge the gracious permission to use and quote from the Royal Archives at Windsor.
177. W.O. 1/924, d'Auvergne to Windham (s.d.).
178. F.O. 95/4, March 21st, 1785.
179. F.O. 26/26.
180. F.O. 95/3, Dumaresq to Nepean, November 12th, 1787–June 23rd, 1788.
181. W.O. 1/395, Dumaresq, February 1790.
182. Ibid.
183. Ibid.
184. Ibid. October 18th, 1790.
185. F.O. 26/26.
186. Ibid.
187. F.O. 95/4.
188. F.O. 27/29, Hailes to Fraser, September 4th, 1788.
189. F.O. 27/31, George Stone to Fraser, February 23rd, 1789.
190. F.O. 27/29, Hailes to Fraser, September 2nd, 1788.
191. Adm. 2/1343, Admiralty to Capt. Pole, August 30th, 1790.
192. H.O. 44/41, letters between Oakes and Nepean, May–June 1790.
193. H.O. 44/43, May 9th, 1790.
194. W.O. 1/395, June 1st, 1790.
195. Windsor Archives, Geo. III, cal. 6255, George III to Pitt, May 26th, 1787, printed in Stanhope, *Life of Pitt*, i. app. xxi.
196. Ibid. cal. 15639.
197. F.O. 95/4.
198. L. Villat, *La Corse de 1768 à 1789* (1924), ii. 408.
199. F.O. 95/4, Masseria, September 28th, 1789.
200. F.O. 95/2, Masseria, October 23rd, November 2nd, November 4th, November 12th, 1789.
201. F.O. 95/4, Masseria, November 5th, 1789. The minister referred to is the marquis Latour-Dupin-Gouvernet, appointed minister of war on August 4th, 1789. Corsica was one of the provinces for which this ministry had a special responsibility.
202. F.O. 28/4, November 23rd, 1789.
203. Suspicions of Russian interest in Corsica were present on the French side also. In a debate on January 21st, 1790, the Corsican Buttafoco told the National Assembly, 'Les Muscovites cherchent un établissement dans la Méditerranée. Ils profiteront des troubles pour s'introduire en Corse' (*Ancien moniteur*, iii. 195).
204. Corsica was declared a part of the French empire by the National Assembly on November 30th, 1789 (*Procès-verbal de l'Assemblée Nationale*, no. 138, p. 6).
205. Windsor Archives, Geo. III, cal. 6647, Intelligence relative to Corsica, December 31st, 1789.
206. F.O. 95/2, Masseria to Nepean, January 10th (mistake for February) 1790.
207. Brit. Mus. Add. MSS. 28065, Paoli to Leeds, January 5th, 1790.
208. Ibid. Paoli to Leeds, May 9th, 1790.
209. F.O. 20/22, Masseria, October 30th, 1790.
210. Ibid. 'His Lordship' refers to Lord Hervey, Envoy Extraordinary at Florence.
211. Ibid.
212. Anson, *Law and Custom of the Constitution*, 4th edn. (1951), ii. *The Crown*, i. 179.
213. Ibid. pp. 179–80.
214. M. A. Thomson, *The Secretaries of State 1681–1782* (1932), pp. 82, 86.
215. In 1794 Bland Burges, one of the under-secretaries at the Foreign Office, reports

the king as saying, 'I cannot but take notice of the difference there is between the red and green boxes I receive: and I have a pleasure in telling you that I find this difference remarkably increased since you took the Northern Department' (*Selections from the Letters and Correspondence of Sir James Bland Burges, Bart.*, ed. J. Hutton [1885], p. 253). The implication is that George III was still referring to the Foreign Office as the 'Northern Department' in 1794, but since a division of labour between northern and southern had appeared inside the Foreign Office, it is also possible that the king was referring to this.

216. Part of this episode has been dealt with by J. Holland Rose, *William Pitt and National Revival* (1914), 578–81.

217. *Memoir of the Right Honourable Hugh Elliot*, by the Countess of Minto (1868), p. 335.

218. *The Despatches of Earl Gower*, ed. O. Browning (1885), pp. 38–9.

219. Ibid. p. 40.

220. P.R.O., G.D. 30/8/102, Pitt to Hugh Elliot, October 1790, printed in Stanhope, *Life of Pitt*, ii. 56–9.

221. Windsor Archives, Geo. III, cal. 6728, Pitt to George III, October 25th, 1790.

222. *Hist. MSS. Comm., Twelfth Report, Appendix, Part ix*, p. 368, George III to Pitt, October 26th, 1790.

223. P.R.O., G.D. 30/8/132, H. Elliot to Pitt, s.d.

224. Ibid. October 26th, 1790. Extracts from this letter are given in Stanhope, op. cit. ii. 59–61.

225. Ibid. November 6th, 1790.

226. Miles, *Correspondence*, i. 150, Miles to Marquess of Buckingham, July 15th, 1790.

227. Ibid. i. 169, 170.

228. Ibid. i. 171, Miles to Rose, October 11th, 1790.

229. Ibid. i. 176–8, Miles to Rose, November 30th, 1790.

230. Miles, *Correspondence*, i. 43.

231. P.R.O. 30/8/159.

232. Miles, *Correspondence*, i. 178, Miles to Buckingham, December 13th, 1790.

233. Ibid. i. 52.

234. *Les Actes des Apôtres*, no. 124, pp. 14–15 (Brit. Mus. F 1357–8; another version in F 259–60, dated 27 juin 1790). This is a pretended letter from Charles de Lameth.

235. *Orléanriade ou le masque rouge déchiré* (Brit. Mus. F 259–60).

236. *Procès-verbal de l'assemblage générale des Saints Martyrs, Confesseurs, Anges, etc., qui a eu lieu en Paradis le 15 novembre 1789*, p. 10 (Brit. Mus. R 195).

237. *Tu ne nous foutras pas dedans, ou Grande Colère de père Duchêne contre les intrigues de Philippe d'Orléans*, p. 7 (Brit. Mus. F 255–6).

238. A.A.E., C.P. Angleterre 571, fos. 60–5, instructions to Orleans, October 13th, 1789.

239. Ibid. fo. 174, La Luzerne to Montmorin, 23 novembre 1789.

240. Ibid.

241. Ibid. vol. 272, fo. 182, La Luzerne to Montmorin, 26 février 1790.

242. Ibid. vol. 273, fo. 146. La Luzerne to Montmorin, 20 avril 1790.

243. Ibid. fo. 284, La Luzerne to Montmorin, 15 juin 1790.

## THE BEGINNING OF THE CHANNEL ISLES
### CORRESPONDENCE 1789–94

1. The literature on royalist movements in Western France is extensive though of varying reliability. Among the most useful books are C. Hettier, *Relations de la Normandie et de la Bretagne avec les îles de la manche pendant l'émigration* (1885); Ch.-L.

Chassin, *Études documentaires sur la révolution française* (11 vols., 1892–1900); L. Dubreuil, *Histoire des insurrections de l'Ouest* (1929); E. Gabory, *L'Angleterre et la Vendée* (1930–2). There are also two unpublished London Ph.D. theses — A. King, 'The relations of the British government and the Émigrés and Royalists of Western France, 1793–5' (1931); and N. F. Richards, 'British Policy and the problem of Monarchy in France, 1789–1801' (1954). All the above have material of some relevance to this paper. Partly because my theme has been a different one from any of those given above, except to a certain extent for the work of Hettier, and partly because all the books are apt to be economical of specific references, I started this little investigation by going over the source material, and except where a note indicates otherwise have taken all my references direct from the Archives. I am indebted to Dr Winifred Edington (Mrs Stokes) for assistance while I was preparing this paper for publication.

2. Cf. 'British Secret Service in France, 1784–92'.
3. Ibid. p. 220. I hope to write more fully of Nepean, for whose remarkable official career it would be difficult to find any parallel in his own day or for some time after, on another occasion.
4. Royal Archives, Windsor, Geo. III cal. 6801–2. I have to acknowledge Her Majesty's gracious permission to quote from the Royal Archives.
5. H.O. 98/2. All H.O., W.O. and F.O. references are to the P[ublic] R[ecord] O[ffice].
6. Ibid.
7. H.O. 98/3. The reference to Cherbourg is to the new harbour works in progress there.
8. H.O. 98/3, Fall to Nepean, January 4th, 1793.
9. W.O. 1/396, Fall to Nepean, January 31st, 1793. A subsequent letter leads one to suppose that this agent may have been Captain Dumaresq. Cf. below n. 23.
10. This was the baron de Gilliers, an émigré from Poitou.
11. H.O. 1/1.
12. H.O. 98/3.
13. Ibid. Fall to Nepean, March 16th, 1793.
14. Ibid. April 30th, 1793.
15. Ibid. Nepean to Fall, March 13th, 1793.
16. W.O. 1/391.
17. François-Augustin-Rénier Pelisson de Jarjayes was in 1791 maréchal de camp and directeur adjoint au dépôt de la guerre: *Biographie nouvelle des contemporains* (1820–25).
18. H.O. 98/24, to Col. Thomas Dundas.
19. Ibid.
20. W.O. 1/395.
21. Cf. p. 215.
22. H.O. 98/4, January 6th, 1793 (misdated 1792).
23. H.O. 98/4, October 24th, 1793. Dumaresq did not cease his espionage activities. He was instructed in April 1795 to draw on Huskisson as formerly on Nepean: W.O. 1/607, J. Dumaresq to W. Huskisson. In 1796 we find the head of the Correspondence writing of him as 'having assisted me in other Services at the recommendation of Earl Balcarres my predecessor in the direction of the Confidential Service here': F.O. 95/605, Bouillon to Windham, February 6th, 1796.
24. Brit. Mus., Huskisson Papers, Add. MS. 38734, fos. 33–4. This document is also cited in C. R. Fay, *Huskisson and his Age* (1951), p. 66.
25. *The Correspondence of the right honourable William Wickham*, ed. W. Wickham (1870), I. 5.

26. Ch.-L. Chassin, *La préparation de la guerre de Vendée, 1789–1793* (1892), iii. 396, n. 5. Chassin's version is followed by Gabory, op. cit. i. 53 ff. A less plausible explanation by Dubreuil, op. cit. i. 255, is that Gaston was merely the *nom de guerre* of one of the more eminent leaders, but there is no real evidence of this.
27. Dubreuil, op. cit. i. 132, 153–4.
28. W.O. 1/388, July 6th, 1793.
29. The whole story of the *Lydia* is told in considerable detail by Duncan in F.O. 26/25.
30. 'Copie des instructions données à M. le Colonel Baron d'Angély', signed by the Hereditary Prince of Orange: F.O. 95/5, May 28th, 1793.
31. His career is summarized in Balteaux, Barroux et Prévost, *Dictionnaire de biographie française*, ii. 1082–3.
32. Archives Nationales, Paris, AF III. 70 (dossier 286). Report by Rocques de Montgaillard, 15 brumaire an VII (November 5th, 1798).
33. *Gedenkstukken der Algemeene Geschiedenis van Nederland von 1795 tot 1840*, ed. H. T. Colenbrander, i. (1905) pp. xxxviii–xxxix.
34. F.O. 95/4.
35. Huskisson Papers, Add. MS. 38764, fos. 53–8.
36. Huskisson Papers, Add. MS. 38734, fo. 68. Cf. Gabory, op. cit. i. 60–2, where however the suggestion that the British government paid no attention to d'Angély is evidently incorrect.
37. F.O. 27/42. Cf. F.O. 97/248, where a letter from the Foreign Secretary to the minister at The Hague acknowledges receipt of the memoir. Another copy was set by Bentinck to Lord Malmesbury on December 1st, 1793: Malmesbury, *Diaries and Correspondence* (1844), iii. 13.
38. W.O. 1/391.
39. [J. J. M. Savary], *Guerres des Vendéens et des Chouans* (1824–7), i. 143. Cf. Chassin, *La Vendée patriote*, i. (1893) 191–3.
40. There are many and varying accounts of these, e.g. Gabory, op. cit. i. 53–7, 62–7; Chassin, *Préparation de la Guerre de Vendée*, iii. 264, 540–1; Dubreuil, *Histoire des insurrections de l'Ouest*, i. 255–8; and the theses by A. King and N. F. Richards cited above.
41. W.O. 1/389; Brit. Mus., Liverpool Papers, Add. MS. 38352, fos. 286–9.
42. W.O. 1/391, Report by Hammelin, June 1793. Information of a plot to deliver the port to the English was given in a letter of March 17th by the local republican commissaire. Chassin, *Préparation de la Guerre de Vendée*, iii. 385–6.
43. W.O. 1/389, Craig to Nepean, August 7th, 1793.
44. Ibid. October 26th, 1793.
45. An account of the Granville affair is given in Gabory, op. cit. ch. v.
46. W.O. 1/389. Cf. Dubreuil, op. cit. i. 257–8, 294. The letter was received on January 1st and a reply sent on February 22nd, 1794; W.O. 1/389.
47. Gabory, op. cit. i. 105.
48. H.O. 98/4.
49. H.O. 98/3, March 13th, 1793.
50. Ibid. April 30th, 1793.
51. H.O. 98/4. A letter from General Conway to Dundas attributed the blame for the failure of co-operation to Craig. Ibid. October 13th, 1793.
52. H.O. 98/4, 98/24, 99/1.
53. H.O. 98/4, to Balcarres, October 17th, 1793.
54. W.O. 1/391, Balcarres to Dundas, November, 4th, 1793.
55. H.O. 98/3, Craig to Nepean, April 30th, 1793.
56. H.O. 98/4, Craig to Nepean, July 16th, 1793.

57. H.O. 98/24, November 16th, 1793.
58. Huskisson Papers, Add. MS. 38769, fo. 358.
59. P.R.O. 30/8/114. Le Comte de Botherel, January 11th, 1794.
60. *Mémoires du comte Joseph de Puisaye* (1803–8), ii. 579 ff.
61. Préfecture de Police, Paris, Aa 265.
62. Brit. Mus., Puisaye Papers, Add. MS. 7991. The administrators of St Malo seized a paper dated December 1st 1793 and signed by Balcarres, which declared, 'le porteur de la présente a la confiance de la cour de Londres, du régent de France, de mylord Moira, du marquis de Dresnay et de moi-même. Vous pouvez avoir confiance en lui, et lui communiquer tout ce que vous croirez convenable. Comptez sur toutes les promesses qu'il vous fera; il en est chargé de M. Pitt, de la cour de Londres et des princes français. C'est notre ambassadeur, ayez-y la plus grande confiance.' Upon which they commented, 'Ainsi ce Prigent que nous avons vu ici marchand de pommes et autres fruits, est devenu ambassadeur': Savary, op. cit., iv. 283.
63. Puisaye, *Memoires*, ii. 579–83.
64. Préf. de Police, Aa 265.
65. There is a concise summary of his career in G. R. Balleine, *A Biographical Dictionary of Jersey* (1948), and a rather romanticized version in H. Kirke, *From the Gun-room to the Throne* (1904). The various contemporary accounts are quite unreliable.
66. *The Case of Philip d'Auvergne a captain in His Majesty's Navy, As submitted to H.M. Ministers* (1803), p. 7.
67. Cf. V. T. Harlow, *The Founding of the Second British Empire, 1763–1793* (1952), pp. 117–20.
68. Royal Archives, Windsor, Geo. III cal. 5763. Lord Sydney to George III, February 14th, 1784; *Case of Philip d'Auvergne*, p. 8.
69. *Case of Philip d'Auvergne*, p. 8.
70. Ibid. In a letter to the French Minister for Foreign Affairs, of December 21st, 1784, concerning a letter for d'Auvergne which had gone astray, the duc de Bouillon says, 'M. d'Auvergne qui est actuellement ici se nomme comme moi. Il est de ma famille': Archives des Affaires Étrangères, Paris, C. P. Angleterre 550, fo. 375.
71. Reports from d'Auvergne sent by Lord Howe to the king, October 22nd, 1787, and May 30th, 1788, have survived. Royal Archives, Windsor, Geo. III cal. 6340, 6439.
72. P.R.O., Bouillon Papers, P.C. 1/115B, J. T. Townshend to Philip d'Auvergne, November 23rd, 1787.
73. *Case of Philip d'Auvergne*, pp. 9–12.
74. W.O. 1/924, d'Auvergne to Windham [1802].
75. *Case of Philip d'Auvergne*, p. 9.
76. F.O. 95/605, d'Auvergne to Windham, November 4th, 1794.
77. e.g. the conveyance of forged *assignats* to France for the use of Puisaye: F.O. 95/604, Bouillon to Pitt, October 22nd, 1794. Bouillon wrote to Windham, November 17th, 1794, 'They [the royalists] have now received safely in our two trips about six millions in assignats': F.O. 95/605. I hope to deal with the question of forged *assignats* on another occasion.
78. Préf. de police, Aa 295, Puisaye to Dufour, September 29th, 1794.
79. Brit. Mus., Windham Papers, Add. MS. 37856, fos. 171–2, August 7th, 1794.
80. Ibid. fos. 366–8, Puisaye to Windham, October 28th, 1794.
81. F.O. 95/604, Bouillon to Nepean, September 11th, 1794.
82. Ibid. Bouillon to Dundas, October 8th, 1794.

83. F.O. 95/605. Bouillon to Windham, November 4th, 1794.
84. F.O. 95/604. Bouillon to Dundas, October 20th, 1794.
85. Cf. Puisaye Papers, Add. MS. 7988, fo. 8, Bouillon to Prigent, October 24th, 1794; Add. MS. 7991, fo. 1, Prigent to Puisaye, December 28th, 1794.
86. H.O. 69/3, Chatham to Bouillon, October 29th, 1794.
87. W.O. 1/607.
88. Puisaye Papers, Add. MS. 7988, fo. 12.
89. H.O. 69/3, Chatham to Bouillon, October 29th, 1794.
90. W.O. 1/924, Bouillon to Windham [1802].
91. F.O. 95/605, Bouillon to Windham, May 24th, 1794.
92. A list of offers to form corps of émigrés, drawn up on March 28th, 1794, is to be found in W.O. 1/388. Leave was granted in the House of Commons, on April 7th, to bring in a Bill 'to enable Subjects of France to enlist as Soldiers in Regiments to serve on the Continent of *Europe*, and in certain other places and to enable His Majesty to grant Commissions to Subjects of *France* to serve and receive Pay as Officers in such Regiments'. *Commons Journals*, April 7th, 1794. I fancy that Woodford was particularly interested in the financial aspect of his work. When, on Windham's resignation in 1801, it became necessary for him to present his accounts, he fled to Rio de Janeiro where the laws against those charged with peculation in the public funds could not follow him: Windham Papers, Add. MS. 37851.
93. F.O. 95/605, Bouillon to Windham, December 28th, 1794.
94. Gabory, op. cit. i. 128, says Prigent embarked with Puisaye on September 23rd, but this date is obviously impossible. Puisaye says it was in the first fortnight of September: *Mémoires*, ii. 607.
95. Puisaye himself, in his account of the first meeting with Pitt, says that Prigent was present, but nothing of the meeting in which Prigent represented him.
96. Stanhope, *Life of Pitt* (1867), ii. 258–9.
97. Préf. de police, Aa 295. Part of his documentation is printed in Savary, op. cit. iv. 273 ff.
98. Bouillon never lost his suspicions. He wrote to Windham, September 13th, 1796, 'I fear much that Prigent has played a double game': F.O. 95/605: 'There is scarcely an Emigrant that has not reclamations against his apparent faithlessness in pecuniary matters': ibid. October 10th, 1796. Of Puisaye, who would hear nothing against Prigent, Bouillon wrote that he was 'taken in with the defence of a flippant spy, whom he calls risibly his aide-de-camp'. Material for a discussion of the case for and against Prigent may be found in Préf. de police, Aa 295; Puisaye Papers, Add. MS. 7991; P.R.O. 30/8/325; Chassin, *Les Pacifications de l'Ouest 1794–1801*, i (1896), 62–5; and Mr M. Hutt tells me of further material in Paris, Archives du Ministère de la Guerre, B 5/25. Prigent must have shown remarkable skill and energy in his innumerable journeys into Brittany. He was captured again in 1808 and executed. There is a full dossier on this last episode of a remarkable career in Archives Nationales, F⁷ 6480–2.
99. Savary, op. cit. iv. 272.
100. W.O. 1/390.

## CARLYLE'S *FRENCH REVOLUTION*

1. J. Symonds, *Thomas Carlyle* (1952), p. 261.
2. Froude, *Thomas Carlyle, a History of his Life in London* (ed. of 1919), I. 27–9.
3. Froude, *Thomas Carlyle, a History of the First Forty Years of his Life* (ed. of 1914), II. 470.

4. Froude, *Thomas Carlyle, A History of the First Forty Years of His Life*, II. 473.
5. *Life in London*, I. 79.
6. Ibid. I. 90.
7. Symonds, p. 157.
8. *Life in London*, I. 56–7.
9. *Early Life*, II. 97.
10. *French Revolution*, I. vi. 1.
11. Hill Shine, *Carlyle and the Saint-Simonians* (1941).
12. I. ii. 7.
13. *The Love Letters of Thomas Carlyle and Jane Welsh*, ed. A. Carlyle 1909), II. 25–33.
14. D. Halévy, *Histoire d'une histoire* (1939), p. 13, n. 2.
15. I. vi. 2.
16. Ibid.
17. III. vi. 2.
18. II. iii. 7.
19. A. Aulard, *Études et leçons*, VIIème Série, V. Carlyle (introduction to a translation of 1913), p. 203.
20. Symonds, p. 149.
21. *Critical and Miscellaneous Essays* (1899), IV. 5. (Parliamentary History of the French Revolution, 1837.)
22. Ibid. p. 6.
23. *Early Life*, p. 337.
24. *Essays*, IV. 3. (Parliamentary History, 1837.)
25. Ibid. pp. 3–5.
26. *Essays*, VI. 175. (On History Again, 1833.)
27. I. iii. 3.
28. Cf. L. M. Young, *Carlyle and the Art of History* (1939).
29. G. P. Gooch, *History and Historians in the Nineteenth Century* (1920), p. 326.
30. A. C. Taylor, *Carlyle: sa première fortune littéraire en France (1825–65)*, 1929, pp. 36–45.
31. *Life in London*, I. 79.
32. III. ii. 8.
33. Aulard, *Études et leçons*, VII. 211.
34. III. iii. 1.
35. III. vii. 6.
36. Cf. Halévy, loc. cit.
37. Michelet, *Histoire de la Révolution française* (1847), II. 250.
38. III. vi. 7.
39. Taylor, p. 90.
40. Ibid. pp. 100–2.
41. Aulard, *Études et leçons*, VII.
42. *Past and Present*, Bk. II, ch. 2.
43. *Essays*, II. 86. (On History, 1830.)
44. This is pointed out by Dr H. Ben-Israel in 'Carlyle and the French Revolution', *The Historical Journal*, i (1958), p. 133, a paper which gives an excellent discussion of the views that have been expressed on the historical merits and defects of Carlyle's history, and a balanced summing-up.

## POLITICAL VERSUS SOCIAL INTERPRETATIONS OF THE FRENCH REVOLUTION

1. *Revue historique,* ccxxxv (1966), pp. 205–9.
2. 'Alfred Cobban s'efforce de démontrer ... que ce sont les paysans pauvres, et non les riches, qui étaient partisans du partage des biens communaux. ... Cette interprétation est diamétralement opposée à celle de la plupart des historiens français, et notamment de Marc Bloch.' (Godechot) 'Pour les prolétaires de la campagne, le partage, cependant, pouvait avoir ses attraits ... L'opération plaisait aux manouvriers, tout prêts à se transformer en défricheurs. Ce sont eux qui, en Lorraine par exemple, mirent à profit la majorité, parfois écrasante, que leur nombre leur donnait dans les assemblées de paroisse, pour imposer aux laboureurs récalcitrants l'application des lois de partage.' (Bloch, *Les caractères originaux de l'histoire rurale française* [1931], p. 229.)
3. e.g. 'Alfred Cobban essaye de montrer que les droits seigneuriaux ne formaient plus, en 1789, qu'une charge insignificante pour les paysans.' (Godechot) 'There is ample evidence that the peasantry was very conscious of the burden they [the seigneurial dues] represented in the years before the French Revolution, and it is probable that the burden was increasing.' (Cobban, p. 52)

   'Alfred Cobban ne reconnaît pas l'existence du groupe socio-professionnel. Pour lui, il n'y a que des pauvres et des riches.' (Godechot) 'To appreciate a man's real position in French society it would have been necessary to know, as well as his legal status, also his actual economic functions, the sources and the extent of his wealth, his mode of life, his profession or office, his family, and during the Revolution even his political affiliations.' (Cobban, p. 21)
4. There is a curious ambivalence in M. Godechot's position. While on the one hand he tells us that the Commission d'Histoire Économique et Sociale de la Révolution has undertaken to draw up a vocabulary of the Revolutionary period, on the other he seems to imply that this task is hardly necessary since the meaning of the terms is already well understood.
5. A. Soboul, 'Problèmes du travail en l'an II', *Annales Historiques de la Révolution française* (1956), p. 238.
6. F. Brunot, *Histoire de la langue française* (1930), VI. i. 306–11.
7. P. Bois, *Paysans de l'Ouest* (1960), pp. 431–2.
8. I have dealt with this in *The Social Interpretation of the French Revolution* (1964), pp. 93–106.
9. Ibid. p. 132.
10. 'Que les Girondins et les Montagnards se soient recrutés dans les mêmes groupes sociaux, Alfred Cobban l'affirme, après M. J. Sydenham: les objections qu'on a opposées à ce dernier sont toujours valables. Connaît-on bien la fortune des uns et des autres?' (Godechot) In fact, what I said was that so far there is no adequate evidence to the contrary.
11. J. McManners, 'France', in *The European Nobility in the Eighteenth Century*, ed. A. Goodwin (1953), p. 26.
12. C. Lefebvre, *Études sur la Révolution française* (1954), p. 261.
13. Cf. note 9 above.
14. In addition to the magisterial *Paysans du Nord*, many other of Lefebvre's earlier writings are significant contributions to social history, among them the post-humously published *Études Orléanaises*. In this he disregarded the political categories and concentrated on a careful and detailed analysis, with which I was

encouraged to find myself almost wholly in agreement — alas, only to read in M. Godechot that Lefebvre's book was no more than an 'aperçu superficiel'.

## THE FRENCH REVOLUTION: ORTHODOX AND UNORTHODOX INTERPRETATIONS

1. A. Goodwin, *English Historical Review* (1966), cccvi.
2. Jacques Godechot, *Revue historique*, ccxxxv (1966), 205–9.
3. Crane Brinton, *History and Theory*, v (1966), 315–20. Subsequent citations from Goodwin, Godechot and Brinton are also taken from these reviews, except where another reference is given.
4. George V. Taylor, 'Noncapitalist Wealth and the Origins of the French Revolution', *American Historical Review*, lxxii (1967), 469–96.
5. A. Soboul, *Précis d'histoire de la Révolution française* (1962), p. 8.
6. R. R. Palmer, *New York Review of Books* (1966).
7. Dr J. Q. C. Mackrell's London Ph.D. thesis, 'The Attack on "Feudalism" in Eighteenth Century French Thought' (1963), which deals with this subject, has unfortunately not yet been published.
8. G. Shapiro, 'The Many Lives of Georges Lefebvre', *American Historical Review*, lxxii (1967).
9. A. Soboul, *La Révolution française* (1965), p. 114.
10. Samuel Bernstein, *Science and Society* (1965), pp. 472–7.
11. G. Rudé, *The New Statesman*, October 2nd, 1964, pp. 504–5.
12. J. Kaplow, *American Historical Review*, lxx (1965), 1094–6.
13. J. Kaplow, *Elbeuf during the revolutionary period* (1964), p. 10.
14. J. Kaplow (ed.), *New Perspectives on the French Revolution* (1965), p. 14.
15. A. Goodwin (ed.), *New Cambridge Modern History*, vol. VIII, p. 4.
16. R. R. Palmer, *New Cambridge Modern History*, vol. VIII, p. 424.
17. The sources in Lefebvre for this analysis are given in my *Social Interpretation of the French Revolution*, pp. 108, 117–18, 165–6.
18. R. R. Palmer, *New York Review of Books*.
19. *The Social Interpretation of the French Revolution* (1964), p. 162.
20. Ibid. pp. 130–31.
21. Ibid. p. 11.
22. Ibid. p. 61.
23. G. Lefebvre, *La Révolution française* (1951), p. 75.
24. In the *Journal of Modern History* (1965), pp. 242–3.

# Index

# Index

# Index

325

# Index

# Index